# Beginning CSS3

David Powers

Apress®

ISBN-13 (pbk): 978-1-4302-4473-8

ISBN-13 (electronic): 978-1-4302-4474-5

President and Publisher: Paul Manning
Lead Editor: Ben Renow-Clarke
Technical Reviewer: Andrew Zack
Editorial Board: Steve Anglin, Ewan Buckingham, Gary Cornell, Louise Corrigan, Morgan Ertel,
    Jonathan Gennick, Jonathan Hassell, Robert Hutchinson, Michelle Lowman, James Markham,
    Matthew Moodie, Jeff Olson, Jeffrey Pepper, Douglas Pundick, Ben Renow-Clarke,
    Dominic Shakeshaft, Gwenan Spearing, Matt Wade, Tom Welsh
Coordinating Editor: Anamika Panchoo
Copy Editor: Linda Seifert
Compositor: SPi Global
Indexer: SPi Global
Artist: SPi Global
Cover Designer: Anna Ishchenko

Distributed to the book trade worldwide by Springer Science + Business Media New York, 233 Spring Street, 6th Floor, New York, NY 10013. Phone 1-800-SPRINGER, fax (201) 348-4505, e-mail orders-ny@springer-sbm.com, or visit www.springeronline.com.

For information on translations, please e-mail rights@apress.com, or visit www.apress.com.

Apress and friends of ED books may be purchased in bulk for academic, corporate, or promotional use. eBook versions and licenses are also available for most titles. For more information, reference our Special Bulk Sales–eBook Licensing web page at www.apress.com/bulk-sales.

Any source code or other supplementary materials referenced by the author in this text is available to readers at www.apress.com. For detailed information about how to locate your book's source code, go to www.apress.com/source-code.

# Contents at a Glance

# Contents

# About the Author

**David Powers** is the author of a more than a dozen highly successful books and video courses on web design and development, including *PHP Solutions: Dynamic Web Design Made Easy, Second Edition* (friends of ED, ISBN: 978-1-4302-3249-0) and *Adobe Dreamweaver CS6: Learn by Video: Core Training in Web Communication* (Peachpit Press, ISBN: 978-0-321-84037-0). He also served as the technical reviewer on *Cascading Style Sheets: Separating Content from Presentation, Second Edition* by Owen Briggs, Steven Champeon, et al. (friends of ED), and *Head First HTML and CSS* by Elisabeth Robson and Eric Freeman (O'Reilly). He is an Adobe Community Professional, and is constantly urging the Dreamweaver development team to improve support for web standards and the latest developments in CSS3.

David first began developing websites in 1994 when, as Editor, BBC Japanese TV, he needed a way to promote his fledgling TV channel with next to no budget. He persuaded the IT department to let him have some space on a web server, and created and maintained a bilingual Japanese-English website, much of it coded by hand. After a career in radio and TV journalism spanning nearly 30 years, he left the BBC at the turn of the century, and continued developing bilingual websites for leading clients, including the Japanese Foreign Ministry and an international consultancy. Since 2006, he's devoted himself full time to writing and teaching.

David has also translated several plays from Japanese. To relax, he enjoys nothing better than some cold sake and sushi.

# About the Technical Reviewer

**Andrew Zack** is the CEO of ZTMC, Inc. (www.ztmc.com), which specializes in search engine optimization (SEO) and Internet marketing strategies. His project background includes almost 20 years of site development and project management experience and over 15 years as an SEO and Internet marketing expert.

Andrew has been very active in the publishing industry, having coauthored *Flash 5 Studio* (Apress, 2001) and served as a technical reviewer on more than ten books and industry publications.

Having started working on the Internet close to its inception, Andrew continually focuses on the cutting edge and beyond, concentrating on new platforms and technology to stay at the forefront of the industry.

# Acknowledgments

My thanks, as always, go to my editor, Ben Renow-Clarke, who suggested I write this book a long time ago, and gently pestered me until I said yes. His perspicacious comments have greatly improved the manuscript. My technical reviewer, Andrew Zack, has also made many helpful suggestions and picked up my errors. Any that remain are my responsibility alone. I'd also like to thank my coordinating editor, Ana Panchoo, for smoothing the whole process over the many months it takes to write a book and see it through the editorial and production process.

Most of all, though, my thanks go to you for taking the trouble to read this book.

# Introduction

CSS3 is the latest version of Cascading Style Sheets, the language that in the hands of a skilled designer turns the ugly duckling of unadorned HTML into the gracious swan of a sophisticated web page. Some web designers will tell you dismissively that CSS3 won't be ready for years. In one sense, they're right. Instead of one massive specification, CSS3 has been broken up into more than 40 modules, some of which are unlikely to gain formal approval for a long time. But the first modules are already complete, while others have reached a high level of stability and are widely implemented by browsers. What's more, CSS3 embraces the whole of the previous version, CSS2.1, a formal standard that's supported by all browsers in widespread use.

This book covers not only the new parts of CSS3, but also those inherited from CSS2.1. Even ancient browsers, such as Internet Explorer (IE) 6 and 7, support most of CSS2.1. So, you'll find large parts of this book relevant even if you still need to support older browsers.

Because CSS is constantly evolving, this book inevitably represents a snapshot in time (August 2012). But I've tried to structure the content in such a way that it will remain relevant even when new modules begin to mature. New modules will add extra features rather than supersede what's covered in this book.

In addition to all the visual properties of CSS2.1, it covers stable features from the following CSS3 modules:

- CSS3 Selectors
- CSS3 Color
- CSS3 Values and Units
- Media Queries (for responsive web design)
- CSS3 Backgrounds and Borders
- CSS3 Text
- CSS3 Fonts
- CSS3 Image Values and Replaced Content (gradients)
- CSS Multi-column Layout
- CSS Transforms
- CSS Transitions
- CSS Animations
- CSS Flexible Box Layout

## Who This Book Is For

The title *Beginning CSS3* indicates that no prior knowledge of CSS is required. However, you should be familiar with HTML and the basic principles of building websites. Each chapter contains a mixture of reference material and hands-on exercises. The reference sections have been designed to make it easy to find properties and values, so the book should continue to be useful even after you have worked through a chapter.

The broad scope of the material covered in this book means that it should also appeal to readers who already have experience of working with CSS and are looking to consolidate their knowledge and learn new features in CSS3.

## How This Book Is Structured

I've split the book into four parts.

**Part I** deals with the basics of CSS: how style rules are structured and attached to web pages; basic selectors; and specifying sizes, colors, and other values.

**Part II** explains how to format text and embed web fonts.

**Part III** covers the main aspects of page layout. It discusses the CSS box model, backgrounds and borders, floats, styling lists, fixed, absolute and relative positioning, and strategies for cross-browser layout.

**Part IV** dives into more advanced techniques, such as responsive web design with media queries, CSS animation, and flex layout.

## Downloading the Code

The code for the examples is available on the Apress website, www.apress.com/9781430244738. A link can be found under the Source Code/Downloads tab. This tab is located underneath the Related Titles section of the page.

You are free to use or adapt the code in your own websites. However, the images remain the copyright of the author and are provided only for use with the exercises.

## Browser Versions Covered

The examples have been tested on a wide range of browsers and operating systems, including Windows XP, Windows 7, and Mac OS X 10.7, as well as Apple and Android touch-screen devices. Where appropriate, the text notes whether a minimum version of a browser is required to support a feature. IE 8 and earlier support only features inherited from CSS2.1.

Windows 8 and IE 10 had not been released when this book went to press, but all the examples in Part IV were tested on the Developer Preview of IE 10. The most recent versions of other browsers used for testing were Firefox 14, Safari 6, Chrome 21, Opera 12.01, Safari in iOS 5.1.1, and the native browser in Android 2.2 and 3.2.

References in the text to Firefox 16 and Opera 12.5 are based on announcements made by the browser manufacturers about changes planned for those versions. For up-to-date information on which browsers support new CSS3 features, check http://caniuse.com/#cats=CSS.

## Errors and Corrections

Every effort has been made to ensure the accuracy of the information in this book, but if something doesn't quite work as expected or you think you have spotted an error, I'll keep a list of known errors and significant updates on my website at http://foundationphp.com/begincss3/. Also check the Errata tab on the book's information page on the Apress website, www.apress.com/9781430244738. If the error isn't listed in either place, submit an error report through the Apress site. In normal circumstances, I try to respond to error reports within 24 hours of them being passed onto me. Submitting errors through the Apress site is the best way to ensure corrections are made to future printings of the book.

# Getting Help

If you need help solving a problem with your own CSS, upload the web page to a temporary location on your website and post a request for help in an online forum. Give the URL of the problem page, and describe the issue briefly. Also mention if the problem is limited to a specific browser. It's only by seeing the HTML, CSS, and other assets in context that others can help troubleshoot problems with the way a page displays.

# Spread the Word

If you find this book useful, consider spending a few minutes spreading the word by writing a brief review on your blog or an online bookstore. Constructive criticism of how the book might be improved is also welcome.

---

▨ **Note**   Shortly before this book was sent to the printers, members of the CSS Working Group informally announced that CSS3 won't be followed by CSS4. This is because new modules, such as Flexible Box Layout, don't have equivalents in earlier versions of CSS, creating difficulties for the formal numbering system. In a couple of chapters, I refer to the draft Selectors Level 4 module as "CSS4 Selectors." I decided to leave those references unchanged because no consensus has emerged on what to call them.

---

# PART I

# CSS Basics

If you come from a graphic design background, the idea of using code to control the look and feel of a website probably sounds bizarre. But it's not as bad as it sounds. Styling a site with Cascading Style Sheets (CSS) involves creating a set of instructions that tell the browser what color, size, and font you want to use for your text; how much whitespace you want around different parts of the page; and so on.

The instructions consist of simple pairs of properties and values. Most properties have intuitive names such as font-size, margin-top, or border-color. Values are specified using keywords or concepts that you're likely to be familiar with, for example pixels and RGB or HSL color formats. If you're not sure what they are, don't worry because everything is explained along the way. The three chapters in Part I provide all the basic knowledge you need to start styling your web pages with CSS.

Chapter 1 explains why CSS separates the style information from the HTML markup of web pages. You'll learn what a style rule looks like, and how to make your styles available to all pages in a website. There are also some hints on how to use browsers' developer tools to understand how styles interact with each other.

Chapter 2 introduces the important concept of CSS selectors. Selectors tell the browser which elements you want to apply the styles to. One of the most important selectors is the type (or tag) selector, which redefines the default look of an HTML element. CSS3 defines more than 40 selectors. This chapter introduces you to a subset of the most widely used, and shows you how to give links unique styles in different parts of a page.

Chapter 3 covers the nuts and bolts of specifying sizes, colors, and other values used in style rules. Don't try to memorize all the details. Come back to it as a reference when necessary.

# CHAPTER 1

# Introducing CSS—the Language of Web Design

Building a website with HTML (Hypertext Markup Language) is only half the story. HTML controls the structure of a web page, using tags such as `<p>` for paragraphs, `<img>` for images, and `<input>` for form elements. This structural role has become even more important with the introduction of semantic elements, such as `<article>` and `<nav>`, in HTML5. But HTML says nothing about how the page should look. That's the role of Cascading Style Sheets (CSS). Even default styles are controlled internally by the browser's own CSS.

Instead of applying styles directly to individual elements, the most common—and efficient—way of using CSS is to create the styles in a separate file. At first, this separation of style information from the content of a web page seems counterintuitive. But it has the following significant advantages:

- Less-cluttered HTML code, making it easier to read and maintain

- Changing the look of multiple pages across a site by editing a single file

- Greater control over the way page elements look

---

**Tip** CSS stands for Cascading Style Sheets, but most web designers say "CSS is. . ." rather than "CSS are. . ." This is because they're referring to CSS as a technology and not to individual style sheets.

---

In the early days of web design, the only way to style elements was with HTML tags, such as `<font>` and `<center>`, and attributes, such as `align` and `size`, which needed to be applied to each element individually. Styling web pages like this not only limited the range of design options, but it also meant you needed to make changes to each element individually. With an external style sheet, you make the change in just one place, and it's automatically applied to all matching elements on every page. It's a blueprint for the website's design. Update the blueprint, and the site updates immediately.

In this chapter, you'll learn about the following:

- A brief history of CSS

- The current state of CSS

- Choosing the tools to help you work with CSS

- How to write style rules and apply them to your web pages

- Using browser-specific prefixes for CSS3

- How to avoid common beginner mistakes

# A Short History of CSS

In the beginning, the Web was simple. The first-ever public web page (see Figure 1-1) consisted of plain, unadorned text. Headings were in large, bold type; links were blue and underlined—and that was it.

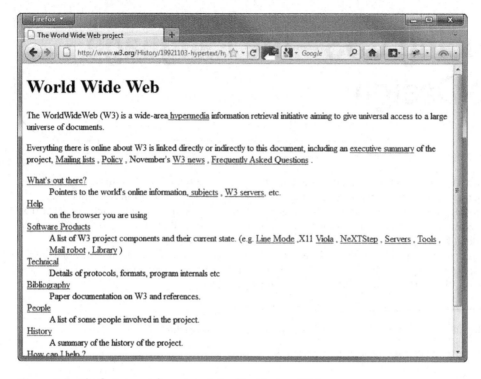

*Figure 1-1.* *The first-ever web page contained just text and links*

---

▓ **Note**　The original, which was created toward the end of 1990, no longer exists, but you can see a copy at www.w3.org/History/19921103-hypertext/hypertext/WWW/TheProject.html.

---

The lack of images and any attempt at styling the page seem odd to us now, but the Web's origins lie in the scientific community, not with artists or graphic designers. It didn't take long before people other than scientists began to demand the ability to include images. Once images began to brighten up web pages, designers began to use their imagination to invent new uses for existing tags. Most notably, the `<table>` tag, which was intended to display scientific data in tabular form, was adapted to provide a grid structure for page layout. HTML was being stretched beyond its limits. Tags such as `<h4>` were no longer used for low-level subheadings, but to display small, bold text. The `<blockquote>` tag, often nested several levels deep, became a way to indent objects, rather than to highlight a quotation from another source. Document structure was thrown to the wind, making it difficult and expensive to maintain web pages or adapt them for other uses, such as printed materials.

The answer was to restore HTML to its original purpose—marking up the structure of the document—and create a new markup language, CSS, devoted to styling the look of a web page. The body responsible for drawing up agreed standards for the Web, the World Wide Web Consortium (W3C), published the first version of this language (CSS1) at the end of 1996, but it wasn't an instant success.

## Why Designers Took So Long to Embrace CSS

According to the W3C, the CSS specification was drawn up in response to "pressure from authors for richer visual control." The demand for better control of web pages was certainly there, but browsers in the late 1990s implemented CSS very poorly or not at all. Only the very brave or foolhardy adopted CSS in the early stages. Nevertheless, the W3C published CSS2 in 1998. CSS2 retained all the features of CSS1 and added some new ones.

Those brave enough to embrace CSS ended up banging their heads on their keyboards in frustration. The specification was a statement of what the W3C thought browsers ought to do. The reality was completely different. Neither of the main browsers, Netscape Navigator or Microsoft Internet Explorer (IE), had good support for CSS. However, Microsoft put a huge effort into improving its browser, sparking off what became known as the browser wars. By the time IE 6 was released in 2001, it supported most of CSS, and won the battle for market share.

With Netscape in terminal decline, adventurous designers began to use CSS in earnest, but IE 6 was far from perfect. Worse, Microsoft sat on its laurels and made no effort to improve CSS support in IE 6 until it began to see its market share eroded by new browsers, such as Firefox, Safari, and Opera. Microsoft's response eventually emerged in the form of IE 7 in 2006. IE 8, which followed in 2009, finally offered support for the whole of CSS2.1 (an updated version of CSS2). In the meantime, the rest of the browser market had already started supporting the next generation of standards, CSS3.

## Understanding the Different Versions of CSS

Because no two browsers ever managed to implement the full CSS2 specification, the W3C issued a revised specification called CSS2.1 in 2002. However, it took a further nine years before CSS2.1 finally received the formal seal of approval in June 2011. Coincidentally, the first part of CSS3—the Color module—became a formal recommendation on the same day as CSS2.1. To speed up the development and adoption of CSS3, the W3C has divided the specification into some 50 modules. Work on some of them is already at an advanced stage. Others are only ideas, and don't yet have any formal proposals.

---

■ **Tip** For an up-to-date list of CSS3 modules and their status, visit www.w3.org/Style/CSS/current-work.

---

The CSS3 Color module expands the type of color formats that you can use in websites to include HSL (hue, saturation, lightness) and alpha transparency. The following year, the Media Queries module also became a formal recommendation. Media queries serve different styles to devices depending on screen width and orientation. Other modules at an advanced stage of development—and widely supported by browsers—at the time of writing include Backgrounds and Borders, and Multi-column Layout. The Background and Borders module makes it easy to add multiple backgrounds to page elements, and to create rounded corners and drop shadows without the need for images. There's also strong support for embedding web fonts.

All the main browser makers now seem committed to implementing CSS3 features as quickly as possible, and the pace at which new versions of browsers are released has rapidly accelerated. This means there's no need to wait for a particular module to gain formal approval. You can begin using many parts of CSS3 in your designs right now. One of the best places to get up-to-date information on which features are supported is the website at http://caniuse.com (see Figure 1-2).

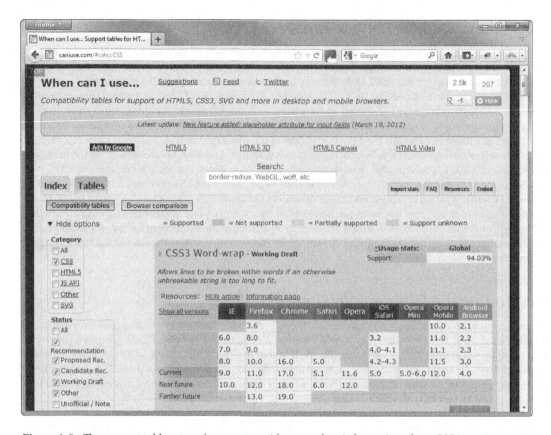

***Figure 1-2.*** *The support tables at caniuse.com provide up-to-date information about CSS3*

Web designers and developers tend to upgrade their browsers much more frequently than other users, who might not even have the freedom to update because of policies imposed by the system administrators at their place of work or study. Choosing whether to use a feature is a decision that only you can make as the designer. If it's important to you that your design looks identical in all browsers, you'll be limited to whatever is supported by the lowest common denominator among your target browsers. However, most people use only one browser, so they won't see the difference—as long as you make sure that the design looks acceptable even in older browsers. Also, many people are now used to seeing websites look different on mobile phones and tablets, so the overall design is more important than pixel-perfect uniformity.

■ **Note** CSS3 builds on the previous versions, preserving existing features and adding new ones. CSS doesn't trigger an error if you use a feature the browser doesn't recognize. Browsers silently ignore CSS properties and values that they don't support.

## So, How Do I Use CSS?

You normally style web pages by creating an external file called a *style sheet*, which contains a series of rules identifying which parts of the page you want to affect and how they should look. Like HTML, CSS is written as plain text. You don't need anything more sophisticated than a text editor, such as Notepad or TextEdit, to start writing

CSS. However, if you're using an HTML editor to build your web pages, you'll almost certainly find that it provides you with code hints or other features, such as code coloring, to help create your style rules. Adobe Dreamweaver (www.adobe.com/products/dreamweaver) and Microsoft Expression Web (www.microsoft.com/expression/products/overview.aspx?key=web), both offer pop-up code hints similar to those shown in Figure 1-3.

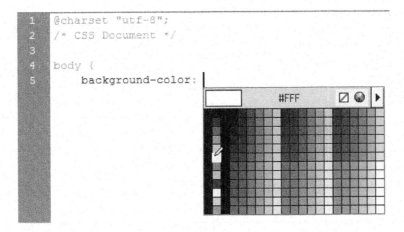

***Figure 1-3.*** *Using CSS code hints in Dreamweaver*

There are also dedicated CSS editors. Among the most popular are Style Master for Windows and Mac (www.westciv.com/style_master/), Espresso for Mac (http://macrabbit.com/espresso/), and Top Style for Windows only (http://svanas.dynip.com/topstyle/index.html).

---

■ **Note**    Your choice of editor is unimportant. This book is strictly software and operating system neutral.

---

## How Do I Write a Style Rule?

Creating a style rule is simple. Figure 1-4 shows the different parts that make up a style rule.

Let's take a look at each part in turn:

- *Selector:* This tells the browser where you want to apply the rule. Figure 1-4 uses a *type selector* (sometimes called a *tag selector*), which redefines the default style of an HTML tag. This example redefines the style of all <p> tags—in other words, paragraphs. You'll learn about other selectors in the next chapter.

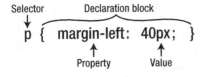

***Figure 1-4.*** *The anatomy of a style rule*

- *Declaration block:* This begins with a left curly brace and ends with a right curly brace. You put your style declarations between these braces. Each declaration consists of a property followed by a colon (:) and value, and ends with a semicolon (;).

- *Property:* This is one of the properties defined in the CSS specification. Most have intuitive names. The property in Figure 1-4 affects the left margin of the element being styled. Property names are not case-sensitive, but they are normally written entirely in lowercase.

- *Value:* This is the value you want to apply to the property. Some properties have a fixed list of values that you can choose from. Others let you specify the value yourself. The example in Figure 1-4 sets the value of the left margin to 40 pixels.

The declaration block in Figure 1-4 contains only one property/value pair, but you can define any number of properties in the same declaration block.

---

■ **Tip**  Strictly speaking, you can leave out the semicolon after the last declaration in a block or if the block contains only one property/value pair. But you should get into the habit of always using a semicolon because you might forget to insert it when later adding extra declarations to the same block. A missing semicolon in the middle of a block is a common cause of CSS failing to work as expected.

---

## Using Browser-specific Prefixes for CSS3 Properties

At the time it was introduced, IE 6 was considered an excellent browser, but it had some terrible bugs that continued to frustrate designers more than 10 years after its release. To avoid a similar situation with CSS3, browser makers have decided to prefix the names of new or experimental properties with the browser-specific identifiers listed in Table 1-1.

*Table 1-1.* *The Main Browser-specific Prefixes for CSS3 Properties*

| Prefix | Browsers |
| --- | --- |
| -moz- | Firefox |
| -ms- | Internet Explorer |
| -o- | Opera |
| -webkit- | Google Chrome, Safari |

For example, when creating a CSS gradient, you need to use three browser-specific prefixes in addition to the standard property like this:

```
div {
    background-image: -moz-linear-gradient(#C24704, #FFEB79);
    background-image: -o-linear-gradient(#C24704, #FFEB79);
    background-image: -webkit-linear-gradient(#C24704, #FFEB79);
    background-image: linear-gradient(#C24704, #FFEB79);
}
```

This might look like a waste of time and effort because the values for the browser-specific versions are identical to the standard property. However, some browsers implemented CSS3 gradients and flexible box layout before the specifications stabilized, and they used different syntax to define the values. Using prefixes like this ensures that incorrect syntax in one browser doesn't affect the way your pages look in other browsers. As noted earlier, browsers ignore properties that they don't recognize. So, Firefox ignores properties prefixed with -ms-, -o-, and -webkit-. The other browsers do likewise, applying only their own prefix. By placing the version without a prefix last, the normal rules of the cascade ensure that all browsers implement the standard property as soon as it's supported.

The CSS3 support tables at caniuse.com (see Figure 1-2) indicate which properties and browser versions require these browser-specific prefixes.

■ **Tip** If the syntax changes, you should normally update only the value for the standard property. The prefixed value will be used by browsers that implemented an earlier syntax. When a CSS property finally stabilizes, you can drop the browser-specific prefixes unless your target browsers still need them.

## Formatting CSS for Ease of Maintenance

Browsers don't care how you format your style rules. As long as you separate each property from its value by a colon, put a semicolon after the value, and surround declaration blocks with curly braces, the browser ignores any whitespace in your style sheet. However, a consistent layout makes your CSS easier to maintain.

Figure 1-4 uses whitespace to make the rule easier to read, but the following is just as valid:

```
p{margin-left:40px;}
```

Spreading everything out even more like this is also acceptable:

```
p {
    margin-left : 40px ;
}
```

However, the following *will not work* because spaces are not permitted in property names or values:

```
p {
    margin - left : 40 px;
}
```

■ **Caution** Although CSS ignores whitespace in style declarations, you cannot put spaces in property names. Nor can there be any whitespace in the value between a number and the unit of measurement. Accidentally putting a space between 40 and px renders the rule invalid and prevents it from working.

## Adding Comments to Your CSS

Style sheets can run to hundreds of lines, so it's often a good idea to add comments to your style sheets to remind you what a particular rule or set of rules is for. Anything between /* and */ is treated as a comment in CSS and is ignored by the browser. For example:

```
/* This is a CSS comment */
```

Comments can be spread over more than one line like this:

```
/* This is a CSS comment that is spread over multiple lines.
   The browser ignores everything until the end of this line. */
```

Comment tags can also be used to disable part of your CSS temporarily. This is a useful technique when experimenting with new ideas or troubleshooting problems. Just put the opening /* and closing */ comment tags around the section that you want to disable. You can disable a single declaration or a whole section at a time. For example, this disables the color and background-color properties in the following rule:

```
body {
    font-family: Arial, Helvetica, sans-serif;
    /* color: #000;
    background-color: #FFF; */
}
```

Just remove the comment tags to restore the rules.

---

■ **Caution**   Comments cannot be nested. As soon as the browser encounters the first */ closing tag, it treats everything else as CSS until it finds another /* opening tag.

---

## Why Are They Called "Cascading" Style Sheets?

The *cascade* in CSS refers to the way that rules are added together and applied cumulatively. Think of the cascade in the literal sense of a waterfall or a river. As a river flows from the mountains to the sea, it starts off as a tiny trickle, but as more water is added through tributaries, it becomes bigger and more powerful. Yet the water in that original trickle is still part of the whole.

CSS works in a similar way. You can create a style rule that trickles down through the whole page. For example, it's common to set the background and text colors in a rule for the body of the page. But lower down, new rules can be added that affect the font or size of the text in paragraphs or headings without changing the color or background. And just like a river can break into a delta as it reaches the sea, you can break the CSS cascade into different strands, so that a sidebar looks different from the main content or footer of the page.

This might sound mysterious at the moment, but all should become clear by the end of this book. The important things to remember are these:

- *Styles trickle down:* A style rule applied to the <body> affects everything inside the page unless something else overrides it.

- *Styles are cumulative:* Most property values are inherited, so you need apply only new ones.

- *Inherited styles can be overridden:* When you want to treat an element or section of the page differently, you can create more detailed style rules and apply them selectively.

In most cases, the order of your style rules doesn't matter. However, the cascade plays an important role when there's a conflict between rules. As a basic principle, style rules that appear lower down in a style sheet or <style> block override any previous rules in the case of a direct conflict. Chapter 2 describes in more detail how to determine which rule takes precedence.

# Where Do I Create My CSS?

Most of the time, you should create style rules in an external style sheet attached to the web page. But styles can also be defined in:

- A `<style>` block

- A style attribute

I'll cover each way of adding styles, but let's begin with the most important—external style sheets.


## Using External Style Sheets

This is the most common and effective way of using CSS. The styles in external style sheets affect all pages to which they're linked.  Typically an external style sheet is used for an entire site or subsection of a site, making it easy to update multiple pages by editing only one file. What's more, the browser caches the style sheets, so they need to be downloaded only once regardless of how many pages are viewed in your site. This speeds up the display of subsequent pages and reduces bandwidth usage. You can link more than one style sheet to a page.

Create your style rules in a separate file, and save the file with the file name extension `.css`. An external style sheet can be anywhere within your website, but the normal practice is to put all style sheets in a dedicated folder called `styles` or `css`.

You attach an external style sheet in the `<head>` section of your web page using a `<link>` tag or a CSS `@import` rule. A `<link>` tag looks like this:

```
<link href="css/basic.css" rel="stylesheet">
```

In HTML5, the `<link>` tag requires two attributes:

> `href` This is the path to the external style sheet.

> `rel` This tells the browser that the file is a style sheet. Note that the value `stylesheet` is written as one word. This attribute also accepts the value `alternate stylesheet`, but it's of little practical value because browsers give no obvious indication of a choice of styles, and the user needs to select the alternate styles manually on each page.

To validate in HTML 4.01 and XHTML 1.0, you also need to add `type="text/css"` in a `<link>` tag. The `type` attribute was dropped in HTML5 because CSS is the only type of style sheet used in web pages.

If you're using an HTML editor, such as Dreamweaver or Expression Web, the `<link>` tag is created automatically when you select the option to attach a style sheet.

The alternative to using a `<link>` tag is to use a CSS `@import` rule. This technique was frequently used in the past to hide styles from older browsers that didn't support `@import`. All current browsers now support `@import`, so there's no real advantage in using it to link a style sheet directly to a web page. However, I have included it here so you know what it's for if you come across it in an existing site. The `@import` rule goes inside an HTML `<style>` block in the `<head>` of the page like this:

```
<style>
@import url(css/basic.css);
</style>
```

The location of the style sheet is specified by putting it between the parentheses of `url()`. The path to the style sheet can optionally be enclosed in quotes.

The main purpose of `@import` is to import styles from one style sheet into another. This can be useful when you organize your rules in several style sheets. Instead of linking each style sheet separately to your web pages, you can link just one, which then imports the rules from the other style sheets. If you do this, the `@import` rule *must* come before any other style rules in the external style sheet. Also, because it's in an external style sheet, you don't wrap it in an HTML `<style>` block. The following code shows how you might import rules into one external style sheet from another:

```
@import url(another.css);
/* Other style rules */
body {
    font-family: Arial, Helvetica, sans-serif;
    color: #000;
    background-color: #FFF;
}
```

---

■ **Caution**  An external style sheet must *not* contain anything other than CSS style rules or CSS comments. You cannot mix HTML, JavaScript, or anything else in a style sheet. If you do, your styles won't work.

---

## Using a <style> Block

Using an HTML `<style>` block limits the style rules to the current page, so this technique should not be used for styles that will be applied to multiple pages. One exception is when you're planning your site's design. Many designers prefer to work in a single page to refine their ideas before moving the styles to an external style sheet. Because they're embedded in the page, these are known as *embedded styles*.

To create a `<style>` block, you write the style rules in exactly the same way as in an external style sheet, and wrap them in a pair of HTML `<style>` tags. For valid HTML 4.01 and XHTML 1.0, the opening tag must contain `type="text/css"` like this:

```
<style type="text/css">
/* Style definitions go here */
</style>
```

You can omit `type="text/css"` from the opening tag in HTML5.

In HTML 4.01 and XHTML 1.0, a `<style>` block can only be in the `<head>` of the page. HTML5 relaxes this restriction, and introduces the concept of *scoped styles* in `<style>` blocks in the body of a page. A scoped `<style>` block in HTML5 applies highly localized styles to the current element and all the element's children (other elements nested inside it).

The idea of allowing scoped styles inside the body of the page is controversial because it violates the principle of separating content from presentation. However, one scenario where scoped styles could be useful is with prestyled components or widgets, such as calendars or date-pickers that you want to drop into a page without needing to update the site's main style sheet.

When using scoped styles, the `<style>` block must come before everything else inside the HTML element to which the styles apply. The opening `<style>` tag requires the `scoped` attribute like this:

```
<div class="calendar">
<style scoped>
/* These styles apply only to the calendar widget */
table {
    font-size: 11px;
    background-color: teal;
}
</style>
    <table>
        <tr>. . . </tr>
    </table>
</div>
```

---

▨ **Note**   At the time of this writing, only the development version of Chrome supports scoped styles.

---

## Applying a Style Directly to an HTML Element

This goes in the opening tag of an HTML element, so it applies to that element alone. This is known as creating an *inline style* and should be avoided because it's the least efficient way to apply CSS. As with all rules, there *is* an exception: some email programs, notably Microsoft Outlook, don't understand style rules unless they're applied this way.

Inline styles use the same properties and values as CSS rules that you put in an external style sheet or a `<style>` block. However, you don't need a selector (the HTML tag itself acts as the selector), and the curly braces are replaced by quotes. For example, you might create the following style rule for `<h1>` tags:

```
h1 {
    font-family: Arial, Helvetica, sans-serif;
    color: #900;
}
```

The equivalent inline style looks like this:

```
<h1 style="font-family: Arial, Helvetica, sans-serif; color: #900;">Heading with an Inline
Style</h1>
```

# Learning to Write CSS Well

The basics of writing a style rule are simple, but CSS can also be infuriatingly complex. The simplicity of CSS lies in the limited number of properties you need to remember. The complexity lies in the fact that you can combine the properties in an infinite number of ways.

My advice is not to rush. I learned CSS by adding or changing one property at a time and viewing the results in a browser. It was a slow, tedious process, but it helped me understand the interaction of the different properties. Once you appreciate the trickle-down, cumulative effect of the cascade, you'll be amazed at the power of CSS. The time spent will be repaid many times over in increased efficiency and easier maintenance of your websites.

Don't succumb to the temptation to skip ahead to later chapters until you have read at least Parts I and II and the first two chapters of Part III.

## Test Your CSS Early in Several Browsers

Don't design for just one browser. Get into the habit of checking your design at an early stage in several browsers—and preferably on different operating systems, including mobile devices. Spotting a problem early on makes it easy to troubleshoot. Not everyone will be viewing your sites in the most up-to-date browsers. If you don't have access to older browsers, ask friends, colleagues, or online forums for help in checking your sites. Also consider using an online browser capture service such as BrowserCam (`www.browsercam.com`) or Adobe BrowserLab (`https://browserlab.adobe.com/en-us/index.html`).

## Use Browser Developer Tools to Inspect Your CSS

All the main browsers have built-in panels that let you inspect the styles not only of your own site but of any public website, giving you a useful insight into how CSS works. In Google Chrome, Safari, or Firefox, right-click the element you want to inspect, and select *Inspect Element* from the context menu. This opens the developer tools with the underlying HTML element highlighted and all the style rules that have been applied to it (see Figure 1-5). Similar tools can be accessed in IE 8 and later by pressing F12, and in Opera by selecting *Tools* ➤ *Advanced* ➤ *Opera Dragonfly*.

***Figure 1-5.** The Developer Tools panel in Chrome*

In the initial stages, you'll find the amount of information overwhelming, but you can toggle individual rules on and off or edit them to see what effect your changes have. Style definitions that have been overridden are displayed with a strikethrough line. Studying your own pages, as well as sites that you admire, greatly increases your understanding of CSS.

■ **Tip**    To gain access to the developer tools in Safari, you need to open the *Preferences* panel from the *Edit* menu in Windows or the *Safari* menu in Mac OS X. In the *Advanced* tab, select the *Show Develop menu in menu bar* check box.

# Summary

This chapter has given you a brief overview of the development of CSS and the advantages of separating styling information from the HTML markup that controls the structure of your web pages. Locating style rules in one or more external files allows you to apply changes instantly throughout a website rather than needing to update each element and page individually. You can also embed styles in a `<style>` block in the `<head>` of the page; and HTML5 introduces the concept of scoped styles for an individual element and its children. Inline styles apply to a single element only, and should be avoided, except for HTML email.

Style rules consist of a selector followed by one or more property/value pairs wrapped in curly braces. The selector identifies the element(s) to which you want the style to apply. In the next chapter, you'll learn about the basic selectors supported by all browsers, including IE 6.

# CHAPTER 2

# Using Basic Selectors

Choosing the right selector is the key to working successfully with CSS. The CSS3 specification defines more than 40 selectors, allowing you to target your styles accurately without the need for extra HTML markup. The latest versions of all browsers support the full range of CSS3 selectors, plus some nonstandard ones. However, not everyone uses the latest browsers, so—at least in the early stages of learning CSS— it makes sense to concentrate on selectors that are supported even by older browsers.

In this chapter, you'll learn about the following:

- How the browser uses the Document Object Model to apply styles

- How to change the default look of HTML elements

- Styling new HTML5 elements in older browsers

- What the difference is between class and ID selectors

- Choosing good names for classes

- How to style links with pseudo-classes

- How to apply styles to different sections of a page using descendant selectors

- How to change the look of the cursor

- How to style the first line or letter using pseudo-elements

- Determining which styles take precedence in case of a conflict

## How Selectors Work

When a browser loads a web page, it reads the HTML tags to build a tree-like outline of the page's structure. This is known as the *Document Object Model* (DOM). Understanding the basic principles of the DOM is essential to many aspects of web design and development. JavaScript manipulates the DOM to add dynamic widgets, such as accordions and tabbed panels, or to load fresh data asynchronously. CSS also relies on the DOM to apply styles to specific elements.

## Understanding the DOM

Listing 2-1 contains the HTML markup for a simple web page, dom.html:

**Listing 2-1.** Exploring the DOM

```
<!doctype html>
<html>
<head>
<meta charset="utf-8">
<title>Understanding the DOM</title>
</head>
<body>
<h1>How the Document Object Model Works</h1>
<p>The <dfn>Document Object Model</dfn> (<abbr title="Document Object Model">DOM</abbr>) creates
a tree-like structure of the page.</p>
</body>
</html>
```

As Figure 2-1 shows, the browser applies some basic styling to different HTML elements. The <h1> heading is rendered in a large, bold font, the words inside the <dfn> tags are italicized, and the contents of the <abbr> element have a dotted underline.

**Figure 2-1.** *The browser adds default styles to the page*

---

■ **Note**   The <dfn> tag is one of the oldest elements in HTML, first mentioned in the HTML 2 specification in 1995, but many web designers have never heard of it. The tag represents the defining instance of a term. With the emphasis on semantic—or meaningful—structure in HTML5, the <dfn> tag deserves to be dusted off and restored to its rightful place in HTML markup.

---

Internally, the browser builds a representation of the DOM like a family tree, as shown in Figure 2-2.

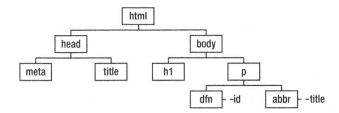

**Figure 2-2.** *The browser sees the page as a hierarchical structure based on the HTML tags*

The family tree analogy is also applied to the relationship between HTML elements. At the top of the family tree in Figure 2-2 is the <html> element, which is known as the *root element*. Next come the <head> and <body> elements, which are the <html> element's *children* or *child elements*. Because they're at the same level of the family tree, the <head> and <body> elements are considered *siblings*. Further down the family tree, the <h1> and <p> elements are also siblings, but they're children of the <body> element and *descendants* of the <html> element. The relationship also works the other way—the <body> element is the *parent* of the <h1> and <p> elements. At the bottom level of Figure 2-2, the <dfn> and <abbr> elements have id and title attributes respectively. Going back up the family tree, all elements in the same branch are the *ancestors* of the <dfn> and <abbr> elements.

The browser uses the DOM as a roadmap to apply styles in accordance with the selector associated with each style rule. You create selectors using the tag and attribute names in various combinations, frequently reflecting the family-tree relationship of different elements. Consequently, it's important not only to have a clear understanding of the DOM, but also to ensure that your HTML is well constructed. If elements are incorrectly nested, the browser is likely to have difficulty reading the roadmap, and your page might not be styled the way you expected. Also, if your markup is overly complex, the browser will have difficulty navigating the DOM. Even if it renders your styles correctly, your pages are likely to load more slowly.

---

■ **Tip** If your styles aren't working the way you expect, always check your HTML markup using the W3C validation service at http://validator.w3.org/. Invalid HTML is one of the main causes of problems with CSS.

---

## The Importance of the DOCTYPE

The first line of the HTML markup in Listing 2-1 looks like this:

```
<!doctype html>
```

This is the HTML5 DOCTYPE preamble, which is required to ensure that the browser renders your styles correctly. The DOCTYPE is case-insensitive, so you can use <!DOCTYPE html> or any other combination of uppercase and lowercase.

If you are using HTML 4.01 or XHTML 1.0, you should use one of the following versions of the DOCTYPE:

```
<!DOCTYPE HTML PUBLIC "-//W3C//DTD HTML 4.01 Transitional//EN"
"http://www.w3.org/TR/html4/loose.dtd">
```

```
<!DOCTYPE HTML PUBLIC "-//W3C//DTD HTML 4.01//EN" "http://www.w3.org/TR/html4/strict.dtd">
```

```
<!DOCTYPE html PUBLIC "-//W3C//DTD XHTML 1.0 Transitional//EN"
"http://www.w3.org/TR/xhtml1/DTD/xhtml1-transitional.dtd">
```

```
<!DOCTYPE html PUBLIC "-//W3C//DTD XHTML 1.0 Strict//EN"
"http://www.w3.org/TR/xhtml1/DTD/xhtml1-strict.dtd">
```

19

The important element in each of these versions is the URL, which points to the Document Type Definition (DTD). Browsers use this reference to the DTD to render CSS in *standards mode*—in other words, according to the CSS specification. Some older HTML editing programs omit the URL like this:

```
<!DOCTYPE HTML PUBLIC "-//W3C//DTD HTML 4.01 Transitional//EN">
```

If you use a shorter version of the HTML 4.01 or XHTML 1.0 DOCTYPE or omit the DOCTYPE altogether, browsers switch to *quirks mode*, which results in widths being applied incorrectly.

---

■ **Note**   Quirks mode is hangover from the days when Internet Explorer interpreted the CSS box model (see Chapter 6) incorrectly. IE 6 corrected the problem, but browsers used the DOCTYPE to switch between quirks and standards mode to prevent breaking the huge number of web pages that had been designed using the wrong interpretation of the standard.

---

The HTML5 DOCTYPE is now the recommended version, which you can safely use in all browsers—even IE 6. It was designed as the shortest string of characters guaranteed to switch all browsers into standards mode.

# Deciding Which Selector to Use

The CSS2.1 specification defines 22 selectors, and CSS3 adds almost as many again. Instead of attempting to cover the full range, I think it makes sense to begin with a subset of the most widely supported. The last four items in Table 2-1 (attribute selectors) are not supported by IE 6, but I've included them in this list because they are so useful and because IE 6 now has an insignificant market share in most parts of the world.

The first column in Table 2-1 follows the convention in the CSS specification of using E and F to represent generic selectors. The meaning should become clear in the descriptions and exercises that follow in the rest of this chapter.

**Table 2-1.** *Basic CSS Selectors Supported by Most Current Browsers*

| Pattern/Selector | Name | Meaning |
|---|---|---|
| * | Universal selector | Matches any element. |
| E | Type selector | Matches any HTML element of type E. The selector consists of the HTML tag name without the angle brackets. For example, h1 selects all <h1> tags. |
| .className | Class | Matches elements with the class attribute className. |
| #someId | ID selector | Matches elements with the id attribute someId. |
| E:link | Link pseudo-class | Matches elements of type E if E is an unvisited link. |
| E:visited | Visited pseudo-class | Matches elements of type E if E is a visited link. |
| E:hover | Hover pseudo-class | Matches elements of type E when the cursor is hovering over it. IE 6 supports this only on links. Other browsers support it on all elements. |
| E:active | Active pseudo-class | Matches elements of type E at the moment the element is being clicked. IE 6 and IE 7 support this only on links. |
| E:focus | Focus pseudo-class | Matches elements of type E when the element currently has focus. Not supported by IE 6 or IE 7. |
| E:first-letter | First-letter pseudo-element | Matches the first letter of element E. |
| E:first-line | First-line pseudo-element | Matches the first line of element E. |
| E F | Descendant selector | Matches any F element that is a descendant of an E element. |
| E[attr] | Attribute selector | Matches elements of type E with the attribute attr. |
| E[attr="x"] | Attribute selector | Matches elements of type E where the value of the attr attribute is exactly "x". |
| E[attr^="x"] | Attribute selector | Matches elements of type E where the value of the attr attribute begins with "x". |
| E[attr$="x"] | Attribute selector | Matches elements of type E where the value of the attr attribute ends with "x". |

# Universal Selector

The *universal selector* is represented by an asterisk (*). It selects any element, but is rarely used except to create hacks to hide styles from IE 6.

# Type Selectors

A *type selector* uses the name of an HTML tag without the angle brackets, and redefines the default look of the tag. For this reason, type selectors are sometimes called *tag selectors*. For example, h1 defines the style of <h1> tags. You can use type selectors for all HTML 4.01 and XHTML 1.0 elements without problem. However, you need to exercise care when using type selectors for new HTML5 elements, as explained in the sidebar "Styling New HTML5 Elements in Older Browsers."

---

## STYLING NEW HTML5 ELEMENTS IN OLDER BROWSERS

HTML5 is designed to be backward compatible, so most browsers allow you to apply CSS to the new HTML5 semantic elements, such as <header>, <section>, and <nav>, even if they don't recognize them. All that's necessary is to add the following rule to your style sheet:

```
article, aside, figure, footer, header, nav, section {
    display: block;
    margin: 0;
    padding: 0;
}
```

This style rule tells the browser to treat the new HTML5 elements the same as a <div>. In other words, the element occupies a line of its own with no extra vertical or horizontal spacing. Unfortunately, IE 6–8 leave HTML5 elements unstyled unless you convince the browser to recognize the new elements by adding the following code just before the closing </head> tag in each page:

```
!--[if lt IE 9]>
<script src="http://html5shim.googlecode.com/svn/trunk/html5.js"></script>
<![endif]-->
```

This code is an Internet Explorer conditional comment (www.quirksmode.org/css/condcom.html) that tells versions of Internet Explorer earlier than IE 9 to load a tiny script created by JavaScript genius, Remy Sharp. The script creates dummy HTML5 elements in the browser's memory. The elements are never displayed, but their existence is sufficient to coax IE 6–8 into styling other HTML5 elements in your page. The link loads the script from Google's content distribution network. If you prefer, you can download the script, and store it on your own web server.

The only disadvantage of this technique is that it relies on JavaScript being enabled in the browser. A detailed survey by Yahoo! in 2010 estimated that about 2 percent of users in the USA have JavaScript disabled (http://developer.yahoo.com/blogs/ydn/posts/2010/10/how-many-users-have-javascript-disabled/). The figure for most other countries was 1.3 percent. Although that's a small proportion, on a busy site it can represent tens of thousands or even millions of users. Consequently, if your target audience is still using IE 6–8, you should probably avoid using the new HTML5 elements.

---

# Class Selectors

A *class selector* applies style rules to elements that have the equivalent class attribute in their opening HTML tag. The selector is created by prefixing the class name by a period. For example, the .warning class selector applies to all elements that have class="warning" in the opening tag. Multiple classes can be applied to the same element by separating the class names by a space in the class attribute, for example, class="warning important".

When choosing class names, try to pick a name that describes what the style is for rather than what it looks like. For example, if you choose boldRed as a class name, it won't make any sense if you decide to use italic instead. You'll either be left with a class that no longer accurately describes it, or you will need to change every instance of the class name in your HTML markup.

Class names must also adhere to the following rules:

- No spaces are permitted.

- The only punctuation characters permitted are the hyphen (-) and underscore (_).

- The name cannot begin with a number or a hyphen followed by a number.

---

■ **Tip** If you're using a language other than English, you can also use accented characters in class names, as long as your pages are encoded as UTF-8. In fact, you can also use Chinese characters or other Asian scripts. When using accented characters or other scripts in an external style sheet, put @charset "utf-8"; on the first line of the style sheet to indicate that it uses UTF-8 encoding.

---

## ID Selectors

An *ID selector* applies styles to elements that have the equivalent id attribute in their opening HTML tag. Unlike classes, which can be applied to multiple elements in the same page, IDs must be unique within a page. It's OK to apply the same ID on different pages, as long as it's used only once on each page.

The selector is created by prefixing the ID with the hash or pound sign (#). For example, #sidebar applies to the element that has id="sidebar" in its opening tag. The rules for naming IDs are the same as for class names.

## Pseudo-classes

A *pseudo-class* doesn't rely on a class attribute in the HTML markup, but is applied automatically by the browser depending on the position of the element or its interactive state. The pseudo-classes listed in Table 2-1 apply mainly to links and form elements.

## Pseudo-elements

Like a pseudo-class, a *pseudo-element* is not identified as such by HTML markup. It applies styles to content based on its position in the HTML hierarchy. The most widely supported pseudo-elements are

:first-letter This applies a style to the first letter of the first line inside a block-level element, such as a paragraph, as long as nothing else precedes it.

:first-line This applies a style to the first line of text in a block-level element. The length expands and contracts dynamically if the text is rewrapped.

---

■ **Note** The CSS3 Selectors specification prefixes pseudo-elements with two colons instead of one. So, :first-letter becomes ::first-letter and :first-line becomes ::first-line. The specification says browsers *must* accept the single-colon prefix for :first-letter and :first-line, as well as for:before and :after, which are covered in Chapters 13 and 15. IE 8 and earlier don't understand the double-colon prefix, so you need use the single-colon versions to avoid styles breaking in older browsers.

---

## Descendant Selectors

A *descendant selector* matches any element that is a descendant of another. To create a descendant selector, separate the two selectors by a space, putting the ancestor first. For example, `#sidebar p` affects only paragraphs that are descendants of an element that has the ID `sidebar`.

## Attribute Selectors

An *attribute selector* matches any element that has a particular attribute in its opening HTML tag. Because IE 6 doesn't support them, attribute selectors have been largely overlooked by web designers. Now that the market share of IE 6 has dropped to insignificant levels in many parts of the world, you should become familiar with them and incorporate them into your styles unless a large part of your target audience is still using IE 6.

You create an attribute selector by putting the attribute—optionally with a value—in a pair of square brackets after a type (tag) selector.

The following sections describe the most common attribute selectors.

### Match Any Value

The simplest type of attribute selector matches an element that contains a particular attribute in its opening tag. The value of the attribute is unimportant. For example, the following style rule adds a five-pixel red border around every image that contains the `alt` attribute:

```
img[alt] {
    border: 5px solid red;
}
```

This can be useful for checking that all images have alternate text before uploading your site. You can see instantly if the `alt` attribute is missing from any images because they won't have a border. Obviously, you would use this only for local testing—unless you like heavy red borders on your images, that is.

### Match an Exact Value

To select elements with attributes that have a specific value, add an equal sign after the attribute followed by the value you want to match. This is particularly useful when styling forms. For example, the following style rule gives all text input fields a width of 250 pixels:

```
input[type="text"] {
    width: 250px;
}
```

### Match the Beginning of a Value

You can select elements by matching only the first few characters of an attribute's value. Precede the equal sign with a caret or circumflex like this:

```
a[href^="http://"] {
    color: red;
}
```

This matches all links where the `href` attribute begins with `http://`. In other words, it matches all external links, except those made over a secure connection.

## Match the End of a Value

To match the last few characters of an attribute's value, precede the equal sign with a dollar sign. For example, the following style rule matches all links to PDF documents, and displays a PDF symbol alongside the link text:

```
a[href$=".pdf"] {
    padding-right: 20px;
    background-image: url(../images/pdficon_small.gif);
    background-repeat: no-repeat;
    background-position: right center;
}
```

---

■ **Note**   Quotation marks around the value of an attribute selector are optional if the value contains only alphanumeric characters.

---

# Grouping Multiple Selectors

To avoid repetition when applying the same styles to several elements, you can group selectors as a comma-separated list. For example, the following style rule changes the color of all headings:

```
h1, h2, h3, h4, h5, h6 {
    color: red;
}
```

# Trying It Out

It's time to put some of that theory to the test. Listing 2-2 shows the HTML markup in the <body> of basic.html, which you'll style using the basic selectors in Table 2-1.

*Listing 2-2.* The <body> Section in basic.html

```
<body>
<h1>Beginning CSS3</h1>
<ul id="nav">
    <li><a href="#">Introducing CSS—the Language of Web Design</a></li>
    <li><a href="#">Specifying Sizes, Colors, and Files</a></li>
    <li><a href="http://apress.com/">Apress—Books for Professionals by Professionals</a></li>
</ul>
<div id="main">
    <h2>Deciding Which Selector to Use</h2>
    <p class="intro">Instead of attempting to cover the full  range of <abbr title="Cascading
Style Sheets">CSS</abbr> selectors, I think it makes sense to begin with a subset of the most
widely supported. The <a href="http://www.quirksmode.org/css/contents.html">compatibility charts
compiled by Peter-Paul Koch</a> provide detailed support information.</p>
    <h3>Type Selectors</h3>
    <p>A <dfn>type selector</dfn> uses the name of an HTML tag without the angle brackets,
and redefines the  default look of the tag. For example, <code>h1</code> defines the style of
<code><h1></code> tags.  You can use type selectors for all HTML 4.01 and XHTML 1.0 elements
without  problem.</p>
```

```
<h3>Class Selectors</h3>
<p>A <dfn>class  selector</dfn> applies style rules to elements that have the equivalent
<code>class</code> attribute in their opening HTML tag. For example, the <code>.warning</code>
class selector applies to all elements that have <code>class="warning</code>" in the opening
tag.</p>
</div>
</body>
```

When viewed in a browser, basic.html looks like Figure 2-3. The browser adds some default styles, such as underlining links and displaying unvisited links in blue and visited ones in purple. Most browsers display the text in the <abbr> tags with a dotted underline, italicize the text in <dfn> tags, and use a monospaced font for the text in <code> tags.

---

■ **Note**    Browsers that use the WebKit rendering engine, such as Safari and Google Chrome, don't display <dfn> elements in italic. Checking the default styling of HTML elements is one of the major challenges of CSS.

---

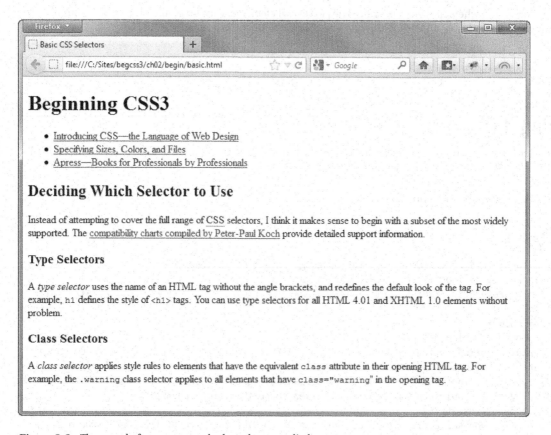

*Figure 2-3.* *The page before custom styles have been applied*

## EXERCISE: REDEFINING THE DEFAULT LOOK OF HTML TAGS

This exercise shows how much you can achieve by redefining the default look of HTML tags with type selectors. Don't worry if you don't understand the properties and values. They will be described in detail in subsequent chapters. In any case, you'll find most of them self-explanatory.

1. Open `basic.html` in the `begin` folder for this chapter.

2. Create a subfolder called `css` within the `begin` folder.

3. Create a new blank file in the `css` folder and save it as `basic.css`.

4. Attach the new style sheet (`basic.css`) to the web page by adding the following `<link>` tag just before the closing `</head>` tag in `basic.html`:

   ```
   <link href="css/basic.css" rel="stylesheet">
   ```

5. Redefine the default settings for the `<body>` tag by adding the following style definition to basic.css:

   ```css
   body {
       background-color: #F7F7F7;
       color: black;
       font-family: "Trebuchet MS", Arial, Helvetica, sans-serif;
   }
   ```

6. Save both pages, and load `basic.html` into a browser. The background color of the page is now a very light gray, the text is black, and the default font has changed. The font affects all text on the page because the headings, paragraphs, and list items are all descendants of the `<body>` tag, so they inherit the style automatically. Strictly speaking, there's no need to specify the text color as black, because that's the default. But it's always a good idea to specify both the background color and text color in the `body` style rule.

7. Change the font and text color for the headings by adding the following rule:

   ```css
   h1, h2, h3 {
       font-family: Tahoma, Geneva, sans-serif;
       color: teal;
   }
   ```

8. Save the style sheet, and reload `basic.html` in a browser. The font and text color of the headings has changed, overriding the `body` rule. The other text still inherits the styles from the earlier rule. The order of the rules isn't important here. The headings have changed because the `h1`, `h2`, and `h3` type selectors target them directly, so they no longer inherit the font or text color from the `<body>`.

9. Change the text color of the `<dfn>` and `<code>` elements by adding the following styles to `basic.css`:

   ```css
   dfn {
       color: maroon;
   }
   ```

```
code {
    color: gray;
}
```

10. To display the `<dfn>` elements in italic in Chrome and Safari, amend the `dfn` style rule like this:

```
dfn {
    color: maroon;
    font-style: italic;
}
```

11. By default, browsers display paragraph text at 16 pixels. Change the font size in the paragraphs like this:

```
p {
  font-size: 14px;
}
```

12. Save the style sheet, and reload `basic.html` in a browser. As Figure 2-4 shows, the text in the paragraphs is smaller, but the size of the headings and list items is unaffected.

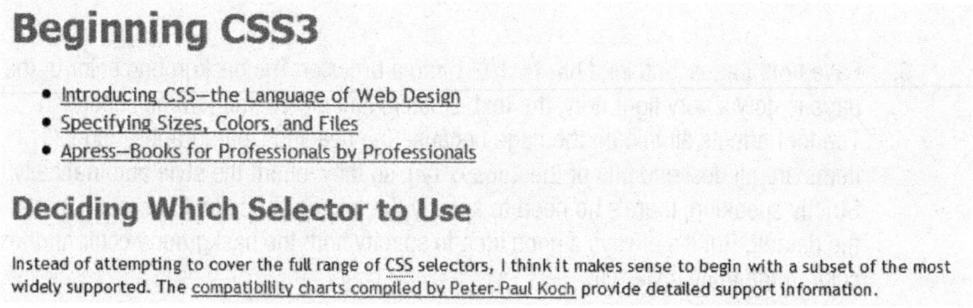

# Beginning CSS3

- Introducing CSS—the Language of Web Design
- Specifying Sizes, Colors, and Files
- Apress—Books for Professionals by Professionals

## Deciding Which Selector to Use

Instead of attempting to cover the full range of CSS selectors, I think it makes sense to begin with a subset of the most widely supported. The compatibility charts compiled by Peter-Paul Koch provide detailed support information.

*Figure 2-4.* *Changing the font size of the paragraphs doesn't affect the other text*

You'll continue making improvements to the look of this page in the remaining exercises

## Styling Links

Links are created using the `<a>` tag in HTML, so you can use a type selector to control the look of links. For example, the following rule makes links bold and red:

```
a {
    font-weight: bold;
    color: red;
}
```

That's fine as far as it goes, but it means that links will look the same, regardless of whether they have been visited or when the mouse passes over a link. The answer is to use pseudo-classes to define how you want links to look dependent on their interactive state. You add the pseudo-class immediately after the type selector like this:

**a:link** Unvisited link

**a:visited** Visited link

**a:hover** Link when the mouse is over it

**a:active** Link at the point of being clicked

**a:focus** Link when it has focus (for example, when accessed by the Tab key)

For the styles to work correctly, the cascade depends on this order being preserved. Many designers use the mnemonic *LoVe-HAte* to remember the correct order of pseudo-classes. The capital letters refer to the first letter of each one—*L* for :link, *V* for :visited, and so on.

It's common to create separate styles for :link and :visited, but the :hover pseudo-class is often combined with the :active and :focus styles.

## EXERCISE: STYLING LINKS IN DIFFERENT SECTIONS

This exercise shows you not only how to apply styles to links with pseudo-classes, but it also demonstrates the effects of inheritance through the cascade. After creating basic styles for all links, you'll learn how to use descendant selectors to apply different styles to links according to where they are in the HTML family-tree hierarchy.

1. Continue working with basic.html and basic.css from the preceding exercise. Alternatively, copy basic_01.html and css/basic_01.css from the end folder for this chapter.

2. Add the following style rule at the bottom of basic.css to set the basic styles for all links:

```
a {
    font-weight: bold;
    text-decoration: none;
}
```

3. Save the style sheet, and reload basic.html in a browser. All links are now bold, and the underline has been removed; but they still retain the browser's default colors.

4. Change the text color for unvisited and visited links by adding the following styles:

```
a:link {
    color: #8D0E6B;
}
a:visited {
    color: #B53392;
}
```

5. Save the style sheet, and test the page again. Unvisited links are deep magenta; visited links are a lighter shade of magenta. If all links look the same, click the last link in the unordered list to visit the Apress website. When you return to basic.html, the color of the link should have changed.

6. Create a rule that groups the :hover, :active, and :focus pseudo-classes like this:

```
a:hover, a:active, a:focus {
    color: #63550A;
    text-decoration: underline;
}
```

7. Save the style sheet, and test the page again. When you mouse over a link, it turns deep brown and the text is underlined to give a visual signal that it's clickable.

8. To style links differently in a specific part of the page, you can use a descendant selector with the pseudo-classes. To keep the code simple, you'll just reverse the colors for the links in the unordered list, which has the ID nav. You'll also apply the same color to both visited and unvisited links. To create a descendant selector, you put the ancestor first—in this case #nav—followed by a space and the selector for the element(s) you want to affect. Add these styles to basic.css:

```
#nav a:link, #nav a:visited {
    color: #63550A;
}
#nav a:hover, #nav a:active, #nav a:focus {
    color: #8D0E6B;
}
```

9. Save the style sheet, and reload basic.html in a browser. The links in the unordered list at the top of the page are now a different color. The descendant selectors affect only links that are descendants of the element with the ID nav.

10. Mouse over one of the links in the unordered list. Not only does the text change color, but it's also underlined (see Figure 2-5), even though the style rule you created in step 8 doesn't set the text-decoration property to underline. The underlining is inherited from the style rule in step 6.

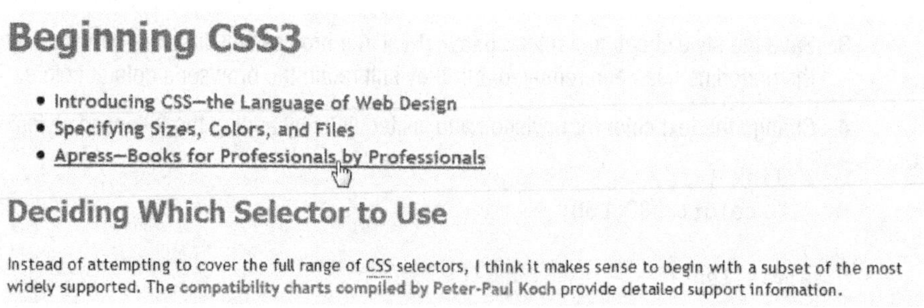

## Beginning CSS3

- Introducing CSS—the Language of Web Design
- Specifying Sizes, Colors, and Files
- Apress—Books for Professionals by Professionals

### Deciding Which Selector to Use

Instead of attempting to cover the full range of CSS selectors, I think it makes sense to begin with a subset of the most widely supported. The compatibility charts compiled by Peter-Paul Koch provide detailed support information.

*Figure 2-5. The underline is inherited from the rule that applies to all links*

11. Turn off the underline by amending the final style rule like this:

```
#nav a:hover, #nav a:active, #nav a:focus {
    color: #8D0E6B;
    text-decoration: none;
}
```

When styling links, there's a danger of removing visual clues that text is clickable. Most users no longer expect blue underlines on links, but choose styles carefully to make links stand out from other text.

## Changing the Look of the Cursor

When you mouse over a link, the browser automatically changes the shape of the cursor from an arrow to a hand. Over ordinary text, the cursor changes to an I-beam, indicating that the text is selectable.

Sometimes, it's convenient to take control over what the cursor looks like. For example, the dotted underline that many browsers display under <abbr> elements is meant to be a visual clue that the meaning of the abbreviation will be displayed as a tooltip if you hover over it. But the visual clue would be much stronger if you changed the cursor to indicate that help is at hand.

To change the look of the cursor, you use the CSS cursor property, which accepts any of the keywords listed in Table 2-2. The examples in the table show how Opera displays cursors in Windows 7. You can test what the cursors look like in different browsers and operating systems by using cursors.html in the ch02 folder.

***Table 2-2.*** *Values Accepted by the cursor Property*

| Keyword | Example | Description |
|---|---|---|
| General Purpose Cursors | | |
| auto | | Browser selects cursor based on current context. |
| default | | Default cursor—usually an arrow. |
| none | | Cursor is hidden. |
| Links and Status Cursors | | |
| context-menu | 🗒 | Context menu is available for the current object. |
| help | | Help is available. |
| pointer | | Indicates a link. |
| progress | | Indicates something is happening, but that user can still interact with the browser. |
| wait | | Indicates the browser is busy and the user should wait. |
| Selection Cursors | | |
| cell | | Indicates a cell or set of cells may be selected. |
| crosshair | | Displays two thin intersecting lines. |
| text | I | Indicates text can be selected. |
| vertical-text | | Indicates vertical text can be selected. |

(*continued*)

*Table 2-2.* (*continued*)

| Keyword | Example | Description |
|---|---|---|
| Drag and Drop Cursors | | |
| alias | | Indicates that an alias or shortcut is to be created. |
| copy | | Indicates that something is to be copied. |
| move | | Indicates that something is to be moved. |
| no-drop | | Indicates that the dragged item cannot be dropped at the current location. |
| not-allowed | | The requested action will not be carried out. |
| Resizing and Scrolling Cursors | | |
| e-resize, n-resize, ne-resize, nw-resize, s-resize, se-resize, sw-resize, w-resize | | Indicates that some edge is to be moved. |
| ew-resize, ns-resize, nesw-resize, nwse-resize | | Indicates a bidirectional resize cursor. |
| col-resize | | Indicates the column can be resized horizontally. |
| row-resize | | Indicates the row can be resized vertically. |
| all-scroll | | Indicates that something can be scrolled in any direction. |

■ **Caution** Not all browsers support the full range of cursor keywords. In my testing, using no-drop caused Safari 5.1 to crash on Windows 7.

Looking at the available keywords in Table 2-2, the most appropriate one for the <abbr> element is help. To display the appropriate cursor when mousing over the abbreviation, use the abbr type selector in combination with the :hover pseudo-class to add the following style rule to basic.css:

```
abbr:hover {
    cursor: help;
}
```

Figure 2-6 shows the help cursor and the tooltip being displayed when the mouse is held over the abbreviation. The tooltip is generated automatically by the browser and cannot be styled with CSS.

■ **Note** Browsers display a tooltip only if you spell out the meaning in the title attribute of the <abbr> tag.

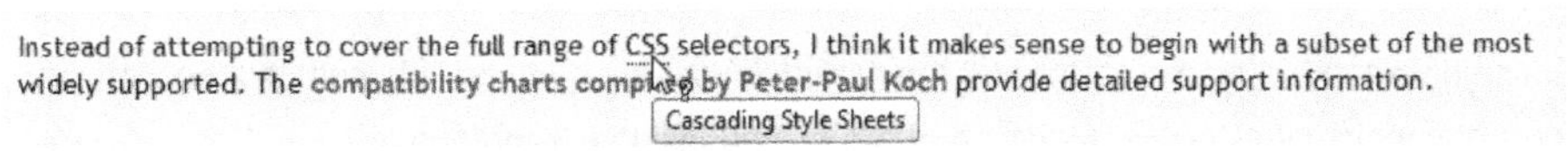

Instead of attempting to cover the full range of CSS selectors, I think it makes sense to begin with a subset of the most widely supported. The compatibility charts compiled by Peter-Paul Koch provide detailed support information.

Cascading Style Sheets

*Figure 2-6.* *The style rule changes the look of the cursor*

You can also use your own custom image for a cursor by setting the location of the image file as the value of the `cursor` property. When specifying a custom cursor, you can list fallback options as a comma-separated list like this:

```
cursor: url(images/awesome.cur), url(images/awesome_cursor.png), pointer;
```

Browsers attempt to display the first value that they can support. For example, if a browser doesn't support images with a `.cur` filename extension, it tries to use the next one. If it can't support that one either, it falls back to the keyword listed at the end.

---

■ **Caution**  Changing a fundamental aspect of the browser such as the cursor can disorient users. But it might be appropriate in situations such as online games.

---

In CSS3, you can optionally add two space-separated numbers after the file to represent the precise position that is being pointed to. The first number specifies the horizontal offset (in pixels) from the top-left corner of the image. The second number specifies the vertical offset. For example, if your cursor image is 24 pixels square, and you want it to be centered over the position being pointed to, you specify the coordinates like this:

```
cursor: url(images/bullseye.cur) 12 12, url(images/bullseye.png) 12 12, default;
```

If you don't specify any offsets, the position being pointed to is at the top-left corner of the image.

---

■ **Note**  The syntax for specifying file locations is explained in Chapter 3

---

## Using Class Selectors

As noted earlier, you create a class selector by prefixing the class name with a period (dot). So, the selector for the `intro` class in `basic.html` is `.intro`. For example, you can use a class selector like this:

```
.intro {
    /* Styles that affect all elements with the intro class */
}
```

You can also use a class selector in a descendant selector like this:

```
.intro a:link {
    /* Styles that affect unvisited links in elements with the intro class */
}
```

You can prefix the class selector with another selector to target elements precisely, for example:

```
p.intro {
    /* Styles for paragraphs with the intro class */
}
```

---

■ **Note**   There is no space between the type selector and the period. If you add a space, it becomes a descendant selector: p .intro selects elements with the intro class that are nested inside paragraphs.

---

Classes can be applied to multiple elements, so using p.intro targets only paragraphs that have the intro class. Any other elements with the same class are ignored, as the following exercise demonstrates.

---

### EXERCISE: TARGETING CLASS SELECTORS

This exercise shows how a class can be applied to different types of elements.

1. Continue working with basic.html and basic.css from the previous exercises. Alternatively, use basic_03.html and css/basic_03.css in the end folder.

2. In basic.html, add **class="intro"** to the opening <li> tag of the first item in the unordered list like this:

   ```
   <li class="intro"><a href="#">Introducing CSS–the Language of Web
   Design</a></li>
   ```

3. In basic.css, use the .intro class selector to create the following style rule:

   ```
   .intro {
   text-transform: uppercase;
   }
   ```

4. Save both files, and load basic.html into a browser. The style rule has turned the text in both elements with the intro class into uppercase, as Figure 2-7 shows.

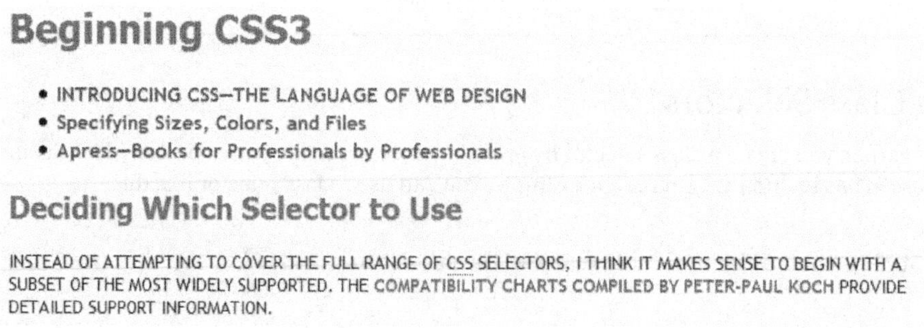

# Beginning CSS3

- INTRODUCING CSS—THE LANGUAGE OF WEB DESIGN
- Specifying Sizes, Colors, and Files
- Apress—Books for Professionals by Professionals

## Deciding Which Selector to Use

INSTEAD OF ATTEMPTING TO COVER THE FULL RANGE OF CSS SELECTORS, I THINK IT MAKES SENSE TO BEGIN WITH A SUBSET OF THE MOST WIDELY SUPPORTED. THE COMPATIBILITY CHARTS COMPILED BY PETER-PAUL KOCH PROVIDE DETAILED SUPPORT INFORMATION.

***Figure 2-7.*** *The class style affects both the list item and the paragraph*

5. Amend the selector to apply only to paragraphs with the intro class:

   ```
   p.intro {
       text-transform: uppercase;
   }
   ```

6. Save the style sheet, and reload basic.html into a browser. This time, only the paragraph is in uppercase (see Figure 2-8).

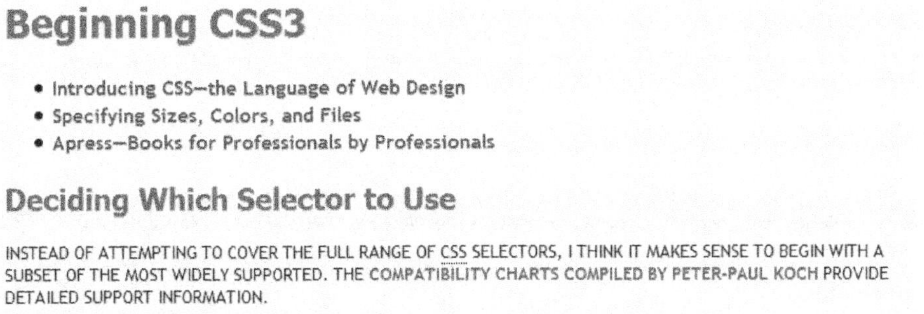

## Beginning CSS3

- Introducing CSS—the Language of Web Design
- Specifying Sizes, Colors, and Files
- Apress—Books for Professionals by Professionals

### Deciding Which Selector to Use

INSTEAD OF ATTEMPTING TO COVER THE FULL RANGE OF CSS SELECTORS, I THINK IT MAKES SENSE TO BEGIN WITH A SUBSET OF THE MOST WIDELY SUPPORTED. THE COMPATIBILITY CHARTS COMPILED BY PETER-PAUL KOCH PROVIDE DETAILED SUPPORT INFORMATION.

*Figure 2-8. The combination of the type and class selector targets only the paragraph*

# Using Pseudo-elements

You append the pseudo-element to the basic selector in the same way as a pseudo-class, for example:

```
p.intro:first-line {
    text-transform: uppercase;
}
```

This applies the style to the first line of any paragraph with the intro class. As Figure 2-9 shows, the length of the first line changes when the browser viewport is resized.

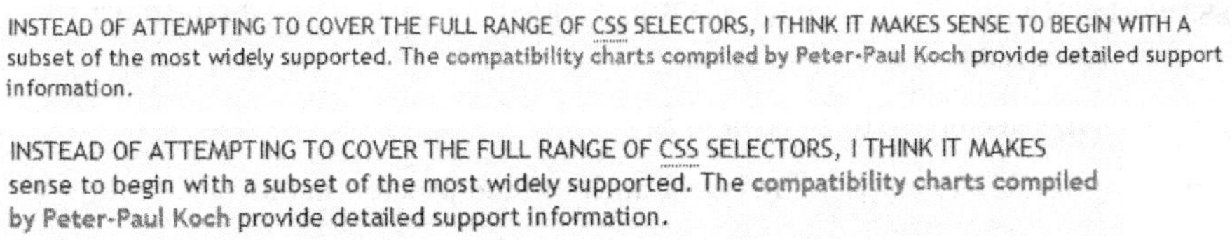

INSTEAD OF ATTEMPTING TO COVER THE FULL RANGE OF CSS SELECTORS, I THINK IT MAKES SENSE TO BEGIN WITH A subset of the most widely supported. The compatibility charts compiled by Peter-Paul Koch provide detailed support information.

INSTEAD OF ATTEMPTING TO COVER THE FULL RANGE OF CSS SELECTORS, I THINK IT MAKES sense to begin with a subset of the most widely supported. The compatibility charts compiled by Peter-Paul Koch provide detailed support information.

*Figure 2-9. The size of the pseudo-element changes dynamically*

To style just the first letter of an element, use the :first-letter pseudo-element like this:

```
p:first-letter {
    font-size: 28px;
}
```

In most browsers, the combination of these two style rules that use pseudo-elements produces the result shown in Figure 2-10

---

■ **Note**  Safari and Google Chrome won't apply two pseudo-elements simultaneously. They apply the :first-letter styles, but ignore the :first-line rule completely. The CSS3 Selectors module says only one pseudo-element may appear per selector, so you can't chain them like this: p::first-letter::first-line. However, it's not clear whether the restriction of one pseudo-element also applies to separate style rules as used here.

---

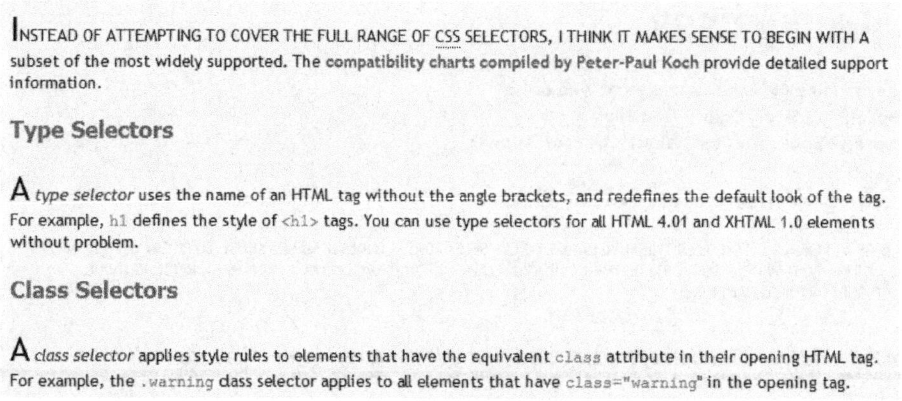

INSTEAD OF ATTEMPTING TO COVER THE FULL RANGE OF CSS SELECTORS, I THINK IT MAKES SENSE TO BEGIN WITH A subset of the most widely supported. The compatibility charts compiled by Peter-Paul Koch provide detailed support information.

### Type Selectors

A *type selector* uses the name of an HTML tag without the angle brackets, and redefines the default look of the tag. For example, h1 defines the style of <h1> tags. You can use type selectors for all HTML 4.01 and XHTML 1.0 elements without problem.

### Class Selectors

A *class selector* applies style rules to elements that have the equivalent class attribute in their opening HTML tag. For example, the .warning class selector applies to all elements that have class="warning" in the opening tag.

*Figure 2-10. The first letter of each paragraph is displayed in a larger font size*

# What Happens When Style Rules Conflict?

As mentioned in Chapter 1, the basic principle of the cascade is that a style definition that comes after another overrides the earlier one in case of a conflict. However, not all selectors are equal. Calculating which style rule wins also depends on a concept known as *specificity*.

You calculate the specificity of a style rule by counting the value of each part of its selector. The CSS2.1 and proposed CSS3 specifications express the values in slightly different ways, but the underlying calculation remains exactly the same. The CSS3 version is easier to understand, so I'll start with that and then explain the CSS2.1 formula so that you know what it means if you ever come across it.

- Count the number of ID selectors in the selector as a.

- Count the number of class selectors, pseudo-classes, and attribute selectors in the selector as b.

- Count the number of type selectors and pseudo-elements in the selector as c.

- Ignore the universal selector.

- String abc together to get the selector's specificity.

- Inline styles always take precedence.

In other words, ID selectors have a value of 100; class, pseudo-class, and attribute selectors each have a value of 10; and type selectors and pseudo-elements have a value of 1.

The CSS2.1 formula expresses each group as a comma-separated list of four numbers. The values are assigned like this:

- Inline style: 1, 0, 0, 0

- ID selector: 0, 1, 0, 0

- Class, pseudo-class, or attribute selector: 0, 0, 1, 0

- Type selector or pseudo-element: 0, 0, 0, 1

Using both formulas, you can calculate the specificity of selectors used in the exercises like this:

```
a                   /* specificity   1 or 0, 0, 0, 1 */
a:link              /* specificity  11 or 0, 0, 1, 1 */
#nav a:link         /* specificity 111 or 0, 1, 1, 1 */
p.intro:first-line  /* specificity  12 or 0, 0, 1, 2 */
```

When you see both formulas alongside each other like this, it becomes obvious that the values are the same if you remove the commas from the CSS2.1 formula.

Selectors that are grouped together to apply the same styles to different elements are counted separately. For example, h1, h2, h3 has a specificity of 1, not 3.

If two rules define different values for the same property, the selector with the higher specificity wins regardless of which order the rules appear in the style sheet. If both selectors have the same specificity, the one lower down the style sheet takes precedence.

---

■ **Note**    Conflicts apply to individual properties, not to the whole style block.

---

For example, basic_05.css in the ch02/end/css folder contains the following styles for links:

```
a:link {                    /* specificity 11 */
    color: #8D0E6B;
}
#nav a:link, #nav a:visited {  /* specificity 111 */
    color: #63550A;
}
```

Both style rules set the text color for links. The second one takes precedence not only because it's lower down the style sheet, but also because it has higher specificity. Try reversing the order of the rules like this:

```
#nav a:link, #nav a:visited {  /* specificity 111 */
    color: #63550A;
}
a:link {                    /* specificity 11 */
    color: #8D0E6B;
}
```

Even though #nav a:link is now higher in the style sheet, it still takes precedence because of its higher specificity. But the selector targets only links in the nav unordered list, so it doesn't affect the other link in the main text.

The concept of specificity can be difficult to grasp. Fortunately, it comes into play only when there's a conflict between styles targeting similar elements. Much of the time, you can forget about it. But when a style isn't applied where you expect it to be, the answer almost always lies in a more specific rule—in other words, one with higher specificity—taking precedence. Using a browser's developer tools to inspect which styles are being applied to an element usually helps trace the source of the problem.

# Summary

This chapter has covered a lot of ground, introducing 16 basic selectors and showing how they can be combined to target styles more precisely. Many beginners tend to rely heavily on classes to apply styles to page elements, but classes have the disadvantage of requiring extra markup in your HTML. As the exercises demonstrated, you can achieve a great deal through the use of type and descendant selectors. You learned how to apply different styles to links depending on the ID of their ancestor. Choosing the right selector for the job isn't always easy, but you should be guided by the principle of using the simplest selector possible. It not only makes your work much simpler, but it also makes it easier for the browser, resulting in pages that load quickly and are more responsive.

In the next chapter, you'll learn how to specify sizes, colors, and the location of files, laying the foundation for a deeper exploration of CSS.

# CHAPTER 3

# Specifying Sizes, Colors, and Files

In the preceding chapter, you used a keyword to set the value of the cursor property. Many CSS properties use predefined keywords, but sizes, colors, and the location of files need to be specified individually. This chapter describes the units of measurement and the syntax used to specify colors and files. CSS3 introduces several new units of measurement, which are only gradually being implemented by browsers, so you need to use them with caution.

In this chapter you'll learn about the following:

- Which units of measurement to use for visual browsers and printers
- Understanding the difference between physical pixels and CSS pixels
- Specifying colors by name
- Which color formats are supported in CSS
- Setting color transparency
- Specifying the location of files, such as background images

This chapter contains a lot of dry, factual information; but it's essential reading for working with CSS. Fortunately, it's relatively short. It should also act as a handy reference.

## Specifying Size and Other Units of Measurement

In CSS, values not expressed as a keyword take one of the following forms:

- Integer
- Number
- Length
- Percentage
- Angle (CSS3)
- Time (CSS3)

### Numeric Values

Using numeric values is straightforward. Some properties expect an *integer*—in other words, a whole number. Others accept either a whole number or a decimal value. The CSS2.1 specification makes no distinction, and refers to both cases as *number*. CSS3 explicitly states when only an integer is accepted. In some cases, the range is limited or only positive numbers can be used.

Numbers must not contain spaces or the thousands separator. Decimal fractions use a decimal point (dot). You can't use a comma as the decimal point, as is common in some European countries.

# Length

The CSS specifications use the term *length* to refer to vertical and horizontal measurements. The CSS3 Values and Units module introduces several new units of measurement, as well as a function that allows the browser to calculate a length value. These new features are not supported by all browsers, so I'll describe them separately to avoid confusion.

## Length Units Supported by All Browsers

Table 3-1 lists the length units in CSS2.1 that are supported by all browsers.

*Table 3-1.* *CSS2.1 Length Units*

| Type | Unit | Description |
| --- | --- | --- |
| Relative Units | | |
| | em | Height of the current font |
| | ex | Half an em in most browsers |
| Absolute Units | | |
| | px | Pixels (1/96 of an inch or 0.265 mm) |
| | in | Inches (2.54 centimeters) |
| | cm | Centimeters (0.394 in) |
| | mm | Millimeters (0.039 in) |
| | pt | Points (1/72 of an inch or 0.353 mm) |
| | pc | Picas (12 points or 4.233 mm) |

Length units are classified as either relative or absolute. A *relative unit* is not a fixed size, but is relative to another length. The relative units in CSS2.1 take their value from the current font size. But CSS3 introduces units that are relative to the browser viewport. An *absolute unit* is anchored to a physical measurement, such as an inch or centimeter.

There must be no space between the number (which can include a decimal fraction) and the unit. The unit of measurement is optional after 0. For example, the following values are correct:

```
0.5em
300px
0px
0
```

The last two examples, 0px and 0, mean the same. Most experienced designers omit the px (or other length unit) but it's perfectly valid to include it. The following examples are incorrect and *will not work*:

```
0.5 em
300 px
0 px
```

Although no unit is required after zero, browsers are likely to interpret the px in the final example as garbage and ignore the style definition.

An *em* is a unit of measurement borrowed from typography. The name originates from the width of the letter M; but in CSS it means the height of the current font, usually including whitespace above and below. So, with a 16-pixel font, one em equals 16 pixels; with a 24-pixel font, it's 24 pixels, and so on. Specifying the width or height of an element in ems adjusts its size in proportion to the size of the font.

---

■ **Caution**  Using em to specify font size can result in ever shrinking text because nested elements inherit the size from their parents, resulting in a multiplier effect. For example, if you set the font size of unordered lists to 0.75em (the equivalent of 12px), the text in a nested list is 0.75 times the size of its parent—in other words, 9px. At the next level, the text shrinks even further (see Figure 3-1).

---

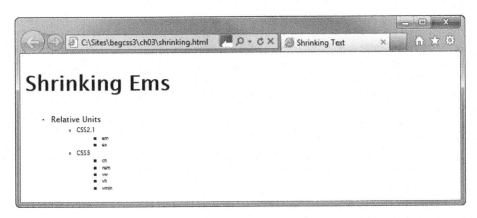

*Figure 3-1. Using em to set the font size can have unexpected results with nested elements*

To avoid this multiplier effect with em, you need to reset the size for nested lists to 1em like this:

```
ul {
    font-size: 0.75em;
}
ul ul {
    font-size: 1em;
}
```

As Figure 3-2 shows, this sets the text in the nested lists to the same size as the previous list, thereby preventing it from shrinking.

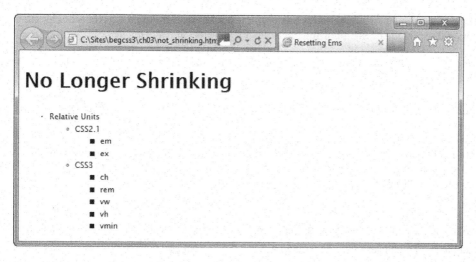

***Figure 3-2.*** *The nested lists now use the same font size as the top level list*

You can examine the HTML and CSS for Figures 3-1 and 3-2 in shrinking.html and not_shrinking.html in the ch03 folder.

---

■ **Note**    The CSS3 `rem` unit described later in this chapter offers a much simpler solution to this problem.

---

The ex unit is meant to be equivalent to the height of a lowercase X in the current font. However, most browsers treat this unit as half an em. It's rarely used.

Of the absolute units, pixels are the only ones that should be used for onscreen display. The other units are intended for use in print style sheets (see Chapter 16).

Originally, pixels were classified as relative units because their size was considered to be relative to the viewing device. However, changes in technology resulted in the need to redefine how pixels are interpreted, as explained in the sidebar "Physical and CSS Pixels."

## PHYSICAL AND CSS PIXELS

In digital imaging, a pixel is the smallest element of a picture that can be represented or controlled (the term is a contraction of "picture" and "element"). Over the years, screen resolutions have improved, cramming more and more dots into the same physical space. As a result, physical pixels have become smaller and smaller. One of the most dramatic changes was the development of the retina display for the iPhone and iPad, which squeezes four pixels into the space where there had previously been only one.

If browsers interpreted pixel units of measurement literally, you would need a magnifying glass to view web pages on high pixel-density screens. Fortunately, that doesn't happen. The CSS specification defines what it calls a *reference pixel*, which aims to standardize how pixel values are displayed when viewed at arm's length. At a distance of 28 inches (71 cm), a reference pixel (or *CSS pixel*, as it's more commonly called) is equivalent to 1/96 inch (0.26 mm). When displayed on a device that's intended to be viewed at a greater distance—a projector, for example—the device is expected to scale up pixel measurements proportionately.

The long and short of it is that using pixels as the unit of measurement should result in roughly the same size, regardless of the physical pixel density of the screen.

Many designers, particularly those who come from a print background, instinctively use points to specify font sizes. A common assumption is that pixels and points are interchangeable. However, both CSS2.1 and CSS3 define a pixel as being equal to 0.75pt.

## Length Units in CSS3

Table 3-2 lists the new length units introduced in CSS3. They are all classified as relative units.

*Table 3-2.* *CSS3 Length Units*

| Unit | Relative to |
|------|-------------|
| ch | The width of the character 0 (zero) in the current font |
| rem | The font size of the root element |
| vw | The viewport's width |
| vh | The viewport's height |
| vmin | The viewport's width or height, whichever is smaller |
| vmax | The viewport's width or height, whichever is larger |

At the time of this writing, the only unit in Table 3-2 with widespread support is rem. It has been available since Firefox 3.6, Chrome 6, Safari 5, IE 9, Android 2.1, and iOS 4.0. It's very similar to the em unit in that it's equivalent to the height of a font. The difference is that it remains relative to the font size of the root element—in other words, the page's default font size. This avoids the multiplier effect that can result in ever-shrinking text when specifying font sizes in em units. With rem units, the scaling is always proportionate to the same value.

The following style rule in rem.html produces the same output as Figure 3-2 in browsers that support the rem unit:

```
ul {
    font-size: 0.75rem;
}
```

The vw, vh, vmin, and vmax units are similar to percentages in that 100vw equals the full width of the viewport, 100vh equals the full height, and 100vmin equals the shorter of the two. When the height or width of the viewport is resized, lengths specified with these units are scaled proportionately. IE 9 implemented an early draft of the specification, in which vmin was called vm. IE 10 uses vmin. Chrome 20 and Safari 6 also support vw, vh, and vmin. The W3C added vmax to the specification as an afterthought. At the time of this writing, it's not supported by any browser.

Firefox is currently the only browser that supports ch correctly.

## Using the calc() Function to Compute Length Values

The situation frequently arises in fluid or flexible layouts where you want to combine absolute values with relative ones. For example, you might want an element to fill 70 percent of the horizontal space, but to have a 10-pixel margin on either side. Because you have no idea how wide the browser viewport will be, it's impossible to know how much horizontal space remains alongside. The CSS3 calc() function is designed to solve such problems.

The calc() function supports the following arithmetic operators:

+ (add)

- (subtract)

/ (divide)

* (multiply)

mod (modulo division)

---

■ **Note** Modulo division produces the remainder of a division. For example, the result of 7 mod 2 is 1. Normally, the operator for modulo division is %, but it was decided to use mod to avoid confusion with percentages.

---

To calculate the width available alongside the element in the preceding example, CSS3 allows you to specify the value like this:

```
calc(30% - 20px)
```

The calc() function is supported in IE 9+ and Firefox 16+. Chrome 19+ and Safari 6 support it on an experimental basis with a browser-specific prefix (-webkit-calc()).

## Percentages

Values specified as percentages use a number immediately followed by the percentage sign (%). There must be no space between the number and %. Percentages are always relative to another value, normally the size of the parent element. Browsers are capable of handling percentages to several decimal places.

## Angles

Angles are used only with CSS3 properties, such as transform. Table 3-3 lists the accepted units.

*Table 3-3.* *Angle Units in CSS3*

| Unit | Meaning |
| --- | --- |
| deg | Degrees |
| grad | Gradians (1/400 of a turn) |
| rad | Radians |
| turn | Turns (360 degrees) |

As with all other units of measurement, there must be no space between the number and unit. Browsers convert angles to the range 0–360°. For example -90deg is the same as 270deg.

## Time

Time units are used only with CSS3 properties. There are just two units, as shown in Table 3-4.

***Table 3-4.*** *Time Units in CSS3*

| Unit | Meaning |
| --- | --- |
| s | Seconds |
| ms | Milliseconds (1/1,000 of a second) |

Again, there must be no space between the number and the unit.

■ **Caution**   When specifying a zero value for an angle or time, you must include the unit of measurement, for example, 0deg, 0s. The only time you can omit the unit after zero is with lengths and percentages.

# Setting Color Values

CSS offers the following options for setting color values:

- Color keywords
- Hexadecimal notation
- RGB (red, green, blue) format
- HSL (hue, saturation, lightness) format (CSS3)
- RGBA (red, green, blue with alpha transparency) format (CSS3)
- HSLA (hue, saturation, lightness with alpha transparency) format (CSS3)

## Color Keywords

CSS3 defines the 16 basic color keywords shown in Figure 3-3. The names are case-insensitive.

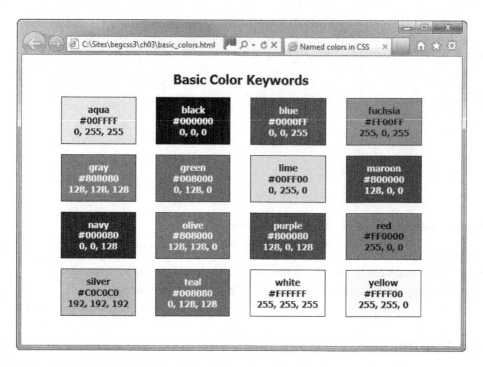

*Figure 3-3. The basic color keywords with hexadecimal and RGB equivalents*

The CSS2.1 specification also includes orange (#FFA500, RGB 255, 165, 0), but it has been dropped from the list of basic color keywords in CSS3. However, it's a moot point, because the CSS3 Color module has extended the definition of nearly 150 color keywords from the Scalable Vector Graphics (SVG) specification to embrace their use in CSS. The SVG color keywords are widely supported by current browsers, so they should be safe to use in your style sheets.

■ **Tip** The basic and extended color keywords together with their hexadecimal and RGB equivalents are in basic_colors.html and extended_colors.html in the ch03 folder.

CSS3 also introduces the keyword currentColor, which acts as a variable. It inherits the value of the parent's color property. So, if color is set to red in the parent element, currentColor is also red. The currentColor keyword is supported by the latest versions of all browsers, but it is not supported by IE 8 or earlier.

## Using Hexadecimal Notation

The most common way of representing color in web design is to use the hexadecimal notation for red, green, and blue (RGB) values. Using hexadecimal numbers allows you to select 256 shades of each value, representing more than 16 million colors. Most graphics and HTML editing programs generate the hexadecimal number for you automatically when you use a color picker or eyedropper tool. If you don't have access to your graphics program (for example, when traveling), you can use online utilities such as www.colorpicker.com or http://kuler.adobe.com.

When using hexadecimal notation, remember the following:

- The color value must begin with the hash or pound sign (#). Omitting the # is a common cause of errors.

- You can use six-digit or three-digit hexadecimal values (see the sidebar "Shorthand Hexadecimal Values" for an explanation of the difference).

- Don't mix up the letter O with 0 (zero) or lowercase L with the number 1. The only letters permitted in hexadecimal values are A–F.

- The letters A–F in a hexadecimal value are case-insensitive. It doesn't matter whether you use uppercase or lowercase, or even a mixture of the two.

## SHORTHAND HEXADECIMAL VALUES

Hexadecimal color values are normally expressed using six digits. The first pair represents the red component of the color; the second pair represents the green component, and the final pair the blue component. In CSS, if all three components contain a pair of identical digits, you can shorten each pair to a single digit. For example, the hexadecimal value for fuchsia is #FF00FF, which contains three pairs of identical digits, so it can be shorted to #F0F. However, #008080 (teal) cannot be shortened, because only the first pair of digits is identical.

## Using RGB Format

As well as using hexadecimal notation to represent RGB values, you can use the rgb() function in a style sheet. You specify the red, green, and blue values as a comma-separated list inside the parentheses.

The rgb() function accepts the values either as numbers in the range 0–255 or as percentages. For example, you can specify red in either of the following ways:

```
rgb(255, 0, 0)
rgb(100%, 0%, 0%)
```

As with hexadecimal notation, you can normally get the correct values from a graphics program's color picker.

## Using HSL Format

A new feature in CSS3 is the ability to specify colors using hue, saturation, and lightness. This color format is favored by many graphic designers because it's more intuitive than the RGB model. Hue is represented by an angle on a color circle, with red at the top (0 degrees), green one-third of the way round the circle in clockwise direction (120 degrees), and blue two-thirds of the way round (240 degrees). Saturation represents the intensity of the color, making it duller or brighter. And lightness makes the color darker or lighter. See www.w3.org/TR/css3-color/#hsl-color for examples.

You specify a color using HSL format with the hsl() function, which takes three comma-separated values, as follows:

- Hue expressed as a number between 0 and 360: This is the angle of the color on the color circle. Browsers are expected to adjust out-of-range numbers, so –120 should be interpreted as 240 (blue).

- Saturation expressed as a percentage: 0% is a shade of gray, and 100% is full saturation.

- Lightness expressed as a percentage: 0% is black, 50% is normal, and 100% is white.

The following example represents red:

```
hsl(0, 100%, 50%)
```

## Creating Transparent Colors with the RGBA and HSLA Formats

The CSS3 Color module extends the RGB and HSL formats to allow you to set the opacity of the color using alpha transparency. To specify a color with alpha transparency, use the rgba() or hsla() function.

Both functions take four comma-separated values. The first three values are the same as for rgb() and hsl(). The fourth value sets the level of transparency, and must be a number between 0 (completely transparent) and 1 (completely opaque). The following examples create semitransparent red:

```
rgba(255, 0, 0, 0.5)
rgba(100%, 0%, 0%, 0.5)
hsla(0, 100%, 50%, 0.5)
```

Setting the alpha transparency of a color not only reduces the color intensity, but it also allows any background to show through. The background becomes more visible the closer the fourth value is to 0.

---

■ **Note**    All browsers except IE 6–8 support rgba(), hsl(), and hsla().

---

# Specifying Background Images and Other Files

A small number of properties, such as background-image and list-style-image, require the URL of the file you want to use. To specify the location of a file, enter the path between the parentheses of url(). You can use either an absolute path or a relative one. The file path can be optionally enclosed in single or double quotes. Whitespace between the parentheses and the file path is also permitted.

The following examples are all valid:

```
url(../../images/grand_canyon.jpg)
url(/images/grand_canyon.jpg)
url("http://www.example.com/images/grand_canyon.jpg")
url( "/images/grand_canyon.jpg" )
url('../../images/grand_canyon.jpg')
url(  '../../images/grand_canyon.jpg'  )
```

If using a relative file path, the location should be relative to the style sheet.

---

■ **Note**    The CSS3 Image Values and Replaced Content module proposes an image() function to specify clipped portions of an image and fallback images, but no browser yet implements it.

---

# Summary

This chapter has provided a comprehensive overview of how to specify CSS property values with units of measurement, as well as colors, and file locations. The CSS specifications refer to horizontal and vertical measurements as "length." The units of measurement listed in Table 3-1 are supported by all browsers, but you should take care when using any of the measurements in Tables 3-2, 3-3, and 3-4 because they're not supported in older browsers, including IE 6–8. When using a value with a unit of measurement, make sure there is no space between the number and the unit.

The new features in the CSS3 Color module, including setting alpha transparency with the rgba() and hsla() functions, are supported in all current browsers except IE 6–8.

You've now covered the essential basics of CSS. In Part II, you get down to more practical aspects of using CSS to improve the look of your web pages.

# Working with Text

Good-looking, readable text is vital to the success of a website. CSS has a large number of properties devoted to formatting text, giving you control not only over fonts and colors, but also allowing you to adjust the distance between lines, words, and individual letters. For many years, one of the most frustrating aspects of styling text on the Web has been the limited range of fonts considered safe to use because browsers rely on what's available on the user's computer. Thankfully, those days are over. You can now embed a wide range of fonts in web pages, either by storing them on your own web server or using a font hosting service.

The CSS3 Text module is still only a working draft. Chapter 4 covers all CSS2.1 text properties and introduces several new ones from CSS3, such as text-shadow, that have already stabilized and are widely supported by browsers.

Chapter 5 shows you how to widen your choice of typeface by using web fonts in your styles, and guides you through the sometimes confusing syntax needed to embed them. The accompanying source files contain several open source fonts for you to practice with.

■ ■ ■

# CHAPTER 4

# Styling Text

Text is the most important element in the vast majority of sites. So, presenting text in a visually pleasing manner is an important part of your design. Not only should the text look good, it must be easy to read—the font needs to be large enough, but not too large, and the text shouldn't look too dense or bunched up. CSS has many properties that affect the appearance of text. Most are very easy to use, and they have an immediate impact on the overall design of a site.

In this chapter, you'll learn about the following:

- Defining which fonts are used for text

- Understanding the different methods to specify font size

- Adding or removing italic and bold face

- Changing the vertical space between lines of text

- Changing the color of text

- Automatically transforming lowercase to uppercase and vice versa

- Indenting the first line of paragraphs

- Increasing and decreasing the horizontal space between words and letters

- Controlling whitespace and line wrapping

- Adding shadows to text

## Selecting and Adjusting Fonts

By default, most browsers display text in Times New Roman, Times, or a similar font. The actual font depends not only on the browser, but also on what's available on the visitor's computer. You'll learn in the next chapter how to increase the range of fonts that can be used in your designs, but for the time being let's concentrate on the basics of styling text in CSS.

The first step is to select the font you want to use, and then to make any adjustments, such as changing its size and whether it's rendered in bold, italic, or small caps. These features are controlled by the properties listed in Table 4-1. Strictly speaking, line-height isn't a font property, but I've included it because it's an integral part of the shorthand font property.

*Table 4-1.* *CSS2.1 Font Properties*

| Property | Initial Value | Inherited | Description |
|---|---|---|---|
| font-family | | Yes | Sets the font and fallback options |
| font-size | medium | Yes | Sets the size of the font |
| font-style | normal | Yes | Controls the display of italic |
| font-variant | normal | Yes | Controls the display of small caps |
| font-weight | normal | Yes | Determines whether the text should be bold |
| line-height | normal | Yes | Sets the vertical distance between lines of text (leading) |
| font | | Yes | Shorthand property that combines all the others in a single declaration |

■ **Note** The properties in Table 4-1 are supported by all browsers. The draft CSS3 Fonts module introduces others, which have varying degrees of support. They're the subject of the next chapter.

## Using font-family to Choose a Range of Alternative Fonts

As a designer, you're likely to have lots of fonts on your computer, but visitors to the sites you design probably won't have half as many. The fonts installed on a computer depend on both the operating system and any other programs that have been installed. If you choose an unusual font for your page, in all likelihood, few of your visitors will ever see the page the way you envisaged. Consequently, you should always choose several alternatives similar in design and proportions to your preferred choice.

The font-family property takes as its value a comma-separated list of fonts like this:

```
font-family: Arial, Helvetica, sans-serif;
```

If any of the font names contain spaces, they must be wrapped in quotes like this:

```
font-family: "Trebuchet MS", Arial, Helvetica, sans-serif;
```

■ **Note** It doesn't matter whether you use single or double quotation marks, but the comma must go outside the quotes.

The browser attempts to display the first available font in the list. In the case of the previous example, the browser tries Arial if Trebuchet MS isn't available on the visitor's computer. If Arial's not available, it tries Helvetica. And if none of the fonts is available, it falls back to the computer's default sans-serif font.

Listing fonts in the font-family property is known as creating a *font stack*. You should always end your font stack with one of the generic font families in Table 4-2.

***Table 4-2.*** *Generic Font Families*

| Name | Example | Description |
| --- | --- | --- |
| sans-serif | Verdana | In typography, serifs are little hooks at the end of strokes (see Figure 4-1). A sans-serif font, such as Verdana, Arial, or Helvetica, has no such hooks. |
| serif | Georgia | A serif font has little hooks at the end of strokes. Typical examples are Georgia, Times, and Times New Roman. |
| cursive | *Viner Hand ITC* | Cursive fonts look handwritten or done with a calligraphic pen. |
| monospace | Consolas | Monospace fonts display all characters the same width. This type of font is typically used to display code examples. |
| fantasy | *Jokerman* | This generic font covers typefaces that don't fall into any other category. |

***Figure 4-1.*** *Hooks on the end of strokes distinguish serif fonts from sans-serif fonts*

---

■ **Tip** Most HTML and CSS editors offer code hints for tried and tested font stacks. If your favorite font isn't listed, choose a font stack that looks similar, and add your own choice at the beginning of the list. If a visitor has that font installed, the browser will use it. Otherwise, it will use one of the fallback options in the font stack. To find out how likely a font is to be available, consult the surveys at www.fluidwebtype.info/web-safe-fonts and www.codestyle.org/css/font-family/sampler-CombinedResults.shtml.

---

## Changing the Size of Fonts

The font-size property controls the size at which a font is displayed. The value can be set using any of the following methods:

- Absolute-size keywords
- Relative-size keywords
- Length
- Percentages

## Using Keywords to Set Font Sizes

In practice, keywords are rarely used to set the value of font-size, but it's important to mention them in case you come across them. Table 4-3 lists the absolute-size keywords together with their recommended scaling factor and HTML equivalents as specified in the draft CSS3 Fonts module.

*Table 4-3.* *Absolute-size Keywords for the font-size Property*

| Keyword | xx-small | x-small | small | medium | large | x-large | xx-large | |
|---|---|---|---|---|---|---|---|---|
| **Scaling factor** | 3/5 | 3/4 | 8/9 | 1 | 6/5 | 3/2 | 2/1 | 3/1 |
| **Equivalent heading** | h6 | | h5 | h4 | h3 | h2 | h1 | |
| **HTML font size** | 1 | | 2 | 3 | 4 | 5 | 6 | 7 |

The default value of font-size is medium, which browsers use for all text other than headings. Although these keywords are rarely used, the scaling factor and equivalent HTML heading sizes provide a useful guideline for setting your own sizes using lengths or percentages. For example, the suggested scaling factor for a level 1 heading is double the size of ordinary text, but the suggested smallest size is three-fifths, not half.

The HTML font sizes in Table 4-3 refer to the size attribute in the deprecated <font> tag. They're included here as a guide in case you need to convert an old site that uses outdated markup.

There are just two relative-size keywords:

        larger

        smaller

Using one of these keywords increases or decreases the size of the font relative to the font size of the parent element. For example, if the parent element has a font size of medium, using larger changes the current element's font to large.

## Using Length to Set Font Sizes

Tables 3-1 and 3-2 in the previous chapter list the units of measurement you can use to specify length. When designing web pages for viewing onscreen, em and px are the most important. The rem unit will gain importance when Internet Explorer (IE) 8 and earlier no longer have a significant market share.

Apart from minor variations between browsers, CSS pixels are a fixed size. As a result, using px is much simpler than em, which is a relative measurement. The default size browsers use for the text in paragraphs is 16px. To make the text slightly smaller, you can set the font size in pixels like this:

```
p {
    font-size: 14px;
}
```

To do the same with em, you need to calculate the ratio of 14px to the default 16px—in other words, 0.875. So the equivalent style rule becomes this:

```
p {
    font-size: 0.875em;
}
```

▪ **Tip**    There's an online calculator that converts pixels to em units at http://riddle.pl/emcalc/.

The `font-size` property is inherited, so if a nested element uses em, it's calculated relative to the inherited value. To demonstrate what this means, em_inheritance.html in the example files for this chapter contains the following markup:

```
<p>The font size in this paragraph is 0.875em.</p>
<div id="ems">
    <p>The font size in this paragraph is also 0.875em, but its parent is set to 1.5em.</p>
</div>
<div id="pixels">
    <p>The font size in this paragraph is 14px. It's not affected by its parent.</p>
</div>
```

The styles for the page look like this:

```
p {
    font-size: 0.875em;
}
#ems {
    font-size: 1.5em;
}
#pixels {
    font-size: 24px;
}
#pixels p {
    font-size: 14px;
}
```

Figure 4-2 shows the output in a browser.

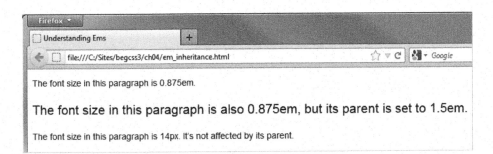

***Figure 4-2.*** *Font sizes specified in ems are relative to any inherited value*

The first style rule uses a type (or tag) selector that redefines all paragraphs and sets their `font-size` property to 0.875em. So, why is the font in the second paragraph so much bigger? This is what happens:

- The first paragraph's font size is reduced to 0.875 of the default size (16px). So, it's displayed at 14px.

- The #ems ID selector sets the `font-size` property for the ems `<div>` to 1.5em. In other words, it becomes one and a half times the default size, or 24px.

- The paragraph nested inside the ems `<div>` inherits its parent's font size (24px), which becomes the equivalent of 1em. It then reduces the size to 0.875em, or 21px.

- The #pixels ID selector sets the font size of the pixels `<div>` to 24px, but this has no effect on the paragraph nested inside. The paragraph gets its size in pixels from the #pixels p descendant selector, which overrides both the original p type selector and the #pixels ID selector.

---

■ **Tip**  It's worth spending some time studying this example, because it illustrates two important principles: inheritance and specificity (see Chapter 2). The #pixels p descendant selector overrides the other selectors not only because it's lower down the styles, but also because it's more specific. Try moving the #pixels p style rule to the top of the `<style>` block. The font sizes remain unchanged. Then change the value to, say, 18px. Only the final paragraph changes size. See also the "Length" section of Chapter 3 for an example of how em units can result in ever shrinking text.

---

As this example shows, using em to set font sizes can be difficult. If you're not careful, changing the font size in a parent element can have a domino effect on the rest of your styles. On the other hand, resizing all text proportionately might be exactly what you want.

To see how rem avoids this multiplier effect, take a look at rem.html. The HTML looks like this:

```
<p>The font size of this paragraph is 0.875rem.</p>
<div id="ems">
    <p>The font size of this paragraph is also 0.875rem, so it's not affected by its
parent's font size.</p>
</div>
```

The font sizes are set like this:

```
p {
    font-size: 0.875rem;
}
#ems {
    font-size: 1.5em;
}
```

Instead of em, the rule for paragraphs uses rem, which is calculated relative to the font size of the root element (usually the `<body>`). If—as in this case—no font size is set for the root element, rem uses the browser default. As Figure 4-3 shows, the multiplier effect is eliminated in a browser that supports rem.

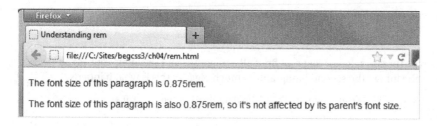

*Figure 4-3. Modern browsers eliminate the multiplier effect with rem units*

## Using Percentages to Set Font Sizes

Using a percentage value changes the font size in relation to the size inherited from any parent or ancestor element, resulting in the same multiplier effect as with em units. The HTML markup in percentages.html looks like this:

```
<p>This paragraph is sized using a percentage.</p>
<div id="parent">
    <p>This paragraph uses the same percentage, but also inherits its parent's font size.</p>
</div>
```

The font sizes are specified with percentages like this:

```
p {
    font-size: 87.5%;
}
#parent {
    font-size: 150%;
}
```

Figure 4-4 shows the output in a browser.

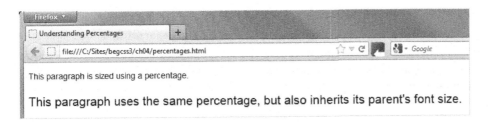

***Figure 4-4.*** *Setting font sizes in percentages also has a multiplier effect on nested elements*

---

■ **Tip** It should be apparent from the results that when used to set the font size, an em is the same as a percentage expressed as a decimal fraction.

---

## Which Method of Setting Font Sizes Should I Use?

In the early stages of learning CSS, there's no doubt that using pixels to specify font sizes is the safest. Trying to compensate for the multiplier effect of ems and percentages will test your patience to the limit. When you specify measurements in pixels, you get what you expect.

Once you feel more comfortable with CSS, start experimenting with percentages. The advantage of using percentages is that they make your designs easily scalable in the browser, which is important for accessibility. Using percentages is also recommended to ensure that type is legible on mobile devices.

Disputes of an almost religious nature have raged over the alleged superiority of a particular method of specifying font sizes. There is no truth in suggestions that ems are "better" than percentages or vice versa. In the end, the browser converts both of them to pixels.

## Using font-style to Italicize Text

The font-style property controls whether text is rendered in italic. It accepts the following values:

**italic** Italicize the text.

**normal** Remove italic.

**oblique** Use an oblique version of the font, if one exists. Otherwise, use italic.

Because very few web-safe fonts have oblique versions, italic and normal are the only values you need. The main use for normal is to remove italic from text that you want to emphasize inside a larger block of text that's already italicized.

## Using font-weight to Make Text Bolder or Lighter

The font-weight property accepts the following values:

**bold** Make the text bold.

**bolder** Make the text bolder in relation to its parent.

**lighter** Make the text lighter in relation to its parent.

**normal** Render the text normally.

One of nine values increasing in steps of 100 from 100 to 900 (400 equals normal, and 700 equals bold).

In practice, the only values you are likely to use are bold and normal. Setting font-weight to normal is useful when you want to display as normal text an element, such as a <th> tag (table heading), that browsers normally render in a bold font.

## Using font-variant to Display Text in Small Caps

In CSS2.1, the font-variant property accepts the following values:

**normal** Render text using the same letter case as in the underlying code.

**small-caps** Render the text in small caps if supported by the font. Otherwise, transform the text to uppercase.

Small caps display lowercase letters as uppercase, but in a smaller size and with slightly different proportions, as shown in Figure 4-5 (the code is in small_caps.html).

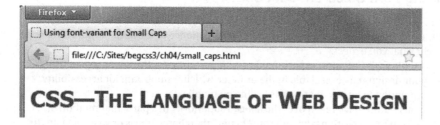

*Figure 4-5. The font-variant property converts the font to small caps*

> ■ **Note**  The draft CSS3 Fonts module envisages a major expansion of the role of the `font-variant` property, controlling ligatures, swashes, stylistic variants, historical forms, and East Asian alternatives. These features are not yet implemented by any browser.

## Adjusting the Vertical Space Between Lines of Text

The `line-height` property controls the vertical space—or leading—between lines of text. Setting the `line-height` property affects the readability of a web page. Too little space and the text looks cramped and is hard to read. Too much space and the reader's eye wanders, making reading equally difficult.

This property accepts a length, percentage, or number. You can also use the keyword `normal` to reset `line-height` to its default value. Negative values are not permitted.

Because of the way `line-height` is calculated and applied by browsers, the most consistent results are achieved by using a number *without* a unit of measurement like this:

`line-height: 1.4;`

The default value applied by browsers varies but is normally in the range of 1.0–1.2. You can use positive values less than 1, but anything smaller than about 0.6 results in lines overlapping each other.

Figure 4-6 shows `line-height.html` with the same paragraph of text displayed with different amounts of vertical space between the lines. The first paragraph uses the browser's default setting. The other three have `line-height` set to `0.8`, `1.4`, and `1.8`, respectively.

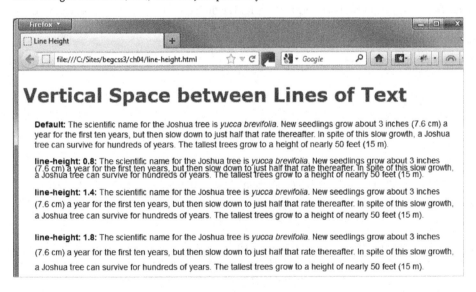

***Figure 4-6.*** *The amount of vertical space between lines of text affects readability*

## Using the Shorthand font Property

CSS shorthand properties let you combine several style declarations into one. Unfortunately, the `font` shorthand property can be difficult to remember, and if you get it wrong, your styles aren't applied.

The `font` shorthand property combines the following properties:

> `font-style` (optional)
>
> `font-variant` (optional)

font-weight (optional)

font-size

line-height (optional)

font-family

The syntax is difficult to remember because the first three items are optional and can be in any order. However, the remaining items *must* come in the prescribed order. If you declare line-height, it must be separated from font-size by a forward slash. Take, for example, the following style rule:

```
p {
    font-style: italic;
    font-weight: bold;
    font-size: 14px;
    line-height: 1.4;
    font-family:"Trebuchet MS", Arial, Helvetica, sans-serif;
}
```

You can convert that to shorthand like this:

```
p {
    font: bold italic 14px/1.4 "Trebuchet MS", Arial, Helvetica, sans-serif;
}
```

Notice that I reversed the order of font-style and font-weight, which is perfectly valid. The shorthand version is shorter and relatively easy to read. However, one of the most common mistakes is to leave out everything except the font-family. The following example *will not work*:

```
/* BAD EXAMPLE */

p {
    font: "Trebuchet MS", Arial, Helvetica, sans-serif;
}

/* END BAD EXAMPLE */
```

---

▓ **Caution**   The font shorthand property is not a synonym for font-family. You must declare both the font size and the font stack, and they must come in that order.

---

There's nothing you can do with the font shorthand property that you can't do with the individual properties. I find that the code completion features in most HTML and CSS editors make it easier to use the more explicit declarations than trying to remember the shorthand syntax. But if you prefer the more succinct way of defining your fonts, the shorthand syntax is supported by all browsers.

# Changing the Color of Text

The color of text is controlled by the color property. You can use any of the color formats described in Chapter 3. The value is inherited, so the color affects the text in all descendant elements unless a more specific rule overrides it. It's considered good practice to set the colors for background and text at the same time because users can set their own default colors in a local style sheet. If your text color doesn't provide sufficient contrast with the user's background, the text will be illegible. Backgrounds are the subject of Chapter 8, but there are no prizes for guessing what the background-color property does. Even if you want the default black text on a white background, you should specify it in the body style rule:

```
body {
    font-family: Arial, Helvetica, sans-serif;
    color: #000;             /* black */
    background-color: #FFF   /* white */
}
```

This sets the font and text color for the whole page, but you can override any of these properties in styles for headings, sidebars, or any other part of the document.

## LOCAL STYLE SHEETS AND THE CASCADE

Some users create local style sheets, usually to compensate for a disability, such as poor vision, color blindness, or dyslexia. For example, a person with poor eyesight could create a local style sheet with the following rule:

```
body {
    font-size: 250% !important;
    background-color: #000; /* black */
    color: #FFF;            /* white */
}
```

This increases the font size to 250%, and displays white text on black. CSS allows you to override the normal rules of specificity (see Chapter 3) for a single style declaration by adding the !important keyword just before the semicolon. In this example, the font size is marked as important, but the background and text color are not.

When browsers encounter a local style sheet, they use the following order of priority (most important first):

1.  Rules marked as important by the user

2.  Rules marked as important by the designer

3.  Rules not marked as important by the designer

4.  Rules not marked as important by the user

If you specify black text on a white background, the browser will honor your styles and ignore the user's preference. The danger is if you specify only the text color as black, and don't bother to specify a background color. In that case, the user's background color and your text color will both be honored—resulting in black text on a black background.

Some designers misuse the !important keyword, adding it liberally to style rules when they fail to resolve a conflict. Don't do it. You should rarely, if ever, use !important in a style sheet.

# Formatting Text

You can format text in a variety of ways using the properties in Table 4-4. The table lists CSS2.1 properties, which are supported by all browsers, plus a selection of properties from the draft CSS3 Text module that have been implemented by some browsers.

***Table 4-4.*** *Text Formatting Properties*

| Property | Initial Value | Inherited | Description |
|---|---|---|---|
| **CSS2.1 properties** | | | |
| letter-spacing | normal | Yes | Adjusts the horizontal space between characters. |
| text-align | | Yes | Controls whether text is aligned to the left or right, centered, or justified. The default in English and other Western European languages is left-aligned. In right-to-left languages, such as Arabic, Hebrew, and Urdu, it's right-aligned. |
| text-decoration | none | No | Draws a line under, over, or through text. |
| text-indent | 0 | Yes | Indents the first line of text. |
| text-transform | none | Yes | Converts text to initial capitals, all uppercase, or all lowercase. |
| vertical-align | baseline | No | Controls the vertical alignment of inline elements, such as <span> and images. |
| white-space | normal | Yes | Controls how spaces and word wrapping are handled. |
| word-spacing | normal | Yes | Adjusts the width of the space character. |
| **CSS3 properties** | | | |
| overflow-wrap | normal | Yes | Preferred name for word-wrap (see "Breaking Overflow Text" later in this chapter). |
| text-align-last | auto | Yes | Sets the alignment of the last line of a text block. |
| text-decoration-color | currentColor | No | Sets the color of underlines, overlines, and line-throughs created by text-decoration. |
| text-decoration-line | none | No | Specifies what line decorations, if any, are added to the text. |
| text-decoration-style | solid | No | Specifies the type of line used for text decoration, for example, solid or wavy. |
| text-overflow | clip | No | Cuts off text that's too long to fit, optionally replacing with ellipsis. Must be used in conjunction with the overflow property (see Chapter 6). |
| text-shadow | none | Yes | Applies one or more shadows to text. |
| word-wrap | normal | Yes | Allows long text, such as a URL, to be broken if it would otherwise overflow. |

## Increasing or Decreasing the Space Between Letters

The letter-spacing property controls the amount of horizontal space between letters. In print terminology, this is known as *tracking*. The property accepts the following values:

**normal** This is the default. It allows the browser to adjust the space between characters to justify text. Setting letter-spacing explicitly to normal cancels any inherited value.

Use a length value with a unit of measurement to specify how much space to add or subtract from the normal spacing between characters. The em unit is particularly useful because it's directly proportional to the font size.

Figure 4-7 demonstrates the effect of this property in letter-spacing.html. The first heading is displayed as normal. In the second, letter-spacing has been set to 0.2em. And the final one uses -0.1em.

***Figure 4-7.*** *Even a small amount of letter-spacing makes a big difference to the look of text*

## Controlling the Space Between Words

Computers have no concept of what constitutes a word, but the word-spacing property adjusts the width of the space character. You use it in exactly the same way as letter-spacing.

---

■ **Note** The CSS3 Text module proposes a space-separated list of up to three values for letter-spacing and word-spacing. One value represents the optimum, minimum, and maximum spacing. With two values, the first represents the optimum and minimum spacing, and the second represents the maximum. If three values are given, they represent optimum, minimum, and maximum respectively. Fine tuning like this is likely to be useful for fully justified text. No browser currently supports multiple values for letter-spacing and word-spacing.

---

## Aligning Text Horizontally

Horizontal alignment is controlled by the text-align property. It accepts the following values:

**left** Align text to the left, and leave ragged ends on the right.

**right** Align text to the right, and leave ragged ends on the left.

**center** Center text, leaving ragged ends on both sides.

**justify** Align text on both sides.

CSS3 adds a new property called text-align-last, which controls the alignment of the last line in a block of text. It accepts the same values as text-align.

Internet Explorer has supported text-align-last since IE 5. In Firefox 12+, it's supported with the browser-specific prefix as -moz-text-align-last. The style rule for the paragraph in text-align-last.html contains the following declarations:

```
p {
    text-align: justify;
    -moz-text-align-last: right;
    text-align-last: right;
}
```

Figure 4-8 shows the result in IE 9. The first two lines of text are justified, and the final line is aligned right. In other browsers apart from Firefox 12+, the final line is aligned left.

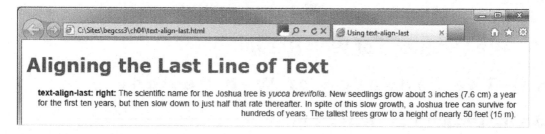

**Figure 4-8.** *Internet Explorer was the first browser to support text-align-last*

## Aligning Text Vertically

Vertical alignment is controlled by the vertical-align property—perhaps one of the least well understood CSS properties. Many newcomers to CSS mistakenly believe it can alter the vertical position of block elements, such as paragraphs. *It can't.* The vertical-align property applies to inline elements, such as images and <span> elements, and moves them in relation to the surrounding text. The HTML <sub> and <super> elements automatically shift text vertically in relation to the rest of the line. As a result, vertical-align is not as useful for text as you might expect.

The property accepts the following values:

**baseline** Align the text to the same baseline as text in the parent element. This is the default value.

**middle** Align the vertical midpoint 0.25em above the baseline of the parent.

**sub** Align text to the proper position for a subscript. This does not alter the size of the font.

**super** Align text to the proper position for a superscript. This does not alter the size of the font.

**text-top** Align the top of the imaginary text box with the top of the text in the parent element.

**text-bottom** Align the bottom of the imaginary text box with the bottom of the text in the parent element.

**top** Align the top of the imaginary text box in line with the top of the parent's text box.

**bottom** Align the bottom of the imaginary text box in line with the bottom of the parent's text box.

**inherit** Vertical alignment is not inherited by default, so use this to apply the same value as the parent element.

You can also use a length or percentage. Both align the bottom of the imaginary text box by the given amount above the bottom of the parent's text box, or below it if a negative value is used. A percentage value is calculated as a proportion of the current line height.

---

■ **Note**   The vertical-align property also controls the vertical alignment of inline blocks and the content in table cells. Inline blocks are covered in Chapter 6, and styling tables is the subject of Chapter 14.

---

## Drawing Lines Under, Above, and Through Text

The text-decoration property controls underlining, strike-throughs, and lines above text. One of its most common uses is to remove the underline from unvisited and visted links. In CSS3, some useful options have been added, such as setting the color and style of the line. But let's start with the way it works in CSS2.1. The text-decoration property accepts the following values:

**none** Remove underlines or cancel any inherited text-decoration rules.

**underline** Underline the text.

**overline** Add a line above the text.

**line-through** Add a line through the center of the text.

**blink** Flash the text on and off. Browsers are not required to support this, and this value has been removed from CSS3.

**inherit** This property is not inherited, so use this to apply the same value as the parent element.

You can use a space-separated list to sandwich text with lines above and below by using both underline and overline in the same style declaration like this:

```
text-decoration: underline overline;
```

Setting the value to line-through has the effect of striking out text. It's the recommended replacement for the deprecated <s> and <strike> HTML tags. In fact, you can go the whole hog and use all three types of lines in the same declaration. Figure 4-9 shows the effect of each type of line.

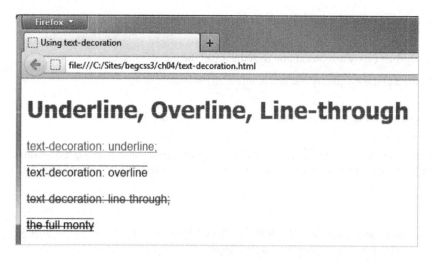

**Figure 4-9.** *The text-decoration property draws a line under, over, or through text or any combination*

In CSS2.1, the color of the line is inherited from the text.

## Changes to text-decoration in CSS3

The CSS3 Text module proposes improvements to the text-decoration property that allow you to set a different color and change the style of the line. CSS3 introduces four new properties:

> **text-decoration-line** This takes the same values as text-decoration in CSS2.1, except blink, which has been dropped.
>
> **text-decoration-color** This sets the color of the line(s).
>
> **text-decoration-style** This sets the style of the line(s). Accepted values are solid, double, dotted, dashed, and wavy. The default is solid.
>
> **text-decoration-skip** This specifies which elements, if any, the line(s) should skip over. Accepted values are none, objects, spaces, ink, and edges. The default is objects, which skips over images and inline blocks. The meaning of spaces is self-explanatory. Specifying ink prevents the line(s) from being drawn over a character. The edges keyword is mainly for use in Chinese. It creates a separate line for each character in a group rather than one solid line.

The text-decoration property itself becomes the shorthand for these four new properties. This ensures backward compatibility with CSS2.1 and older browsers. However, it means you need to be careful when using the new properties in combination with text-decoration because the shorthand version overrides any previously set values.

To maintain cross-browser compatibility, you need to specify text-decoration first for older browsers, followed by the new properties to enhance the display in browsers that understand them. If you put text-decoration last, the other properties won't be applied.

Currently, no browser supports text-decoration-skip. However, Firefox has supported the three other CSS3 properties with the -moz- browser-specific prefix since version 6. It's also a good idea to follow the browser-specific versions with the official properties so they'll be used as soon as browsers support them, for example like this:

```
.under {
    text-decoration: underline;
    -moz-text-decoration-color: red;
    -moz-text-decoration-style: wavy;
    text-decoration-color: red;
    text-decoration-style: wavy;
}
```

Figure 4-10 shows how Firefox renders text-decoration_css3.html.

**Figure 4-10.** *CSS3 offers an increased range of options for text-decoration*

When browsers fully support the CSS3 implementation of text-property, you'll be able to consolidate the values for any combination of text-decoration-line, text-decoration-color, text-decoration-style, and text-decoration-skip into a single shorthand declaration. For example, the preceding under class can be rewritten like this:

```
.under {
    text-decoration: underline red wavy;
}
```

However, even when browsers start to support this CSS3 shorthand, you won't be able to use it if you want your style to be rendered in older browsers. For the foreseeable future, you need to use the CSS2.1 version of text-decoration followed by the individual CSS3 properties for cross-browser compatibility.

## Indenting the First Line of Text

The text-indent property takes a length or a percentage and indents the first line of text in each block by the amount specified. When the value is a percentage, the indentation is a percentage of the parent element's width. Figure 4-11 shows what happens when you set text-indent for paragraphs to 40px (see text-indent.html).

***Figure 4-11.*** *The text-indent property automatically indents the first line in each text block*

---

■ **Tip**    You can't use `text-indent` to indent an entire block of text. You'll learn how to do that in Chapter 6 by adjusting the text's padding or margins.

---

If you specify a negative value for `text-indent`, it creates a hanging indent with the first line protruding to the left, as shown in Figure 4-12.

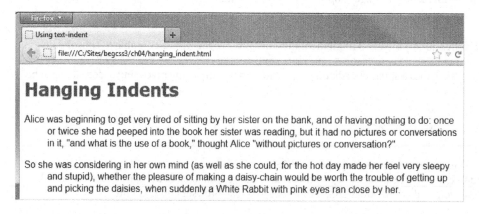

***Figure 4-12.*** *A negative value for text-indent creates a hanging indent*

Compare Figures 4-11 and 4-12. The `text-indent` property affects only the first line, shifting it right or left relative to the remaining text. The hanging indent is made possible by the fact that the paragraphs have a left margin of 40 pixels (margins are covered in Chapter 6). Without the margin, the text in the hanging indent would disappear off the left of the browser window.

## Switching Between Uppercase and Lowercase

The text-transform property converts text to use initial caps, all lowercase, or all uppercase. It's supported by all browsers, and accepts the following values:

**capitalize** Convert to uppercase the first letter after every space.

**lowercase** Convert all characters to lowercase.

**uppercase** Convert all characters to uppercase.

**none** No conversion.

The text-transform property is inherited, so it affects all child elements. Set the value to none in a child element to turn off an inherited text transformation rule.

## Controlling Whitespace and Line Wrapping

Browsers automatically close up sequences of spaces, ignore new lines in HTML, and wrap text at the right edge. The white-space property gives you control over the handling of whitespace and new lines. It accepts the following values:

**normal** This is the default value and is used to cancel any inherited value.

**pre** Preserve all spaces and new lines in the HTML.

**nowrap** Prevent the browser from automatically wrapping text.

**pre-line** Close up sequences of whitespace as in normal text, but honor new lines.
Not supported in IE 6–7.

**pre-wrap** Preserve sequences of whitespace and new lines, but automatically wrap text
when the border is reached. Not supported in IE 6–7.

Using pre has a similar effect to <pre> tags in HTML, but with the advantage of preserving the current font. It's useful for displaying poetry without the need to insert <br> tags at the end of each line. You can also use spaces to indent lines.

There are examples of each value of white-space in white-space.html. Figure 4-13 shows the results. The section with the gray background illustrates the effect of text wrapping.

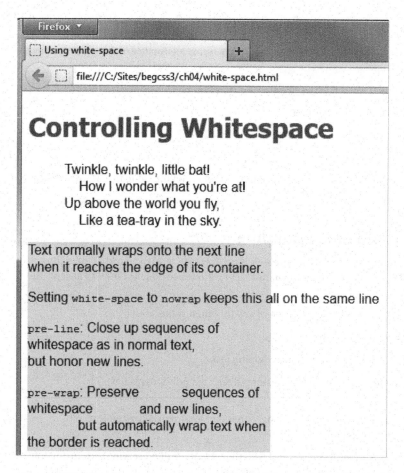

**Figure 4-13.** *The white-space property overrides the browser's default handling of spaces and new lines*

## Dealing with Text That's Too Long

If text is too long to fit into the space available, browsers let it overflow, destroying the design and sometimes making the text illegible. CSS lets you deal with the overflow by breaking the text or hiding it.

# Breaking Overflow Text

When there are no spaces in text, such as with a long URL, the browser is unable to break it, resulting in an ugly overflow. All browsers in current use support the `word-wrap` property to handle this situation. It accepts the following values:

**normal** This is the default. Lines may break only at normal word break points.

**break-word** Lines can break at arbitrary points if no break points can be found.

---

■ **Note** Although `word-wrap` has been supported by browsers for many years (it first appeared in IE 5.5 in 2000), it was never officially part of the CSS specification. When the W3C decided to include it in the CSS3 Text module, it insisted on calling the property `overflow-wrap` because it's a more accurate description of what the property does. However, browser manufacturers objected to a name change purely for the sake of linguistic accuracy. After much debate, the W3C caved in and accepted `word-wrap` as an official synonym for `overflow-wrap`. Although `overflow-wrap` remains the W3C's preferred name, it's currently not supported by any browser. Use `word-wrap` instead.

---

# Hiding Overflow Text

To hide overflow text, the overflow property needs to be set to `hidden` (the overflow property is covered in more detail in Chapter 6). This simply clips the text. A more elegant way to handle the overflow is to add the `text-overflow` property, and set its value to `ellipsis`. For example, the third paragraph in `overflow_text.html` uses the following class:

```
.ellipsis {
    overflow: hidden;
    text-overflow: ellipsis;
}
```

Figure 4-14 shows examples of the same text being broken over several lines using `word-wrap`, clipped by setting overflow to `hidden`, and the excess text being replaced by an ellipsis using a combination of the overflow and `text-overflow` properties.

---

■ **Note** The `text-overflow` property is supported by IE 6+, Firefox 7+, Opera 11+, and all versions of Safari and Chrome.

---

**Figure 4-14.** *CSS lets you break or hide text that's too long to fit*

## Adding Shadows to Text

The text-shadow property does exactly what you expect—it adds a shadow to text without the need to embed the text in an image. In fact, it can add multiple shadows to text. It was originally part of the CSS2 specification, but was dropped from CSS2.1 because no browsers supported it. Ironically, once it had been dropped, most browsers then implemented it. The only exception was Internet Explorer, which supports text-shadow only since IE 10.

---

■ **Note** Because of its CSS2 origins, there's no need to use a browser-specific prefix with text-shadow.

---

The text-shadow property expects the following values:

> A length specifying the horizontal offset of the shadow. A positive value moves the shadow to the right of the text, a negative one moves it to the left.

> A length specifying the vertical offset of the shadow. A positive value moves the shadow below the text, a negative one moves it above.

> An optional length specifying the shadow's blur radius. Negative values are not allowed.

> The color of the shadow. If no color is specified, the shadow is the same color as the text.

The order of the three length values is fixed, but the color value can come before or after them. Although the color is optional, omitting it usually produces unsatisfactory results. To create a realistic shadow, it's best to use a color with alpha transparency. All browsers that support text-shadow also support the rgba() and hsla() color formats.

The styles in text-shadow.html contain the following classes:

```
.no-blur {
    text-shadow: 0.1em 0.1em rgba(0,0,0,0.4);
}
.blur {
    text-shadow: 0.1em 0.1em 0.2em rgba(0,0,0,0.4);
}
.color-blur {
    text-shadow: 0.1em 0.1em 0.2em rgba(0,102,102,0.4);
}
```

Figure 4-15 shows the result in a browser.

**Figure 4-15.** *Adding a blur radius to a text shadow produces a more subtle effect*

All classes use the same horizontal and vertical offsets, which position the shadow 0.1em (one-tenth the height of the font) to the right of the text and below it. The first two classes use the same color (black with 40 percent alpha transparency), but only the second one has a blur radius, which softens the effect. The final class uses a similar color to the text.

## Adding Multiple Shadows to Text

You can add more than one shadow to text by creating a comma-separated list of shadow definitions. Figure 4-16 shows examples of text effects using multiple shadows in text-shadow_multi.html.

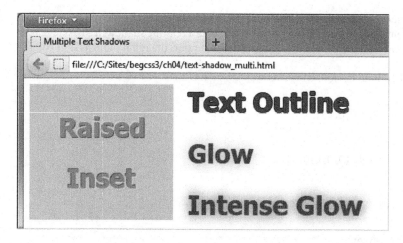

***Figure 4-16.*** *Multiple shadows on text produce a variety of effects without the need for images*

Multiple shadows are rendered with the first one on top and each subsequent one painted behind its predecessor. So, if you want shadows to overlap, smaller ones must be listed first.

## Creating Raised and Inset Text

To create the raised and inset letterpress effect similar to the one on the left of Figure 4-16, you need to choose four related colors ranging from light to dark. The lightest and darkest colors are used for the shadows. Use the darker of the remaining colors for the text, and the lighter one for the background.

I used the following colors to create the effect in Figure 4-16:

>  #FFE79B Light yellow (shadow)

>  #FFE79B Mustard (background)

>  #CCAA3F Dark mustard (text)

>  #7F744D Brown (shadow)

For a raised effect, use the lightest color to create a 1px shadow to the top left of the text, and the darkest color to the bottom right. For an inset effect, use the colors the other way round. The styles in `text-shadow_multi.html` look like this:

```
.raised {
    text-shadow: -1px -1px #FFE79B, 1px 1px #7F744D;
}
.inset {
    text-shadow: -1px -1px #7F744D, 1px 1px #FFE79B;
}
```

---

■ **Caution**   The contrast between the text and background color might not be sufficient for users with color blindness or partial vision. This technique is best reserved for decorative effect on nonessential text.

---

## Outlining Text

At the time of this writing, there is no agreed way of adding a stroke to text. The CSS3 Text module proposed a `text-outline` property, but it was dropped. WebKit browsers, such as Safari and Chrome, support a nonstandard `-webkit-text-stroke` property, but there are currently no signs of it being adopted by the W3C or other browsers. However, you can fake adding an outline to text by adding a 1px shadow to all four sides like this:

```
.outline {
    text-shadow: -1px 0 #000, 0 1px #000, 1px 0 #000, 0 -1px #000;
}
```

This is a rather clumsy solution, but at least it works in all browsers that support `text-shadow`. Unfortunately, using just two shadow definitions (`-1px -1px #000`, `1px 1px #000`) doesn't produce quite as good a result. You can compare the different effects in outline.html. The difference is subtle, but noticeable.

## Using Multiple Shadows for a More Intense Effect

The last two examples in `text-shadow_multi.html` demonstrate a surprising feature of the `text-shadow` property. If shadow definition uses a blur radius, repeating the same definition multiple times intensifies the effect. The last two examples use the following styles:

```
.glow {
    text-shadow: 0 0 0.4em #6F9;
}
.intense-glow {
    text-shadow: 0 0 0.4em  #6F9, 0 0 0.4em #6F9, 0 0 0.4em #6F9;
}
```

The `glow` class creates a green text shadow with no offsets and a `0.4em` blur radius. The `intense-glow` class simply repeats the same definition three times, resulting in a more intense effect (see Figure 4-16).

# Summary

CSS gives you an impressive toolbox to style and format text, and more features are being added by browsers as CSS3 evolves. Browsers depend on the fonts available to them, so you need to create a font stack to offer a choice of fonts with similar characteristics, finishing with a generic font family. In addition to choosing fonts, font-related properties allow you to control the size and whether the font should be displayed as bold, italic, or small caps.

As well as setting fonts, you have many formatting options, such as changing the horizontal space between individual characters and words using `letter-spacing` and `word-spacing`. You can also change the vertical space between lines of text with `line-height`; draw lines under, over, and through text with `text-decoration`; indent the first lines of text with `text-indent`; control whitespace and overflow text with `white-space` and `text-overflow`; and add multiple effects with `text-shadow`.

In the next chapter, you'll learn how to increase the range of font options using embedded fonts and related properties.

■ ■ ■

# CHAPTER 5

# Embedding Web Fonts

For many years, web designers—frustrated by the narrow range of web-safe fonts—have been demanding the ability to embed different fonts in their web pages. It's hard to believe, but Internet Explorer (IE) 4 was the first browser to support embedded fonts way back in 1997. Two main factors prevented other browsers from following suit: IE used a proprietary technology for web fonts; and font foundries were concerned about fonts being downloaded and reused without paying license fees.

The situation began to change rapidly after 2008–2009, when all major browsers finally offered support for CSS @font-face rules that specify the location of font files. This sparked the creation of many new fonts designed specifically for embedding in web pages. At the same time, font foundries began to relax their attitude toward embedded fonts. Not every font is available for embedding in web pages, but you now have a much wider range to choose from.

In this chapter, you'll learn about the following:

- Which font formats are necessary for cross-browser compatibility

- Checking whether a font's license allows it to be used in a website

- How to specify the location of font files with @font-face

- Specifying bold and italic fonts

- Restricting the range of characters downloaded by the browser

- How to adjust the relative size of fallback fonts

Using web fonts rather than images for text has several advantages, the most important being that it makes the text content immediately accessible to assistive technology for the blind and search engines. If the text needs to be changed, you just change it in the HTML rather than creating a new image.

## Adding Web Fonts to Your Sites

To add nonstandard fonts to your web pages: you can either use a font hosting service to deliver the fonts from a content distribution network (CDN), or you can store the font files on your own web server.

Most fonts are protected by copyright, so you can't upload font files to your website without first checking the license and seeing if there are any restrictions on its use. Even if you have paid for a font, you cannot assume that you have the right to use it in a website. It might be restricted to use on your local computer. Having said that, there are hundreds of fonts that you can use—and many of them are available free of charge.

### Using a Font Hosting Service

Font hosting services, such as Typekit (https://typekit.com/), Fontdeck (http://fontdeck.com/), WebINK (www.extensis.com/en/WebINK), and Google web fonts (www.google.com/webfonts), offer a wide range of web fonts. Google offers more than 500 fonts free of charge, but most other font hosting services charge an annual subscription or scaled fees depending on the number of visitors to your sites. The hosting service should provide detailed instructions of how to use the fonts. Normally, all you need to do is to include a link to the CDN in your web pages and add the font name at the beginning of the relevant font stack(s) in your style sheet. Other advantages include:

- A wide choice of fonts from a single source.

- No need to worry about licensing issues; the hosting service handles them for you.

- Reduced bandwidth consumed by your web server.

A potential drawback is that the CDN might be down or network latency might result in a delay in the fonts being loaded.

## Storing Fonts on Your Own Server

The alternative is to store the font files on your own web server. This increases the amount of bandwidth consumed when someone accesses your web pages, but it gives you greater control. There's no danger of the fonts not being rendered if the CDN is down or if you forget to renew your font hosting subscription.

If you choose to store the fonts on your own server, you need to handle all the technical and licensing details yourself. It's not particularly difficult, but there are some oddities to which you need to be alert. The main problems are the need to supply multiple formats for cross-browser compatibility, and the way that embedded fonts handle bold and italic.

The rest of this chapter is devoted to these issues.

# Choosing the Right Font Formats

Fonts come in a variety of formats. Table 5-1 lists the main formats and the browsers that support them.

***Table 5-1.*** *Font Formats and Browser Support*

| Format | Extension | Support |
| --- | --- | --- |
| Embedded Open Type (EOT) | .eot | IE 4+ |
| TrueType (TTF) & OpenType (OTF) | .ttf, .otf | IE 9 +, Firefox 3.5+, Chrome 4+, Opera 10+, iOS4.2+ |
| Web Open Font Format (WOFF) | .woff | IE 9+, Firefox 3.6+, Chrome 5+, Safari 5.1+, Opera 11+ |
| Scalable Vector Graphics (SVG) | .svg | Chrome 17+, Safari 5+, Opera 11.6+, iOS 3.2+, Android 3+ |

It's expected that WOFF will become the dominant format. It has the backing of many font foundries, and was adopted as a candidate recommendation by the W3C in August 2011. However, for cross-browser support, you'll also need EOT and TTF, and possibly SVG. Internet Explorer supports TTF and OTF only if the font's embedding permissions are set to installable.

---

▨ **Tip** Font Squirrel (`www.fontsquirrel.com`) offers a wide range of web fonts that are free for commercial use. Most are supplied as an @font-face kit, which contains all formats needed for cross-browser compatibility. The companion Fontspring site (`www.fontspring.com`) performs a similar service for commercial fonts.

---

# Checking the License

Although most modern browsers support OpenType and TrueType fonts, many font foundries expressly forbid embedding them in web pages. So, it's important to check the license. Because each font designer, foundry, and distributor has different rules regarding the use of fonts, it's impossible to give blanket advice in a book. Check with the supplier. If in doubt, don't use the font in your website. Using a font in violation of the license could turn into an expensive mistake.

The Font Squirrel and Fontspring websites have a prominent link to the license that applies to each font, so you can check its conditions before deciding whether to download it. Many fonts on the Font Squirrel site use the SIL Open Font License (`http://scripts.sil.org/OFL`), which allows the font to be used and redistributed freely as long as it is not sold separately. All web fonts used in this chapter come under this license. Other fonts are governed by individual licenses that impose simple requirements, such as adding an acknowledgment and link to the font creator's website in your style sheet.

# Embedding Fonts with @font-face

Before you can use a web font in your styles, you need to tell the browser where to find the necessary font files with an @font-face rule.

## Basic Syntax

An @font-face rule is made up of what the CSS specification calls *descriptors*, which define the location and style characteristics of the font. The basic syntax looks like this:

```
@font-face {
    font-family: font_name;
    src: location [format];
}
```

The font-family descriptor defines the name of the web font. You can choose any name you want. If it contains spaces, the name must be wrapped in quotes. If you choose the name of a font that already exists on a user's computer, the font specified in the @font-face rule takes precedence.

The src descriptor tells the browser where to find the font files. Specify multiple values for different font formats as a comma-separated list.

You can try to load a local version of the font if it exists on the user's system by inserting the font's full name or Postscript name between the parentheses after local(). The required name differs according to the font and operating system, so the CSS specification recommends using both.

However, the normal practice is to load the font files from your web server. You specify the location by inserting the path between the parentheses after url(), as described in "Specifying Background Images and Other Files" in Chapter 3. The files must be located on the same domain as the website.

After the location, you can add an optional format() declaration, using one of the format strings listed in Table 5-2.

**Table 5-2.** *Font Format Strings*

| Font Format | Format String |
|---|---|
| EOT | "embedded-opentype" |
| TrueType | "truetype" * |
| OpenType | "opentype" * |
| WOFF | "woff" |
| SVG Font | "svg" |

*\* The truetype and opentype font strings are regarded as synonymous.*

## "Bulletproof" @font-face Syntax

Although the basic @font-face syntax is fairly straightforward, browser bugs complicate the situation. Thanks to the efforts of Paul Irish and other talented web developers, a "bulletproof" workaround has been devised. It involves using two src descriptors like this:

```
@font-face {
    font-family: 'My Font';
    src: url('myfont.eot');
    src: url('myfont.eot?#iefix') format('embedded-opentype'),
        url('myfont.woff') format('woff'),
        url('myfont.ttf') format('truetype'),
        url('myfont.svg') format('svg');
}
```

The first src descriptor takes just the path to the EOT font file. The second src descriptor consists of a comma-separated list of font file locations, each with a format() declaration. The list begins with the path to the EOT file again, but with ?#iefix appended to it. The order of the remaining formats isn't important, but it's recommended to list WOFF next.

The need for two src descriptors for EOT is because of a bug in IE 8 and earlier, which fail to load the font if more than one format is listed. Adding ?#iefix tricks older versions of IE into treating the rest of the descriptor as a query string, so the font is loaded correctly. However, the bug was fixed in IE 9, which is why you need a separate src descriptor for EOT. It's messy, but it works.

If you're not worried about older browsers seeing the web fonts, you can use just the WOFF format like this:

```
@font-face {
    font-family: 'My Font';
    src: url('myfont.woff') format('woff');
}
```

## Specifying Bold and Italic

A potentially confusing aspect of embedding web fonts is that the font-family property in an @font-face rule identifies only a single font, not the whole family with its bold, italic, and other versions, such as expanded or condensed. If you want the other versions of the same family, you need to create separate @font-face rules for each one. You can either give each font face a different name, or you can reuse the same name and specify its characteristics using extra descriptors.

# Using Different Names

The Aurulent Sans font (www.fontsquirrel.com/fonts/Aurulent-Sans) designed by Stephen G. Hartke is available in four styles: regular, italic, bold, and bold italic. To demonstrate what happens when you use different names for the fonts, different.css in the ch05/styles folder contains the following style rules:

```css
@font-face {
    font-family: 'AurulentSans Regular';
    src: url('fonts/AurulentSans-Regular-webfont.eot');
    src: url('fonts/AurulentSans-Regular-webfont.eot?#iefix') format('embedded-opentype'),
        url('fonts/AurulentSans-Regular-webfont.woff') format('woff'),
        url('fonts/AurulentSans-Regular-webfont.ttf') format('truetype'),
        url('fonts/AurulentSans-Regular-webfont.svg') format('svg');
}
@font-face {
    font-family: 'AurulentSans Bold';
    src: url('fonts/AurulentSans-Bold-webfont.eot');
    src: url('fonts/AurulentSans-Bold-webfont.eot?#iefix') format('embedded-opentype'),
        url('fonts/AurulentSans-Bold-webfont.woff') format('woff'),
        url('fonts/AurulentSans-Bold-webfont.ttf') format('truetype'),
        url('fonts/AurulentSans-Bold-webfont.svg') format('svg');
}
body {
    font-family: 'AurulentSans Regular', sans-serif;
}
.bold {
    font-family: 'AurulentSans Bold', sans-serif;
}
```

The @font-face rules assign different names to the regular and bold versions of the font. The body selector applies the regular font to all text, and the bold class uses the bold font.

---

■ **Note**    I've used a class for bold text to show what happens if the browser can't find the correct font weight.

---

This style sheet is attached to different.html, which contains the following HTML markup in the <body> of the page:

```html
<h1>The Lobster Quadrille</h1>
<h1 class="bold">The Lobster Quadrille</h1>
<p>"Will you walk a little faster?" said a whiting to a snail.</p>
<p><b>"Will you walk a little faster?" said a whiting to a snail.</b></p>
<p class="bold">"Will you walk a little faster?" said a whiting to a <b>snail</b>.</p>
```

The page contains the same level 1 heading twice and the same paragraph three times. Figure 5-1 shows how Chrome 21 on Windows renders the page.

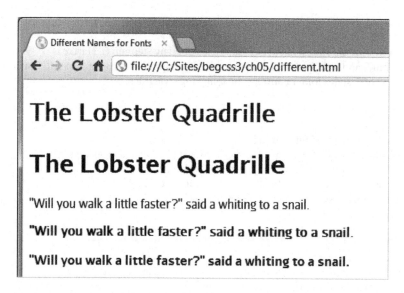

**Figure 5-1.** *Chrome synthesizes bold text*

Normally, browsers render <h1>, <b>, and <strong> elements in bold. It's clear from Figure 5-1 that Chrome has attempted to do so with the first heading and the second paragraph. However, if you compare the two headings, there's a marked difference between the synthesized bold and the genuine bold font. The difference isn't quite so clear between the second and third paragraphs, although the synthesized version results in the text being marginally wider. Internet Explorer and Opera also synthesize bold text.

However, if you view the same page in Safari 5.1, there's no attempt to synthesize bold text. As Figure 5-2 shows, it renders both the first heading and the second paragraph using the regular version of the font.

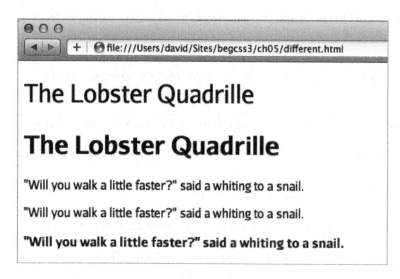

**Figure 5-2.** *Safari 5.1 does not synthesize bold text*

Safari 6 and Firefox handle the fonts yet another way. They not only synthesize the bold text, but they also double the effect when they encounter <b> tags in text that's rendered in the genuine bold font. Look closely at the word "snail" in the third paragraph in Figure 5-3. The font is heavier than the rest of the sentence.

*Figure 5-3. Firefox not only synthesizes bold text, it doubles the effect with <b> tags*

In this example, I've used only bold text, but all browsers handle italic the same way. If a genuine italic face isn't found, all except older versions of Safari render a synthetic version.

Figure 5-4 shows the difference between synthetic and genuine italic in Firefox.

|  | Regular | Bold |
| --- | --- | --- |
| Synthetic: | *faster* | ***faster*** |
| Italic: | *faster* | ***faster*** |

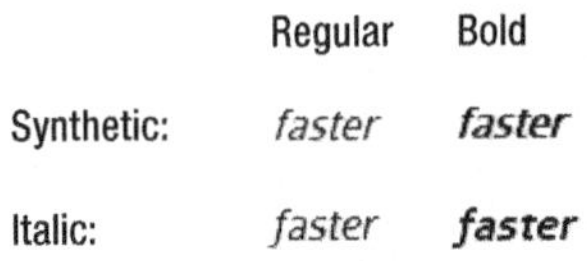

*Figure 5-4. Comparison of synthetic and genuine italic in Firefox*

Failure to synthesize bold and italic in older versions of Safari was an incorrect interpretation of the specification, as explained in the side bar "To Synthesize or Not to Synthesize."

## TO SYNTHESIZE OR NOT TO SYNTHESIZE

The draft CSS3 Fonts module specifies a new `font-synthesis` property, which controls whether a browser is allowed to synthesize bold or italic. The property accepts the following values:

- `none`: All synthetic faces are disallowed.

- `weight`: Synthetic bold is allowed.

- `style`: Synthetic italic is allowed.

The default value is `weight style`, which allows the browser to synthesize both bold and italic. At the time of this writing, no browser has yet implemented the `font-synthesis` property.

The use of a class for bold type in the preceding example was purely for demonstration purposes. The styles in different2.css assign the bold and italic faces like this:

```
/* Omitted: four @font-face rules defining regular, bold, italic, and bold italic fonts. */

body {
    font-family: 'AurulentSans Regular', sans-serif;
}
/* Headings and bold text */
h1, h2, h3, h4, h5, h6, b, strong {
    font-family: 'AurulentSans Bold', sans-serif;
}
/* Regular italic */
i, em {
    font-family: 'AurulentSans Italic', sans-serif;
}
/* Bold italic */
b i, h1 i, strong em {
    font-family: 'AurulentSans BoldItalic', sans-serif;
}
```

The first three rules use type selectors to redefine the look of the body, headings, and bold and italic elements. Defining the rule for bold italic is slightly more problematic, because it depends on how elements are nested. This example uses descendant selectors for `<i>` tags nested inside `<b>` or `<h1>` elements, and for `<em>` nested inside `<strong>`. However, if the tags are nested the other way round, the descendant selectors need to be reversed.

The HTML markup inside the `<body>` of different2.html looks like this:

```
<h1>The Lobster <i>Quadrille</i></h1>
<p>"Will you walk a little <i>faster</i>?" said a whiting to a snail.</p>
<p><b>"Will you walk a little <i>faster</i>?" said a whiting to a snail.</b></p>
```

Figure 5-5 shows how the page is rendered in Firefox 14 (left) and IE 9 (right).

**Figure 5-5.** *Firefox 14 doubles the italic even when the correct face is used*

What appears to be happening in Firefox is that it applies the correct font, but also synthesizes the italic, resulting in double italic. This is clearly a bug that will hopefully be eliminated in a later version.

## Using Different Names with Descriptors

The alternative way of using @font-face is to create a family of fonts by using the same value for font-family in each rule and describing the font's characteristics with font-weight and font-style.

The values for the font-weight and font-style descriptors are the same as for the similarly named properties described in Chapter 4. The default for both is normal, so you need to include the descriptor in an @font-face rule only if you want to use a different value.

The styles in same_name.css look like this:

```
@font-face {
    font-family: 'Aurulent Sans';
    src: url('fonts/AurulentSans-Regular-webfont.eot');
    src: url('fonts/AurulentSans-Regular-webfont.eot?#iefix') format('embedded-opentype'),
        url('fonts/AurulentSans-Regular-webfont.woff') format('woff'),
        url('fonts/AurulentSans-Regular-webfont.ttf') format('truetype'),
        url('fonts/AurulentSans-Regular-webfont.svg') format('svg');
}
@font-face {
    font-family: 'Aurulent Sans';
    src: url('fonts/AurulentSans-Bold-webfont.eot');
    src: url('fonts/AurulentSans-Bold-webfont.eot?#iefix') format('embedded-opentype'),
        url('fonts/AurulentSans-Bold-webfont.woff') format('woff'),
        url('fonts/AurulentSans-Bold-webfont.ttf') format('truetype'),
        url('fonts/AurulentSans-Bold-webfont.svg') format('svg');
    font-weight: bold;
}
@font-face {
    font-family: 'Aurulent Sans';
    src: url('fonts/AurulentSans-Italic-webfont.eot');
    src: url('fonts/AurulentSans-Italic-webfont.eot?#iefix') format('embedded-opentype'),
        url('fonts/AurulentSans-Italic-webfont.woff') format('woff'),
        url('fonts/AurulentSans-Italic-webfont.ttf') format('truetype'),
        url('fonts/AurulentSans-Italic-webfont.svg') format('svg');
    font-style: italic;
}
```

87

```
@font-face {
    font-family: 'Aurulent Sans';
    src: url('fonts/AurulentSans-BoldItalic-webfont.eot');
    src: url('fonts/AurulentSans-BoldItalic-webfont.eot?#iefix') format('embedded-opentype'),
        url('fonts/AurulentSans-BoldItalic-webfont.woff') format('woff'),
        url('fonts/AurulentSans-BoldItalic-webfont.ttf') format('truetype'),
        url('fonts/AurulentSans-BoldItalic-webfont.svg') format('svg');
    font-weight: bold;
    font-style: italic;
}
body {
    font-family: 'Aurulent Sans', sans-serif;
}
```

Each @font-face rule uses 'Aurulent Sans' as the value for font-family, and—with the exception of the first one—uses font-weight and/or font-style to describe the font's characteristics. The first rule defines the regular font, so the descriptors default to normal.

The HTML markup in same_name.html is identical to different2.html. Figure 5-6 shows how it's rendered by Firefox 14.

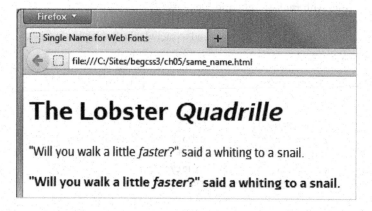

**Figure 5-6.** *The double italic effect in Firefox is eliminated by building a font family with descriptors*

Building a font family like this with descriptors not only simplifies your subsequent CSS and HTML markup, but it also eliminates the double italic effect in Firefox. So, if you're planning to use web fonts for the main text in a website, this is the better way to use @font-face. However, if you plan to use web fonts only for special effects on a limited number of elements, using different names for each font face makes your styles easier to understand. Neither method is inherently superior to the other.

---

■ **Note** You can also use the font-stretch descriptor in an @font-face rule to specify a condensed or expanded version of a font. It accepts the following values: normal, ultra-condensed, extra-condensed, condensed, semi-condensed, semi-expanded, expanded, extra-expanded, and ultra-expanded.

---

# Specifying a Range of Characters

Embedding web fonts increases the download size of your web pages, so it's important to use them only where it makes a significant improvement to the design. You can also limit the range of characters that a browser downloads, which can be particularly useful when dealing with nonalphabetic languages such as Chinese or Japanese, or if you want only a small number of symbols from a larger font.

You control the range of characters in an @font-face rule with unicode-range, which expects one or more Unicode ranges as a comma-separated list. A Unicode range always begins with U+ followed by one of the following formats:

- A hexadecimal number representing a single code point, for example U+A5 (¥).

- Two hexadecimal numbers separated by a hyphen representing a consecutive range, for example U+590-5ff represents the code range for Hebrew.

- A range where trailing ? characters represent any single digit, for example U+30?? represents the code range for Japanese hiragana and katakana.

---

■ **Note**   The hexadecimal digits in a Unicode range are case-insensitive. U+A5 and U+a5 have the same meaning.

---

At the time of this writing, unicode-range is supported by the latest versions of all browsers except Firefox and Opera. The styles in range.html contain the following @font-face rule to define a font called Limelight Quotes, which uses unicode-range to select only left and right double quotes from the Limelight font (www.fontsquirrel.com/fonts/limelight) designed by Eben Sorkin.

```
@font-face {
    font-family: 'Limelight Quotes';
     src: url('styles/fonts/Limelight-webfont.eot');
     src: url('styles/fonts/Limelight-webfont.eot?#iefix') format('embedded-opentype'),
        url('styles/fonts/Limelight-webfont.woff') format('woff'),
        url('styles/fonts/Limelight-webfont.ttf') format('truetype'),
        url('styles/fonts/Limelight-webfont.svg#LimelightRegular') format('svg');
    unicode-range: U+201c-d;
}

.quote {
    font-family: 'Limelight Quotes', serif;
    font-size: 150%;
}
```

---

■ **Tip**   There's a list of Unicode code points at http://en.wikipedia.org/wiki/List_of_Unicode_characters.

---

The quotes in the main heading in the page are wrapped in <span> tags and assigned the quote class like this:

```
<h1><span class="quote">&#8220;</span>Turtle Soup<span class="quote">&#8221;</span></h1>
```

Figure 5-7 shows the result in Chrome.

**Figure 5-7.** *Browsers that support unicode-range download only the quotes, not the full font*

The problem with using `unicode-range` is that it's not currently supported by Firefox or Opera, so those two browsers download the entire font rather than the characters you want. However, British web developer Drew McLellan has devised a crafty technique to prevent Firefox and Opera from downloading the whole font (`http://24ways.org/2011/unicode-range`). It involves creating a second `@font-face` rule that specifies a local font as the source of the same `font-family` descriptor like this:

```
@font-face {
    font-family: 'Limelight Quotes';
    src: local(Georgia);
    unicode-range: U+270C;
}
```

In the second `@font-face` rule, `unicode-range` specifies an obscure symbol that will never be used in your page. Firefox and Opera treat the second rule as overriding the first, but other browsers simply add the new `unicode-range` value to the existing one. But because the font is local, there's nothing to download, so the rule is harmless. Figure 5-8 shows the result in Firefox.

**Figure 5-8.** *The second @font-face rule prevents Firefox from downloading the web font*

# Adjusting Relative Font Sizes

When building a font stack, it's difficult to find fallback fonts that have exactly the same proportions as your first-choice font. To increase legibility, the CSS3 Fonts module provides the `font-size-adjust` property, which adjusts the font size so that the height of lowercase letters is the same regardless of the font used.

Figure 5-9 demonstrates the effect of using `font-size-adjust` in Firefox, which at the time of this writing is the only browser that supports it.

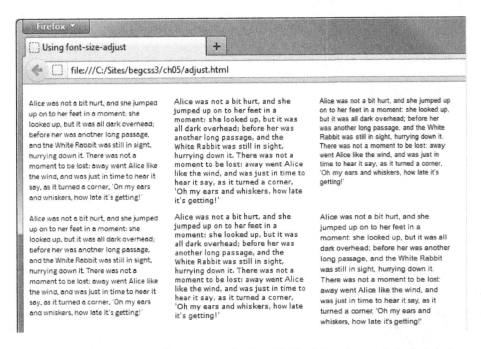

***Figure 5-9.*** *Using font-size-adjust changes the size of fallback fonts to match the first choice*

The first row displays three fonts at 9px without adjustment: a web font called Nobile (`www.fontsquirrel.com/fonts/Nobile`) designed by Vernon Adams, Verdana, and generic sans-serif. Verdana is a good match as a fallback font for Nobile, but the generic sans-serif is much smaller, making it difficult to read. The second row uses `font-size-adjust` to change the aspect ratio of each font to match that of Nobile. A font's *aspect ratio* is defined as being equal to the height of a lowercase "x" divided by font size. Changing the aspect ratio of the generic sans-serif text in the second row with `font-size-adjust` makes it easier to read. It also occupies a similar amount of vertical space as the other fonts.

Finding the aspect ratio of a font is done by trial and error using two identical characters at a large size surrounded by a border. The styles in aspect_ratio.html in the ch05 folder look like this:

```
body {
    font-family: Nobile, Verdana, sans-serif;
}
span {
    border: 1px solid red;
    font-size: 200px;
}
```

```
.adjust {
    font-size-adjust: 0.5;
}
```

The Nobile font is defined by @font-face rules in an external style sheet. The <body> of the page contains the following HTML:

```
<p><span>b</span><span class="adjust">b</span></p>
```

Both letters are wrapped in <span> tags that add a one-pixel red border around them. The second <span> is modified by the adjust class, which sets font-size-adjust to 0.5.

Figure 5-10 shows what aspect_ratio.html looks like in Firefox.

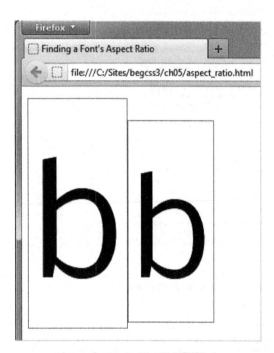

***Figure 5-10.*** *You need to change the value of font-size-adjust until both borders are equal in height*

Because Nobile has a higher aspect ratio, the second border isn't as tall as the first. To find the font's aspect ratio, you need to change the value of font-size-adjust in the adjust class and refresh the page in the browser until both borders are the same height. In the case of Nobile, this happens when font-size-adjust is set to 0.57. So, that's its aspect ratio.

Although finding the aspect ratio of your first-choice font involves a little guesswork, it's easy enough to do, and it's a one-time operation. All that's necessary is to add font-size-adjust to the same style rule as your font stack, and set its value to the aspect ratio of the first font like this:

```
body {
    font-family: Nobile, Verdana, sans-serif;
    font-size-adjust: 0.57;
}
```

Adding `font-size-adjust` to your styles won't make any difference to the look of your normal text—as long as you use the correct aspect ratio for the first font in your font stack. However, it ensures that the relative size of the text remains constant if a fallback font is used.

## Summary

Now that web fonts are widely supported by browsers, using images for typographic effects should soon become a thing of the past. Fonts increase the size of the download, but that's often compensated by no longer needing to use images. However, just because you can embed web fonts with `@font-face`, don't go overboard. Mixing a large number of different fonts on a page can destroy the design.

If you plan to use a web font for the main text, use the same name for `font-family` and specify bold and italic faces with the `font-weight` and `font-style` descriptors. Although most browsers synthesize bold and italic, using the correct font faces produces better results. To minimize the download burden on users, don't forget that you can limit the range of characters with `unicode-range`.

That concludes Part II. In the next part, we'll take an in-depth look at page layout with CSS.

# PART III

■ ■ ■

# CSS Page Layout

Page layout is one of the most challenging aspects of CSS. Unlike print, you don't know in advance what size screen your web pages will be viewed on. You also have no control over which browser is used. Old, less capable browsers tend to cling to a significant proportion of market share for many years. CSS3 proposes new techniques, such as Flexible Box Layout (covered in Chapter 22), but until a sufficient proportion of browsers supports them, you need to stick to the tried-and-tested techniques that work cross-browser.

Chapter 6 lays the foundation for this part with an in-depth discussion of the CSS box model, showing how to add whitespace around HTML elements, and explaining the difference between margins and padding. You'll also learn how width and height are calculated, and how to deal with content that's too big for its container. This is arguably the most important chapter in the book.

Chapter 7 introduces the concept of floats, which are used to flow text around images and position elements horizontally alongside each other. It also shows how to create a two-column layout with a sidebar.

Chapters 8 and 9 describe how to add backgrounds and borders to elements. You'll learn how to position background images accurately, as well as modern techniques to add rounded corners and drop shadows without the need for images or complex markup.

In Chapter 10, you'll learn how to style ordered and unordered lists, and convert an unordered list into a smart looking navigation bar.

Chapter 11 demystifies the secrets of CSS positioning, a subject that confuses many beginners. You'll learn how to fix elements within the browser window, and how to lock elements into position using a combination of relative and absolute positioning.

Rounding out Part III is an extensive review of cross-browser layout techniques in Chapter 12, showing how to create one-, two-, and three-column layouts using floats and CSS table display.

# CHAPTER 6

■ ■ ■

# Understanding the CSS Box Model

The basic principle underlying web page layout is a concept known as the CSS box model, which regards every HTML element as a box. The position of each box is determined by the *flow* of the web page—in other words, the order in which the HTML elements appear in the source code. There are two main types of boxes: block-level and inline. A *block-level* box or element—such as a <div>, heading, or paragraph—normally occupies all available horizontal space, beginning on a line of its own and pushing subsequent elements down onto a new line. On the other hand, an *inline box* or element—such as a <span> or image—sits alongside preceding and subsequent inline elements.

Often, this behavior is exactly what you want, but there are many occasions when it's not. CSS allows you to change the way elements are displayed, so you can put block-level elements alongside one another or convert inline elements to act like block-level ones. You can even remove elements completely from the flow of the page. The box model controls the width and height of elements, as well as the horizontal and vertical space around them. Understanding the box model is the key to successful page layout. The basic elements are very simple, but they often work in a counterintuitive way. The aim of this chapter is to guide you through the mysteries of the box model to lay a solid foundation for the rest of the book. If there's one chapter you really need to get to grips with, this is it!

In this chapter, you'll learn about:

- The different components of the box model
- Controlling width and height
- Using the CSS3 box-sizing property for width and height calculations
- Creating vertical and horizontal space with padding and margins
- Centering elements
- Using the display property to change the default layout of an element
- Controlling visibility and overflow

---

■ **Note**   This chapter is based mainly on the CSS2.1 box model, which is likely to remain the basis for CSS layout for the foreseeable future. Work on the CSS3 box model resumed in early 2012 after being abandoned for nearly five years, so it's not as far advanced as other parts of CSS3.

---

# Introducing the Components of the Box Model

The CSS box model consists of the following components:

> *Content* This is the content of an HTML element, such as a paragraph, image, `<div>`, or `<span>`.

> *Padding* Horizontal and vertical space surrounding the content.

> *Border* A border drawn around the padding.

> *Margin* Horizontal and vertical space outside the border.

Figure 6-1 shows how these components fit together.

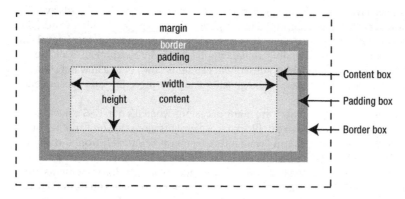

**Figure 6-1.** *The standard CSS box model*

Browsers apply default values to individual elements. For example, paragraphs have default top and bottom margins, but no padding or border, whereas `<div>` elements have no padding, border, or margins. You can use CSS to adjust the padding, border, and margins independently on each side of an element to control its look and layout.

Figure 6-1 looks perfectly logical. Padding goes around the content, the border goes around the padding, and the margin goes around the border. What confuses many people is the way in which width and height are calculated. Another complicating factor is the behavior of adjacent vertical margins. First, let's take a look at width and height.

---

■ **Caution**    If you use an incomplete DOCTYPE or none at all, Internet Explorer 8 and earlier switch to quirks mode, which uses an incorrect version of the box model. See "The Importance of the DOCTYPE" in Chapter 2.

---

## Setting Width and Height

The width and height properties set the horizontal and vertical dimensions of an element. The default value of both properties is auto, which means that the element expands or contracts to fit the natural size of the content. Another four properties allow you to constrain the dimensions of an element within a specified range. Table 6-1 describes the width- and height-related properties.

*Table 6-1.* *CSS Width and Height Properties*

| Property | Initial Value | Inherited | Description |
|---|---|---|---|
| width | auto | No | Sets the width for an element. Can be applied to any element, except inline text, or table rows. If no value is specified, the element expands horizontally as far as possible to accommodate the element's content. |
| min-width* | 0 | No | Sets a minimum width for an element. |
| max-width* | none | No | Sets a maximum width for an element. |
| height | auto | No | Sets the height for an element. Can be applied to any element, except inline text, or table columns. If no value is specified, the element expands vertically as far as possible to accommodate the element's content. |
| min-height* | 0 | No | Sets a minimum height for an element. |
| max-height* | none | No | Sets a maximum height for an element. |

*\* Internet Explorer 6 does not support the min- and max- properties.*

All six properties accept values expressed as a length (for example, pixels or ems) or as a percentage. When a percentage is used, the width or height is calculated as a percentage of the parent element's width or height.

The default for min-width and min-height is 0, whereas the default for max-width and max-height is none. Although these sound just two ways of saying the same thing, 0 means "there is no minimum," and none means "there is no maximum." So, unless you specify a minimum, the element will collapse to nothing if it has no content. If you specify no maximum, the element will expand horizontally or vertically as far as it can to accommodate its content.

■ **Caution** In the standard box model, width and height refer to the dimensions of the *content*, not the element's overall size. Padding and borders are *added* to the width and height, not included.

## Using Padding and Margins to Add Space Around Elements

Both padding and margins add vertical and horizontal space around elements. Sometimes, it doesn't matter which you use, because they appear to have the same effect. However, there are important differences, as described in Table 6-2.

**Table 6-2.** *Differences Between Padding and Margins*

| Feature | Padding | Margins |
| --- | --- | --- |
| Background | The content's background stretches into padding. | The background of the content's parent element shows through margins. |
| Border | Padding goes inside the border. | Margins go outside the border. |
| Collapsing | Padding never collapses. | Adjacent vertical margins collapse. |

To demonstrate the differences, the styles in comparison.html in the ch06 folder add a background color to the `<body>` of the page, which contains two `<div>` elements. Both `<div>` elements have the same width, background color, border, and margins, but the first one also has 20 pixels of padding.

As Figure 6-2 shows, the white background of the first `<div>` element extends to the gray border and shows through the padding. What's more, the overall width of the first `<div>` is 40 pixels greater than the second one because the padding is added outside the content. The light yellow background of the page shows through the margins of both `<div>` elements.

**Figure 6-2.** *Padding adds breathing space around the content inside an element*

The styles in comparison.html look like this:

```
body {
    background-color: #FFC;
    color: #000;
    font-family: "Lucida Sans Unicode", "Lucida Grande", sans-serif;
}
#padded, #notpadded {
    width: 300px;
    background-color: #FFF;
```

```
    border: 2px solid #999;
    margin: 20px;
}
#padded {
    padding: 20px;
}
```

■ **Note**   Backgrounds and borders are covered in depth in Chapters 8 and 9.

## Specifying Padding

Padding can be added to almost any element. However, the only table elements that can have padding are the table itself and individual table cells. Table 6-3 lists the properties used for padding.

*Table 6-3.* *CSS Padding Properties*

| Property | Initial Value | Inherited | Description |
| --- | --- | --- | --- |
| padding-top | 0 | No | Adds padding to the top of an element. |
| padding-right | 0 | No | Adds padding to the right of an element. |
| padding-bottom | 0 | No | Adds padding to the bottom of an element. |
| padding-left | 0 | No | Adds padding to the left of an element. |
| padding | 0 | No | Shorthand property. Accepts between one and four values. |

All properties listed in Table 6-3 accept a length, such as px or em, or a percentage. Negative values are not allowed. Although padding is never inherited, you can use the keyword inherit to apply the same value as the parent element.

The properties are listed in clockwise order because that's the order used by the shorthand property, which takes between one and four values. This is how it works:

*One value* Applies equally to all four sides.

*Two values* The first one applies to the top and bottom, and the second one to the left and right.

*Three values* The first one applies to the top, the second one to the left and right, and the third one to the bottom.

*Four values* The values are applied in clockwise order starting from the top.

Confused? Don't be. Take my advice, and forget about using three values. Concentrate on one, two, and four. The way to remember the rest is simple:

- Always start at the top.

- Go clockwise.

If there's only one value, it's easy—it applies to the top and all other sides.

If there are two values, the first one applies to the top. Then, going clockwise, the next one applies to the right side. The same two values are repeated in the same order as you continue going round the clock. So, the first one is applied to the bottom, and the second one to the right.

If there are four values, you start at the top, and go clockwise to the right, bottom, and left. Some designers use the mnemonic **TRouBL**e to remember this, but I think that clockwise is much simpler.

The styles in comparison.html use the shorthand version like this:

```
#padded {
    padding: 20px;
}
```

This has exactly the same meaning as the following:

```
#padded {
    padding-top: 20px;
    padding-right: 20px;
    padding-bottom: 20px;
    padding-left: 20px;
}
```

I think you'll agree that the shorthand version is much simpler to write. Once you get used to the shorthand, it also tends to be a lot easier to read. In this example, I've listed the properties in clockwise order, but the order is not important when setting padding for individual sides.

---

■ **Caution**    When using percentage values for padding, the values are based on the width of the *parent* element—even for top and bottom padding. For example, if you have a paragraph that's 400px wide, specifying padding as 10% does not add 40px of padding on the left and right. The actual amount depends on how wide the containing element is. If there is no containing element, the padding is 10 percent of the width of the page.

---

## Specifying Margins

Specifying margins is very similar to padding. There are separate properties to control the margin independently on each side of an element, as well as a shorthand property. They're listed in Table 6-4.

*Table 6-4.* CSS Margin Properties

| Property | Initial Value | Inherited | Description |
| --- | --- | --- | --- |
| margin-top | 0 | No | Sets the top margin of an element. |
| margin-right | 0 | No | Sets the right margin of an element. |
| margin-bottom | 0 | No | Sets the bottom margin of an element. |
| margin-left | 0 | No | Sets the left margin of an element. |
| margin | 0 | No | Shorthand property. Accepts between one and four values. |

Margins can be set using a length, such as px or em, or a percentage. If you use a percentage, the value is based on the width of the parent element in the same way as with padding. You can also use the inherit keyword to apply the same margin(s) as the parent element.

An important difference between padding and margins is that you can use negative values for margins. This means that you can reduce the gap between elements or move an element further to the left—the opposite of indenting.

The margin properties also accept the keyword auto, which tells the browser to calculate the margin automatically. However, for the browser to be able to do so, the element *must* have a width. The width can be set either in the HTML (for example, through the width attribute of an image) or with the CSS width property.

---

■ **Tip**   The default CSS value of all margin properties is 0, but browsers add their own default margins to many page elements. If you're having difficulty adjusting the gap between elements, the problem might be caused by a default margin. Some web developers use what's known as a *reset style sheet* to eliminate default margins and padding. I prefer to change only those values where I need to override the defaults. To learn more about reset style sheets, see http://meyerweb.com/eric/tools/css/reset/.

---

## Understanding How Vertical Margins Collapse

Every element has a top margin and a bottom margin, even if it's set to zero. When block-level elements follow one another, adjacent vertical margins collapse or overlap each other. The best way to understand this is with a practical exercise.

---

### EXERCISE: INSPECTING MARGINS AND THE BOX MODEL

All modern browsers have tools that let you inspect CSS and other aspects of a web page. For this exercise, I'm going to use the Developer Tools in Google Chrome.

1.  Open comparison.html in Google Chrome. Right-click the first block of text, and select *Inspect Element* from the context menu. This opens the Developer Tools with the HTML for the padded <div> selected, as shown in Figure 6-3.

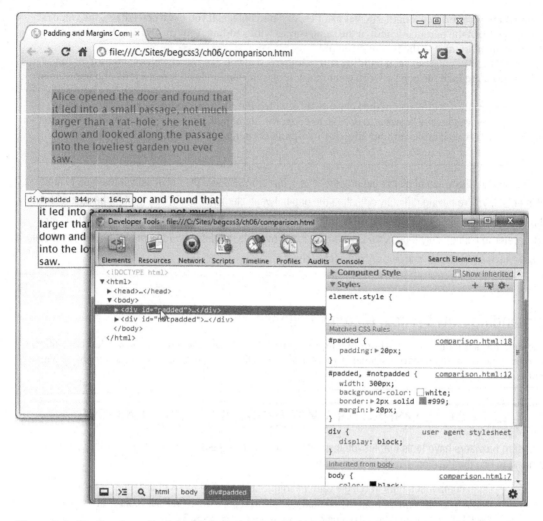

**Figure 6-3.** *The Developer Tools highlight the content, padding, and margins in different colors*

2.  Position your mouse pointer over the HTML for the <div> in the Developer Tools panel to show the highlighting for the content, padding, and margins. Notice that, although the declared width is 300px, the tooltip shows the dimensions of the <div> as 344px × 164px. The extra 44px come from 20px of padding and the 2px border on each side.

3.  Next, look at the highlighting for the margins. It extends all the way to the top of the page and to the top border of the next <div>, but there's a small gap on the left and right.

4.  Move your mouse pointer so that it's over the <body> tag in the Developer Tools panel. The margin highlighting changes to a narrow line wrapped around both <div> elements, as shown in Figure 6-4. This is the 8px default margin that all browsers add to a web page.

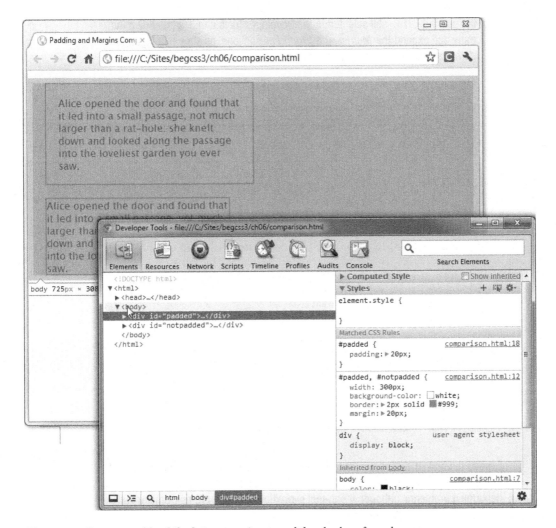

**Figure 6-4.** *Browsers add a default 8px margin around the <body> of a web page*

5. Move your mouse pointer back over the HTML for the padded <div> in the Developer Tools panel. It should be obvious that the gap on the left and right is accounted for by the 8px margin on the <body>. What might not be quite so obvious is why the margin highlighting in Figure 6-4 is pushed away from the top of the page. The reason is that the top margins on the <body> and the padded <div> have been collapsed, and the 20px margin on the <div> overlaps the smaller margin, pushing it away from the top.

6. Position your mouse pointer over the second <div> in the Developer Tools panel. Then move it back over the first <div>. As you switch between them, the highlighting should make it obvious that the bottom margin of the first <div> occupies the same space as the top margin of the second one.

7. With the padded `<div>` still selected in the Developer Tools panel, scroll down the right pane and expand the *Metrics* and *Properties* sections, as shown in Figure 6-5. The *Metrics* section shows a diagrammatic representation of the `<div>` element's box model.

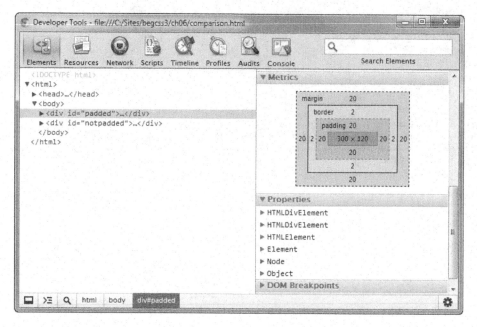

**Figure 6-5.** *The Developer Tools panel displays a diagram of the box model of the selected element*

8. Expand the first `HTMLDivElement` in the *Properties* section. This displays a long list of the element's attributes in alphabetical order. Examining this list can be useful for debugging problems, although it can feel overwhelming if you're not familiar with the Document Object Model (DOM).

9. Scroll down to locate `offsetLeft`. Its value is 28, indicating that the `<div>` is 28px from the left of the screen. The next property, `offsetParent`, is `HTMLBodyElement`, confirming that the 8px comes from the `<body>`. Immediately following is `offsetTop`, which is 20. So, the `<div>` is 28px from the left, but only 20px from the top of the page. The difference is accounted for by the way adjacent vertical margins collapse, but horizontal ones do not.

Understanding how adjacent vertical margins collapse is vital to successful page layout with CSS. Using a browser's tools to highlight margins greatly simplifies troubleshooting problems with the vertical space between elements.

■ **Note** The draft CSS3 box model proposes adding support for text that runs from top to bottom—as is traditional in Chinese and Japanese, and making collapsing margins dependent on the direction of the content. The rules remain unchanged for horizontal text—adjacent vertical margins collapse, while horizontal ones are preserved. For vertical text, the rules are reversed.

## Isn't There an Easier Box Model?

You're not alone if you think that the CSS box model is counterintuitive. Surely it would be much easier to calculate width and height from the outer edge of one border to the outside of the opposite border? In other words, include padding and borders in the overall dimensions. In fact, that's how Internet Explorer interpreted the CSS specification when it first supported CSS. However, the web standards community generally agreed that IE's version of the box model was wrong. All other browsers implemented the box model as described in Figure 6-1, and Microsoft fell in line when it released IE 6 in 2001.

So, for more than a decade, web designers have grown accustomed to calculating width and height by deducting the dimensions of padding and borders. But CSS3 offers a way of turning back the clock to the original Microsoft box model using the `box-sizing` property, which accepts the values listed in Table 6-5.

**Table 6-5.** *Values Accepted by the box-sizing Property*

| Value | Description |
| --- | --- |
| content-box | Width and height apply only to the content box (see Figure 6-1). This is the default. |
| padding-box* | Width and height include both content and padding. |
| border-box | Width and height include content, padding, and borders. |

*\* This value might be dropped from the final specification.*

Because `content-box` results in the standard box model described at the beginning of this chapter, and `padding-box` might be dropped from the final specification, `border-box` is the only value of interest. Setting `box-sizing` to `border-box` makes width and height calculations more intuitive by including padding and borders, as shown in Figure 6-6.

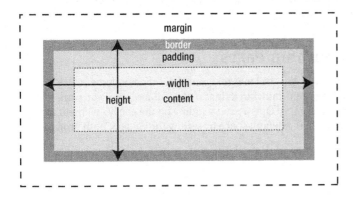

**Figure 6-6.** *Setting box-sizing to border-box changes the way width and height are calculated*

---

■ **Tip**   The default values of padding and borders are zero, so you don't need to declare them.

---

The box-sizing property is not inherited, so you can apply it to individual elements. Alternatively, you can apply it to all elements using the universal selector like this:

```
* {
    -moz-box-sizing: border-box;
    -webkit-box-sizing: border-box;
    box-sizing: border-box;
}
```

Opera 7+ and IE 8+ support box-sizing without a prefix—as do the most recent versions of Safari and Chrome—but you need the -moz- and -webkit- prefixes for cross-browser support.

In early 2012, Paul Irish, one of the most influential front-end web developers, publicly endorsed this technique to avoid dealing with the complexities of the standard box model (http://paulirish.com/2012/box-sizing-border-box-ftw/). However, it's not a perfect solution. The main problems with setting box-sizing to border-box are as follows:

- The box-sizing property is not supported by IE 6 and IE 7. If a significant proportion of visitors to your sites use either of these browsers, your design will break.

- Some browsers, notably Firefox, don't support min-height and max-height when box-sizing is set to border-box.

---

■ **Note**   Fashions in web development come and go. My instinct is to stick with the standard box model while problems remain with the implementation of box-sizing with border-box. Throughout the rest of this book, I use the standard box model.

---

# Using Margins to Improve Page Layout

CSS allows you to adjust the margins on each side of every element individually, giving you considerable control over horizontal and vertical space between elements. When used in combination with the float property, which you'll learn about in the next chapter, margins are one of the most important tools in current page layout. In this section, I'll describe some of the most common uses of margins.

## Removing the Default Margin from Your Pages

As you saw in the preceding exercise, browsers add an eight-pixel margin around the <body> element (see Figure 6-4). Most of the time, this default margin is unimportant, but it does make a difference if you want to use images that go right to the edge of the page. Older versions of Opera used padding on the <body> element instead of a margin, so it's become standard practice to remove the default space by setting the value of both properties to zero like this:

```
body {
    margin: 0;
    padding: 0;
}
```

■ **Note**   It's been many years since Opera stopped using padding on the <body> element. However, setting its value to zero does no harm.

## Centering Block-level Elements

As you learned in Chapter 4, you center text elements using the text-align property and setting its value to center. The draft CSS3 box model proposes introducing a similar property, tentatively called alignment or block-align, for block-level elements. But until the specification is implemented by browsers, you center a block-level element by giving it a declared width and setting the left and right margins to auto.

The styles in centered.html in the ch06 folder set the width of a <div> to 400px, and use the margin shorthand property to set its top and bottom margins to 20px and left and right margins to auto like this:

```
#centered {
    background-color: #FFF;
    border: 2px solid #999;
    width: 400px;
    margin: 20px auto;
    padding: 20px;
}
```

As Figure 6-7 shows, the <div> remains centered regardless of the size of the browser window.

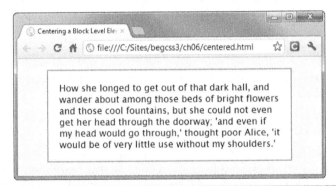

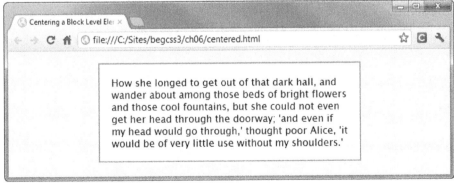

***Figure 6-7.*** *Specifying a width and setting horizontal margins to auto centers a block-level element*

---

■ **Tip**    Setting both horizontal margins to auto also centers a block-level element that has a max-width property.

---

To center the entire content of a web page, it's common to wrap everything inside the <body> in a <div>, give the <div> an ID such as wrapper, and set its width and horizontal margins like this:

```
#wrapper {
    width: 100%;
    max-width: 1000px;
    margin: 0 auto;
}
```

Alternatively, give the <body> a width and set its horizontal margins to auto like this:

```
body {
    width: 100%;
    max-width: 1000px;
    margin: 0 auto;
    padding: 0;
}
```

Both approaches work equally well in modern browsers. However, giving the <body> a width presents a problem if you want to give the margins a different background unless you also add a background to the <html> element. Although all browsers support styling the <html> element separately from the <body>, the CSS3 Borders and Backgrounds module specifically recommends against doing so (www.w3.org/TR/css3-background/#special-backgrounds). The safer approach is to use a wrapper <div>.

---

■ **Tip**    Setting the width of the <body> or a wrapper <div> to 100% in combination with max-width ensures that the page fills the full width of the screen on mobile devices, but never grows too wide on a desktop.

---

## Using Margins to Indent Text

In the past, the <blockquote> tag was frequently used to indent text. Apart from using a tag for a purpose that was never intended, the big limitation of <blockquote> is that it creates a 40-pixel margin on both sides of the text. If you nest <blockquote> tags, the text in the center steadily becomes narrower and narrower. Using CSS margins eliminates that problem, because you can set the margin on each side to the exact amount you want. For example, you can control the margins on paragraphs like this:

```
p {
    margin-top: 0;
    margin-right: 10px;
    margin-bottom: 0.5em;
    margin-left: 50px;
}
```

Alternatively, the same margins can be declared using the shorthand property:

```
p {
    margin: 0 10px 0.5em 50px;
}
```

These rules apply to all paragraphs, but you can create a class or use a descendant selector to apply a different amount of indentation to paragraphs in a particular section of a page.

## Using Negative Margins

CSS permits negative values for margins. This means that you can reduce the gap between elements, or move an element further to the left—the opposite of indenting. When using negative margins, you need to be careful, because doing so could result in elements overlapping or being hidden offscreen.

---

■ **Caution** In the days before widespread support for web fonts, a common technique known as *image replacement* used negative margins and other CSS tricks to hide text offscreen. The idea was to provide alternative content for search engines and screen readers for the blind when text was embedded in an image. Google's guidelines specifically warn that using CSS to hide text can "cause your site to be perceived as untrustworthy since it presents information to search engines differently than to visitors." (http://support.google.com/webmasters/bin/ answer.py?hl=en&answer=66353)

---

## EXERCISE: STYLING A PAGE WITH MARGINS

In this exercise, you'll create some basic styles to restrict the width of a page, center its content, and indent the paragraphs using techniques described in the previous sections. You'll also make use of text properties from Chapter 4. Use destinations.html in the ch06/begin folder as your starting point.

1. Create a blank file and save it as destinations.css.

2. Attach destinations.css to destinations.html by adding a `<link>` tag in the `<head>` of the page like this:

```
<title>Mediterranean Destinations</title>
<link href="destinations.css" rel="stylesheet">
</head>
```

3. Create a style rule for the `<body>` to remove the default margin and padding. Also, specify the `font-family` property like this:

```
body {
    margin: 0;
    padding: 0;
    font-family: "Lucida Sans Unicode", "Lucida Grande", sans-serif;
}
```

4. The content is in a `<div>` with the ID `wrapper`. Create an ID selector to center the `<div>` and fill the full width of the screen on small devices, but not exceed 650px.

```
#wrapper {
    width: 100%;
    max-width: 650px;
    margin: 0 auto;
}
```

5. Create a style to indent the paragraphs by 30 pixels like this:

```
p {
    margin-left: 30px;
}
```

6. Save the style sheet, and view destinations.html in a browser. The content should be centered with the paragraphs slightly indented from the headings.

7. Resize the browser window so that it's less than 650 pixels wide. The headings and right side of the paragraphs are uncomfortably close to the edge of the page, as shown in Figure 6-8.

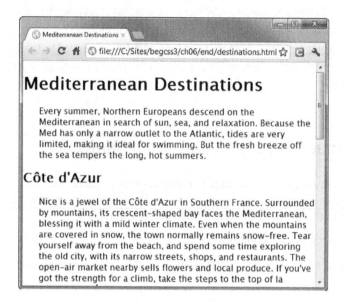

**Figure 6-8.** *When the browser viewport is narrow, the text is too close to the sides*

8. Center the main heading using the text-align property, and set its value to center:

```
h1 {
    text-align: center;
}
```

9. Move the other headings away from the edge of the screen by adding a small horizontal margin. You need to add the margin on both sides in case you have a long heading that stretches across the full width of a narrow screen. Use a group selector for <h2> and <h3> elements like this:

```
h2, h3 {
    margin-left: 10px;
    margin-right: 10px;
}
```

10. Amend the style rule for the paragraphs to add a similar right margin, and increase the left margin by 10px to compensate for the margin on the headings:

```
p {
    margin-left: 40px;
    margin-right: 10px;
}
```

11. Save the style sheet, and reload destinations.html in the browser. The text is no longer jammed against the sides of the screen, as Figure 6-9 shows.

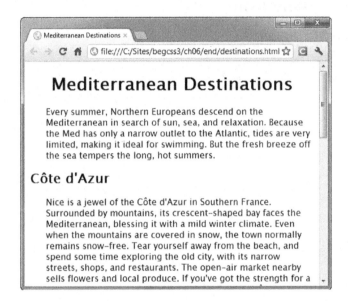

**Figure 6-9.** *The text has been moved off the edges of the browser window*

12. The horizontal space looks OK, but there's too much vertical space between the second level headings and the following paragraphs. Amend the h2, h3 style rule like this:

```
h2, h3 {
    margin-left: 10px;
    margin-right: 10px;
    margin-bottom: 0.5em;
}
```

13. Save the style sheet and reload the page. The distance between the headings and paragraphs barely changes.

14. Try changing the value of margin-bottom to 0.25em, and test it again. It makes no difference.

15. Use the developer tools in your browser to inspect one of the <h2> elements. For example, in Chrome, right-click a heading and select *Inspect Element* from

113

the context menu. Then select the HTML for the heading in the Developer Tools panel. As Figure 6-10 shows, the highlighting around the heading reveals that the bottom margin doesn't occupy the full vertical space between the heading and the following paragraph. It's the top margin on the paragraph that's causing the gap.

***Figure 6-10.*** *Using the browser's developer tools helps explain what's causing the gap*

16. Remove the top margin from the paragraphs by amending their style rule like this:

```
p {
    margin-left: 40px;
    margin-right: 10px;
    margin-top: 0;
}
```

17. Save the style sheet and test the page again. The vertical gap between the headings and the following paragraphs is now much smaller, but the space between individual paragraphs remains unchanged. This is because the default bottom margin still occupies the space between paragraphs.

The styles created in this exercise use type selectors to redefine the default margins around the <body>, paragraphs, and headings. The exercise also demonstrated the importance of checking the size of adjacent vertical margins when trying to adjust the distance between block-level elements.

# Changing Layout with the display Property

As I explained at the beginning of this chapter, CSS treats all elements as boxes, the two main types being block-level and inline. The other types of boxes supported by all browsers are table elements and list items. It's likely that other types of boxes will be added in the CSS3 box model, but in this chapter I intend to concentrate on what browsers currently implement rather than speculate on what might happen in the future.

You should be familiar with table elements and list items from HTML. Table elements are organized in rows and columns. In the table box model, the height of each row and width of each column are determined by the tallest and widest elements, respectively. What distinguishes the list item box model is the presence of a marker box for the bullet or number alongside the content block.

By default, every HTML element is treated as one of these types of boxes: block-level, inline, table element, or list item. However, the display property gives you the power to change an element's box type by using one of the values listed in Table 6-6.

**Table 6-6.** *Values Supported by the display Property*

| Value | Description |
| --- | --- |
| block | Treats the element as block-level. |
| inline | Treats the element as inline. |
| inline-block | Treats the element as a block, but displays it inline. The block's height and vertical padding and margins affect the height of the line in which it is displayed. |
| list-item | Used internally by browsers to create list items. Of no practical value to web designers. |
| none | Removes the element and *all* its contents from display. You cannot override this value in a child element. |
| table, inline-table, table-row, table-cell, table-caption, table-column, table-column-group, table-row-group, table-header-group, table-footer-group | Causes the element to behave like the equivalent table element. Not supported in IE 6 or IE 7. See Chapter 12 for a more detailed description. |

■ **Note** CSS2.1 also proposed run-in as a value for the display property. This treats a block-level element like a run-in headline, which begins on a new line of its own, but allows the next block-level element to run straight on. The W3C dropped it from the final specification because no browser managed to support it completely.

The display property is not inherited, so you can also use the inherit keyword to apply the same value as the element's parent.

## Understanding the Difference between inline and inline-block

An important aspect of the box model as it applies to inline text elements is that margins and padding do not affect the line height of the surrounding text unless you set the display property to inline-block. Horizontal margins and padding increase the distance before and after the inline element, but the vertical distance remains unchanged.

The text in display1.html in the ch06 folder contains two <span> elements. By default, browsers treat <span> elements as inline, but the display property of the second one is set to inline-block. The style rules add margins and padding on all sides of both <span> elements and make the text bold like this:

```
span {
    margin: 20px;
    padding: 20px;
    font-weight: bold;
}
#inline-block {
    display: inline-block;
}
```

As Figure 6-11 shows, both <span> elements are surrounded by horizontal space, but only the one displayed as an inline block affects the vertical space around it.

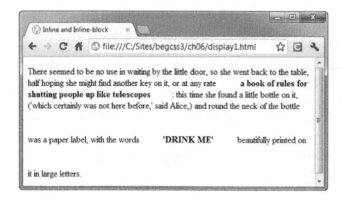

***Figure 6-11.*** *Setting display to inline-block affects the line height of the surrounding text*

The lack of vertical space around the first <span> gives the misleading impression that browsers ignore vertical margins and padding applied to inline text. The styles in display2.html add a background color and border to both <span> elements. As Figure 6-12 shows, the padding and border around the first <span> element are rendered normally and overlap the text in the surrounding lines.

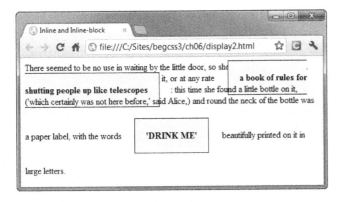

**Figure 6-12.** *The vertical padding is still rendered on inline text elements*

Examine display2.html closely (or compare Figures 6-11 and 6-12), and observe the following:

- The background and border of the inline <span> obscures the preceding line.
- The next line is displayed over the background and border of the inline <span>.
- The text in the inline <span> wraps normally, splitting the box over multiple lines.
- If you resize the browser window, the inline block is never split.

In other words, setting the display property to inline-block gives the element all the characteristics of a block-level element, but displays it inline. You can verify this in display3.html, which adds the width, text-align, and vertical-align properties to the style rule applied to both <span> elements like this:

```
span {
    margin: 20px;
    padding: 20px;
    font-weight: bold;
    background-color: #FF9;
    border: 1px solid #000;
    width: 150px;
    text-align: center;
    vertical-align: top;
}
```

As Figure 6-13 shows, the inline <span> remains unaffected, whereas the inline block is a different width with the text centered. Its position in relation to the surrounding text has also been affected by the vertical-align property.

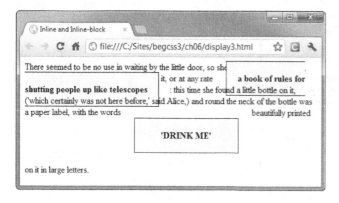

**Figure 6-13.** *The alignment and width of the inline block have been changed*

---

■ **Note**   The `vertical-align` property also affects inline elements. However, since the alignment is in relation to the surrounding line, the only values that affect inline text elements are `sub` and `super`.

---

These examples might seem rather impractical, but they have been designed to demonstrate the different behavior of inline text elements and inline blocks. The following exercise offers a more practical use for inline blocks when styling a form.

## EXERCISE: USING THE DISPLAY PROPERTY TO STYLE FORM LABELS

In this exercise, you'll take a simple HTML form and use the `display` property to style the labels. Setting the value to `inline-block` and giving the labels a declared width makes it easy to align text fields vertically. However, applying the same styles to all labels isn't always appropriate, so you'll use descendant and attribute selectors to apply different styles where necessary.

Use form.html and form.css in the ch06/begin folder as your starting point. The style sheet contains only the following style rule, which sets the font, background color, and text color for the page:

```
body {
    font-family: "Lucida Sans Unicode", "Lucida Grande", sans-serif;
    color: #000;
    background-color: #FFF;
}
```

1.   Open form.html and load it into a browser. As Figure 6-14 shows, the text fields are not aligned vertically, and there's a border around the set of radio buttons. The border is added automatically by browsers because the radio buttons are wrapped in a <fieldset>.

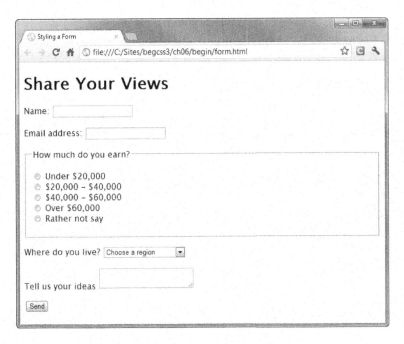

**Figure 6-14.** *Apart from the font, the form is unstyled*

2. To align the text fields vertically, set the `display` property of the labels to `inline-block` and give them a fixed width. Also use a bold font by adding the following type selector to form.css:

```
label {
    display: inline-block;
    width: 140px;
    font-weight: bold;
}
```

3. To increase the width of the text input fields, you need to use an attribute selector to avoid affecting other `<input>` elements, such as the radio buttons and submit button. Add the following style definition to form.css:

```
input[type="text"] {
    width: 250px;
}
```

4. Save form.css and reload form.html in a browser. The labels are now bold, and the two text fields at the top of the form are vertically aligned and wider. But the same styles have been applied to all labels. Using bold text for the radio button labels looks wrong, and the fixed width wraps the text. As Figure 6-15 shows, the result looks a mess.

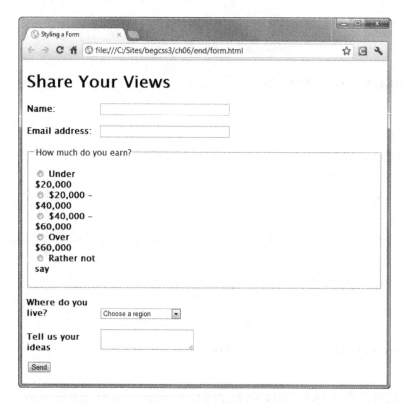

**Figure 6-15.** *The improvements to the text input labels don't suit the rest of the form*

5.  The radio button labels are nested inside a `<fieldset>` element, so you can use a descendant selector to reset the `font-weight` and `width` properties like this:

    ```
    fieldset label {
        font-weight: normal;
        width: auto;
    }
    ```

6.  Remove the margin, padding, and border from the `<fieldset>` like this:

    ```
    fieldset {
        margin: 0;
        padding: 0;
        border: none;
    }
    ```

7. You can use the `<legend>` element of the `<fieldset>` as the label for the radio group by setting its font to bold. You also need to remove the left padding from the `<legend>` to align it correctly with the other labels. Add the following style rule:

```
legend {
    font-weight: bold;
    padding-left: 0;
}
```

8. Save form.css, and reload form.html in the browser. As Figure 6-16 shows, the radio button group now looks much better. The `<label>` elements now stretch their natural width, and the `<legend>` identifies the whole group.

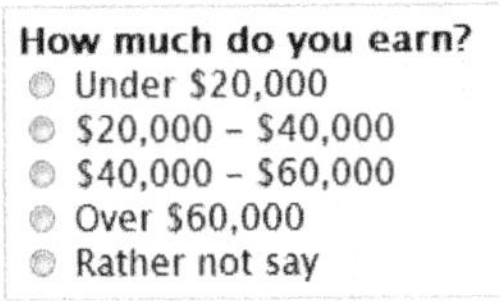

**How much do you earn?**
- ⊘ Under $20,000
- ⊘ $20,000 – $40,000
- ⊘ $40,000 – $60,000
- ⊘ Over $60,000
- ⊘ Rather not say

**Figure 6-16.** *The restyled fieldset*

9. Using a bold font is fine for the labels for the `<select>` menu and `<textarea>`, but the wrapped text looks odd. Although you could increase the width of all labels, it would create too large a gap for the text input fields at the top of the form. Instead, create attribute selectors for the last two labels using their `for` attribute to identify them. Set their `display` property to `block` and their `width` property to `auto` like this:

```
label[for="region"], label[for="ideas"] {
    display: block;
    width: auto;
}
```

10. To finish styling the form, add a couple of style rules to set the width and height of the `<textarea>`, and to indent the form like this:

```
textarea {
    height: 100px;
    width: 300px;
}
form {
    margin-left: 60px;
}
```

11. Save form.css, and reload form.html in a browser. It should look like Figure 6-17.

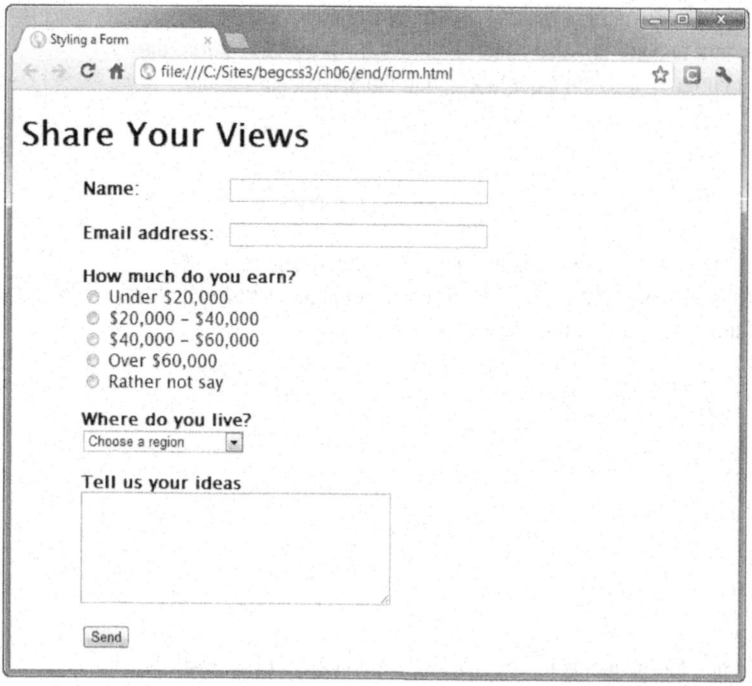

**Figure 6-17.** *Changing the display property of the labels results in a clean form layout*

Setting the `display` property for the last two labels to `block` forces them to display on a separate line. As a result, the `<select>` menu and `<textarea>` are vertically aligned with their labels rather than with the text input fields. I think this looks fine, but you could add a left margin to both elements if you prefer. Examine the style rule commented out at the bottom of form.css if you're not sure how to do it.

This exercise has used type, descendant, and attribute selectors, avoiding the need for classes or IDs in the HTML markup. The styles are rendered correctly in all browsers, except IE 6, which doesn't understand attribute selectors. If you need to support IE 6, use classes in place of attribute selectors.

## Using the display Property to Hide Elements

Setting the `display` property to `none` hides the affected element and all its children in a visual browser. The elements remain in the underlying HTML source, but they're removed completely from the flow of the document, and any subsequent elements move up to take their place. Hiding content like this is commonly used in conjunction with JavaScript in interactive widgets, such as accordions and tabbed panels. When the user clicks a trigger element, a JavaScript function changes the value of the `display` property to `block`, thereby revealing the content. Such techniques are particularly useful in designs for mobile phones, where screen real estate is limited.

The HTML in display4.html in the ch06 folder contains three paragraphs. The styles contain two classes: `hide`, which sets the `display` property to `none`, and `show`, which sets the `display` property to `block`. When the page loads, a JavaScript function runs automatically and applies the `show` class to the second paragraph, and adds a link at the end of the first paragraph, as shown in Figure 6-18.

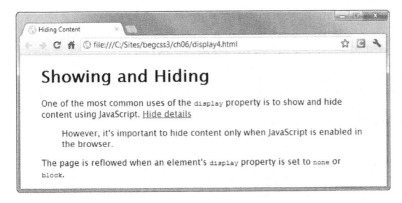

***Figure 6-18.*** *The link at the end of the first paragraph toggles the display of the second paragraph*

When "Hide details" is clicked, the JavaScript function replaces the show class with the hide class, changing the second paragraph's display property from block to none. As a result, the paragraph is removed from display, and the third paragraph moves up into its place, as shown in Figure 6-19.

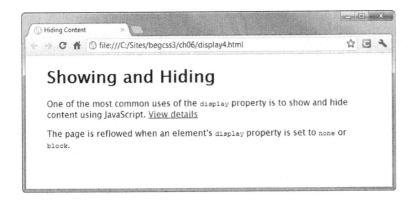

***Figure 6-19.*** *The middle paragraph is removed completely from the page*

Clicking "View details" switches the classes applied to the second paragraph, restoring it and moving the third paragraph back down to make room for it.

---

▓ **Note** Controlling CSS with JavaScript is beyond the scope of this book, but the code is included in the ch06 folder for you to examine. If you'd like to learn more about using JavaScript to enhance your web pages with dynamic effects, take a look at *DOM Scripting: Web Design with JavaScript and the Document Object Model, 2nd Edition* by Jeremy Keith with Jeffrey Sambells (friends of ED, ISBN: 978-14302-3389-3).

---

# Controlling Visibility

As explained in the preceding section, setting an element's display property to none hides it and all its children by removing them completely from the flow of the document. The CSS box model also has a visibility property, which can be used to hide elements. However, when the visibility property is used to hide an element, it doesn't remove it from the document flow. A space is left where the element would normally be. Another important difference is that the visibility of child elements can be controlled independently.

The visibility property accepts the values listed in Table 6-7.

**Table 6-7.** *Values Accepted by the visibility Property*

| Value | Description |
|---|---|
| visible | The element is visible. This is the default. |
| hidden | The element is not visible, but the layout of surrounding elements is not affected. Child elements are also hidden, but this can be overridden by setting their visibility property to visible. |
| collapse | Used only with table elements. See Chapter 14 for a description. |

To demonstrate the difference between using display and visibility to hide elements, visibility.html in the ch06 folder is an adaptation of display4.html (see Figures 6-18 and 6-19). Instead of setting the display property to none and block respectively, the hide and show classes set the visibility property to hidden and visible like this:

```
.show {
    visibility: visible;
}
.hide {
    visibility: hidden;
}
```

When you load visibility.html in a browser, the JavaScript function applies the show class to the second paragraph, which has the ID details. This makes the paragraph visible, as shown in Figure 6-20.

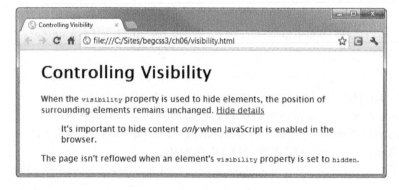

**Figure 6-20.** *The second paragraph is visible when the page first loads*

The word "only" is wrapped in `<i>` tags, making it a child element of the details paragraph. A separate style rule sets its visibility property to visible like this:

```
#details i {
    visibility: visible;
}
```

When you click "Hide details," the JavaScript function sets the class of the second paragraph to hide, setting its visibility property to hidden. However, the page layout remains unchanged. Moreover, as Figure 6-21 shows, "only" remains visible because it's controlled by a separate style rule.

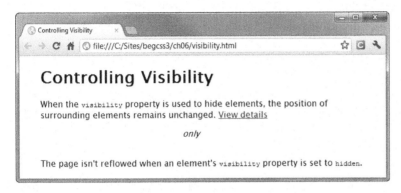

***Figure 6-21.*** *The child element and page layout are not affected*

---

▪ **Tip** Beginners often confuse visibility and display because both hide elements, but in very different ways. Remember that visibility doesn't remove an element from the document flow, whereas display does.

---

# Handling Content That's Too Big

Browsers automatically wrap text when it reaches the specified width or at the right edge of the browser window if no width is specified. But what if you've specified a height and the text is too long, or if you use an image that's too big for the containing element? By default, the content spills over. To control content that's too big for its container, use one of the properties listed in Table 6-8.

***Table 6-8.*** *Properties that Control Overflow*

| Property | Initial Value | Description |
|---|---|---|
| overflow | visible | Controls the horizontal and vertical overflow of a block or inline block. |
| overflow-x | visible | Controls the horizontal overflow of a block or inline block. |
| overflow-y | visible | Controls the vertical overflow of a block or inline block. |

The overflow property is part of CSS2.1. The other two properties are part of CSS3, but are supported by all browsers in current use (including IE 6). All three properties accept the values listed in Table 6-9.

***Table 6-9.*** *Values Accepted by Overflow Properties*

| Value | Description |
| --- | --- |
| visible | The content flows outside the box. |
| hidden | Content that is too big is clipped. No scrollbars are provided. |
| scroll | Content that is too big is clipped. Scrollbars are provided, even if not needed. |
| auto | Scrollbars should be provided if the content is too big, but actual implementation is left up to the browser. |

The overflow properties are not inherited, so you can also use the inherit keyword. In CSS3, it's proposed that overflow should be a shorthand property for overflow-x and overflow-y. If one value is supplied, it applies to both horizontal and vertical overflow. If two values are supplied, the first should apply to horizontal overflow, and the second to vertical overflow.

---

■ **Caution**    At the time of this writing, browsers support overflow with only a single value. Using two values results in the style rule being ignored. If you need to apply different values to horizontal and vertical overflow, set overflow-x and overflow-y independently.

---

The ch06 folder contains six files that show how the overflow properties work. Each file contains five <div> elements that are 150px wide and 200px high with a solid red border. To demonstrate the difference between text, which wraps automatically, and images, the <div> elements in three files contain only text. The remaining files contain a mixture of text and images.

In overflow.html and overflow_image.html, the overflow property has the following effects:

- When overflow is set to auto and the content is smaller than the box, no scrollbars are generated.

- When overflow is set to auto and the content is larger than the box, text generates only a vertical scrollbar. Because images can't be wrapped, both horizontal and vertical scrollbars are generated when necessary.

- When overflow is set to hidden, no scrollbars are generated. Excess content is inaccessible.

- When overflow is set to scroll, horizontal and vertical scrollbars are always generated.

- When overflow is set to visible, excess content overlaps the box.

This is exactly what you would expect from the descriptions in Table 6-9. However, using overflow-x and overflow-y on their own produces some surprising results. Figure 6-22 shows how browsers handle overflow-x with text.

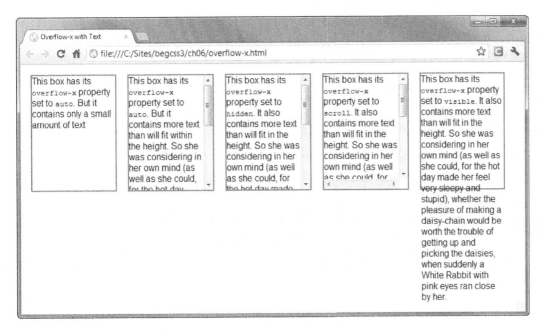

**Figure 6-22.** *Browsers generate a vertical scrollbar for text, even when only overflow-x is set*

As Figure 6-22 shows, Chrome generates a vertical scrollbar for text that's too large to fit the box when overflow-x is set to auto, hidden, or scroll. All other browsers in widespread use do the same. In the case of scroll, the horizontal scrollbar is understandable, because the specification says the scrollbar should be added even if it's not needed. However, it's not clear whether the vertical scrollbars are an incorrect interpretation of the specification.

Figure 6-23 shows the effect of using the same values with overflow-x when an image is too large for the box (see overflow-x_image.html).

**Figure 6-23.** *Oversized images also generate a vertical scrollbar with overflow-x*

The effect of using hidden with overflow-x is easier to understand on an image. The middle box in Figure 6-23 doesn't have a horizontal scrollbar, so the horizontal overflow is genuinely hidden.

The behavior of overflow-y with text is more straightforward. Figure 6-24 shows the results in overflow-y.html. Vertical scrollbars are generated by oversized text with auto and by scroll. But hidden results in no scrollbars, leaving the oversized text inaccessible.

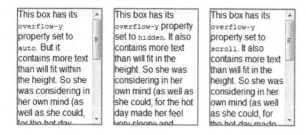

**Figure 6-24.** *Controlling vertical overflow with text works as expected*

Notice that only a vertical scrollbar is generated by setting overflow-y to scroll.

When scrollbars are generated by the overflow properties, they're drawn inside the containing box. However, WebKit-based browsers on Mac OS X 10.7 (Lion), iOS 5, and Android don't draw any scrollbars. Figure 6-25 shows overflow-x.html in Chrome on a Mac. A narrow scrollbar indicator appears when you mouse over a scrollable element, but the content fills the box. On iOS 5 and Android, the content can be scrolled, but no indicator appears.

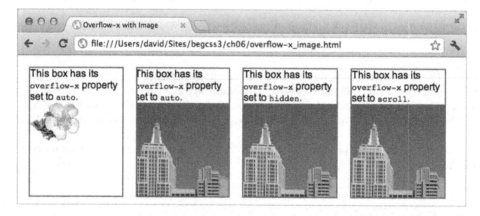

**Figure 6-25.** *No scrollbars are displayed in Chrome and Safari on Mac OS X*

All browsers provide a scrolling mechanism when needed, but the lack of scrollbars in some browsers means you need to test your design carefully when using overflow properties.

# Summary

The CSS box model lies at the heart of page layout, making this arguably the most important chapter in this book. In the standard box model, width- and height-related properties apply only to the content of an element. Padding, borders, and margins are added outside the content. Setting the CSS3 box-sizing property to border-box allows you to change this behavior by including padding and borders inside an element's dimensions. However, the box-sizing property isn't universally supported, so it should be used with caution.

Whichever box model you choose, padding adds horizontal and vertical space around the content of an HTML element, but inside any border. Padding uses the same background as the content and never collapses.

Margins go outside an element's border, but adjacent vertical margins overlap and collapse to the size of the largest margin. The background of the parent element shows through margins. Horizontal and vertical space around an element can be controlled independently on each side by using specific properties, such as `padding-top` and `margin-left`, or by using the `padding` and `margin` shorthand properties. As long as an element has a declared width, you can center it by setting its left and right margins to `auto`.

In addition to setting the `width` and `height` properties, you can limit the dimensions of an element within a range by using `min-width`, `max-width`, `min-height`, and `max-height`, which are supported by all browsers except IE 6.

Browsers treat most elements as block-level or inline boxes, but the `display` property allows you to change the default box type. Setting `display` to `none` hides an element and all its children by removing it completely from the document flow. Setting `visibility` to `hidden` also hides an element, but it leaves a space where the element would normally be. The overflow properties control what happens when an element's content is too big.

There's a lot of information to absorb in this chapter. Take your time to make sure it sinks in. In the next chapter, you'll learn about another fundamental aspect of current page layout—using the `float` property to flow text around images and position block-level elements alongside each other.

# CHAPTER 7

## Floating Elements for Layout

As I explained in the preceding chapter, CSS treats HTML elements as boxes. Block-level elements force whatever follows them down the page, even if there's sufficient room alongside. Inline elements sit alongside their neighbors, but if one element is taller than the rest, it affects the line height. For example, images are treated as inline elements. Inserting one in a block of text forces the text to align with the bottom of the image, as shown in Figure 7-1.

### Côte d'Azur

Nice is a jewel of the Côte d'Azur in Southern France. Surrounded by mountains, its crescent-shaped bay faces the Mediterranean, blessing it with a mild winter climate. Even when the mountains are covered in snow, the town normally remains snow-free.

Tear yourself away from the beach, and spend some time exploring the old city, with its narrow streets, shops, and restaurants. The open-air market nearby sells flowers

*Figure 7-1. Text doesn't automatically flow around an image*

To get text to flow around an image, you need to use the float property, which takes an element out of the normal flow of the document and moves it to one side to make room for whatever follows. So, if you float an image to the left, the following text flows into the empty space created on the right. The same happens with block-level elements. When you float a block-level element, as long as there's sufficient space alongside the floated block, the following elements are no longer forced onto a new line, and they can move up. Floating a <div> element alongside another is a common technique for creating a main content area and sidebar.

Learning how to use the float property is an essential skill in current web page layout. The basic principles are very simple, but floating elements can have unexpected consequences.

In this chapter, you'll learn how to do the following:

- Float images to the left and right, and flow text around them

- Prevent headings and other elements from moving up alongside floated elements

- Examine the interaction of margins with floated elements

- Add a caption to a floated image

- Use float to add a sidebar to a page

# How to Float an Element

You can float any element, unless its display property is set to none, or it uses absolute or fixed positioning (see Chapter 11). The float property accepts the values listed in Table 7-1.

***Table 7-1.*** *Values Accepted by the float Property*

| Value | Description |
| --- | --- |
| left | The element generates a block that is floated to the left inside its parent. Following elements move up into the empty space on the right. |
| right | Same as left, but the block is floated to the right and other elements fill the space on the left. |
| none | The element is not floated. This is the default value. |

Because float is not inherited, you can also use the inherit keyword to force inheritance from the parent element. The main purpose of none is to override another style rule. For example, CSS3 media queries (see Chapter 17) allow you to serve different styles depending on a device's features, such as screen width. For desktop monitors, your styles will probably float images left or right. But on a mobile phone, you could set float to none, and use other styles to center the image.

■ **Note**  The draft CSS3 Box Model module proposes adding top, bottom, start, and end as acceptable values for the float property. However, at the time of this writing, browsers support only the values listed in Table 7-1.

## Using float to Flow Text Around Images

The old-school way of flowing text around an image was to add the align attribute in the <img> tag, and set its value to left or right. It did the job, but no space was left between the image and the surrounding text. To compensate, you needed to use the hspace attribute, but this adds the same amount on both sides of the image. Similarly, the vspace attribute adds the same vertical space on the top and bottom of an image, destroying the layout, as shown in Figure 7-2 (see align_attr.html in the ch07 folder).

## Côte d'Azur

Nice is a jewel of the Côte d'Azur in Southern France. Surrounded by mountains, its crescent-shaped bay faces the Mediterranean, blessing it with a mild winter climate. Even when the mountains are covered in snow, the town normally remains snow-free.

Tear yourself away from the beach, and spend some time exploring the old city, with its narrow streets, shops, and restaurants. The open-air market nearby sells flowers and local produce. If you've got the strength for a climb, take the steps to the top of la Colline du Château (Castle Hill) for a great panorama of la Baie des Anges (Bay of Angels).

***Figure 7-2.*** *You can't control the individual margins around images with HTML attributes*

Using the align, hspace, and vspace attributes is no longer permitted in HTML5. Even if that weren't the case, CSS gives you much greater control, because you can adjust the margins independently on each side of the image. I usually add the following class definitions to my style sheet:

```
floatleft {
    float: left;
    margin: 3px 10px 3px 0;
}
.floatright {
    float: right;
    margin: 3px 0 3px 10px;
}
```

This adds a 3px margin to the top and bottom of the image and a 10px margin between the image and surrounding text. Both classes use the margin shorthand property, which lists the values in clockwise order starting from the top. So, the 10px in the floatleft class represents the right margin, and in the floatright class, it's the left margin.

To align an image on the left, just add the floatleft class to the <img> tag like this:

```
<p><img src="images/nice_seafront.jpg" alt="Nice seafront" width="400" height="266"
class="floatleft">Tear yourself away. . . </p>
```

As Figure 7-3 shows, the left edge of the image in floatleft.html remains flush with the main body of the text, but there's a small gap on the right between the image and the text.

## Côte d'Azur

Nice is a jewel of the Côte d'Azur in Southern France. Surrounded by mountains, its crescent-shaped bay faces the Mediterranean, blessing it with a mild winter climate. Even when the mountains are covered in snow, the town normally remains snow-free.

Tear yourself away from the beach, and spend some time exploring the old city, with its narrow streets, shops, and restaurants. The open-air market nearby sells flowers and local produce. If you've got the strength for a climb, take the steps to the top of la Colline du Château (Castle Hill) for a great panorama of la Baie des Anges (Bay of Angels).

***Figure 7-3.*** *Controlling the individual margins with CSS results in cleaner lines*

To move the image to the other side, floatright.html changes the class from floatleft to floatright (see Figure 7-4).

## Côte d'Azur

Nice is a jewel of the Côte d'Azur in Southern France. Surrounded by mountains, its crescent-shaped bay faces the Mediterranean, blessing it with a mild winter climate. Even when the mountains are covered in snow, the town normally remains snow-free.

Tear yourself away from the beach, and spend some time exploring the old city, with its narrow streets, shops, and restaurants. The open-air market nearby sells flowers and local produce. If you've got the strength for a climb, take the steps to the top of la Colline du Château (Castle Hill) for a great panorama of la Baie des Anges (Bay of Angels).

***Figure 7-4.*** *Floating the image to the right results in text flowing round the left*

If you prefer a wider or narrower margin, simply adjust the values in the class definitions.

In Figures 7-3 and 7-4, the image is the first element inside a paragraph, which acts as its parent. Consequently, the image floats to the left or right of the paragraph, and the text flows around it. When the text gets to the end of the floated image, it flows underneath. However, you can insert an image anywhere you like inside a paragraph. Figure 7-5 shows what happens if I move the image to the beginning of the third sentence and float it to the left.

Tear yourself away from the beach, and spend some time exploring the old city, with its narrow streets, shops, and restaurants. The open–air market

nearby sells flowers and local produce. If you've got the strength for a climb, take the steps to the top of la Colline du Château (Castle Hill) for a great panorama of la Baie des Anges (Bay of Angels).

A short distance to the west of Nice is Antibes, an ancient walled city with a maze of narrow streets. Alongside the port packed with luxury yachts, locals play cards and boules to while away the hours.

*Figure 7-5. The next paragraph also flows around the floated image*

Even though the image extends below its parent paragraph, the next paragraph moves into the empty space alongside the floated element. In this instance, it's almost certainly what you want. But Figure 7-6 shows what happens in short_para.html, when a short paragraph is followed by a heading.

Antibes was the favorite haunt of great literary figures, such as Guy de Maupassant, Nikos Kazantzakis, and Graham Greene. In 1946, Pablo Picasso established a studio in the Château Grimaldi, which now houses the Picasso Museum with nearly 250 of his works.

## Monaco and Monte Carlo

Close to the Italian border lies the tiny city state of Monaco, home to the rich and famous. Surrounded on three sides by France and by the

*Figure 7-6. The heading tries to wrap around the floated image*

Obviously, one solution is to make sure you have sufficient content to flow alongside your images. However, you can't always predict how much text you'll have. So you need a way to prevent this type of layout problem.

## Preventing Elements from Moving Alongside a Floated Element

To force an element to move down below a floated element, such as an image, use the clear property, which accepts the values listed in Table 7-2.

***Table 7-2.*** *Values Accepted by the clear Property*

| Value | Description |
| --- | --- |
| left | Forces the element to a new line below any left-floated elements. |
| right | Forces the element to a new line below any right-floated elements. |
| both | Forces the element to a new line below any floated elements. |
| none | Floats act normally. This is the default, but it can be used to override an earlier rule that uses the clear property. |

Because clear is not inherited, you can use the inherit keyword to make a child element act the same way as its parent.

The image in Figure 7-6 is floated left, so setting the heading's clear property to left in float_clear.html prevents it from moving into the space alongside the image, as shown in Figure 7-7.

Antibes was the favorite haunt of great literary figures, such as Guy de Maupassant, Nikos Kazantzakis, and Graham Greene. In 1946, Pablo Picasso established a studio in the Château Grimaldi, which now houses the Picasso Museum with nearly 250 of his works.

### Monaco and Monte Carlo

Close to the Italian border lies the tiny city state of Monaco, home to the rich and famous. Surrounded on three sides by France and by the

***Figure 7-7.*** *The heading now occupies a line of its own*

Although the clear property has separate values for clearing left- and right-floated elements, it's often convenient to set clear to both to avoid having to change the value if you decide to alter your layout and float elements in the opposite direction. For example, by using the following style for <h2> headings, it doesn't matter if the preceding image is floated left or right:

```
h2 {
    clear: both;
}
```

Although using the clear property solves the problem of the heading trying to move into the space alongside a floated image, there's another problem. The gap between the bottom of the image and the heading in most browsers is very small. To understand why, you need to examine the page in a browser's developer tools.

## EXERCISE: EXAMINING FLOATS AND MARGINS

In this exercise, you'll use a browser's developer tools to examine what happens to the margins around a floated element. Use the browser of your choice, but in the instructions and screen shots, I'll be using the Safari Web Inspector panel on Windows. The Developer Tools panel in Chrome works identically.

1. Load float_clear.html in the ch07 folder into a browser, and scroll down to the "Monaco and Monte Carlo" heading.

2. Right-click the heading and select *Inspect Element* from the context menu.

3. Highlight the heading's margins, as shown in Figure 7-8.

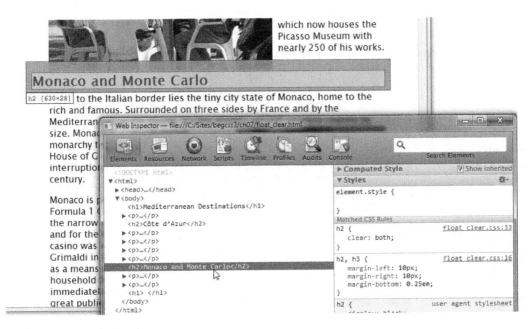

*Figure 7-8.  Use the browser's developer tools to inspect the heading's margins*

4. Note how the heading's top margin heading overlaps the bottom of the image.

5. With the heading still selected, expand the *Metrics* pane in the right column of the Web Inspector panel. As Figure 7-9 shows, the heading's top margin is 19px. (I collapsed the *Styles* pane to take the screen shot.)

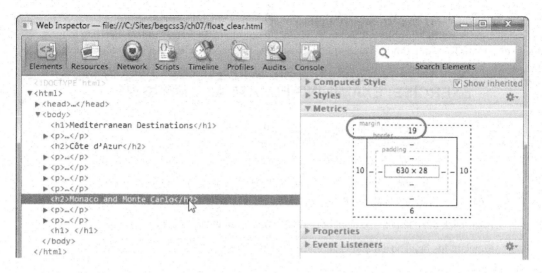

*Figure 7-9. The Metrics pane exposes the dimensions of the heading's box model*

6. Right-click the image and select *Inspect Element* to highlight the image's margins, as shown in Figure 7-10.

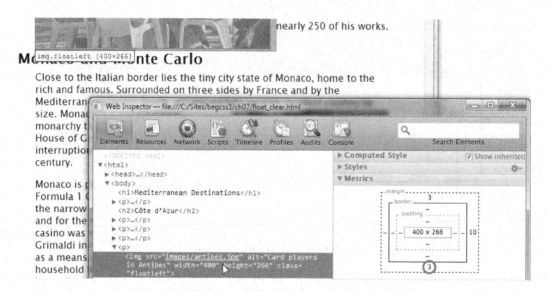

*Figure 7-10. The floated image's bottom margin creates the gap between the image and heading*

What this exercise has just shown is that the browser ignores the 19px top margin on the heading and uses the image's 3px bottom margin instead. This isn't a bug. It's what the CSS specification says should happen when you use clear to move an element below a floated one.

When you float an element, it's removed from the normal document flow. Although it looks as though the heading follows the image, it actually follows the preceding paragraph. Because the paragraph is too short to flow around the image, the heading's top margin isn't big enough to fill the gap. So the browser adds just enough extra to push it below the floated image. But it doesn't add the default margin as well. That's why the gap between the image and the heading is only 3px. In fact, if the image didn't have a bottom margin, there would be no gap at all.

To increase the gap, you would need to add a larger bottom margin to the image. One way to do so would be to give the image an ID and create a special rule. Or if you anticipate this happening frequently, you could create a special class. A simpler solution would be to move the image or increase the amount of text.

While you still have the page open, right-click the paragraph alongside the image, and select *Inspect Element*. Notice how the highlighting of the paragraph's margins overlaps the image completely to the left, as shown in Figure 7-11.

**Monaco and Monte Carlo**

*Figure 7-11. The paragraph's margins are not affected by the floating image*

What's happening is that the paragraph's content has been displaced by the float, but the block-level box created by the paragraph still occupies its normal place. This has important implications for adding backgrounds and borders to elements when floats are involved. I'll come back to those issues in Chapter 9, which deals with borders in detail.

In the example shown in Figure 7-11, the paragraph is the image's parent element, so it's perhaps not surprising that the paragraph's box stretches the full width. But this behavior applies to all block-level elements, except tables—which have a box model of their own. When a block-level element flows alongside a floated element, its notional box occupies its normal place, and only the content is displaced. If it didn't, there would be a 40px horizontal gap between the image and the second paragraph in Figure 7-5, because all paragraphs in the page have a 40px left margin.

---

■ **Note** A table's margins do not extend underneath a floated element. If a left-floated element has a right margin of 10px, and a table with a left margin of 20px moves alongside, the gap between them is 30px because horizontal margins don't collapse.

---

# Centering an Image

The float property doesn't have an option for centering an element. But while we're on the subject of aligning images, this seems like a logical place to explain how to center an image.

As I explained in the previous chapter, you center a block-level element by giving it a width and setting its left and right margins to auto. Browsers automatically obtain the dimensions of an image, even if you don't specify the width and height attributes in the <img> tag. But images are inline elements, so setting the left and right margins to auto has no effect on its own. However, all you need to do is to set the image's display property to block, and it's centered. So, in addition to the floatleft and floatright classes, I usually add the following class to my style sheets:

```
.imgcentered {
    margin: 10px auto;
    display: block;
}
```

Figure 7-12 shows what happens in imgcentered.html when the imgcentered class is applied to the same image as in Figures 7-3 and 7-4.

## Côte d'Azur

Nice is a jewel of the Côte d'Azur in Southern France. Surrounded by mountains, its crescent-shaped bay faces the Mediterranean, blessing it with a mild winter climate. Even when the mountains are covered in snow, the town normally remains snow-free.

Tear yourself away from the beach, and spend some time exploring the old city, with its narrow streets, shops, and restaurants. The open-air market

*Figure 7-12.* *The image is centered above its parent paragraph*

Although it looks as though the image has been inserted between the two paragraphs, the <img> tag is nested inside the beginning of the second paragraph like this:

```
<p><img src="images/nice_seafront.jpg" alt="Nice seafront" width="400" height="266"
class="imgcentered">Tear yourself away. . .</p>
```

So what happens if you center an image in the middle of a paragraph? Figure 7-13 shows center_break.html, where the image has been placed at the beginning of the third sentence.

Tear yourself away from the beach, and spend some time exploring the old city, with its narrow streets, shops, and restaurants. The open-air market nearby sells flowers and local produce.

If you've got the strength for a climb, take the steps to the top of la Colline du Château (Castle Hill) for a great panorama of la Baie des Anges (Bay of Angels).

**Figure 7-13.** *The image breaks the paragraph in two*

As you can see, the text is broken at the point the image was inserted into the text, so you need to put the image at a convenient break point, such as the end of a sentence.

## Adding a Caption to an Image

As the old saying goes, an image is worth a thousand words. But a few choice words added to an image as a caption can make all the difference. HTML5 introduces two new tags, ⟨figure⟩ and ⟨figcaption⟩, specifically designed to handle images with captions. You wrap the image inside a ⟨figure⟩ element together with its caption in a ⟨figcaption⟩ element. Instead of floating the image, you float the ⟨figure⟩ element.

---

■ **Note**  IE 6–8 don't support ⟨figure⟩, ⟨figcaption⟩, and other HTML5 elements. The following discussion describes how they work in modern browsers, including IE 9+. Later in this chapter, I'll explain a cross-browser solution for adding a caption to an image.

---

Unfortunately, you can't use the ⟨figure⟩ and ⟨figcaption⟩ tags inside a paragraph because they're regarded as block-level elements—or *flow content* to use the HTML5 terminology for elements that are used in the body of a document. In the past, browsers have been very forgiving if you break the rules, so you might be tempted to nest a ⟨figure⟩ and ⟨figcaption⟩ inside a paragraph like this (the code is in nested_figure.html):

```
<p><figure class="floatleft"><img src="images/nice_seafront.jpg" alt="Nice seafront"
width="400" height="266">
    <figcaption>Nice seafront from la Colline du Château</figcaption>
</figure>Tear yourself away. . .</p>
```

As Figure 7-14 shows, the left side of the image is no longer flush with the paragraphs.

## Côte d'Azur

Nice is a jewel of the Côte d'Azur in Southern France. Surrounded by mountains, its crescent-shaped bay faces the Mediterranean, blessing it with a mild winter climate. Even when the mountains are covered in snow, the town normally remains snow-free.

Tear yourself away from the beach, and spend some time exploring the old city, with its narrow streets, shops, and restaurants. The open-air market nearby sells flowers and local produce. If you've got the strength for a climb, take the steps to the top of la Colline du Château (Castle Hill) for a great panorama of la Baie des Anges (Bay of Angels).

Nice seafront from la Colline du Château

A short distance to the west of Nice is Antibes, an ancient walled city with a maze of narrow streets. Alongside the port packed with luxury yachts, locals play cards and boules to while away the hours.

*Figure 7-14. The <figure> breaks out, even though it is nested inside the paragraph*

To understand why, you need to use the browser's developer tools again. When you inspect the HTML in a browser's developer tools, you're not looking at the page's source code, but at the markup generated by the browser. Figure 7-15 shows the HTML Safari generates when the page is rendered.

Because <figure> is flow content—in other words, a block-level element—Safari has automatically closed the opening <p> tag (highlighted in Figure 7-15). The <figure> and the following text are then rendered outside the paragraph. Finally, an opening <p> tag is inserted to match the closing one (also highlighted in Figure 7-15).

All modern browsers render the HTML the same way. As a result, when the <figure> element is floated to the left, its parent element is the <body>, not the paragraph that it was incorrectly nested inside. That's why the image and its caption are no longer left-aligned with the paragraphs.

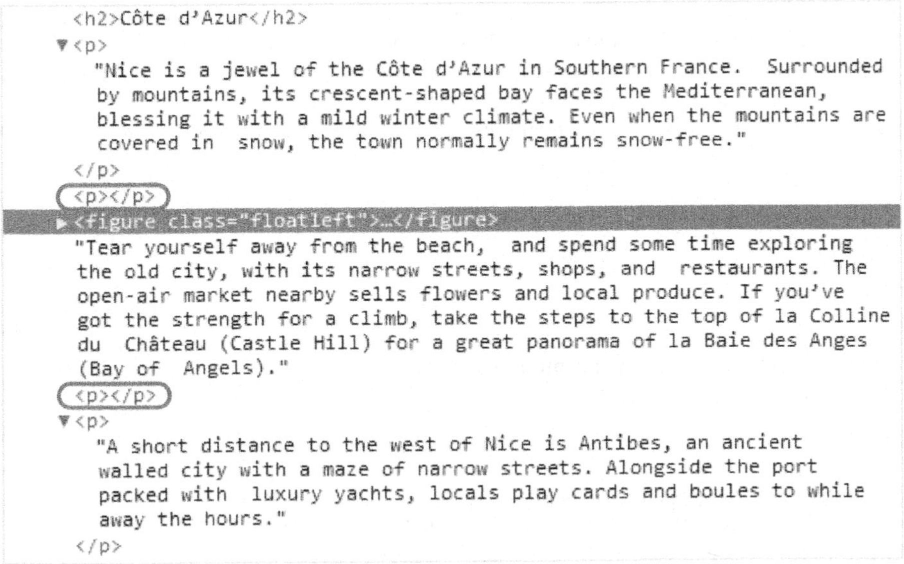

```
    <h2>Côte d'Azur</h2>
▼ <p>
    "Nice is a jewel of the Côte d'Azur in Southern France.  Surrounded
    by mountains, its crescent-shaped bay faces the Mediterranean,
    blessing it with a mild winter climate. Even when the mountains are
    covered in  snow, the town normally remains snow-free."
    </p>
  ( <p></p> )
  ▶ <figure class="floatleft">...</figure>
    "Tear yourself away from the beach,  and spend some time exploring
    the old city, with its narrow streets, shops, and  restaurants. The
    open-air market nearby sells flowers and local produce. If you've
    got the strength for a climb, take the steps to the top of la Colline
    du  Château (Castle Hill) for a great panorama of la Baie des Anges
    (Bay of  Angels)."
  ( <p></p> )
▼ <p>
    "A short distance to the west of Nice is Antibes, an ancient
    walled city with a maze of narrow streets. Alongside the port
    packed with  luxury yachts, locals play cards and boules to while
    away the hours."
    </p>
```

*Figure 7-15. The browser has generated two empty paragraphs*

To insert an image with a caption, you need to put the <figure> element between paragraphs like this (see figcaption.html):

```
<p>Nice is a jewel. . .</p>
<figure class="floatleft"><img src="images/nice_seafront.jpg" alt="Nice seafront"
width="400" height="266">
    <figcaption>Nice seafront from la Colline du Château</figcaption>
</figure>
<p>Tear yourself away. . .</p>
```

Because the <figure> element is outside the paragraphs, you need to adjust the margins in the classes that float elements to the left and right. The styles in figcaption.css contain these definitions:

```
figure.floatleft {
    margin-left: 40px;
}
figure.floatright {
    margin-right: 10px;
}
```

---

■ **Caution**    There's no space in the selector in the preceding style rules. If you put a space between the type selector and the class, it becomes a descendant selector. For example, figure .floatleft targets any element to which the floatleft class has been applied and which is nested at any level inside a <figure> element, whereas figure.floatleft, selects only <figure> elements to which the floatleft class has been applied. That tiny space makes a huge difference in meaning.

---

These rules inherit the float and margin values from the earlier floatleft and floatright classes, but override the left and right margins, respectively. Prefixing the classname with the figure type selector like this has higher specificity (11) than the classname on its own (10). So, these rules apply only to <figure> elements, whereas the existing classes can be applied to any other element you want to float.

Browsers don't apply default styles to <figcaption> elements, so figcaption.css contains this style:

```
figcaption {
    display: block;
    font-weight: bold;
    padding: 10px;
    text-align: center;
}
```

Figure 7-16 shows the result in figcaption.html in a modern browser.

## Côte d'Azur

Nice is a jewel of the Côte d'Azur in Southern France. Surrounded by mountains, its crescent-shaped bay faces the Mediterranean, blessing it with a mild winter climate. Even when the mountains are covered in snow, the town normally remains snow-free.

Tear yourself away from the beach, and spend some time exploring the old city, with its narrow streets, shops, and restaurants. The open-air market nearby sells flowers and local produce. If you've got the strength for a climb, take the steps to the top of la Colline du Château (Castle Hill) for a great panorama of la Baie des Anges (Bay of Angels).

**Nice seafront from la Colline du Château**

A short distance to the west of Nice is Antibes, an ancient walled city with a maze of narrow streets. Alongside the port packed with luxury yachts,

***Figure 7-16.*** *The image and caption are floated and styled correctly*

---

■ **Tip** Most browsers that support the new HTML5 tags add a large default margin to the <figure> element. In Chrome, it's 1em on the top and bottom, and 40px on both sides. The space around the image in Figure 7-16 is much smaller because the margin property in the floatleft class overrides the browser default for <figure>. If your layout doesn't look the way you expect, it's always a good idea to use the browser's developer tools to check whether browser defaults have been applied to one or more elements.

---

Alas, not everyone uses a modern browser. IE 8 and earlier don't recognize the new HTML5 elements, so they completely ignore any styles that you apply to them. Instead, the page looks like Figure 7-17.

the town normally remains snow-free.

 Nice seafront from la Colline du Château
Tear yourself away from the beach, and spend some time exploring the old city, with its narrow streets, shops, and restaurants. The open-air market

**Figure 7-17.** *Older versions of Internet Explorer fail to style HTML5 elements*

There are two ways to tackle this problem. One is to create dummy HTML5 elements in the browser's memory using the solution described in "Styling New HTML5 Elements in Older Browsers" in Chapter 2. It definitely works, but it relies on JavaScript being enabled in the user's browser. The alternative is to use <div> elements and to assign them the same classnames as the new HTML5 elements, as described in the next section.

## Using Multiple Classes on an Element

Instead of using the HTML5 <figure> and <figcaption> elements, you can create figure and figcaption classes, and apply them to <div> elements. It's a completely cross-browser solution, and it doesn't rely on JavaScript. The HTML class attribute accepts multiple values. Just separate each classname with a space like this (the code is in figcaption_safe.html):

```
<div class="figure floatleft"><img src="images/nice_seafront.jpg" alt="Nice seafront"
width="400" height="266">
    <div class="figcaption">Nice seafront from la Colline du Château</div>
</div>
```

---

■ **Note**  The order of classnames in the class attribute is not important. Any conflicts are resolved using the normal rules of the cascade and specificity.

---

When an element uses two or more classes, you chain them together to create a CSS selector. For example, the following selector styles an element that has the figure and floatleft classes applied to it:

.figure.floatleft

As with the class attribute in the HTML markup, the order of the classnames in the selector is unimportant. The following selector means exactly the same:

.floatleft.figure

---

■ **Note** As in the preceding section, if you put a space between the two parts, it becomes a descendant selector. To style elements that have both classes applied to them, there must be no space in the selector. It's a subtle, but important difference.

---

The styles for the figure and figcaption classes in figcaption_safe.css are exactly the same as in figcaption.css apart from the selectors. The amended rules look like this:

```
.figure.floatleft {
    margin-left: 40px;
}
.figure.floatright {
    margin-right: 10px;
}
.figcaption {
    display: block;
    font-weight: bold;
    padding: 10px;
    text-align: center;
}
```

If you test figcaption_safe.html in a browser, it looks the same as Figure 7-16.

---

■ **Note** I have added an Internet Explorer conditional comment to set the width of the wrapper `<div>` to 650px for IE 6, which doesn't support the `max-width` property. There's another problem with IE 6 that I explain in "Dealing with the IE 6 Double-margin Bug" at the end of this chapter.

---

## Making the Images and Captions Adapt to the Screen Width

The style rule for the wrapper `<div>` sets its maximum width to 650px. If the browser viewport is narrower, the text automatically reflows. The images and captions need to be equally adaptive. The simple way to scale the images is to remove the width and height attributes from the `<img>` tags, and to give the figure class (or `<figure>` elements) a percentage width. At the same time, you need to set the maximum width of the images to 100% to prevent them from spilling out of their containers.

In figcaption_adapt.html, the width and height attributes have been removed from the `<img>` tag:

```
<div class="figure floatleft"><img src="images/nice_seafront.jpg" alt="Nice seafront">
    <div class="figcaption">Nice seafront from la Colline du Château</div>
</div>
```

Two new style rules have been added to figcaption_adapt.css:

```
.figure {
    width: 61.5%
}
.figure img {
    max-width: 100%;
}
```

The percentage width for the figure class is based on dividing the width of the wrapper `<div>` (650px) by the width of the image (400px), and multiplying by 100:

```
400 ÷ 650 × 100 = 61.5
```

Figure 7-18 shows how the image and caption are scaled down proportionately when the browser window is narrower than 650px. Removing the dimensions from the `<img>` tag ensures that the image's aspect ratio is preserved. The image is distorted if you leave in the height attribute,

**Nice seafront from la Colline du Château**

Tear yourself away from the beach, and spend some time exploring the old city, with its narrow streets, shops, and restaurants. The open-air market nearby sells flowers and local produce. If you've got the strength for a climb, take the steps to the top of la Colline du Château (Castle Hill) for a great panorama of la Baie des Anges (Bay of Angels).

*Figure 7-18. The image and caption are scaled when the browser window is resized*

---

■ **Note**  IE 6 doesn't support `max-width`. If you need to support IE 6, add a style rule for `.figure img` in an Internet Explorer conditional comment setting `width` to 100%, as in figcaption_adapt.html.

---

Lower down the page is a much narrower image. Instead of being 400px wide and 266px high, its dimensions are the other way round. As a result, the figure `<div>` is too wide when the page is viewed in a normal desktop browser. To fix this, you need to work out the correct percentage width like this:

```
266 ÷ 650 × 100 = 40.9
```

The styles in figcaption_adapt.css contain a portrait class to set the width for the figure `<div>` surrounding the image:

```
.portrait {
    width: 40.9%;
}
```

The portrait class is added to the HTML markup for the image and its caption like this:

```
<div class="figure floatright portrait"><img src="images/casino.jpg" alt="Monte Carlo Casino">
    <div class="figcaption">Monte Carlo casino</div>
</div>
```

This is a case where the cascade plays a vital role. Both the figure and portrait classes try to set the width of the <div>, and they have equal specificity (10). The portrait class takes precedence because it comes after the figure class in figcaption_adapt.css like this:

```
.figure {
    width: 61.5%
}
.figure img {
    max-width: 100%;
}
.portrait {
    width: 40.9%;
}
```

As Figure 7-19 shows, the narrower width is applied correctly to the <div>, which scales automatically when the browser viewport is resized.

## Monaco and Monte Carlo

Close to the Italian border lies the tiny city state of Monaco, home to the rich and famous. Surrounded on three sides by France and by the Mediterranean on the fourth, it's the world's second smallest country by size. Monaco is a constitutional monarchy that has been ruled by the House of Grimaldi with only brief interruptions since the thirteenth century.

Monaco is perhaps best known for the Formula 1 Grand Prix that roars through the narrow streets and tight corners, and for the Monte Carlo Casino. The casino was established by the House of Grimaldi in the mid–nineteenth century as a means of saving the ruling household from bankruptcy. It wasn't immediately successful, but gained great publicity in 1873 when Joseph Jagger became the man who "broke the bank at Monte Carlo." The bank

**Monte Carlo casino**

*Figure 7-19. The portrait class applies the correct width to the figure <div>*

If you reverse the order of the portrait and figure class definitions in the style sheet, the figure class takes precedence.

■ **Tip** Rather than rely on the cascade, you can create a rule with higher specificity. In this case, you could use .figure.portrait (or .portrait.figure) as the selector. Then it wouldn't matter which order the classes are defined in the style sheet. Combining the two classnames in the selector has higher specificity than .figure on its own, and it affects only elements that have both classes applied to them.

## Adding a Sidebar Using the float and margin Properties

Most web page layouts intended for viewing on a desktop consist of two or more columns—one for the main content, and the other(s) for less important information or advertising. In the bad old days, tables were used to create the columns. CSS3 promises better methods, but until they're more widely supported, the most common approach is to use the float property. There are several patterns for creating columns and sidebars, which I'll go into in detail in Chapter 12. In this section, I'll concentrate on just one—creating a wide margin and floating a <div> into it.

The basic technique is very simple. You wrap the content of the page in two <div> elements, one for the sidebar, and the other for the main content. Of course, if you don't need to support IE 6–8, you can use the new HTML5 elements, such as <aside> for the sidebar, and <section> or <article> for the main content. You give the main content a wide margin to make room for the sidebar, and then float the sidebar into the space created by the margin.

The downside of this technique is that the sidebar needs to come before the main content in the HTML markup. However, it has the advantage of being simple to implement, and you can switch the sidebar from left to right by changing just a couple of properties.

---

### EXERCISE: ADDING A SIDEBAR

This exercise shows how to add a sidebar to a page by creating a wide margin alongside the main content and floating the sidebar into the margin. It uses sidebar_begin.html in the ch07 folder and sidebar_begin.css in ch07/styles as its starting point. The finished versions are in sidebar_left.html and sidebar_left.css, and in sidebar_right.html and sidebar_right.css.

The page is basically the same as used in previous examples in this chapter, but content for the sidebar has been added after the main heading and ahead of the existing content. The sidebar is in a <div> element with the ID aside, and the existing content has been wrapped in a <div> with the ID main.

1. To make room for the sidebar, change the maximum width of the wrapper <div> from 650px to 1000px:

```
#wrapper {
    width: 100%;
    max-width: 1000px;
    margin: 0 auto;
}
```

2. To preserve the width of the main content if the sidebar is shorter, you need to create a new style rule using an ID selector. Previously, the main content was 650px wide, which is 65% of 1000px, leaving 35% for the sidebar. So the new rule that needs to be added to the style sheet looks like this:

```
#main {
    width: 65%;
    margin-left: 35%;
}
```

3. You need to assign a width to the sidebar and float it into the space on the left alongside the main content. Although 35% of the `wrapper` `<div>` width is available, filling it completely will make the page look too crowded. Make the sidebar a little narrower like this:

```
#aside {
    float: left;
    width: 32%;
}
```

4. Save the style sheet, and load the page into a browser. The sidebar is where you would expect, but most of the main content has disappeared (see Figure 7-20).

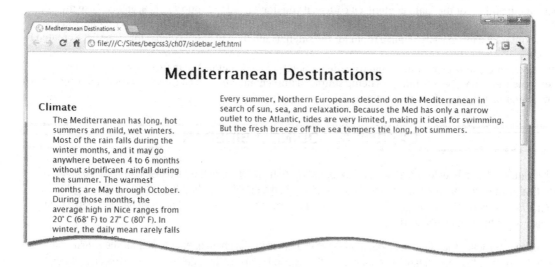

***Figure 7-20.*** *Only the first paragraph of the main content remains at the top of the page*

5. Scroll down the page. The first `<h2>` heading in the main content has been pushed down below the sidebar, as shown in Figure 7-21.

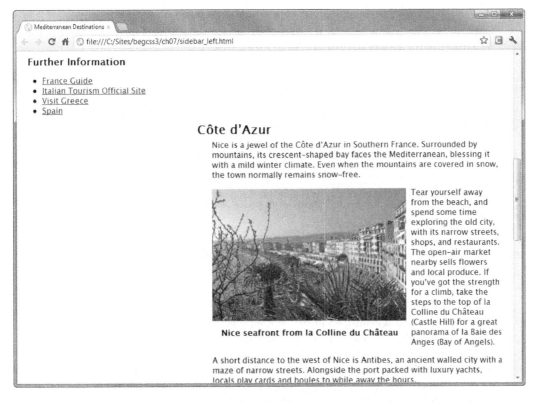

*Figure 7-21. The heading and all following content has been pushed below the sidebar*

The following style rule is causing the problem:

```
h2 {
    clear: both;
}
```

This rule was added to the style sheet in "Preventing Elements from Moving alongside a Floated Element" earlier in this chapter (see Figure 7-6). However, the sidebar is floated to the left, so the first heading in the main content is pushed all the way down the page. The fact that the heading is in a different section of the page doesn't make any difference.

There are several ways to solve this problem. One is to change the value of the clear property to right, and to float the problem image to the right. Alternatively, you could move the image, remove it altogether, or add some extra text to prevent the heading from floating up alongside the image. In fact, I not only floated the problem image to the right, but I also added some extra text. As a result, this rule is no longer needed.

6. Delete the following style rule:

```
h2 {
    clear: both;
}
```

7. Save the style sheet, and reload the page in a browser. The main content now displays correctly, but the heading at the top of the sidebar is not aligned with the first paragraph of the main content, as Figure 7-22 shows.

*Figure 7-22. The top of the sidebar is not in alignment with the main content*

8. The misalignment is caused by the default top margin on the "Climate" heading. Because the sidebar is floated, it's treated as a separate block, and the top margin pushes the heading away from the top of the block. To remove its top margin without affecting the other headings in the sidebar, you can use the :first-child pseudo-class, which styles an element that is the first child of its parent. The :first-child pseudo-class is supported by all browsers except IE 6. Add the following rule to the style sheet to align the sidebar with the main content:

```
h3:first-child {
    margin-top: 0;
}
```

9. To switch the sidebar to the right, all that's necessary is to move the wide margin to the right of the main content, and to float the sidebar to the right. Make the changes highlighted in the following two rules:

```
#main {
    width: 65%;
    margin-right: 35%;
}
#aside {
    float: right;
    width: 32%;
}
```

10. Save the style sheet, and load the page into a browser. As Figure 7-23 shows, the sidebar is now on the right.

**Figure 7-23.** *Changing just two properties moves the sidebar to the right*

This layout displays as expected in all browsers except IE 6. If you need to support IE 6, amend the styles in the Internet Explorer conditional comment in the `<head>` of the web page. Change the `width` in the `#wrapper` rule to 1000px. You also need to add an ID selector for the `main` `<div>` changing `margin-left` or `margin-right` to 34%. This is because IE 6 has problems with percentage widths that add up to exactly 100%. Reducing the overall total to 99% solves the problem. However, IE 6 has another problem with floated elements, which is discussed in the next section.

## Dealing with the IE 6 Double-margin Bug

IE 6 is rapidly fading into insignificance in most parts of the world, but if you still have to support it, you need to be aware of the double-margin bug. If you add a horizontal margin to an element and then float it to the same side, IE 6 doubles the margin. For example, the `.figure.floatleft` style used in this chapter adds a 40px left margin to a `<div>` and then floats it to the left. IE 6 doubles the margin to 80px, indenting the image and caption, as shown in Figure 7-24.

## Côte d'Azur

Nice is a jewel of the Côte d'Azur in Southern France. Surrounded by mountains, its crescent-shaped bay faces the Mediterranean, blessing it with a mild winter climate. Even when the mountains are covered in snow, the town normally remains snow-free.

**Nice seafront from la Colline du Château**

Tear yourself away from the beach, and spend some time exploring the old city, with its narrow streets, shops, and restaurants. The open-air market nearby sells flowers and local produce. If you've got the strength for a climb, take the steps to the top of la Colline du Château (Castle Hill) for a great panorama of la Baie des Anges (Bay of Angels).

**Figure 7-24.** *The double-margin bug indents the image and caption in IE 6*

In this case, the effect isn't critical, but it can have a disastrous effect when multiple elements are floated alongside each other. Fortunately, the solution is very simple and it doesn't have an adverse effect on other browsers.

When you add a margin to an element and float it to the same side, set its display property to inline. IE 6 then applies the correct margin. Of course, this is necessary only if you have to support IE 6.

# Summary

Floating elements to the left or right is an important CSS layout technique. The basic principles are simple. The floated element moves as far left or right as permitted by its parent element. Subsequent content moves up to fill the available space alongside the floated element. The clear property prevents elements from moving up alongside a float. Where floats can be difficult to understand is how the margins of surrounding elements interact with the floated element. However, using a browser's developer tools to highlight the margins usually reveals which margin you need to adjust.

In this chapter, you also learned how to apply multiple classes to an element and how to style them by chaining class selectors. Then you saw how to create a two-column layout by adding a wide margin to one side of the main content and floating the sidebar into the empty space. This technique relies on the sidebar coming before the main content in the HTML markup, but Chapter 12 demonstrates other techniques where the main content comes first. Finally, you learned how to fix the IE 6 double-margin bug.

The next chapter looks in depth at adding background colors and images to your web pages.

# CHAPTER 8

■ ■ ■

# Adding Backgrounds

The secret of good web design is drawing the visitor's eyes to important parts of the page. Background colors and images help to break up the page and focus attention. Although some images are an important part of the page content, and need to be embedded in the HTML using <img> tags, others are simply decorative touches that should be added through CSS. Using CSS for background images not only keeps your HTML markup less cluttered and easier to maintain, but it also gives you a considerable amount of control over position and size.

The CSS3 Backgrounds and Borders module became a candidate recommendation in April 2012, and it may well have been formally approved by the time you read this. In other words, the features described in this chapter can be used with confidence in recent browsers. However, older browsers—particularly IE 8 and earlier—support only the CSS2.1 specification. Fortunately, CSS2.1 covers the most important aspects, such as background color and images, the position of background images, and basic controls over how images are repeated. The CSS3 features can be described as "nice to have" rather than essential.

Because backgrounds and borders are such a large subject, I've split them into separate chapters. This one deals with background colors and images. Chapter 9 looks at borders.

In this chapter, you'll learn about the following:

- Changing the background color of an element
- Adding background images and controlling how they repeat
- Adjusting the position of background images
- Using CSS sprites to display icons
- Changing the extent of a background
- Scaling background images
- Dealing with older browsers that don't support CSS3 features

## Controlling Backgrounds with CSS

CSS2.1 has six properties that handle backgrounds. CSS3 improves the functionality of some of the existing properties and adds another three. Because they're so widely supported, all nine properties are listed in Table 8-1.

*Table 8-1. CSS Background Properties*

| Property | Initial Value | Description |
|---|---|---|
| background-color | transparent | Sets the background color of an element. |
| background-image | none | Sets the background image(s) of an element. IE 6–8 allow only one image. |
| background-repeat | repeat | Controls how background images repeat if smaller than the element. By default, images tile horizontally and vertically. |
| background-attachment | scroll | Determines whether the background image remains in a fixed position or scrolls with the page. |
| background-position | 0% 0% | Determines the background image's horizontal and vertical position. The default is the top left of the element. |
| background-origin | padding-box | Determines the point from which background-position is measured. Not supported by IE 6–8. |
| background-clip | border-box | Determines the area covered by the background. Not supported by IE 6–8. |
| background-size | auto | Controls the size of background images. Not supported by IE 6–8. |
| background | See individual properties | Shorthand property for setting all background properties in a single declaration. |

Apart from background-color, all the individual properties are concerned with background images. The background properties are not inherited, but the background of a parent element remains visible because the default value of background-color is transparent.

## Changing the Background Color of an Element

As you might expect, the background-color property takes as its value a color, which can be expressed in any of the ways described in "Setting Color Values" in Chapter 3, namely:

- A 3- or 6-digit hexadecimal number
- A color keyword
- An rgb() value
- An hsl() value
- A color with alpha transparency specified as an rgba() or hsla() value

Hexadecimal numbers, color keywords, and rgb() values are supported by all browsers. So, it's a good idea to choose one of them unless you want to use a background color with alpha transparency. For example, the background color for the <body> in background_alpha.html in the ch08 folder (see Figure 8-1) is defined using hexadecimal notation like this:

***Figure 8-1.*** *The body uses a solid background color, but the text background is translucent*

```
body {
    margin: 0;
    padding: 0;
    font-family: "Lucida Sans Unicode", "Lucida Grande", sans-serif;
    color: #000;
    background-color: #D2E1E6;  /* light blue */
}
```

## Setting a Background Color with Alpha Transparency

Modern browsers support alpha transparency, which creates a translucent effect that can produce a more pleasing result than a solid block of color in some circumstances. For example in Figure 8-1, the sea is partially visible through the white background behind the text. This is achieved by setting the alpha transparency of the white background to 0.8.

To set a background color with alpha transparency, you need to use an rgba() or hsla() value, which IE 8 and earlier don't support. So, if you use one of these values on its own, older versions of Internet Explorer ignore the background color and display the text on top of the background image, making it very difficult to read.

To avoid this problem, first define a fallback style for IE 6–8 using hexadecimal notation, a color keyword, or an rgb() value. Then follow it with an rgba() or hsla() value like this:

```
background-color: #FFF;
background-color: rgba(255, 255, 255, 0.8);
```

Browsers ignore values they don't understand. So, an old browser should apply the first value (#FFF or solid white), and ignore the second one. But a modern browser that understands rgba() applies the rules of the cascade, and uses the second value (translucent white) to override the first one.

This works as expected in IE 8 and any other mainstream browser. IE 8 uses the solid color, others use the translucent one. However, IE 6 and IE 7 don't play ball. They ignore both colors, leaving the text without an independent background.

Fortunately, the solution is simple: use background-color for the fallback color and the background shorthand property for the color with alpha transparency. The styles for the <div> that contains the text in background_alpha.html look like this:

```
#sailing {
    background-color: #FFF;
    background: rgba(255, 255, 255, 0.8);
    width: 230px;
    padding: 10px;
    margin-left: 230px;
}
```

This keeps all browsers happy. As Figure 8-2 shows, IE 6 uses the hexadecimal value and displays a solid white background behind the text. IE 7 and IE 8 do the same. All other mainstream browsers use the rgba() value and render a translucent background as in Figure 8-1.

---

■ **Note** The background-color property works only with solid and translucent colors. It can't be used to apply a gradient. CSS3 treats gradients as images. You'll learn about CSS gradients in Chapter 19.

---

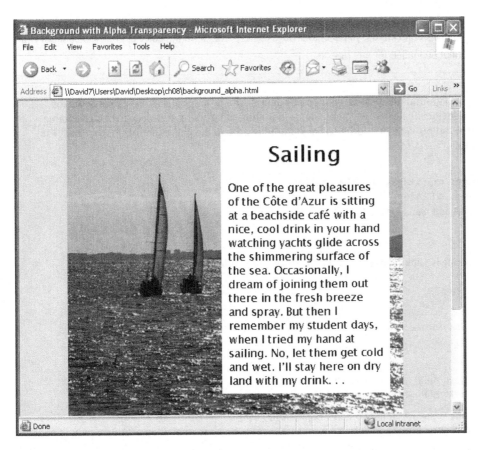

**Figure 8-2.** *It's important to provide a fallback background color for IE 6–8*

# Using Background Images

The remaining background properties deal with adding and controlling the behavior of background images. There's also the background shorthand property, which allows you to define all aspects of an element's background (including color) in a single declaration. First, let's look at how you add background images.

## Adding Background Images

The background-image property defines the source of an element's background image(s). It accepts two possible values, namely:

> **url()** The path to the image goes between the parentheses as described in "Specifying Background Images and Other Files" in Chapter 3.

> **none** No background image. This is the default value.

All browsers in widespread use—with the exception of IE 8 and earlier—support multiple background images on the same element. To specify more than one image, separate each url() value with a comma. If the background images overlap, the first one is drawn on top with each subsequent one behind the previous one.

---

■ **Tip**   When adding a background image, you should always specify a background color to preserve contrast with the text if the image cannot be loaded for any reason.

---

When you add a background image to an element, by default, the browser places the image at the top left of the element and automatically tiles (repeats) the image both horizontally and vertically to fit all available background space. This can be useful for adding a background texture to the page. The rule for the <body> in tiling.html looks like this:

```css
body {
    background-image: url(images/bg_tile.jpg);
    background-color: #D2E1E6;
    font-family: "Lucida Sans Unicode", "Lucida Grande", sans-serif;
    color: #000;
}
```

The image, bg_tile.jpg is 50px square, but as Figure 8-3 shows, it fills the entire page.

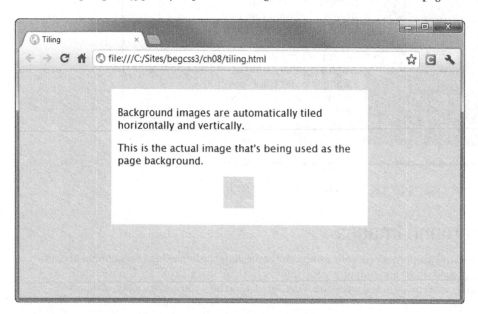

*Figure 8-3.* *A seamless tile can provide an interesting background texture for a page*

The background image is only 523 bytes, so it adds virtually nothing to the overall size of the page.

---

■ **Tip**   The image hasn't been stretched by the browser. I created the seamless edges for the tile in Photoshop using the Offset filter, setting the horizontal and vertical values to half the width and height, and selecting *Wrap Around*. I then cleaned up the inner sections with the Clone Stamp Tool. There's also a wide choice of online pattern generators at http://singlefunction.com/15-online-background-generators/.

---

Obviously, it doesn't make any sense adding multiple background images to an element if they tile automatically to fill all available space. Because the first image appears on top, subsequent images would always be hidden. However, you can control the default tiling behavior.

I'll come back to the subject of multiple background images later in this chapter after describing the other background properties.

## Controlling How Background Images Repeat

The property that controls the way background images are repeated is called background-repeat. I'll begin by describing the CSS2.1 version because it works in all browsers, including IE 8 and earlier. Then I'll describe the enhanced CSS3 features supported by more recent browsers.

### Values that Work in All Browsers

The background-repeat property accepts the following values in all browsers:

> **repeat** This is the default value. It repeats the image both horizontally and vertically to fill all available space.

> **repeat-x** This repeats the image horizontally only.

> **repeat-y** This repeats the image vertically only.

> **no-repeat** Display the image once only.

Setting the value of background-repeat to repeat-x tiles the background image across the horizontal axis only. This can be useful for creating a gradient background. The background image needs to be only a thin slice. For example, the background image in repeat-x.html is only 20px wide. If you set the background color to the same as the bottom of the image, it gives the appearance of a continuous color (see Figure 8-4). The style rule for the <body> in repeat-x.html looks like this:

```
body {
    background-image: url(images/gradient.jpg);
    background-repeat: repeat-x;
    background-color: #C1FEFF;
    color: #000;
    font-family: Tahoma, Geneva, sans-serif;
}
```

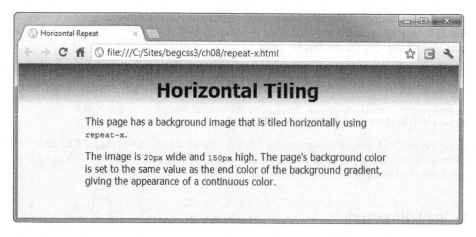

*Figure 8-4. The gradient is created by a narrow image being tiled horizontally*

■ **Note** This technique of creating a gradient background relies on using an physical image. Chapter 19 describes how to generate gradients without an image.

Setting the value of background-repeat to repeat-y tiles the background image along the vertical axis only. This can be useful for creating a decorative border as in repeat-y.html (see Figure 8-5).

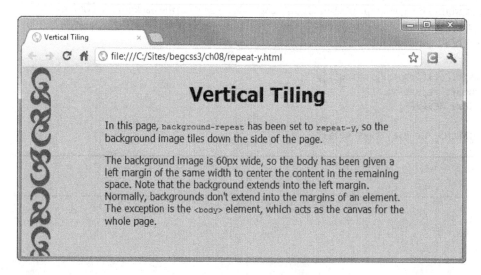

*Figure 8-5. The border is created by tiling a background image along the vertical axis*

The style rule for the <body> in repeat-y.html looks like this:

```
body {
    background-image: url(images/border.png);
    background-repeat: repeat-y;
    background-color: #CCC;
    color: #000;
    font-family: Tahoma, Geneva, sans-serif;
    margin-left: 60px;
}
```

An interesting feature about repeat-y.html is that the background color and background image are displayed in the 60px left margin of the <body>. The normal rule is that backgrounds do not extend into an element's margins. However, the background of the <body> covers the whole viewport.

■ **Note** Although browsers allow you to set different background properties for the <body> and <html> elements, the recommendation in the CSS3 specification is to add a background only to the <body> element.

If you set background-repeat to no-repeat, it's displayed once as in no-repeat.html (see Figure 8-6).

*Figure 8-6. You can also set a background image to display just once*

The styles for the <body> in no-repeat.html look like this:

```
body {
    background-image: url(images/flower.png);
    background-repeat: no-repeat;
    background-color: #EFECCA;
    color: #000;
    font-family: Tahoma, Geneva, sans-serif;
    margin-left: 60px;
}
```

# New Features in CSS3

In CSS2.1, background images simply tile in the specified direction and are cut off at the edge if they don't fit exactly. CSS3 addresses this issue with two new values for the `background-repeat` property. Both repeat the background image a sufficient number of times to cover the available space. But they differ in how they then treat the background.

> **space** Any space left over is evenly distributed between the images.

> **round** The images are rescaled to fit the background.

To demonstrate the difference, space_round.html adds a background image to two `<div>` elements like this:

```
#space, #round {
    background-image: url(images/flower2.png);
    background-color: #EFECCA;
    /* other styles omitted */
}
#space {
    background-repeat: space;
}
#round {
    background-repeat: round;
}
```

As Figure 8-7 shows, IE 9 spaces out the background images in the `<div>` on the left, but it marginally scales them down on the right to fit more in.

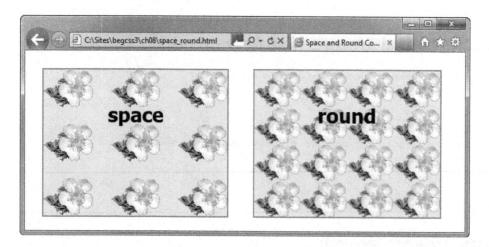

***Figure 8-7.*** *The new CSS3 values prevent background images from being clipped*

In addition to the new values for `background-repeat`, the CSS3 specification allows you to specify either one or two values.

In the case of one value, `repeat-x` and `repeat-y` work as before. In other words, they repeat the background image across only one axis. However, other values are applied to both axes. Each style rule in space_round.html uses a single value, so it applies in both directions.

If you specify two values, the first one applies to horizontal axis and the second one to the vertical axis. For example, the values for background-repeat in bg_repeat_2vals.html have been amended like this:

```
#space {
    background-repeat: space repeat;
}
#round {
    background-repeat: round repeat;
}
```

Figure 8-8 shows the result in IE 9. In the <div> on the left, the horizontal images are spaced out, but the vertical ones are not. Also, the images in the final row are cut off. In the <div> on the right, the horizontal rows are not cut off, but the bottom of the final row is.

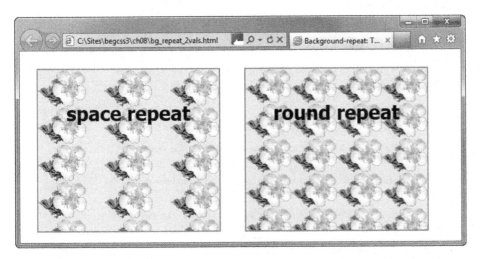

**Figure 8-8.** *Specifying two values to the background-repeat property affects each axis differently*

■ **Note**    At the time of this writing, only IE 9+ and Opera 10.5+ support space and round. Firefox and earlier versions of IE treat both single and double values as repeat. WebKit-based browsers, such as Chrome and Safari, accept double values, but treat space and round as no-repeat.

## Controlling Background Images During Scrolling

The background-attachment property controls what happens to background images when the page or element is scrolled. It accepts the following values:

> **scroll** This is the default value. The background is fixed with regard to the element, so it scrolls with the page.

> **fixed** The background is fixed in relation to the browser viewport, so it remains in the same position when the page is scrolled. Not supported by IE 6.

**local** The background is fixed in relation to the element's contents. If the element has a scrollbar, the background scrolls with the contents. This value is new in CSS3. Not supported by IE 6–8. At the time of this writing, Firefox is the only modern browser that doesn't support it.

The best way to understand how these values work is to look at some examples.

Figure 8-9 shows what happens when you set background-attachment to fixed. The background image in fixed.html is displayed at the top left of the page, and it remains in that position even when you scroll to the bottom of the page.

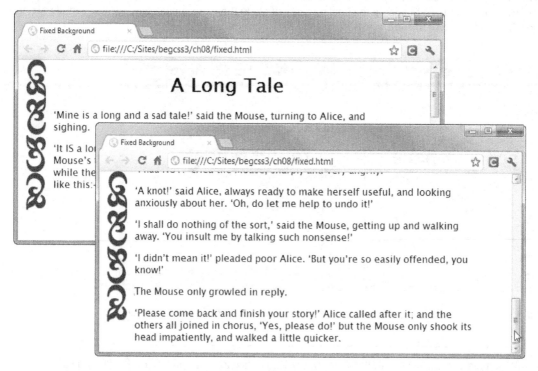

*Figure 8-9. The background image remains fixed in the browser viewport when the page is scrolled*

The styles in fixed.html add the fixed background image to the page like this:

```
body {
    /* Other styles omitted */
    background-image: url(images/border.png);
    background-repeat: no-repeat;
    background-attachment: fixed;
}
```

The only browser that doesn't support fixed is IE 6. It simply ignores the background-attachment property, and the background image scrolls with the page in the normal way.

The new local value allows you to attach a background to an element that has scrollbars so that it scrolls with the content. For example, the <div> with the ID tail in local.html has the following styles that give it a fixed width and height and set its overflow-y property to auto. It also has a background image that's displayed once and has its background-attachment property set to local like this:

```
#tail {
    white-space: pre;
    font-family: "Trebuchet MS", Arial, Helvetica, sans-serif;
    border: double 4px #900;
    height: 350px;
    width: 250px;
    margin: 0 auto;
    overflow-y: auto;
    background-image: url(images/border.png);
    background-repeat: no-repeat;
    background-attachment: local;
}
```

Figure 8-10 shows what happens when you scroll the content of the <div> in local.html. The background image scrolls with the content.

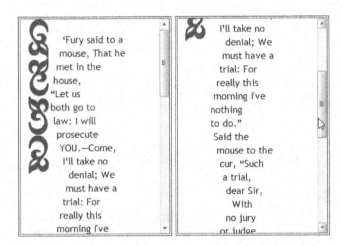

***Figure 8-10.*** *Setting background-attachment to local scrolls the background with the content*

At first, this seems counterintuitive. Surely it should scroll when you set background-attachment to scroll? To show what happens, the value of background-attachment in scroll.html has been changed to scroll. Otherwise, the styles are identical to local.html. Figure 8-11 shows the result.

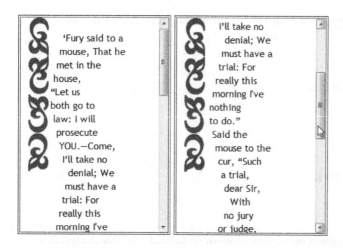

***Figure 8-11.*** *The background image is attached to the element rather than its content*

When I first tested this in a browser, I thought it might be a bug, but it's not. In CSS2.1, the only values for background-attachment were fixed and scroll. The choice of "scroll" was intended to indicate that the background scrolls along with the containing block. And to do so, it needs to be fixed to the element rather than its content.

---

■ **Tip**    The easy way to remember the meaning of scroll is that the background remains attached to the element, but that it scrolls with the rest of the page.

---

## Controlling the Position of Background Images

By default, browsers place the top-left corner of background images at the top left of the element, and apply the background to the whole element (unless you restrict it using background-repeat). However, the background-position property allows you to specify new offsets for the background image to place it exactly where you want. CSS3 introduces two other properties: background-origin and background-clip, which give you control over where the offsets are measured from and how far the background extends

You specify the offsets for background-position using any combination of the following:

Lengths, such as pixels and ems

Keywords

Percentages

Table 8-2 lists the keywords and their percentage equivalents.

***Table 8-2.*** *Keywords and Percentage Values for the background-position Property*

| Keyword | Percentage Equivalent |
|---------|----------------------|
| left | 0% |
| center | 50% |
| right | 100% |
| top | 0% |
| bottom | 100% |

The center keyword applies to both the horizontal and vertical axes.

In CSS2.1, background-position expects one or two values, whereas the CSS3 syntax accepts up to four values. Not all browsers support the CSS3 syntax. So, to avoid confusion, I'll concentrate first on the CSS2.1 syntax, which works in any browser.

## CSS2.1 Syntax

The background-position property expects one or two values.

- If you use one value, the other value is automatically set to center or 50%.

- If you use two keywords, the horizontal and vertical values can be in either order.

- If you use any other combination of two values, the first one must specify the horizontal offset and the second one the vertical offset.

---

■ **Tip** When using two values, make a habit of always putting them in the order: horizontal, vertical. Although specifying background-position as top right is valid, 0% right is not.

---

Using lengths is straightforward. If you specify background-position as 30px 50px, the top-left corner of the background image is placed 30px horizontally and 50px vertically from the top left of the element. Negative values move the top left of the image in the opposite direction, effectively cutting it off.

Keywords are also intuitive. Specifying right top positions the top-right corner of the image at the top right of the element. Specifying center positions the center of the image at the center of the element.

However, percentages are calculated not only in relation to the background, but also in relation to the image itself. That's why the percentage equivalent of right is 100%. It's not only 100% of the background width, but also 100% of the image width. This applies to all percentages. For example, if you specify background-position as 30% 80%, it locates the point at 30% of the image's width and 80% of its height at 30% of the background width and 80% of its height.

To illustrate how this works, I have created position_percent.html, which uses the HTML5 <canvas> element and JavaScript to draw a grid. Each vertical and horizontal line represents 10% of the element's width and height. The background image, checker.png, is a 10 × 10 checkerboard, so each block represents 10 percent of its width or height. The styles set its background-position to 30% 80%.

As Figure 8-12 shows, the third vertical line of the canvas sits exactly between the third and fourth horizontal blocks of the checkerboard, and the eighth horizontal line of the canvas is between the eighth and ninth vertical blocks of the checkerboard.

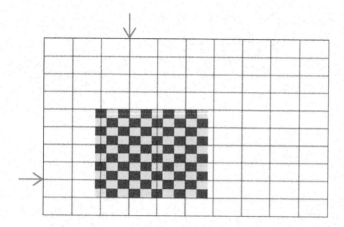

**Figure 8-12.** *The 30% and 80% positions of both the element and the background image coincide*

Try it yourself by loading position_percent.html into a JavaScript-enabled browser that supports the <canvas> element (all modern browsers do). Experiment by changing the percentage values for background-position. Figure 8-13 shows that when you change the value to 90% 10% the top-right 10 percent of the background image is proportionately distanced from the top right of the element.

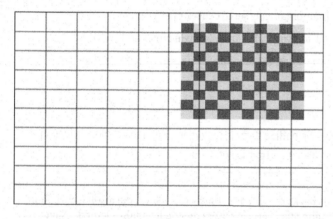

**Figure 8-13.** *The background image is now positioned at 90% horizontally and 10% vertically*

Using percentage values for background-position can be difficult to understand, but they're particularly useful in fluid layouts. Background images are visible only within the element to which they are applied, and not through the element's margins. Any excess is hidden. To demonstrate the effect, fluid.html contains two <div> elements, one with its width set to 80%, and the other set to 60%. Both use the same background image, which is 1200px wide. The image consists of a dark gradient that occupies the left quarter. The remaining three quarters is a light color. The image tiles vertically, and its background-position is set to 25% top. The styles look like this:

```
#box1, #box2 {
    background-image: url(images/fluid_bg.png);
    background-repeat: repeat-y;
    background-position: 25% top;
    height: 30px;
    margin-bottom: 20px;
}
```

```
#box1 {
    width: 80%;
    margin-left: 5%;
}
#box2 {
    width: 60%;
    margin-left: 10%;
}
```

The left margin of the `<div>` elements has been set to align the 25% mark of each one. As Figure 8-14 shows, the dark gradient always fills the left quarter of each `<div>` even when the browser is resized.

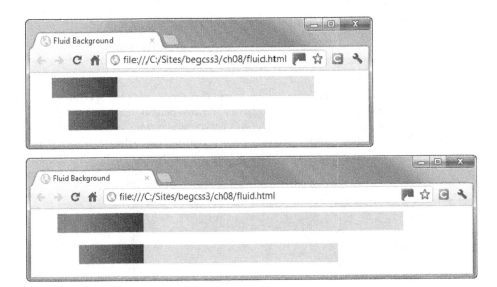

***Figure 8-14.*** *The proportions of the background image remain unchanged at different widths*

## Using Negative Offsets with CSS Sprites

Because background images are cut off when they extend beyond the element to which they're applied, you can combine multiple images in a single file and then use negative `background-position` offsets to display only a portion of the background image—a technique known as using a *CSS sprite*. The main advantages of CSS sprites are that they reduce the number of requests to the web server, and they often result in smaller image sizes, speeding up the download of the page. Most major sites, including Amazon, YouTube, and Apple, use them to consolidate their icons.

When designing a CSS sprite, you need to take into account where the individual images are going to be used. The sprite shown in Figure 8-15 contains five icons stacked at 40px intervals.

**Figure 8-15.** *A CSS sprite combines multiple background images in a single file*

In sprites.html, each icon is displayed as the background image in padding added to the left or right of the text. That's why the icons are stacked vertically. If they were arranged horizontally, neighboring icons would appear behind the text. The first three icons are designed to be added as background images to the left of text, so they're aligned to the left of the sprite. The last two are designed to go on the right of text, so they're aligned right.

Figure 8-16 shows the icons in use. Each one is displayed independently, even though it's part of the larger image.

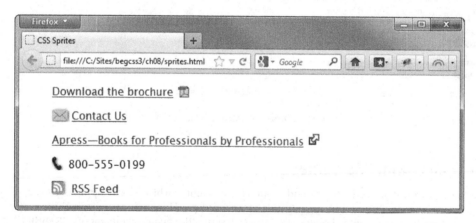

**Figure 8-16.** *Only the part of the sprite that fits into each element's background is displayed*

The styles in sprites.html look like this:

```
.icons {
    background-image: url(images/icons.png);
    background-repeat: no-repeat;
}
.rss {
    padding-left: 30px;
}
.phone {
```

```
        padding-left: 25px;
        background-position: left -40px;
}
a[href^='mailto:'] {
        padding-left: 30px;
        background-position: left -80px;
}
a[href$='.pdf'] {
        padding-right: 24px;
        background-position: right -120px;
}
a[href^="http://"] {
        padding-right: 25px;
        background-position: right -160px;
}
```

The icons class specifies the background image and prevents it from repeating. The class is applied to each block of text. The RSS icon is at the top left of the sprite, so there's no need to set a value for background-position in the rss class. The other style rules set the horizontal position to left or right, and then use a negative vertical position. Designing the sprite with the top of each icon 40px apart made the calculations easy. The styles for the email, PDF, and external link icons all use attribute selectors, which IE 6 doesn't recognize. If you need to support IE 6, use classes instead.

---

■ **Note** CSS3 introduces image fragments that allow you to select just one part of a CSS sprite like this: **image**('images/icons.png**#xywh=0,0,20,20**'). The first two numbers are the horizontal and vertical coordinates (in pixels from the top left of the sprite, and the last two numbers are the width and height (also in pixels) of the section you want. At the time of this writing, no browser has implemented the new image() notation.

---

## CSS3 Syntax

In CSS3, background-position accepts up to four values. Using one or two values works exactly the same as in the CSS2.1 syntax. Using three or four values offers greater flexibility by specifying where the offsets are calculated from using the keywords listed in Table 8-2 in the preceding section. Follow the keyword with the size of the offset from that position. For example, instead of always calculating the image's position from the top left, you can specify offsets from the bottom right. Positive values represent an inward offset. Negative values represent an outward offset. If you omit a value after the keyword, it's assumed to be zero.

The styles in css3_position.html use the same background image for three <div> elements. The position of each one is specified like this:

```
#box1 {
        background-position: right 30px bottom 30px;
}
#box2 {
        background-position: right bottom 30px;
}
#box3 {
        background-position: right -20px bottom -20px;
}
```

This syntax is currently supported in IE 9+, Firefox 13+, and Opera 10.5+. As Figure 8-17 shows, IE 9 displays the image in the first `<div>` 30px from the bottom-right corner. In the second `<div>`, there's no value after `right`, so the right offset defaults to zero, positioning the background image hard against the right side. The final `<div>` uses negative offsets from the bottom right, partially hiding the image.

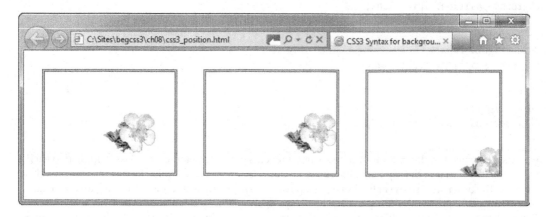

***Figure 8-17.*** *In CSS3, you can specify where the offsets are calculated from*

## Changing Where the Background Begins and How Far It Extends

The new CSS3 `background-origin` property controls the *background positioning area*, which determines where the offsets for `background-position` are calculated from. Closely related is the `background-clip` property, which controls the *background painting area*—in other words, the extent of the background. Both properties are supported in the latest versions of all browsers in widespread use, but not in IE 8 or earlier.

The `background-origin` and `background-clip` properties accept the following properties, which are explained diagrammatically in Figure 8-18:

> `border-box` (default for `background-clip`)
>
> `padding-box` (default for `background-origin`)
>
> `content-box`

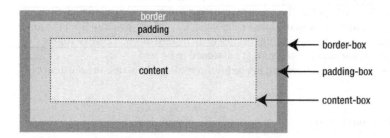

***Figure 8-18.*** *The values for background-origin and background-clip are based on the CSS box model*

Figure 8-19 shows how IE 9 offsets the background image differently in three `<div>` elements in background-origin.html. The left one uses `border-box`, which tucks the background image under the translucent border. The middle `<div>` uses the default `padding-box`, which puts the image inside the border. The right `<div>` uses `content-box`, which puts the image inside the padding.

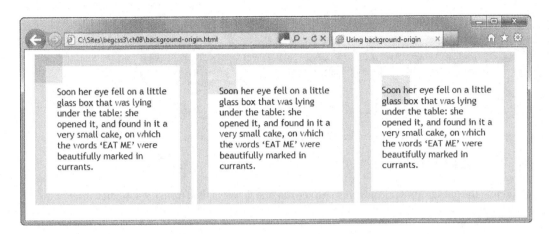

***Figure 8-19.*** *The value of background-origin determines where the background begins*

What might come as a surprise is that the whole area of each `<div>` is covered by the background image if you comment out the `background-repeat` property in background-origin.html like this:

```
#box1, #box2, #box3 {
    width: 200px;
    padding: 20px;
    border: 20px rgba(255, 0 , 0 , 0.2) solid;
    float: left;
    margin-left: 10px;
    background-image: url(images/bg_tile.jpg);
    /* background-repeat: no-repeat; */
}
```

Because bg_tile.jpg is a seamless background image, it's impossible to see what's going on, so I've used a different background image in background-origin_rpt.html (see Figure 8-20).

**Figure 8-20.** *The image is repeated, but starts from a different position*

If you examine the backgrounds closely, you can see that the flower is tiled from the top-left corner of the first <div>; but in the middle <div> it begins from inside the border; and the first whole flower in the final <div> begins under the content.

---

■ **Note** When a background image is repeated, it tiles in *both* directions along the vertical and/or horizontal axis. The background-position and background-origin properties determine only its starting point. They have no control over the background painting area.

---

To control the extent of the background, you need to use the background-clip property, which affects both background colors and images. The styles in background-clip.html set the background painting area in each <div> like this:

```
#box1 {
    background-origin: border-box;
    background-clip: border-box;
}
#box2 {
    background-origin: padding-box;
    background-clip: padding-box;
}
#box3 {
    background-origin: content-box;
    background-clip: content-box;
}
```

Figure 8-21 shows how the background in the left <div> extends under the border. In the middle <div>, it's painted inside the border. And in the right <div>, the background is confined to the content.

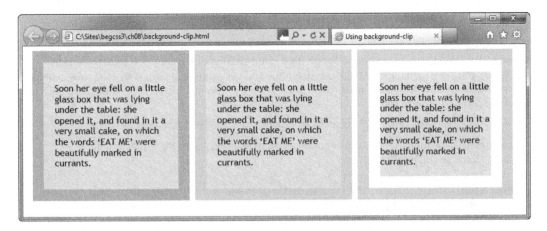

***Figure 8-21.*** *The background-clip property controls the extent of the background*

Background images appear in front of the background color. So, the image hides the color if you add a background color to the `<div>` elements in background-clip.html. However, when `background-clip` is set to `content-box`, the padding inherits the background color of the parent element rather than the color set on the element itself.

In background-clip_bg.html, the dark red background color of the `<div>` is hidden, but the light gray background of the `<body>` shows through the padding between the text and the border. Even in glorious monochrome, you should be able to see the padding and `<body>` are the same shade in Figure 8-22.

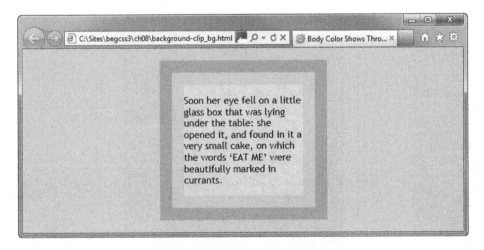

***Figure 8-22.*** *The parent's background color shows through the padding*

177

## Setting the Size of Background Images

When adding a background image to an element, it's important to realize that the background is simply that. The element won't increase in size to accommodate that great image you've chosen. If you want the image to be displayed in full, you need to make sure the element is wide and tall enough. At least, that's the case in older browsers. CSS3 gives you more flexibility with the `background-size` property, which is supported by all browsers in widespread use except IE 8 and earlier.

The `background-size` property accepts the following values:

> **contain** Scale the image to the largest possible size so that both its width and height fit into the background positioning area.

> **cover** Scale the image to its smallest size so that both its width and height can completely cover the background positioning area.

> One or two lengths or percentages.

> When using lengths or percentages, the first value sets the width of the background image, and the second sets its height. If only one value is given, the height is treated as `auto`. Percentages are relative to the background positioning area as determined by `background-origin`. The `contain`, `cover`, and `auto` keywords all preserve the image's aspect ratio.

The difference between `contain` and `cover` is best shown through actual examples. Figure 8-23 shows two 300px square `<div>` elements, both with the same background image (the code is in size_keywords.html). The image is 500px × 667px. The `<div>` on the left sets `background-size` to `contain`, the one on the right sets it to `cover`.

*Figure 8-23.* *The same background image is resized differently without losing its aspect ratio*

Using `contain` results in the whole image being used, but it doesn't necessarily fill the entire background. On the other hand, using `cover` fills the background, but doesn't necessarily use the whole image. If you look at the coastline in both images, they're the same, but the lower section of the image on the right is cut off.

The actual result depends on the comparative dimensions of the background image and element. What's more, `background-size` can be combined with all the other background properties to produce different effects. For example, setting `background-position` to `center` shifts the yachts into the upper third of the `<div>` on the right in Figure 8-23.

## EXERCISE: ADDING BACKGROUNDS TO A PAGE

In this exercise, you'll add background images and colors to a page using properties described in this chapter. The main purpose is to highlight common problems caused by the interaction of vertical margins and backgrounds. Use destinations_begin.html and styles/destinations_begin.css in the ch08 folder as your starting point. The web page contains an Internet Explorer conditional comment to fix problems with IE 6's lack of support for max-width and rounding of percentage widths (see Chapter 7 for a more detailed explanation). The finished files are called destinations.html and destinations.css.

1. In the body style rule, change the background color to light blue and add the light blue seamless tile, bg_tile.jpg, as a background image like this:

```
body {
    margin: 0;
    padding: 0;
    font-family: "Lucida Sans Unicode", "Lucida Grande",
    sans-serif;
    color: #000;
    background-color: #D2E1E6;
    background-image: url(../images/bg_tile.jpg);
}
```

2. To make it easier to add a background image to the main heading, wrap it in a `<div>` with the ID header:

```
<div id="header">
    <h1>Mediterranean Destinations</h1>
</div>
```

3. Create a style rule for the header `<div>` using an ID selector. Use yachts_banner.jpg as the background image, which should not repeat. The image is 127px high, so you need to specify a height to ensure the `<div>` is tall enough to display the full image. The style rule looks like this:

```
#header {
    background-image: url(../images/yachts_banner.jpg);
    background-repeat: no-repeat;
    height: 127px;
}
```

4. Save the style sheet, and load the web page into a browser. The seamless tile covers the whole background of the page, and the image of the yachts acts as the background to the main heading. The background color isn't visible because it's covered by the seamless tile, but it will act as a fallback if the tile can't be loaded. The big problem is a large gap at the top of the page, even though the body style rule sets the page's margins and padding to zero.

5. Use the browser's developer tools to inspect the heading. As Figure 8-24 shows, the `<h1>` element has large top and bottom margins. Adjacent vertical margins collapse to the size of the largest margin. As a result the `<div>` and its background are pushed away from the top of the page.

179

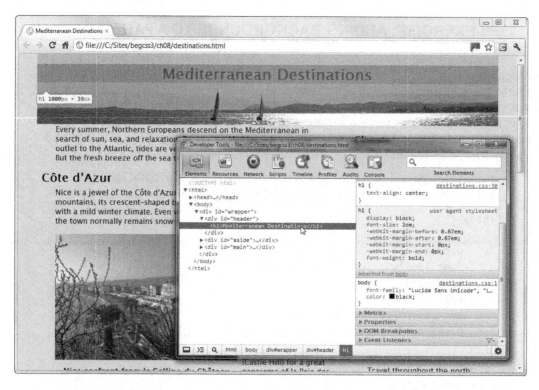

**Figure 8-24.** *The heading's top margin pushes the <div> away from the top of the page*

6. To eliminate the gap, remove the top margin from the `<h1>` element, and replace it with padding. Amend its style rule like this:

```
h1 {
    text-align: center;
    margin-top: 0;
    padding-top: 20px;
}
```

7. Add a white background color to the `main` and `aside` `<div>` elements. Also give them a top margin to move them away from the banner image behind the heading.

```
#main {
    width: 65%;
    margin-right: 35%;
    background-color: #FFF;
    margin-top: 15px;
}
#aside {
    float: right;
    width: 32%;
    display: inline;
    background-color: #FFF;
    margin-top: 15px;
}
```

8. Save the style sheet, and test the page again. As Figure 8-25 shows, the problem with the gap at the top of the page has been solved, but the text is too close to the top of the main and aside <div> elements.

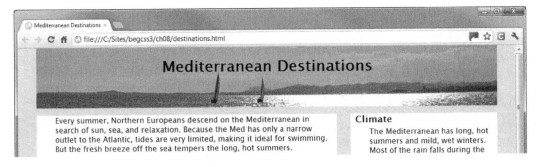

**Figure 8.**25. *The main content and sidebar need headroom*

9. The lack of space is caused by style rules that remove the top margin from paragraphs and from the first <h3> heading in the sidebar. Delete or comment out the following style rule:

```
h3:first-child {
    margin-top: 0;
}
```

10. Restoring the top margin to the heading in the sidebar resolves the problem, but adding a top margin to the first paragraph in the main content seems to have no effect. What explains the different behavior? The sidebar is floated, so it's removed from the normal flow of the document. As a result, the top margin is applied *inside* the <div>. However, the main content is not floated, so the rule of collapsing vertical margins applies. Any margin on top of the first paragraph overlaps the 15px top margin on the main <div>. To create a gap between the white background and the text, you need to add padding to the <div>. It also needs some breathing space at the bottom, so amend the #main style rule like this to add 18px padding at the top and bottom, but none on the sides:

```
#main {
    width: 65%;
    margin-right: 35%;
    background-color: #FFF;
    margin-top: 15px;
    padding: 18px 0;
}
```

The interaction of margins and backgrounds can be puzzling at times. Thankfully, browser developer tools make it easy to inspect where a margin is being applied. Frequently, the solution is to use padding instead of a margin. Unlike adjacent vertical margins, padding never collapses.

# Using the background Shorthand Property

Instead of individual properties, you can wrap the definition in a single declaration using the background shorthand property. All browsers support the CSS2.1 syntax, which combines the following properties:

background-color

background-image

background-repeat

background-attachment

background-position

Values can be in any order. Omitted values use the initial value listed in Table 8-1 at the beginning of this chapter. For example, the body style rule in fixed.html contains four background properties:

```
body {
    background-color: #FFF;
    color: #000;
    font-family:"Lucida Sans Unicode", "Lucida Grande", sans-serif;
    margin-left: 60px;
    max-width: 600px;
    background-image: url(images/border.png);
    background-repeat: no-repeat;
    background-attachment: fixed;
}
```

They can be combined in a single shorthand rule as a space-separated list like this:

```
body {
    color: #000;
    font-family:"Lucida Sans Unicode", "Lucida Grande", sans-serif;
    margin-left: 60px;
    max-width: 600px;
    background: url(images/border.png) fixed no-repeat #FFF;
}
```

In this example, there's no value for background-position, so it defaults to 0% 0%—in other words, the top left of the element.

---

■ **Caution** The background shorthand property automatically resets all values to their defaults before assigning the values given in the declaration. This can have unexpected consequences if you use the shorthand version at the end of a style rule that already contains individual background properties.

---

To illustrate the problem with using the background shorthand property after individual properties in the same style rule, shorthand_override.html contains the following style:

```
body {
    color: #000;
    font-family:"Lucida Sans Unicode", "Lucida Grande", sans-serif;
    margin-left: 60px;
```

```
    max-width: 600px;
    background-image: url(images/border.png);
    background-repeat: no-repeat;
    background-attachment: fixed;
    background: #EFECCA; /* This overrides the individual background properties */
}
```

If you load shorthand_override.html into a browser, you'll see there's no background image at the top left of the page. However, the image is rendered correctly if you move the shorthand property above the individual properties like this:

```
body {
    color: #000;
    font-family:"Lucida Sans Unicode", "Lucida Grande", sans-serif;
    margin-left: 60px;
    max-width: 600px;
    background: #EFECCA; /* This does not affect the individual background properties */
    background-image: url(images/border.png);
    background-repeat: no-repeat;
    background-attachment: fixed;
}
```

---

■ **Tip**  Don't use background as quick way of adding a single value, such as color. The shorthand is great for grouping several values, but it's easy to override existing values by mistake.

---

Modern browsers that support the new CSS3 background properties accept a more complex version of the background shorthand property. It accepts a space-separated list of values in the same way as the CSS2.1 syntax, but with the following additions:

- The value for background-size must be preceded by a value for background-position, with the two values separated by a forward slash.

- Because background-origin and background-clip accept the same values (border-box, padding-box, and content-box), if only one of those values is given, it applies to both background-origin and background-clip. If two values are given, the first one sets background-origin, and the second background-clip.

- Separate the lists of values for multiple background images with commas, beginning with the foremost image.

- Only one background color is permitted. If multiple images are specified, only the final list of values can contain a color.

Putting so many values in a single declaration makes the CSS3 version of the background shorthand much more difficult to write and understand.

The styles in css3_shorthand.html contain the following example of the shorthand property:

```
background: url(images/yachts.jpg) center / contain no-repeat padding-box content-box #D2E1E6;
```

This is equivalent to the following individual properties:

```
background-image: url(images/yachts.jpg);
background-position: center;
background-size: contain;
```

```
background-repeat: no-repeat;
background-origin: padding-box;
background-clip: content-box;
background-color: #D2E1E6;
background-attachment: scroll; /* default value */
```

Using the individual properties is more verbose, but is probably much easier to maintain. Figure 8-26 shows how IE 9 renders the background.

***Figure 8-26.*** *IE 9 renders the CSS3 background shorthand property faultlessly*

Opera and Chrome also display css3_shorthand.html correctly. However, at the time of this writing, Firefox and Safari fail. Instead, they ignore the background completely and just display the border and text. This is because browsers must ignore any style declaration that contains an invalid value. Of course, in this case, the value isn't invalid. It's just that the browser doesn't understand it. By the time you read this, the latest versions of Firefox and Safari will probably have caught up with the CSS3 background shorthand values. However, older browsers never will.

The failure of IE 6–8 to understand the CSS3 shorthand syntax for multiple backgrounds makes it possible to add multiple background images in modern browsers while providing a fallback in older ones.

# Adding Multiple Background Images to an Element

CSS3 allows you to add multiple background images to an element by listing the image sources as a comma-separated list. The first image in the list is displayed at the front, and all subsequent images are displayed behind. Obviously, adding multiple images to an element only makes sense if you control the default repeat pattern and other background properties. Consequently, in CSS3-compliant browsers all background properties except background-color accept a comma-separated list of values, which need to be in the same order as the images. If a property has only one value, the same value applies to all images.

The styles in multiple_images.html add two background images to a `<div>` like this:

```
#box {
    /* Other styles omitted */
    background-image: url(images/yachts.jpg), url(images/stripe.png);
    background-position: center;
    background-size: contain, auto;
    background-repeat: no-repeat, repeat;
    background-origin: padding-box, border-box;
    background-clip: content-box, border-box;
    background-color: #D2E1E6;
}
```

This adds yachts.jpg as the first image, with stripe.png behind. There's only one value for `background-position`, so it applies to both images. In the remaining declarations, the first value applies to yachts.jpg, and the second one to stripe.png. The values for yacht.jpg reset its size, prevent it from repeating, and change its background positioning and painting areas. The other image, stripe.png, is automatically tiled and covers the whole element. Finally, the background color is set to light blue. Figure 8-27 shows the result in a modern browser (left) and in IE 8 (right).

**Figure 8-27.** *Modern browsers support multiple background images, but older versions of IE don't*

Older browsers regard commas as invalid in background property values, so they don't even display the first background image. If I hadn't included `background-color`, there would be no background at all in the screen shot on the right of Figure 8-27.

In some cases, you might accept the background color as being sufficient fallback for older browsers. However, you can exploit older browsers' inability to understand CSS3 shorthand to provide a single background image as fallback. To do so, you need to specify the single image and other background properties first as individual properties. Then you add the background shorthand for the multiple images.

The styles in multiple_images_safe.html show how this is done:

```
#box {
    /* Other styles omitted */
    background-image: url(images/yachts.jpg);
```

```
    background-position: left 15%;
    background-color: #D2E1E6;
    background: url(images/yachts.jpg) center / contain no-repeat padding-box content-box,
               url(images/stripe.png) #D2E1E6;
}
```

I've adjusted background-position for older browsers to compensate for the fact that the image won't be resized. As Figure 8-28 shows, this produces an acceptable result even in IE 6.

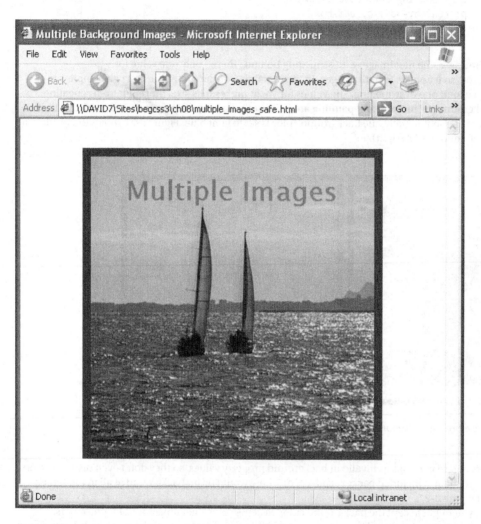

**Figure 8-28.** *Older browsers ignore the shorthand declaration and display the single background image*

In browsers that understand the CSS3 shorthand syntax, the result is identical to the screen shot on the left of Figure 8-27. The shorthand for yachts.jpg is basically the same as in css3_shorthand.html, which was explained in the preceding section. The only difference is that it doesn't contain the color because only the final list of values can contain a color. The shorthand for stripe.png omits all other values because it uses the defaults to fill the entire background. The color is included only as a fallback in case stripe.png cannot be loaded.

# Summary

CSS gives you considerable control over background images, particularly in CSS3-compliant browsers that support the new background-size, background-origin, and background-clip properties. But even in older browsers, you can position background images with great accuracy. Background images are displayed only inside the element they're attached to. Any excess is hidden by the element's margins, making it possible to combine multiple images in a CSS sprite and use background-position to display only one. You can also add a patterned background by repeating a tiny image across the horizontal or vertical axes or both.

In this chapter, you also learned how to use the background shorthand property in combination with individual properties to provide a fallback option for older browsers. In the next chapter, we'll look at borders, the other half of the CSS3 Backgrounds and Borders module.

# CHAPTER 9

■ ■ ■

# Adding Borders and Drop Shadows

All browsers support basic borders, but the CSS3 Backgrounds and Borders module offers a wider range of options. In the past, the only way to add rounded corners or drop shadows to an element was by nesting it in other elements and adding background images. In a CSS3-compliant browser, no images are involved. It's all done with a simple style rule. For more ambitious decorative borders, CSS3 makes it possible to use images without nested elements. The CSS3 features are widely supported, except in IE 8 and earlier.

In this chapter, you'll learn how to do the following:

- Control the color, style, and width of borders on different sides of an element
- Add translucent borders with a fallback for older browsers
- Get rid of borders around image links and image maps
- Prevent borders and backgrounds from running under floated elements
- Add rounded corners to an element
- Create drop shadows and inset shadows
- Use an image to create a decorative border
- Remove the focus rectangle from links without compromising accessibility

## Creating Basic Borders

Because CSS gives you control over the color, style, and width of each side of an element, there are no fewer than 20 properties just for basic borders. The reason there are so many is to reduce the amount of typing. Most properties are shorthand versions. Once you know the basic principles, you can choose whichever best suits your needs. However, let's start by looking at the individual properties.

### Setting Individual Border Properties

Individual properties allow you to set each aspect of an element's border(s) independently. Table 9-1 lists the individual border properties that are supported by all browsers in current use.

**Table 9-1.** *Individual Border Properties Supported by All Browsers*

| Property | Initial Value | Description |
| --- | --- | --- |
| border-top-color | currentColor | Sets the color for the top border. |
| border-right-color | currentColor | Sets the color for the right border |
| border-bottom-color | currentColor | Sets the color for the bottom border. |
| border-left-color | currentColor | Sets the color for the left border |
| border-top-style | none | Sets the style for the top border. |
| border-right-style | none | Sets the style for the right border. |
| border-bottom-style | none | Sets the style for the bottom border. |
| border-left-style | none | Sets the style for the left border. |
| border-top-width | medium | Sets the width of the top border. |
| border-right-width | medium | Sets the width of the right border. |
| border-bottom-width | medium | Sets the width of the bottom border. |
| border-left-width | medium | Sets the width of the left border. |

The color properties accept any color value, but for cross-browser compatibility, it's best to use hexadecimal notation, a color keyword, or rgb(). If you specify a color with alpha transparency using rgba() or hsla(), IE 6–8 ignore the color and use the text color instead. To specify an opaque fallback color for older browsers, you need to use shorthand properties as described later in this chapter. Browsers also use the text color if you don't set a color for the border.

The style properties accept any of the following keywords: none, hidden, dotted, dashed, solid, double, groove, ridge, inset, or outset. Although none is the default value, it's also useful for suppressing an unwanted border. The hidden value is used with table borders and is discussed in Chapter 14.

Using solid and double produces consistent results in all browsers, but there are minor differences between browsers and operating systems in how the other styles are rendered. There is no way to control the spacing of the dots and dashes, but browsers normally create symmetrical corners for dotted and dashed. Examples of the styles are in border_styles.html in the ch09 folder. Figure 9-1 shows the page rendered in Chrome in Windows 7.

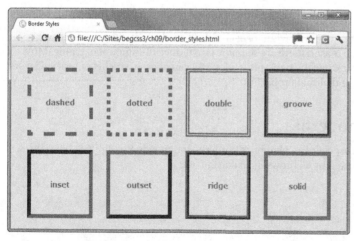

**Figure 9-1.** *Examples of different border styles as rendered in Chrome*

The width properties accept a length or one of the keywords thin, medium, or thick. The actual values of the keywords are not fixed, but they are consistent throughout a page. Negative values or percentages are not valid.

Because each element has four sides, creating a border with these individual properties involves setting at least four of them to specify the style for each side. And you need all 12 to specify a width and a color different from the text. Thankfully, shorthand properties simplify the creation of multiple borders, but setting a single border can be useful. For example, you can add a border to the bottom of < h1> headings like this:

```
h1 {
    color: #933;
    padding-bottom: 3px;
    border-bottom-style: solid;
    border-bottom-width: 10px;
}
```

This adds a 10px solid border under a heading. It's usually a good idea to add a small amount of padding to the bottom of the text to add a little space for descenders that go below the baseline. There's no need to add border-bottom-color unless you want to use a different color from the text.

Another use for bottom borders is to add a double underline to text by creating a class like this:

```
.important {
    border-bottom-style: double;
    border-bottom-width: 3px;
}
```

Just wrap the text in a <span> and apply the class to it to create the double underline. Again, there's no need to specify a color because the browser uses the same color as the text.

---

■ **Note**   The preferred way to create double underlines is with text-decoration-style, as described in Chapter 4. However, until this property is more widely supported, using a bottom border is the only cross-browser solution.

---

You can also use a single left border to highlight text. For example, the following style rule creates a teal rectangle alongside an <h2> heading:

```
h2 {
    border-left-color: teal;
    border-left-style: solid;
    border-left-width: 20px;
    padding-left: 10px;
    margin-left: 30px;
}
```

Figure 9-2 shows all three examples in a browser (the code is in single_borders.html).

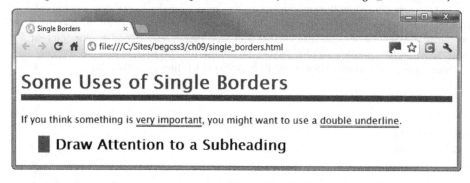

***Figure 9-2.*** *Single borders can be used to highlight text*

Note that the border under the main heading stretches the full width of the page. There's a proposal in the draft CSS3 box model to create a new fit-content value for the width property. In the meantime, the simplest way to make the border under a heading match the width of the text is to wrap the text in <span> tags, and create a descendant selector like this:

```
h1 span {
    color: #933;
    padding-bottom: 3px;
    border-bottom-style: solid;
    border-bottom-width: 10px;
}
```

## Using Border Shorthand Properties

To avoid unnecessarily verbose style rules, CSS provides not one, but eight shorthand properties for defining borders, as listed in Table 9-2. Their meaning and use is fairly straightforward.

***Table 9-2.*** *Border Shorthand Properties*

| Property | Description |
| --- | --- |
| border-color | Defines the color of each border. |
| border-style | Defines the style of each border. |
| border-width | Defines the width of each border. |
| border-top | Sets the color, style, and width of the top border. |
| border-right | Sets the color, style, and width of the right border. |
| border-bottom | Sets the color, style, and width of the bottom border. |
| border-left | Sets the color, style, and width of the left border. |
| border | Sets the same color, style, and width for all four borders. |

The border-color, border-style, and border-width shorthand properties accept up to four values following the same formula as the shorthand for margins and padding:

> *One value:* Applies equally to all four sides.

> *Two values:* The first applies to the top and bottom, and the second to the left and right.

*Three values:* The first applies to the top, the second to the left and right, and the third to the bottom.

*Four values:* The values are applied in clockwise order starting from the top.

The `border-top`, `border-right`, `border-bottom`, and `border-left` shorthand properties accept a space separated list of the color, style, and width values that you want to apply to that side. The values can be in any order. Omitted values use the initial value listed for the individual property in Table 9-1.

Using the shorthand properties, the styles in single_borders.html could be simplified like this:

```
h1 {
    color: #933;
    padding-bottom: 3px;
    border-bottom: solid 10px;
}
.important {
    border-bottom: double 3px;
}
h2 {
    border-left: teal solid 20px;
    padding-left: 10px;
    margin-left: 30px;
}
```

The border shorthand property also takes a space separated list of color, style, and width values, which can be in any order. The same value is applied to all four sides of the element. If a value isn't specified, the initial value for the individual property is applied.

If you want the same border on all four sides, the `border` shorthand is clearly the best option. For example, the following definition creates a 4px double red border around an element:

```
border: 4px double #F00;
```

It couldn't be much simpler.

---

■ **Tip**   The default border style is none. If you forget to specify a style, no border is created, even if you set a color and/or width. To make a border invisible, but preserve its width, set its color to `transparent`. This can be useful to prevent an element from moving if you display a border only when you mouse over it.

---

## Combining Shorthand Properties

You can mix the border shorthand properties to achieve the effect you desire. For example, the styles in combined_shorthand.html use `border-style` and `border-width` to add a top and bottom border to a paragraph in the same way as the preceding Tip like this:

```
.tip {
    text-indent: 0;
    padding: 1em 0;
    font-family: "Lucida Sans Unicode", "Lucida Grande", sans-serif;
    border-style: solid none;
    border-width: 1px;
}
```

The border-style shorthand has two values, so the first one applies a solid border to the top and bottom, while the second one sets the left and right borders to none. The border-width then sets the border on all sides to 1px. This doesn't affect the horizontal alignment of the paragraph because border-style has eliminated the left and right borders. So, in effect, the 1px border is added only to the top and bottom. If you find this difficult to comprehend, you can achieve exactly the same effect with the following styles:

```
border-top: solid 1px;
border-bottom: solid 1px;
```

Whichever way you choose, it's not necessary to specify a color because it's the same as the text.

The flexibility of the shorthand properties is very convenient, but you need to be careful when using the border shorthand property in combination with other border properties.

Browsers tend to use different colors for the inset and outset border styles, so it's usually better to create a custom style to add an embossed or indented border. This requires a solid border that's the same width on all four sides. The only property that needs to be adjusted on different sides is the color. The styles in border_override. html use the border shorthand property in combination with border-color shorthand to create an embossed effect like this:

```
#correct {
    border: solid 6px;
    border-color: #5C9D9D #003636 #003636 #5C9D9D;
}
```

The border property sets the style and width of all four borders to solid and 6px. The border-color property then sets the colors for each side independently. This works because border-color is setting the value that was missing from the border shorthand

However, the style rule for the indented border not only changes the order of colors, but also puts the border property last like this:

```
#incorrect {
    border-color: #003636 #5C9D9D #5C9D9D #003636;
    /* This overrides the border-color properties */
    border: solid 6px;
}
```

As Figure 9-3 confirms, putting the border property last overrides border-color. Instead, a white border is used, picking up the color from the text.

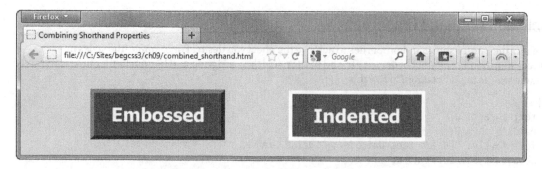

**Figure 9-3.** *The order of the shorthand properties affects the result*

■ **Caution**   The border shorthand property resets omitted values to their defaults.

## Setting a Fallback Border Color for Alpha Transparency

As noted earlier, IE 6–8 don't support the rgba(), hsl(), or hsla() color formats. For cross-browser compatibility, it's best to avoid hsl() altogether when setting border colors. But if you want to use alpha transparency in a border, you can set an opaque fallback color first followed by a shorthand property that uses rgba() or hsla(). For example, border_alpha.html contains a <div> that's styled like this:

```
#description {
    width: 300px;
    padding: 5px 10px;
    margin-left: 30px;
    background-color: #FFF;
    background: rgba(255,255,255, 0.9);
    background-clip: padding-box;
    border: 15px solid;
    border-color: rgb(217,79,17);
    border-color: rgba(217,79,17,0.6);
}
```

As Figure 9-4 shows, a browser that understands rgba() uses the second border-color declaration, allowing the background image to show through. Note also that background-clip has been set to padding-box. This is necessary to prevent the background color from extending under the border.

*Figure 9-4.* *The background image is visible through the translucent border*

Because the same border is used on all sides, an alternative way of specifying the fallback color and translucent borders is to use the border shorthand for both:

```
border: rgb(217,79,17) 15px solid;
border: rgba(217,79,17,0.6) 15px solid;
```

This combination produces a translucent border in a modern browser and an opaque one in an older browser.

---

■ **Note**    The style for the fallback color must come first. Although you can use the individual border properties listed in Table 9-1 for the fallback color, you must use one of the shorthand properties in Table 9-2 for the rgba() or hsla() version. If you use individual properties for both, older browsers ignore both styles.

---

## Getting Rid of Borders Around Image Links and Image Maps

In the early days of the Web, using images as links was a novel idea. So, browsers automatically added a blue border around image links to indicate they were clickable. However, using images as links is now commonplace, and the blue border tends to destroy the visual harmony of the page. As a result, most browsers no longer add a blue border. However, older browsers do, as does IE 9. Some browsers also add a border around image maps—images with hotspots defined in a <map> element that act as links.

The old-school way of eliminating these borders was to add border = "0" in each <img> tag. However, this is invalid in HTML5. Moreover, it's much more efficient to add the following rule to your style sheet:

```
a img, img["usemap"] {
    border: none;
}
```

This is a group selector that targets images nested inside <a> tags or that are linked to an image map with the usemap attribute. One simple rule that removes all borders around image links and image maps.

## Preventing Borders and Backgrounds from Extending Under Floats

When you add a border and/or background to an element, it stretches underneath any element floated alongside. This is because only the content is displaced by the float. Figure 9-5 shows what happens when a <div> with a background and border moves up alongside a floated image in border_float.html.

# Nice Market

Nice has a great open-air market just one block away from the seafront at the eastern end of town. It's a real local market, with locally grown produce, and it's used by the townspeople and local restaurants.

### How to Find It

The market is in the Cours Saleya, just off the Quai des Etats Unis, near the Old Town (Vieille Ville). It's open daily from 6 a.m. Try to get there early—or at least during the morning. On Mondays, the flowers and food make way for antiques.

***Figure 9-5.*** *The border and background extend under the floated image*

Fortunately, the solution is very simple. Just add the overflow property to the style rule that adds the background and/or border, and set its value to hidden (the code is in the #location style rule in border_float_fix.html). As Figure 9-6 shows, this neatly solves the problem.

# Nice Market

Nice has a great open-air market just one block away from the seafront at the eastern end of town. It's a real local market, with locally grown produce, and it's used by the townspeople and local restaurants.

### How to Find It

The market is in the Cours Saleya, just off the Quai des Etats Unis, near the Old Town (Vieille Ville). It's open daily from 6 a.m. Try to get there early—or at least during the morning. On Mondays, the flowers and food make way for antiques.

***Figure 9-6.*** *The background and border now flow alongside the floated image with the text*

Setting overflow to hidden works in all browsers in widespread use. However, if you need to support IE 6, you need to set the Microsoft proprietary zoom property to 1 in the relevant style rule. Because zoom is not needed (or supported) by other browsers, you can use an Internet Explorer conditional comment in the <head> of your page like this (the selector needs to be the same as in your main style sheet):

```
<!--[if lte IE 6]>
<style>
#location {
    zoom: 1;
}
</style>
<![endif]-->
```

# Adding Rounded Corners and Drop Shadows Without Images

Creating rounded corners and drop shadows once took a lot of patient effort, but now takes just a few seconds. Both features are part of CSS3, so they don't work in IE 6–8 or older versions of other browsers. But because these effects are purely decorative, there's no need to provide a fallback.

---

▌ **Tip**   If you really need a fallback for older versions of IE, try CSS PIE (http://css3pie.com/).

---

## Creating Rounded Corners With border-radius

If you're tired of being boxed in by angular designs, the border-radius and related properties might be just what you've been waiting for. In spite of the name, an element doesn't need to have a border for you to give it rounded corners. You can adjust each corner individually or apply the same values to each one. What's more, you can set the horizontal and vertical radii of each corner separately, so you're not limited to uniform shapes. This fine degree of control can make the syntax seem overwhelming at first, but it's not difficult. What's more, there are visual tools available to do the calculations for you.

Table 9-3 lists the properties for creating rounded corners.

*Table 9-3.* *Rounded Corner Properties*

| Property | Initial Value | Description |
|---|---|---|
| border-top-left-radius | 0 | Rounds an element's top-left corner. |
| border-top-right-radius | 0 | Rounds an element's top-right corner. |
| border-bottom-right-radius | 0 | Rounds an element's bottom-right corner. |
| border-bottom-left-radius | 0 | Rounds an element's bottom-left corner. |
| border-radius | | Sets the values for all corners in a single declaration. |

---

▌ **Note**   If you need to support iOS Safari 3.2 or Android 2.1, use the -webkit prefix in addition to the standard property.

---

## Rounding Individual Corners

The individual properties take one or two lengths or percentages, which are used to calculate the curve applied to the corner. Percentages are relative to both the element's width and height.

- A single length creates an evenly rounded curve.

- A single percentage creates an evenly rounded curve only if the element is a square. Otherwise, the browser calculates the percentage values of the width and height, and treats them as two values.

- With two values, the first sets the horizontal radius of a quarter ellipse and the second sets the vertical radius.

- If any value is 0, the corner is square.

In the following example, each corner is set using a different method.

```
#box1 {
    background-color: #006;
    width: 200px;
    height: 150px;
    border-top-left-radius: 25px;
    border-top-right-radius: 30%;
    border-bottom-left-radius: 50% 30%;
    border-bottom-right-radius: 100px 45px;
}
```

The top-left corner is shaped using a single length, which produces an evenly rounded curve. The top-right corner uses a single percentage, but the element isn't square. So, the browser calculates 30% of the width (60px) and 30% of the height (45px). The resulting values are used as the horizontal and vertical radii of a quarter ellipse. The bottom two corners create identical curves using percentages and lengths. Figure 9-7 shows the result.

*Figure 9-7. Examples of setting different corner curves*

Percentages remain proportional to the element. Lengths produce a consistently sized curve.

## Using border-radius Shorthand

The border-radius shorthand property sets all four corners in a single declaration. Using it can be either fiendishly complex or blissfully simple. Let's start with a simple example, which is probably the way most people use it. In radius_shorthand.html, two <div> elements are styled like this:

```
#box1 {
    background-color: #006;
    width: 200px;
    height: 150px;
    border-radius: 25px;
}
#circle {
    background-color: #900;
    width: 150px;
    height: 150px;
    border-radius: 50%;
}
```

In both cases, border-radius takes just one value, which is applied to all four corners. In the first case, a length is used, producing an evenly rounded curve on each corner. In the second case, the border-radius of a square is set to 50%, producing a circle as shown in Figure 9-8.

***Figure 9-8.*** *Using border-radius with a single value applies the same curve to all corners*

Using border-radius with more than one value is less straightforward. First let's deal with using the same value for the horizontal and vertical radii of each curve.

> *Two values:* The first applies to the top-left and bottom-right corners. The second applies to the top-right and bottom-left corners.

> *Three values:* The first applies to the top-left corner. The second applies to the top-right and bottom-left corners. The third applies to bottom-right corner.

> *Four values:* The values are applied to each corner in a clockwise direction starting from the top left.

It's when you want to use different values for horizontal and vertical radii that the border-radius shorthand becomes mind-numbingly complex, taking 2–8 values. Unless you want to apply the same values to each corner, it's probably much easier to use the individual properties for each corner. Still, I'll explain how it works and let you make up your own mind.

The values for the horizontal and vertical radii are separated by a forward slash. However, you don't specify each pair separately. All horizontal values come before the slash, and all vertical values come after. And this is where the syntax becomes really complex—you don't need to use the same number of values before and after the slash. So, for example, you could have three horizontal values before the slash and two vertical ones after the slash. The rules regarding which corners the values apply to are the same as just described for two, three, and four values.

The following styles for #box1 using border-radius shorthand have exactly the same meaning as the individual rules for #box2 (the code is in radius_shorthand2.html):

```
#box1 {
    border-radius: 20% 10% 40% / 15% 30%;
}
#box2 {
    border-top-left-radius: 20% 15%;
    border-top-right-radius: 10% 30%;
    border-bottom-right-radius: 40% 15%;
    border-bottom-left-radius: 10% 30%;
}
```

■ **Tip**   You might find it easier to create rounded corners using one of the many free border-radius generators online, such as those at http://border-radius.com/ or http://css3gen.com/border-radius/.

## Using border-radius With Background Images

When you apply border-radius to an element that has a background image, the image is clipped by the curve, and the parent element's background shows through. For example, in radius_bg_image.html, the following style rule adds a background image to a <div> and applies a 50% curve to all corners:

```
#photo {
    /* Other styles omitted */
    background-image: url(images/weaver.jpg);
    background-repeat: no-repeat;
    border-radius: 50%;
}
```

As Figure 9-9 shows, the rounded corners are also applied to the background image. Setting border-radius to 50% on an element that has one dimension greater than the other produces an oval shape.

### Lee's Tapestry Works

The Arthur H Lee and Sons tapestry works in the North End of Birkenhead was an important employer in the town for more than 60 years until it closed in 1970. The weavers and embroiderers who worked there created wall hangings for ocean liners, Chester Cathedral, and royalty around the world. The tapestries were of unrivalled quality, often made up of millions of stitches.

The tapestry works no longer exists. After it closed, it was demolished, and a supermarket now stands on the site. However, the tapestries created by its skilled workers will endure for centuries.

*Figure 9-9.*  *Rounded corners also affect background images*

## How Borders Interact With Rounded Corners

When you use border-radius in combination with a border, the outer edge of the border is rounded. But the border's inner shape depends on the border width and size of the border radius.

The example in border_alpha.html earlier in this chapter (see Figure 9-4) uses a 15px translucent border around a < div>. If you set border-radius to the same value as the border width or less, the outer radius is curved, but the corners of the padding box remain square, as shown in Figure 9-10 (the code is in rounded_alpha_15.html).

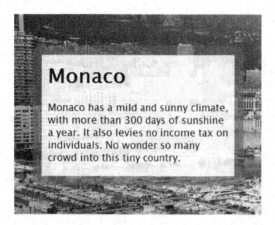

**Figure 9-10.** *Although the border has rounded external corners, the inner shape of the border is square*

However, as soon as the border-radius exceeds the width of the border, the inner border is also rounded. With an opaque border, there's no problem. But Figure 9-11 shows what happens with translucent borders. The element's background retains its rectangular shape and protrudes into the border (the code is in rounded_alpha_40.html).

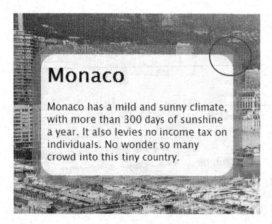

**Figure 9-11.** *The rectangular background remains visible through a translucent border*

■ **Note**    Even if you increase the size of the rounded corners, the background never extends beyond the border.

When borders of different widths meet, the inner and outer curves are smoothed automatically. However, the specification doesn't lay down any rules about smooth transitions between colors. It simply specifies the region in which the transition takes place. In all my tests, there's a straight line where one color ends and the next begins. Figure 9-12 shows examples of how rounded corners are rendered on borders of different widths and colors (the code is in rounded_different.html).

***Figure 9-12.***  *Rounded corners can also be applied to borders of different widths and colors*

## Applying Rounded Corners to Various Border Styles

So far, all the examples of border-radius have shown only solid borders and elements without a border. However, rounded corners can be applied to any border style. As with color transitions, it's left up to the browser to decide how to treat the style on the curve. Figure 9-13 shows how Chrome handles the different styles (the code is in radius_styles.html).

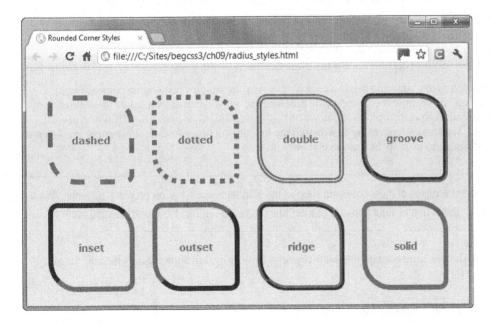

***Figure 9-13.***  *How Chrome applies rounded corners to different border styles*

Rounded corners work well across all browsers with double and solid borders. However, other border styles produce dramatically different effects. Figure 9-14 shows how IE 9 (left) and Firefox 14 (right) handle rounded corners on dashed and dotted borders.

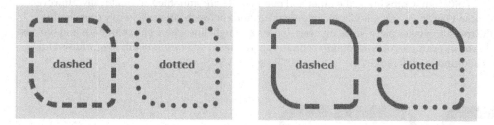

*Figure 9-14.* *Rounded corners on dashed and dotted borders in IE 9 (left) and Firefox 14 (right)*

The color transitions on groove, inset, outset, and ridge border styles are also less than satisfactory when used with rounded corners.

## Adding Drop Shadows With box-shadow

The box-shadow property adds one or more drop shadows to an element. You specify a shadow using 2–4 space-separated lengths, which represent the following values (in this order):

*Horizontal offset:* A positive value positions the shadow to the right. A negative value positions it to the left.

*Vertical offset:* A positive value moves the shadow down. A negative value moves it up.

*Blur radius:* If omitted or set to 0, the shadow has a crisp edge. Negative values are not allowed.

*Spread distance:* A positive value causes the shape to expand in all directions. A negative value (used with an inset shadow) causes it to contract. To create a spread effect without setting a blur radius, the third length must be set to 0.

In addition to these lengths, you can specify a color. Otherwise, the shadow is the same color as the element's text. By default, the shadow is drawn outside the element, but you can draw it inside the element by adding the inset keyword. To specify multiple shadows on the same element, separate the definition of each shadow with a comma. The shadow effects are drawn with the first one on top, and each subsequent one layered behind. If you want shadows to overlap, list the smaller ones first.

---

■ **Note** The most recent versions of most browsers support the standard box-shadow property. However, Android 4 (Ice Cream Sandwich), Safari 5, and older versions of iOS Safari need the -webkit browser-specific prefix.

---

The styles for box-shadow.html contain the following rules (for clarity, I'm showing only the standard property):

```
#drop1 {
    box-shadow: 5px 5px 7px rgba(0,0,0,0.3);
}
```

```
#drop2 {
    box-shadow: -5px -5px 7px rgba(0,0,0,0.3);
}
```

Both rules set box-shadow using three lengths. The first two set the horizontal and vertical offsets, respectively. In #drop1, the values are positive, so the shadow is to the right and down from the element. In #drop2, the values are negative, so the shadow is to the left and up. The third value sets the blur radius of the shadow to 7px. Finally, the color is set to black with 30 percent alpha transparency. Figure 9-15 shows the result. Notice that the shadows follow the rounded corners of the elements.

**Figure 9-15.** *Negative values for the offsets produce a reverse shadow*

■ **Tip** Using a color with alpha transparency usually produces a more realistic shadow. All browsers that support box-shadow also support the rgba() and hsla() color formats.

The next two rules add the inset keyword:

```
#inset1 {
    box-shadow: inset 10px 10px 10px rgba(0,0,0,0.3);
}
#inset2 {
    box-shadow: inset -10px -10px 10px rgba(0,0,0,0.3);
}
```

As Figure 9-16 shows, positive values draw the shadow from the left and top sides of the element. Although this might appear odd, the shadow itself is being moved to the right and down. Similarly, the negative values are being moved to the left and up, so the shadow comes from the bottom-right corner.

**Figure 9-16.** *Inset shadows are drawn inside the element*

Adding a fourth length to the box-shadow values spreads the shadow color out in all directions by the amount specified. However, the spread is affected by the horizontal and vertical offsets. So, if the spread is smaller than the offsets, it's displayed only on the same sides as the shadow. If it's greater than the offsets, it appears on all sides. The following style rules add a 4px and 12px spread, respectively.

```
#spread1 {
    box-shadow: 5px 5px 7px 4px rgba(0,0,0,0.3);
}
#spread2 {
    box-shadow: 5px 5px 7px 12px rgba(0,0,0,0.3);
}
```

In both rules, the horizontal and vertical offsets are 5px. As Figure 9-17 shows, the 4px spread of the first rectangle is hidden behind the element on the left and top, but the 12px spread of the second rectangle is visible on all sides.

**Figure 9-17.** *The offsets affect the position of the spread shape*

## Simulating Multicolored Borders

Combining a spread shape with offsets and a blur radius rarely produces an attractive effect. However, using multiple spread shapes with no offset or blur offers an easy way to create multicolored borders. The box-shadow property accepts multiple shadow effects as a comma-separated list. Each subsequent effect is painted behind the preceding one, so the smallest one must come first followed by the others in increasing sizes. The style rule for the heading <div> in multiple_spreads.html looks like this:

```
#heading {
    text-align: center;
    width: 20em;
    padding: 0.5em 1em;
    background-color: #DCEBDD;
    margin: 30px auto;
    border-radius: 20px;
    box-shadow: #A0D5D6 0 0 0 5px,
                #789AA1 0 0 0 10px,
                #AD9A27 0 0 0 15px,
                #304345 0 0 0 20px;
}
```

The horizontal and vertical offsets and blur radius in each value are set to 0. The spread value in each one is incremented by 5px, producing the result seen in Figure 9-18. The <div> has rounded corners, so the spread colors added by box-shadow follow the same outline.

**Figure 9-18.** *Using multiple spreads of increasing sizes creates the impression of a multicolored border*

# Using Border Images

For a more decorative border, you need to use an image. In CSS2.1, this involves creating up to nine images and wrapping the element in a complex series of < div> elements. CSS3 simplifies the process by using just one image, which the browser automatically slices into nine sections (see Figure 9-19) to build the border. If you use Adobe Flash or Fireworks, this concept will be familiar to you as 9-slice scaling.

*Figure 9-19.* *The border is created by utilizing different sections of a single image*

The browser positions the four corner slices, and scales or tiles each side to fill the width and height. The dimensions of the border image aren't important. You just need a design that can be sliced this way.

---

■ **Note** The browser doesn't physically slice the image. It masks the individual sections when using them.

---

At the time of this writing, Chrome is the only browser with full support for border images. Of the other mainstream browsers, Safari, Firefox, and Opera have implemented enough to be usable, but Internet Explorer has no support at all.

Although Firefox and Opera currently support only the shorthand border-image property, I'll describe the individual properties first because they make the shorthand easier to understand.

## Individual Properties for Border Images

There are five individual properties for border images, as described in Table 9-4.

**Table 9-4.** *Individual Properties for Border Images*

| Property | Initial Value | Description |
|---|---|---|
| border-image-source | none | Specifies the image to use for borders. |
| border-image-slice | 100% | Sets the inward offsets from each side of the image, dividing it into four corners, four edges, and a center section. |
| border-image-width | 1 | Sets the amount of space allocated to the border image on each side. |
| border-image-outset | 0 | Specifies how far the border image should extend beyond the border box. |
| border-image-repeat | stretch | Specifies how the slices are scaled and tiled along the horizontal and vertical edges. |

The first two properties, border-image-source and border-image-slice, are required. The other properties are optional.

## Specifying the Image and Its Slices

The border-image-source property tells the browser which image to use for the borders. You specify the image in the normal way with url().

The border-image-slice property defines how the image should be sliced up. It expects 1–4 numbers or percentages that indicate how much of each side should be used for the border. The values are treated in a similar way to margin and padding shorthand, namely:

> *One value:* Applies to all sides.

> *Two values:* The first value applies to the top and bottom, and the second to the right and left sides.

> *Three values:* The first value applies to the top, the second to the right and left sides, and the third one to the bottom.

> *Four values:* The values apply to each side starting from the top and moving clockwise.

The unusual aspect of using numbers with border-image-slice is that they're not followed by a unit of measurement, such as px or em. This is because the property is intended to be used with scalable vector graphics (SVG) as well as JPEG, PNG, or GIF images. When using an ordinary image, the value is the number of pixels measured from the edge that you want to use as the slice. If you're using an SVG image, the numbers are vector coordinates.

Percentage values for top and bottom are relative to the image's height. Those for the right and left are relative to the image's width.

According to the specification, the center slice should be discarded. To preserve the center slice, add the fill keyword.

## Controlling the Size and Position of the Border Image

The border-image-width property sets the width of the slices, *not* the width of the border. It's a subtle, but important difference. Border images are normally displayed within the element's border box (see Figure 8.18 in Chapter 8). If you don't create a border around the element using the properties described at the beginning of this chapter, there's no space between the border and padding boxes. Consequently, the image won't be displayed or will be squeezed to almost nothing. Figure 9-20 shows what happens when using border images generated from 24px slices without setting a default border to accommodate them (the code is in border-image1.html).

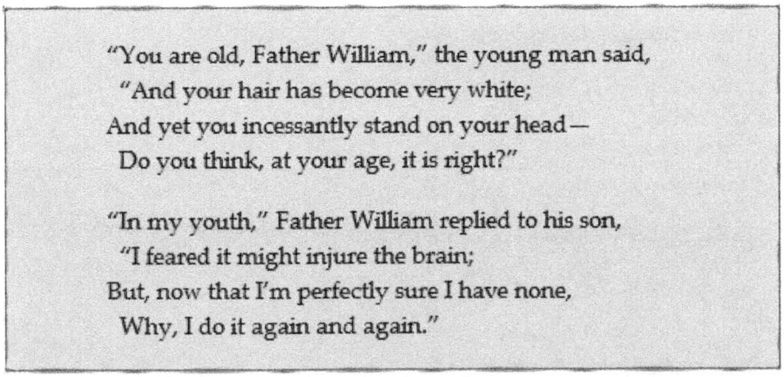

> "You are old, Father William," the young man said,
>   "And your hair has become very white;
> And yet you incessantly stand on your head—
>   Do you think, at your age, it is right?"
>
> "In my youth," Father William replied to his son,
>   "I feared it might injure the brain;
> But, now that I'm perfectly sure I have none,
>   Why, I do it again and again."

**Figure 9-20.** *The border image is squeezed because the element doesn't have a default border*

The `border-image-width` property accepts up to four values, which are allocated to each side in the same way as slices. The values can be specified as lengths, percentages, or numbers. A number represents a multiple of the computed `border-width`. Percentages are relative to the width or height of the border box for horizontal and vertical slices, respectively.

The examples in border-image2.html and border-image3.html illustrate the difference between setting `border-image-width` on its own and creating a default border. The style rule for the `<div>` in border-image2.html looks like this:

```
#poem {
    /* Other styles omitted */
    border-image-source: url(images/frame1.png);
    border-image-slice: 24 fill;
    border-image-width: 24px;
}
```

The value of `border-image-width` is set to `24px`, which is the same as the slices. However, there's no default border around the element. On the other hand, border-image3.html omits `border-image-width`, but specifies a basic border in addition to the border image like this:

```
#poem {
    /* Other styles omitted */
    border: 24px double #4B8896;
    border-image-source: url(images/frame1.png);
    border-image-slice: 24 fill;
}
```

In border-image2.html (Figure 9-21, left), the border image is no longer squeezed because it has been given a width. But there's no room in the border box, so it's displayed *inside* the `<div>`. However, in border-image3.html (Figure 9-21, right), `border-image-width` is not set, so the default value (1) is applied. This is a multiple of the computed `border-width`, which the border shorthand property sets to `24px`. Because the border box is the same width as the slices, the border image overrides the `24px double` border, which is displayed only in browsers that don't support border images.

209

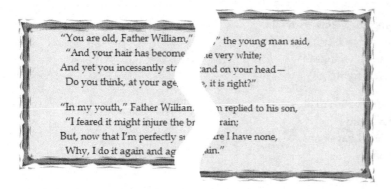

**Figure 9-21.** *The border image is displayed inside the element if you don't create a default border*

As border-image3.html demonstrates, there's no need to set `border-image-width` if you create a default border that's the same size as the slices. The main value of `border-image-width` is if you want to scale the image slices. Setting `border-image-width` to 12px in the preceding examples would rescale them to half their natural size.

The role of `border-image-outset` is to allow the border image to extend beyond the border box. For example, border-image4.html sets both `border-image-width` and `border-image-outset` to 24px without creating a default border. This has a similar effect to the styles in border-image3.html. The crucial difference is that the top border is cut off by the top of the page. A normal border interacts with surrounding elements, altering their relative positions. But `border-image-outset` puts the border image outside the border box. As a result, it can be clipped by an ancestor or the viewport.

## Setting How the Slices Fill the Sides

By default, the browser stretches each slice so that it fills the gap between the corners. It does so without changing the height for the top and bottom slices, or the width for the right and left slices. However, the `border-image-repeat` property lets you specify how to handle the slices with the following keywords:

> `stretch` This is the default. The slices are scaled along the axis to fill the gap.

> `repeat` The image is tiled from the center of the side to fill the gap.

> `round` The image is rescaled if necessary to fill the gap an exact number of times.

> `space` The image is repeated an exact number of times to fill the gap. If there's insufficient space for an exact number, the extra space is distributed evenly leaving a gap between individual tiles. This value is currently not supported by any browser.

If you use one keyword, it applies to all sides. If you use two keywords, the first applies to the top and bottom, and the second applies to the right and left.

All the preceding examples have omitted `border-image-repeat`, so the default `stretch` has been used. Choosing the best option(s) depends entirely on the image you're using. For the pattern used in the example files, round is best for all four sides, but border-image5.html (see Figure 9-22) sets the top and bottom to `stretch` and the sides to round like this:

```
border-image-repeat: stretch round;
```

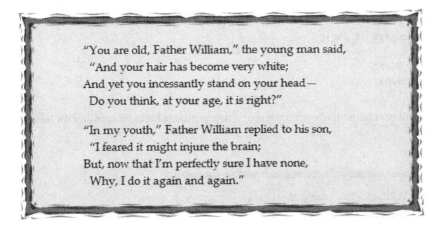

**Figure 9-22.** *Different repeat values have been set for the horizontal and vertical slices*

## Using the Shorthand Property for Border Images

The shorthand border-image property combines the five individual properties in a single declaration. At the time of this writing, only Chrome has full support for the shorthand property. Firefox, Safari, and Opera have incomplete support and require browser-specific prefixes. However, by the time you read this, any shortcomings will hopefully have been ironed out. So, I'll begin by describing the full syntax, followed by what currently works cross-browser.

### Full Shorthand Syntax

The shorthand syntax combines the individual properties like this:

```
border-image: source slices / width / outset repeat;
```

As explained in the preceding section, only the image source and slices are required. The other three values are optional. However, note the following rules:

- If you include 1–4 values for width, they must follow the values for slices, separated by a forward slash.

- To include 1–4 values for outset, they must follow the width values, separated by a forward slash.

- You cannot specify values for outset without also setting width.

- If you omit width and outset, there should be no slash between any of the values.

Although the border slices in frame1.png are all 24px wide, I have assigned three values each to the width and outset properties in border-image6.html to demonstrate how to use the full shorthand syntax like this:

```
#poem {
    /* Other styles omitted */
    -webkit-border-image: url(images/frame1.png) 24 fill / 18px 12px 24px / 6px 12px 12px↵
        round stretch;
    border-image: url(images/frame1.png) 24 fill / 18px 12px 24px / 6px 12px 12px↵
        round stretch;
}
```

The shorthand is the equivalent of using the following individual properties:

```
border-image-source: url(images/frame1.png);
border-image-slice: 24 fill;
border-image-width: 18px 12px 24px;
border-image-outset: 6px 12px 12px;
border-image-repeat: round stretch;
```

As Figure 9-23 shows, the result isn't particularly attractive, but it demonstrates how you can alter the width and position of individual sides.

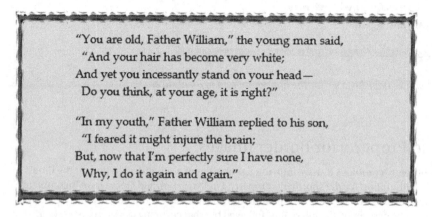

**Figure 9-23.** *Different widths have been applied to the slices*

The full shorthand syntax in the preceding example is currently supported only in Chrome. Safari requires the -webkit prefix and almost gets it right. However, Safari doesn't yet support the fill keyword. The styles in border-image7.html are identical to the preceding example, except that the fill keyword has been removed. If you test border-image7.html in Chrome, the center slice is discarded, and the white background of the page shows through. Currently, Safari incorrectly displays the center slice.

## Most Widely Supported Syntax for Border Images

Until Firefox and Opera implement the full specification, the most reliable cross-browser way of using border images is to use an incomplete version of the shorthand property, omitting the width and outset values. In fact, unless you need to scale the slices, this is probably all that you will need most of the time. Like Safari, Firefox and Opera require browser-specific prefixes, and they don't support the fill keyword. However, unlike Safari, they don't simply ignore fill. If you use it, they refuse to display the border image.

The style rule in border-image8.html specifies a fallback border for older browsers together with the border-image shorthand optimized for the current level of browser support like this:

```
#poem {
    /* Other rules omitted */
    border: 24px double #4B8896;
    -moz-border-image: url(images/frame1.png) 24 round;
    -o-border-image: url(images/frame1.png) 24 round;
    -webkit-border-image: url(images/frame1.png) 24 fill round;
    border-image: url(images/frame1.png) 24 fill round;
}
```

This sets the image source to frame1.png, makes all slices 24px wide, and sets the repeat value for all sides to round. The last two declarations include the fill keyword to ensure that the center slice is displayed. Although the current version of Safari doesn't support it, you need to include fill in case a later version does. Figure 9-24 shows the result in Firefox.

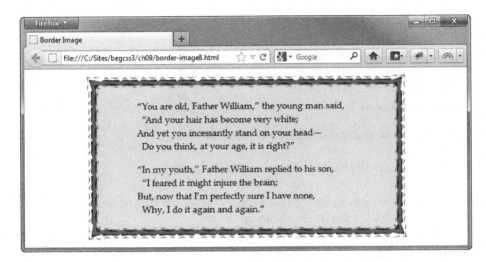

**Figure 9-24.** *Firefox 12+ supports a limited version of border-image*

By the time you read this, Firefox and Opera might have added support for fill. If they're still using the browser-specific properties, the preceding code will result in the center slice being discarded. To prevent the page background from showing through, it's a good idea to add a background color to the style rule. The border image contains transparent sections, so also set background-clip to padding-box by adding the following to the style rule (the code is in border-image9.html):

```
background-color: #DCEBDD;
background-clip: padding-box;
```

Browsers that don't support border images also use the background color, so it serves a dual purpose.

## Avoiding Problems With the Center Slice

The center section of frame1.png is filled with a solid color, so it doesn't matter how you set the repeat pattern for the sides. However, frame2.png has a vertical gradient. Figure 9-25 shows the ugly banding of the gradient when you set the repeat pattern for all sides to round (the code is in border-image10.html).

"You are old, Father William," the young man said,
"And your hair has become very white;
And yet you incessantly stand on your head—
Do you think, at your age, it is right?"
"In my youth," Father William replied to his son,
"I feared it might injure the brain;
But, now that I'm perfectly sure I have none,
Why, I do it again and again."

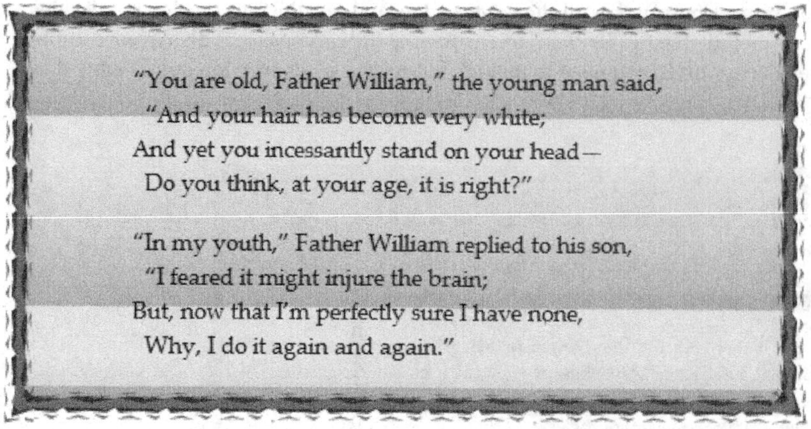

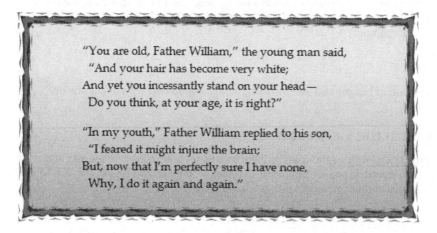

***Figure 9-25.*** *Using round as the repeat value for all four sides also affects the center section*

The banding is caused by the repeat value for the right and left sides. To prevent this problem, you need to set the second repeat keyword to `stretch` like this (see border-image11.html):

```
-moz-border-image: url(images/frame2.png) 24 round stretch;
-o-border-image: url(images/frame2.png) 24 round stretch;
-webkit-border-image: url(images/frame2.png) 24 fill round stretch;
border-image: url(images/frame2.png) 24 fill round stretch;
```

As Figure 9-26 shows, this eliminates the banding of the center section, but it changes the pattern along the sides. In this case, I think that the stretched version looks acceptable, but it might not work for all patterns.

"You are old, Father William," the young man said,
"And your hair has become very white;
And yet you incessantly stand on your head—
Do you think, at your age, it is right?"
"In my youth," Father William replied to his son,
"I feared it might injure the brain;
But, now that I'm perfectly sure I have none,
Why, I do it again and again."

***Figure 9-26.*** *The gradient is no longer banded, but the pattern on the sides is elongated*

# Styling Outlines

An outline is similar to a border in that it's drawn around an element, but it differs in the following ways:

- An outline doesn't add to the overall width or height of an element. It's drawn on top of other styles.

- An element can have both an outline and a border. Browsers normally draw the outline outside the border.

- All sides of an outline must be the same. They can't be styled independently.

- The outline of an inline element surrounds the whole element. Unlike a border, it doesn't break when the element wraps to another line (see Figure 9-27).

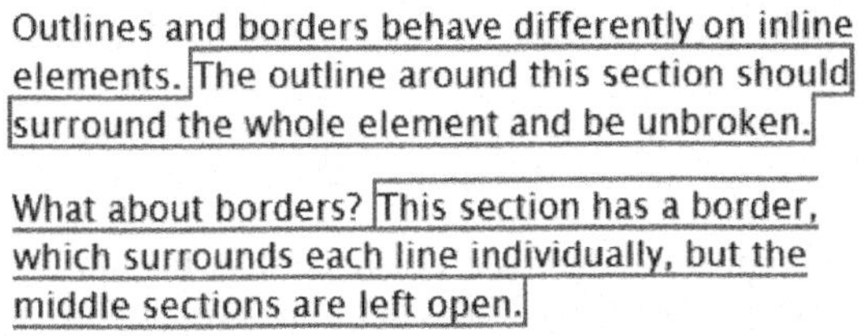

Outlines and borders behave differently on inline elements. The outline around this section should surround the whole element and be unbroken.

What about borders? This section has a border, which surrounds each line individually, but the middle sections are left open.

*Figure 9-27. Most browsers draw an outline as an irregular box around inline elements*

There are three individual properties for outlines and a shorthand one, as described in Table 9-5.

*Table 9-5. Outline Properties*

| Property | Initial Value | Description |
|---|---|---|
| outline-width | medium | Sets the width of the outline using a length or one of the keywords thin, medium, or thick. |
| outline-style | none | Sets the style of the outline using the same keywords as border-style except hidden. |
| outline-color | invert | Sets the color of the outline using any color format. The default is invert, which performs a color inversion of the pixels on the screen to ensure the outline is visible. If the browser doesn't support color inversion, it defaults to the same color as the current text. |
| outline | | Shorthand property that sets all three values in a single declaration. |

Perhaps the most common use of the properties in Table 9-5 is not to add an outline, but to remove it. Most browsers automatically add a dotted line around links and other clickable elements when they have focus. This is known as a *focus rectangle*, an accessibility feature designed to help people who use the keyboard to navigate around websites. Although it's there for an important reason, many designers find the focus rectangle aesthetically unacceptable.

One way to deal with the focus rectangle is to use `outline-color` to make it blend better with your design. If you adopt this approach, it's important to make sure the rectangle is still perceptible.

The other approach is to remove the focus rectangle on links, but to use the `:focus` pseudo-class to apply the same style as `:hover` like this:

```
a {
    outline: none;
}
a:hover, a:active, a:focus {
    color: #8E2800;
    text-decoration: underline;
}
```

This removes the focus rectangle, but ensures that when someone tabs to the link, it's styled the same way as on hover. It's a win-win situation. You preserve the unity of your design, but someone using keyboard navigation still gets a strong visual clue as to which link currently has focus.

# Summary

CSS has a large number of options for creating borders. Older browsers support only plain borders, but most modern browsers offer a much wider choice, allowing you to create rounded corners, drop shadows, and decorative borders using images. Although older browsers don't get the benefit of the shiny new features in CSS3, the sky won't fall in if they see only straight corners without shadows. The main point to remember about creating borders is that the default border style is none. If you forget to specify a style, no border is created.

The syntax for border images can be confusing at first because `border-image-width` sets the width of the slices, not of the border box where the slices are displayed. Remember to create a basic border the same width as the image slices. In modern browsers, the border image overrides the basic border, which acts as a fallback for older browsers. Although Chrome is the only browser that currently implements all aspects of border images, the main parts are supported by all other browsers in widespread use except Internet Explorer.

In the next chapter, we'll take an in-depth look at styling lists. Although there's a draft CSS3 Lists module, the W3C describes it as being at the exploratory stage. However, the CSS2.1 features are stable and well implemented in all browsers.

# CHAPTER 10

## Styling Lists and Navigation Menus

HTML provides tags for three different types of lists: unordered (`<ul>`), ordered (`<ol>`), and definition (`<dl>`). Unordered lists are normally displayed as a series of bullet points; ordered lists are numbered; and definition lists are presented as a word or phrase followed by its definition, indented on the following line. Figure 10-1 shows examples of all three (the code is in lists.html in the ch10 folder).

CSS regards the components of definition lists as block-level elements, so it has no special properties to deal with them. You style definition lists with text properties, padding, margins, borders, and backgrounds as required. Unordered and ordered lists use the same properties, but CSS provides extra ones to control the bullets or numbers alongside each list item.

Using these extra properties in combination with the `display` property, it's easy to convert an unordered list into a navigation menu, as you'll learn how to do later in this chapter. Many designers now regard this as the preferred way to build navigation for their sites. This isn't simply a design trick. Even without any styling, a bulleted list is a logical and visually acceptable way of presenting a series of links to other parts of a website. A series of nested lists provides a structured outline of a website's hierarchy, with the top level indicating the site's main sections, and the nested lists acting as submenus.

In this chapter, you'll look first at the properties used for styling unordered and ordered lists, and then at creating a navigation bar. In particular, you'll learn how to

- Control the type of bullets and numbers used for a list
- Decide whether the bullet or number is displayed as a hanging indent
- Replace standard bullets with your own images
- Embed an encoded image in a style sheet
- Create a navigation bar from an unordered list

Apart from embedding encoded images, the techniques in this chapter are supported by all browsers in widespread use, including IE 6.

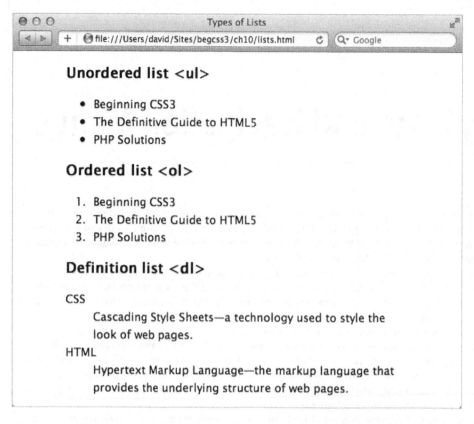

**Figure 10-1.** *The three types of lists supported in HTML*

# Styling Unordered and Ordered Lists

CSS has three individual properties and a shorthand property designed to style bulleted and numbered lists. They are listed in Table 10-1.

**Table 10-1** *List Properties in CSS*

| Property | Initial Value | Description |
|---|---|---|
| list-style-type | disc | Determines the type of symbol used. By default, unordered lists use a solid disc, and ordered lists use a number followed by a period (dot). |
| list-style-position | outside | Controls whether the symbol or number is displayed as a hanging indent (default) or nested inside the list item. |
| list-style-image | none | Allows you to use your own image in place of an automatically generated symbol. |
| list-style | See individual properties | Shorthand property that lets you specify all properties in a single declaration. |

All properties in Table 10-1 are inherited, so the same values are used by nested lists unless you create specific rules to override them.

# Changing the Symbol or Number

The list-style-type property controls the symbol or number for both unordered and ordered lists.

## Unordered Lists

When used with unordered lists, list-style-type offers a choice of just three symbols: disc (default), circle, and square. Figure 10-2 shows what they look like in Safari on Mac OS X (see list_type_ul.html).

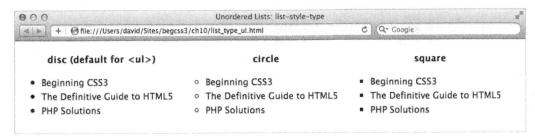

**Figure 10-2.** *There's a limited choice of symbols for unordered lists*

The symbol uses the same color as the text. There's no mechanism for changing the color of the symbol other than to wrap the content of each list item in a <span> like this:

```
<ul>
    <li><span>Beginning CSS3</span></li>
    <li><span>The Definitive Guide to HTML5</span></li>
    <li><span>PHP Solutions</span></li>
</ul>
```

Then create two style rules, one for the list, and the other for the <span> elements:

```
ul {
    list-style-type: square;
    color: #F00;
}
li span {
    color: #000;
}
```

This uses red squares as the bullet symbol and displays the text in black. However, wrapping every list item in <span> elements is an ugly hack. A better solution is to use an image to replace the symbol, as described later in this chapter.

## Ordered Lists

There's a much wider choice of symbols for ordered lists. All browsers except IE 6 and IE 7 support the 11 keywords listed in the CSS2.1 specification: decimal (default), decimal-leading-zero, lower-roman, upper-roman, lower-greek, lower-alpha, upper-alpha, lower-latin, upper-latin, armenian, and georgian. Figure 10-3 shows the sequences each keyword produces (see list_type_ol.html).

As you can see in Figure 10-3, lower-alpha and lower-latin are synonymous, as are upper-alpha and upper-latin. However, it's better to use lower-alpha and upper-alpha because IE 6 and IE 7 support only decimal, lower-roman, upper-roman, lower-alpha, and upper-alpha. For all other keywords, they revert to the default decimal (1, 2, 3, and so on).

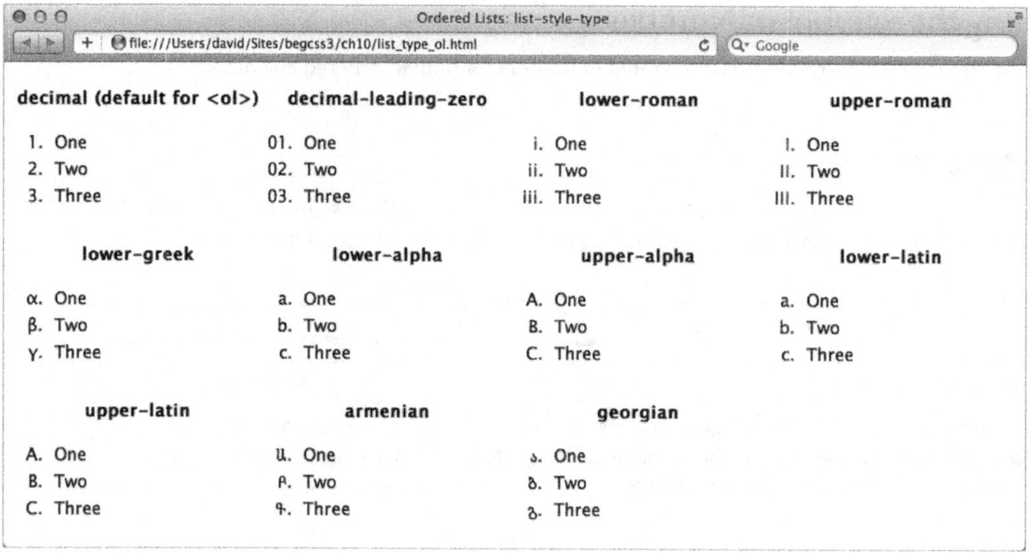

**Figure 10-3.** *There's a wide choice of numbering systems for ordered lists*

Page encoding has no effect on the symbols displayed. Setting `list-style-type` to armenian or georgian displays traditional Armenian and Georgian numbering even with page encoding that doesn't support either of these alphabets.

---

■ **Caution**   If you use disc, circle, or square with an ordered list, the symbol is displayed instead of a number or letter. However, it doesn't work the other way round. Using one of the keywords for an ordered list with an unordered list results in the default disc (solid circle) being displayed.

---

Some browsers support even more keywords that were originally part of the CSS2 specification, but were dropped from CSS2.1. Figure 10-4 shows examples of extra keywords supported by Safari and Chrome (the code is in list_type_extra.html). Firefox 14 supports all except upper-greek, whereas IE 9 supports only upper-greek.

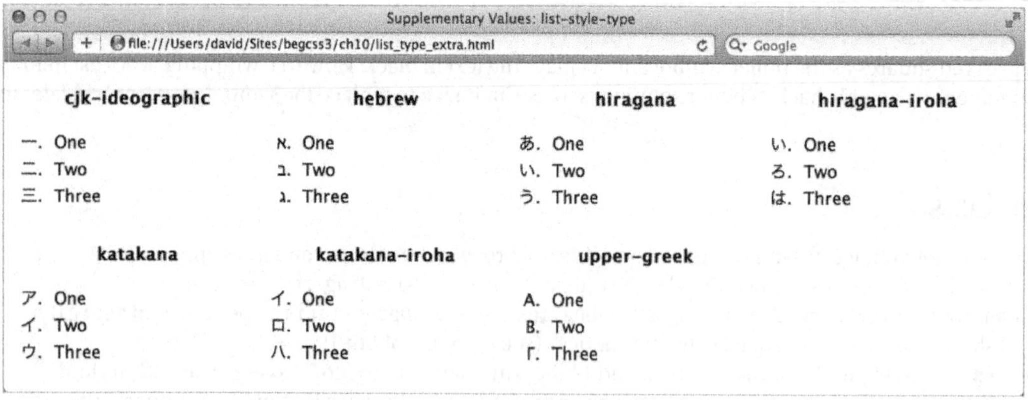

**Figure 10-4.** *Some browsers support keywords that were dropped from CSS2.1*

## Suppressing the Symbol

In addition to all these keywords is perhaps the most important one: none. This enables you to suppress the symbol or number, which opens up the way to convert a list into a navigation bar.

## Nested Lists

With unordered lists, browsers automatically change the symbol for each new level of nesting, as shown in Figure 10-5 (see nested_ul.html).

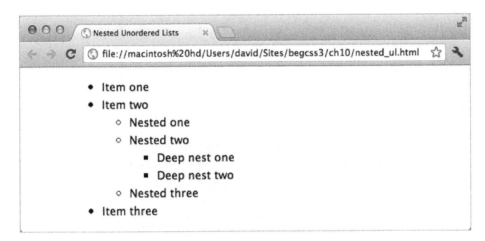

***Figure 10-5.*** *Browsers automatically change the symbol when unordered lists are nested*

■ **Note** The automatic sequence of symbols for unordered lists is fixed. It doesn't change if you reset the top-level symbol.

Ordered lists keep track of the current number, starting again at 1 when moving to a deeper level, and resuming the sequence when backing out of a nested list. Although this is convenient, the numbers are difficult to follow because each level of nesting uses the default decimal value for list-style-type (see Figure 10-6 and nested_ol.html).

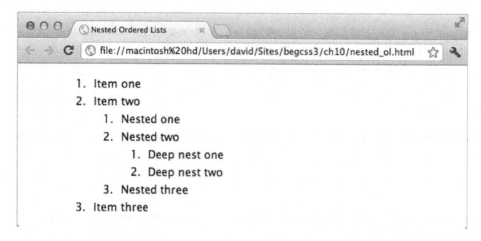

*Figure 10-6.* *The default numbering of nested ordered lists can be confusing*

To make the numbering easier to follow, use descendant selectors to set list-style-type like this:

```
ol ol {
    list-style-type: lower-alpha;
}
ol ol ol {
    list-style-type: lower-roman;
}
```

This produces the output shown in Figure 10-7 (see nested_ol_styled.html). The top-level ordered list takes the default decimal value, so no style is needed. The first descendant selector, ol ol, targets ordered lists nested one level deep; and the second one, ol ol ol, targets ordered lists at the next level.

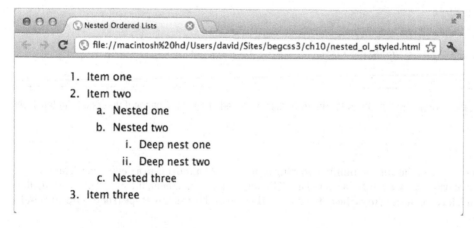

*Figure 10-7.* *Changing the numbering of nested lists makes the sequences easier to follow*

■ **Tip**  As you have just seen, ordered lists resume the sequence when you back out of a nested list. However, if you follow a list with a paragraph or any other type of element, the sequence always restarts at 1. To continue a numeric sequence after a break, use the `start` attribute in the opening `<ol>` tag. For example, `<ol start = "4">` continues a list at item 4. The `start` attribute was deprecated in HTML 4.01 and XHTML 1.0 in favor of CSS. Unfortunately, the CSS method of resuming numbering after a break is complex. Thankfully, the W3C saw the error of its ways, and restored the `start` attribute to HTML5. Chapter 15 explains how CSS counters work.

## Changing the Position of the Symbol

The `list-style-position` property accepts just two values, namely:

> `inside` This tucks the bullet or number inside the list item, so that it is flush with the left edge in left-to-right languages like English.

> `outside` This is the default position, which puts the bullet or number outside the list item like a hanging indent.

The styles in list-style-position.html include the following class:

```
.inside {
    list-style-position: inside;
}
```

The class has been applied to the unordered and ordered lists on the right of Figure 10-8. As a result, the symbols and numbers are tucked into the first line of each item. The lists on the left use the default style, which leaves the bullets and numbers outside the list items.

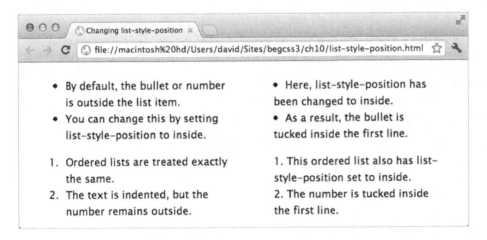

***Figure 10-8.*** *The symbol or number can be positioned outside the list item or tucked into the first line*

## Replacing the Symbol with Your Own Image

The list-style-image property allows you to replace the symbol with an image of your own. Although it works with both ordered and unordered lists, the same image is used for every item. So, in practical terms, it makes sense only with unordered lists.

As explained earlier in this chapter, displaying the symbol in a different color from the text involves wrapping each list item in a <span>. The alternative is to use list-style-image to replace the default with a custom image.

In replace_bullet.html, an image of a red square is used as the symbol for an unordered list like this:

```
ul {
    list-style-image: url(images/redsquare.png);
}
```

As Figure 10-9 shows, the image is used in place of the default disc. You won't be able to see the different color in the printed book, but you can check the file in the ch10 folder. The image used in this example is 16px × 14px, which produces a larger square than the default bullet. It's an odd size because a 2-pixel transparent border was added to one side to move it away from the text. As a general rule, the height of the image shouldn't exceed the font size of the text.

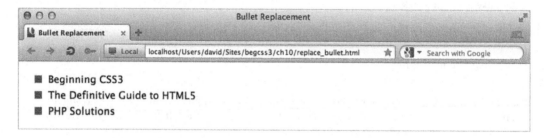

**Figure 10-9.** *Using a custom image solves the problem of using a different color from the text*

When using a custom image, it's recommended that you leave list-style-type at its default value (or choose another one), rather than setting it to none. This ensures that a symbol is still displayed even if the image is missing or the user is browsing with images turned off. To make sure a square is used instead of a disc, amend the previous style rule like this:

```
ul {
    list-style-image: url(images/redsquare.png);
    list-style-type: square;
}
```

## Embedding an Encoded Image in the Style Sheet

A disadvantage of using an image to replace bullets in unordered lists is that the image needs to be downloaded by the browser. Although redsquare.png in the preceding example is only 216 bytes, it adds an extra request to the server. With only one image, it's not a significant burden, but it can begin to add up if you use many images.

In Chapter 8, you learned about CSS sprites as a technique for reducing the number of server requests for small images. Unfortunately, you can't use a CSS sprite with list-style-image. However, you can use a *data URI* (Uniform Resource Identifier). This is a version of the image encoded as text using an encoding system known as base64. It's suitable for only small images, but is supported by all browsers in widespread use except IE 7 and earlier.

The simple way to convert an image to a data URI is to use an online converter, such as the one at http://dopiaza.org/tools/datauri/. You then simply replace the path to the image as the value of url() in the style rule like this (the code is in datauri.html):

```
ul {
    list-style-image:url(data:image/png;base64,iVBORwOKGgoAAAANSUhEUgAAABAAAAAOAQMAAAAc4Q↵
7JAAAAA3NCSVQICAjb4U/gAAAABlBMVEXZAAD///+Q6NI6AAAAnRSTlP/AOW3MEoAAAAJcEhZcwAADsMAAA7DAcdv↵
qGQAAAAWdEVYdENyZWFOaW9uIFRpbWUAMDUvMjcvMTJc5/NzAAAAHHRFWHRTb2ZOd2FyZQBBZG9iZSBGaXJld29ya3↵
MgQ1M26LyyjAAAABFJREFUCJlj+P+fAYgOMBNEAESTDSFz7scaAAAAAElFTkSuQmCC); /* red square */
    list-style-type: square;
}
```

In a modern browser, this produces the same result as in Figure 10-9. IE 6 and IE 7 don't understand data URI, so they display the default square instead. The obvious disadvantage of a data URI is that it's not human readable, so it's a good idea to add a comment to remind yourself what the image looks like.

---

■ **Tip** The CSS3 image() notation described in "Using Negative Offset with CSS Sprites" in Chapter 8 allows you to specify image fragments. Once browsers support image(), the need for data URI is likely to go away.

---

## Using Larger Images

You're not restricted to discs, circles, and squares. For example, list-style-image.html uses an image of a wine glass as the symbol for an unordered list like this:

```
ul {
    list-style-image: url(images/redwine.png);
}
```

As Figure 10-10 shows, the base of the image is aligned with the baseline of the text in each item. Also, the image is displayed at its full height, increasing the gap between list items.

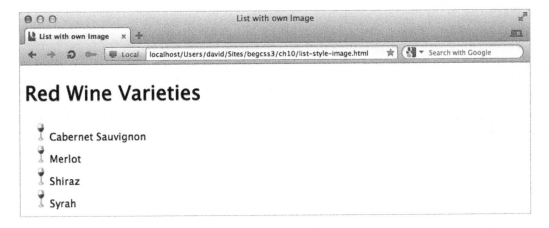

***Figure 10-10.*** *The custom image affects the line height of the list items*

Moreover, there's no mechanism for positioning the image. So, you need to choose the image carefully or design it so that it blends well with the text of the list items.

The alternative is to suppress the default symbol by setting list-style-type to none, and to use a background image. This means that no bullet will be displayed if there's a problem with the image or images are turned off, but it usually produces better results.

The styles in list_bg_image.html look like this:

```
ul {
    list-style-type: none;
}
ul li {
    padding: 0.35em 0 0.35em 25px;
    background-image: url(images/redwine.png);
    background-repeat: no-repeat;
    background-position: left;
}
```

The styles for the list items add a small amount of padding to the top and bottom, and 25px on the left. The background image is displayed in the left padding. Only the horizontal value is set for background-position, so the vertical value defaults to center. This results in the images aligning with the center of the text, as shown in Figure 10-11.

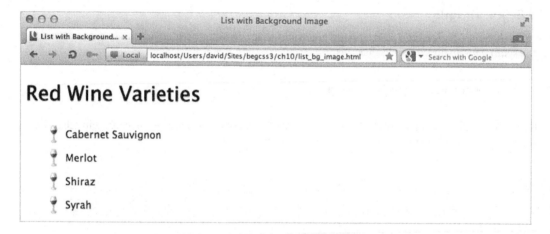

*Figure 10-11. Background images can be positioned accurately alongside list items*

■ **Caution**    If the list item contains multiple lines, the styles in the preceding example center the image vertically alongside the whole list item. To ensure the background image is always positioned alongside only the first line of longer items, you need to specify the vertical position as well.

## Using the list-style Shorthand Property

The list-style shorthand property accepts the same values as the individual list-style-type, list-style-position, and list-style-image properties. You can define all three values, separated by a space, or just one or two. Any value that is omitted uses the initial value listed in Table 10-1. For example, the following style tells the browser to replace the default symbol with redsquare.png, but to display a standard square symbol if the image can't be found or images are turned off:

```
ul {
    list-style: url(images/redsquare.png) square;
}
```

This has exactly the same meaning as using the individual properties like this:

```
ul {
    list-style-image: url(images/redsquare.png);
    list-style-type: square;
}
```

# Creating a Navigation Bar from a List

Several years ago, the only way to create an attractive navigation bar was to design everything in a graphics editor. If you wanted a rollover effect, you needed to create at least two images for each button. I always seemed to nudge something accidentally, and ended up with text out of alignment, meaning I had to start all over again. It was back to the drawing board each time you wanted to make a change to the menu.

CSS has made life a lot easier, because you can often use image elements as backgrounds and handle all the text with HTML and CSS. Thanks to the display property, you can turn links into large, clickable blocks. Add some rounded corners and a drop shadow, and before you know it, a humble link looks like a menu button.

Unordered lists are the ideal container for navigation links, because they can be nested, allowing you to create a hierarchy of top-level items with individual submenus. In this chapter, I'm going to deal only with single-level navigation bars. Then in Chapter 11, I'll show you how to display submenus using CSS Positioning.

## Creating a Vertical Text-based Navigation Bar

When converting an unordered list into a vertical navigation bar, you don't need to worry about long menu items. As long as the horizontal space allocated to the navigation bar is wide enough to accommodate two words of average length, long text simply wraps onto another line, and the style rules create a taller button. Assuming you want the navigation bar to fill the entire width of its container element, the process involves the following steps:

1. Remove the bullet and all margins and padding from the unordered list.

2. Remove all margins from the list items.

3. Set the display property of the links to block.

4. Style the links with padding, background color, and borders.

That's all there is to it. So, let's put the theory into practice.

---

### EXERCISE: CREATING A VERTICAL NAVIGATION BAR

In this exercise, you'll convert an unordered list of links in the sidebar of a page into a vertical navigation bar. Use as your starting point vertical_begin.html and styles/vertical_begin.css in the ch10 folder. The finished menu is in vertical_end.html and styles/vertical_end.css.

The page is based on the Mediterranean Destinations file that has been used in previous chapters, but I have added some rounded corners and drop shadows. I have also reduced the width of the sidebar and main content area to add a 1% margin on the left and right, respectively, to move them away from the edge of the page when the viewport is less than 1000px.

1. Give the unordered list at the top of the aside `<div>` the ID nav by amending the opening `<ul>` tag:

```
<div class="rounded shadow" id="aside">
    <ul id="nav">
        <li><a href="#">Home</a>
```

2. Create an ID selector in the style sheet to remove the bullets from the unordered list. Also, give it a top margin of 20px, but zero the other margins and padding like this:

```
#nav {
    list-style-type: none;
    margin: 20px 0 0;
    padding: 0;
}
```

3. Make sure the individual list items don't have any margins by adding the following style rule:

```
#nav li {
    margin: 0;
}
```

4. Next comes the key to this technique. Add a rule to set the display property of links inside the nav unordered list to block. This makes the link fill the entire width of the list item, turning it into a clickable button. The effect will become obvious when you add a background color later. The rule looks like this:

```
#nav a {
    display: block;
}
```

5. Amend the style rule to add some padding to the links, remove the underline, use a bold font, and a light gray text color:

```
#nav a {
    display: block;
    padding: 0.5em 15px;
    text-decoration: none;
    font-weight: bold;
    color: #F2F2F2;
}
```

6. To make the links look like buttons, add background colors for the normal and hover states:

```
#nav a:link, #nav a:visited {
    background-color: #071726;
}
#nav a:hover, #nav a:active, #nav a:focus {
    background-color: #326773;
}
```

7. Save the style sheet, and test the page in a browser. The links are now solid blocks of color, as shown in Figure 10-12.

***Figure 10-12.*** *Setting the display property to block makes the whole link clickable*

8. To distinguish between the links, give them a border with harmonious colors. Putting a lighter color on the top and left, and a darker color on the right and bottom gives the illusion of embossed buttons. Amend the `#nav a` style rule like this:

```
#nav a {
    display: block;
    padding: 0.5em 15px;
    text-decoration: none;
    font-weight: bold;
    color: #F2F2F2;
    border: 2px solid;
    border-color: #606B74 #02060B #02060B #606B74;
}
```

9. To make the buttons seem inverted when the mouse is hovering over them, the border on the top and left needs to be a darker color, and the right and bottom a lighter one:

```
#nav a:hover, #nav a:active, #nav a:focus {
    background-color: #326773;
    border-color: #142A2F #61797F #61797F #142A2F;
}
```

10. Save the style sheet, and test the navigation menu again. It should now look like Figure 10-13.

***Figure 10-13.*** *Adding harmonious color borders gives the links an embossed look*

11. The navigation bar looks good in all browsers except one—IE 6. It inserts a wide gap between each menu item. If IE 6 is no longer on your support list, you don't need to worry about it. The menu is perfectly usable. It just doesn't look as good. However, if you're still supporting IE 6, the fix is easy. Just set the `display` property of the list items to `inline`. This closes up the gaps in IE 6 and has no effect on other browsers. Amend the style rule for the list items like this:

```
#nav li {
    margin: 0;
    display: inline;
}
```

This exercise assumes that you want the vertical navigation bar to fill the entire width of a container, such as the sidebar. If you want the menu to be narrower than its containing element, add the `width` property to the style rule for the unordered list or change the values of its left and right margins.

## Creating a Horizontal Text-based Navigation Bar

The basic principles behind creating a horizontal navigation bar are the same as for a vertical one. However, you need to give the menu items a width and float them left. Unfortunately, this poses problems with long menu items. If one or more items are too long to fit into the declared width, the buttons end up different heights.

## EXERCISE: CREATING A HORIZONTAL NAVIGATION BAR

In this exercise, you'll convert an unordered list into a horizontal navigation bar. Most of the styles are the same as for a vertical navigation bar. Because the menu items are floated, you need to adjust the position of the following content. Although there are a couple of ways to achieve this, only one produces a satisfactory cross-browser solution.

You'll need to use the browser's developer tools to inspect margins and height. I suggest using Safari or Chrome to start with. If you have access to IE 9 or later, you'll also use its developer tools to inspect a problem unique to Internet Explorer.

Use horizontal_begin.html and styles/horizontal_begin.css in the ch10 folder as your starting point. The files are the same as in the preceding exercise, but the unordered list has been moved to between the header `<div>` and the sidebar. The finished menu is in horizontal_end.html and styles/horizontal_end.css.

1. The unordered list has been given the ID nav. Create an ID selector to remove the bullets. Also, give it a top margin of 15px, but zero the other margins and padding like this:

```
#nav {
    list-style-type: none;
    margin: 15px 0 0;
    padding: 0;
}
```

2. There are six links. If you leave a 1% gap between each one, with a similar gap at both ends, the remaining space is 93%. Dividing that figure by six gives you a width of 15.5% for each menu item. Create a style for the list items, setting their width

and left margin. Float the list items left, and center the text. The resulting style rule looks like this:

```
#nav li {
    width: 15.5%;
    margin-left: 1%;
    float: left;
    text-align: center;
}
```

3.  Next, create a style rule for the links in the list items. This is basically the same as you created for the horizontal menu, but with a little less horizontal padding. Also, instead of creating embossed borders, give the menu items rounded corners and a drop shadow with the following style rule:

```
#nav li a {
    display: block;
    padding: 0.5em 5px;
    text-decoration: none;
    font-weight: bold;
    color: #F2F2F2;
    border-radius: 8px;
    -webkit-box-shadow: 3px 3px 3px rgba(51,51,51,0.3);
    box-shadow: 3px 3px 3px rgba(51,51,51,0.3);
}
```

4.  Add background colors for the normal and hover states:

```
#nav a:link, #nav a:visited {
    background-color: #071726;
}
#nav a:hover, #nav a:active, #nav a:focus {
    background-color: #326773;
}
```

5.  Save the style sheet, and test the page in a browser. As Figure 10-14 shows, there are two problems. The *Eastern Mediterranean* link is split over two lines, creating a button that's much taller than the others. Also, the main `<div>` is tucked behind the menu, which is why the first line of text has moved into the space alongside the tall menu item.

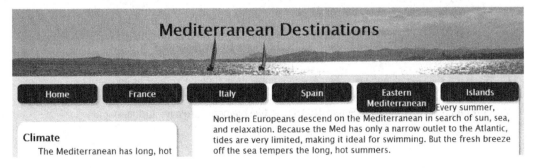

***Figure 10-14.*** *The long item and the position of the main `<div>` need fixing*

6. Rather than doing complex calculations to equalize the heights of the long and short items, the most practical approach is to shorten the item that's split over two lines. Change *Eastern Mediterranean* to **East Med**.

7. Use your browser's developer tools to inspect the `nav` unordered list. In Chrome or Safari, right-click one of the menu items, and select *Inspect Element* from the context menu. Then click the `<ul>` element in the panel that opens. As Figure 10-15 shows, its height is zero. That's because all the list items are floated.

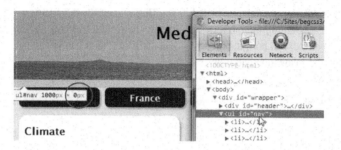

**Figure 10-15.** *Floating the list items reduces the height of the unordered list to zero*

8. Repeat the previous step to inspect the `main <div>` in the browser's developer tools. You should see that its top margin of `15px` overlaps the top margin of the `nav` unordered list. At first, this seems inexplicable. Although adjacent vertical margins collapse, the `aside <div>` comes between the unordered list and the `main <div>` in the underlying HTML. However, both the `aside <div>` and all the content of the unordered list are floated, which removes them from the normal flow of the document. As a result, the top margins of the `nav` unordered list and the `main <div>` are considered to be adjacent—and that's why they overlap.

9. Select one of the list items in the developer tools to find its height. In Chrome, it's `36px`.

10. To move the `main <div>` back into position, add the existing `15px` top margin to the height of the list item (`36px`), plus another `15px` to move it below the menu—a total of `66px`. Amend the top margin in the `#main` style rule like this:

```
#main {
    width: 64%;
    margin: 66px 1% 10px 35%;
    background-color: #FFF;
    padding: 18px 0;
}
```

11. Save the style sheet, and view the page in a browser. In Safari, Firefox, Chrome, and Opera, the tops of the sidebar and main content are in alignment. In IE 9, there's a 5px difference, as shown in Figure 10-16. The two elements are even further out of alignment in IE 6 and IE 7.

***Figure 10-16.*** *There's a slight, but perceptible misalignment with the sidebar in IE 9*

12. In IE 9, press *F12* to launch the developer tools. If you don't have access to Windows, just read the following steps to understand what's causing the misalignment.

13. In the *HTML* section on the left, expand `<body>`, and select one of the `<li>` items.

14. Click the *Layout* button on the right to display a diagrammatic representation of its box model. As Figure 10-17 shows, the list item's dimensions in IE 9 are 155px × 40.59px. This is approximately 5px taller than in other browsers.

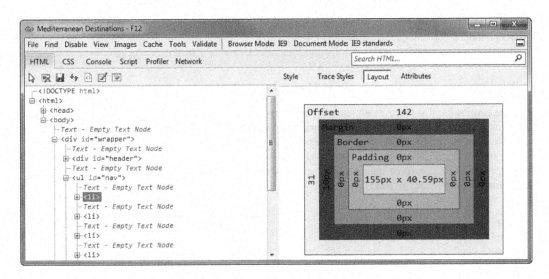

***Figure 10-17.*** *Inspecting the size of a list item in IE 9's developer tools*

15. One way to fix this would be to create an Internet Explorer conditional comment to set a different top margin for IE 9. You would also need a different one for IE 6 and IE 7. Doing so would work, but it's an unsatisfactory solution. What's more, IE 10 doesn't support conditional comments, so you can't rely on them to solve problems with IE 10 and later. Fortunately, there's an alternative.

16. Change the top margin of the main `<div>` back to 15px:

```
#main {
  width: 64%;
  margin: 15px 1% 10px 35%;
  background-color: #FFF;
  padding: 18px 0;
}
```

17. Give the nav unordered list a height of 40px:

```
#nav {
    list-style-type: none;
    margin: 15px 0 0 0;
    padding: 0;
    height: 40px;
}
```

When you give the unordered list a fixed height, the top margin of the main <div> and the unordered list are no longer adjacent to each other, and no longer collapse. As a result, the top margin of the main <div> positions the <div> correctly below the menu in all browsers. An important lesson to take away from this exercise is the need to use the developer tools in different browsers to solve discrepancies in layout.

▓ **Note** If you need to support IE 6, amend the #nav li style rule to set display to inline. You also need to add #nav li to the IE conditional comment to change the width property from 15.5% to 15.3% because rounding errors prevent IE 6 from handling percentages that add up to exactly 100%.

## Using CSS Sprites in a Navigation Bar

The preceding examples use just text and background colors to style the links in an unordered list. Once you have styled the links as clickable buttons, there's nothing stopping you from adding a background image or using CSS sprites for rollover effects (see Chapter 8 for an explanation of CSS sprites).

There's a very basic example of using a CSS sprite for a navigation menu in sprite_nav.html. The styles for the unordered list are very similar to those used for the horizontal menu in the preceding example. The styles for the unordered list and list items look like this:

```
#nav {
    list-style-type: none;
    margin: 0;
    padding: 0;
    height: 2.3em;
    border-bottom: #5B4625 3px solid;
}
#nav li {
    width: 220px;
    height: 2.3em;
    margin: 0;
    float: left;
}
```

The bullets are removed from the unordered list by setting list-style-type to none, and its margins and padding are set to zero. The list is also given a fixed height. The list items are given a fixed width and are floated left, but they also need a fixed height in order to make room for the background images.

The styles for the links look like this:

```
#nav a {
    display: block;
    text-decoration: none;
    font-family: "Arial Black", Gadget, sans-serif;
```

```
    font-size: 18px;
    font-weight: bold;
    padding: 5px 5px 6px 35px;
    color: #900;
    background-image: url(images/sprite.png);
    background-repeat: no-repeat;
    background-position: left top;
}
#nav a:hover, #nav a:active, #nav a:focus {
    background-position: left -90px;
    color: #060;
}
```

The only significant difference from the previous examples is the addition of a background image. In the normal state the image's background-position is left top, but in the hover state it changes to left -90px. This moves the sprite 90px up to reveal a green ball in place of the red one (see Figure 10-18).

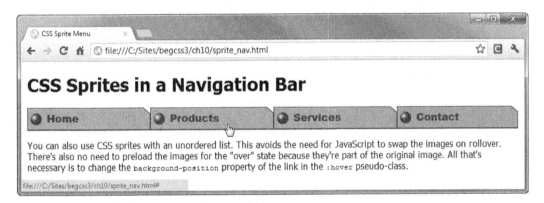

*Figure 10-18.* *You can use a CSS sprite to change the background on hover*

This is only a very basic example to demonstrate the principle. I hope it inspires you to experiment with designs of your own.

# Summary

There are just three CSS properties and one shorthand property for styling lists. The list-style-type property lets you change the symbol or number, or remove it completely. The symbols for unordered lists are limited to disc, circle, and square, but there's a much wider choice for ordered lists. Changing the type of number for nested lists improves readability. The list-style-position property determines whether the symbol or number should be outside the list item or tucked into the first line. And the list-style-image property lets you use a custom image for unordered lists. Unfortunately, there's no way of fine-tuning the position of the image, so it's sometimes preferable to use a background image instead.

It's become a common convention to convert an unordered list into a navigation menu by setting list-style-type to none to remove the bullets. The links inside the list items can be turned into clickable buttons by setting their display property to block, and giving them a background color. To create a horizontal menu, give the list items a defined width, and float them left. It's a good idea to give the unordered list a height to avoid alignment problems with subsequent elements. The list items also need a height if you plan to use background images or CSS sprites.

In the next chapter, we'll unravel the mysteries of CSS positioning and create a CSS drop-down menu without the need for JavaScript.

# CHAPTER 11

■ ■ ■

# Positioning Elements Precisely

In this chapter, I'm going to discuss *CSS positioning* (sometimes referred to as CSS-P), which not only removes an element from the flow of the document, but also allows you to position it with pinpoint accuracy. However, CSS positioning is rarely appropriate for laying out complete pages. Web design is different from print layout, where the dimensions of the page are immutable. Web pages need to be flexible.

The role of CSS positioning lies in creating effects, such as text disappearing behind a static image as you scroll the page and elements that overlap each other. It's also useful for creating tooltips and drop-down menus.

This chapter covers the following:

- Understanding the different types of positioning

- Understanding the significance of the containing block

- Fixing an element within the browser viewport

- Using a combination of relative and absolute positioning to prevent misalignment

- Setting the stacking order of positioned elements with z-index

- Creating tooltips and drop-down menus without JavaScript

- Using the clip property to mask an element

## How Does CSS Positioning Work?

The float property that you learned about in Chapter 7 takes an element out of the normal flow of the document, but its position is still controlled by where it appears in the markup. You can't arbitrarily float an image alongside text that's in a completely different part of the page.

CSS positioning takes a different approach by allowing you to remove an element from the flow of the document and place it wherever you want on the page. But there's a catch—and a pretty serious one at that. Once an element has been positioned, it ceases to interact with other elements on the page. So, you can't flow other content around it or use margins to separate it from other elements that remain in the document flow. The positioned element resides on a separate layer in front of the normal content. This introduces a third dimension that allows you to make elements overlap.

To position an element, you use the position property in combination with the other properties listed in Table 11-1.

***Table 11-1.*** *Properties Used for CSS Positioning*

| Property | Initial Value | Description |
|---|---|---|
| position | static | Controls how an element is positioned. When set to absolute or fixed, the element is removed completely from the normal flow of the document. When set to relative, the element is moved relative to its position in the normal flow, but a space is left where it would normally have been. The default value, static, means the element remains in the normal flow and is not positioned. |
| top | auto | Specifies the top offset of a positioned element. A positive value moves the element down. A negative value moves it up. |
| left | auto | Specifies the left offset of a positioned element. A positive value moves the element to the right. A negative value moves it to the left. |
| right | auto | Specifies the right offset of a positioned element. A positive value moves the element to the left. A negative value moves it to the right. |
| bottom | auto | Specifies the bottom offset of a positioned element. A positive value moves the element up. A negative value moves it down. |
| z-index | auto | Sets the stacking order of positioned elements. If elements are in the same stacking context, ones with a higher z-index appear in front. |
| clip | auto | Defines the area of an absolutely positioned element that remains visible. |

▦ **Caution**　The W3C's CSS Mobile Profile, which was drawn up before the rapid spread of smartphones and tablets, lists all the properties in Table 11-1 as being optional on a mobile device. Most smartphones and tablets do support CSS positioning, but you cannot rely on it completely when designing for mobile devices.

## Understanding the Different Types of Positioning

The position property requires one of the following values:

**absolute** This removes the element, including any child elements, completely from the flow of the document, and positions it at the specified offsets. If the element is nested inside another positioned element, the offsets are calculated with reference to the positioned parent. Otherwise, the offsets are calculated with reference to the page.

**fixed** This is similar to absolute, but the offsets are always calculated with reference to the browser viewport.

**relative** This moves the element relative to its normal position in the document flow, but without affecting the position of other elements.

**static** This leaves the element in the normal document flow.

The position property is not inherited, so you can use the inherit keyword if you want a child element to inherit the same type of positioning as its parent.

The only time you need to use static is if you want to override another style rule to make an element act like normal HTML. For example, in a print style sheet that inherits styles from a screen style sheet, it's normal to reset position to static for positioned elements to ensure they print out correctly (print style sheets are covered in Chapter 16).

■ **Note**  For an element to be considered positioned, its position property must be set to absolute, fixed, or relative. An element that has its position property set to static is not considered to be positioned.

## Identifying the Containing Block

Web pages are made up of boxes or blocks nested inside each other. In the normal flow of the document, the size and position of a nested element are determined by its parent—or *containing block*.

With CSS positioning, an element's containing block isn't necessarily the same as its parent. It depends on the value assigned to the position property:

- If an element's position is absolute, the containing block is the nearest *positioned* ancestor. In other words, the containing block *must* have a position of absolute, fixed, or relative. If no such element exists, the page is the containing block.

- If an element's position is fixed, the containing block is the browser viewport.

- If an element's position is relative, the containing block is the nearest block level ancestor—in other words, its parent.

■ **Tip**  Most of the confusion surrounding CSS positioning stems from not understanding the role of the containing block, particularly with regard to absolute positioning. Keep reading, and all should become clear.

## Setting the Offsets of a Positioned Element

You specify where an element is positioned by setting offsets from its containing block with the top, right, bottom, and left properties, all of which accept a length or a percentage. The offsets are calculated from the same sides of the element and its containing block. Figure 11-1 shows an example of a positioned element with the following offsets:

```
top: 100px;
left: 150px;
```

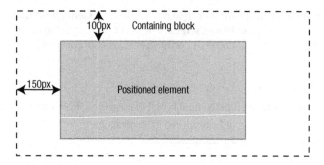

*Figure 11-1.* *The offsets of a positioned element are calculated from the sides of its containing block*

In this example, the top of the positioned element is 100px below the top of the containing block, and the element's left edge is 150px to the right of the containing block's left side.

If you don't specify an offset or you use the keyword auto, the element occupies the position it normally would, unless it's prevented from doing so by another offset. For example, if you don't set a value for the left offset, the left edge of the element is where it would be in the normal flow of the document. But a specific value for the right offset could move the entire element, shifting the left edge to a different position.

---

■ **Note**    Percentage values for top and bottom are relative to the containing block's height. Values for right and left are relative to the containing block's width. Unlike a background image, setting left to 50% doesn't center a positioned element. It positions the element's left edge halfway across the containing block.

---

Don't be confused by the expression "containing block." It doesn't constrain where the element can be displayed. In fact, it's quite common to display a positioned element outside its containing block by using negative offsets. Figure 11-2 shows an example of an element being positioned outside its containing block by setting top to -500px.

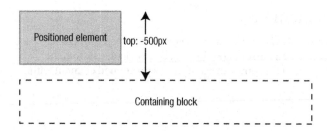

*Figure 11-2.* *Setting a negative offset moves the element out of its containing block*

No offset for left is set, so the left edge of the element remains aligned with the left edge of the containing block—in other words, where it would have been in the normal flow of the document.

# Fixing Elements Inside the Browser Window

When you set an element's position property to fixed, the offsets tell the browser where to position the element in relation to the browser window. When you scroll the page, the element remains where you placed it, but other content scrolls behind. If you don't set a right or left offset, the element remains in the same position horizontally as it would be normally. How this works is best seen through an example.

## EXERCISE: CREATING A FIXED HEADER AND MENU

In this exercise, you'll make the header and horizontal navigation menu of a page remain onscreen while the rest of the page is scrolled. Use as your starting point fixed_begin.html and styles/fixed_begin.css in the ch11 folder. The finished files are fixed_end.html and styles/fixed_end.css.

1.  Add the position property to the #header style rule, and set its value to fixed.

```
#header {
    background-image: url(../images/yachts_banner.jpg);
    background-repeat: no-repeat;
    height: 127px;
    position: fixed;
}
```

2.  Save the style sheet, load the page into a browser, and start scrolling. As Figure 11-3 shows, the header isn't displayed full width, and it's pushed away from the top, but it remains in the same position with the other content scrolling behind.

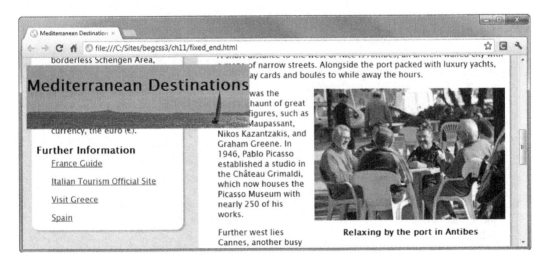

*Figure 11-3.* *The header needs adjusting, but it remains in a fixed position while the other content scrolls*

3.  Scroll back to the top of the page, and use the browser's developer tools to inspect the nav unordered list, which is used as the horizontal menu. As Figure 11-4 shows, the gap between the header and the top of the browser window is identical to the 15px top margin of the unordered list.

241

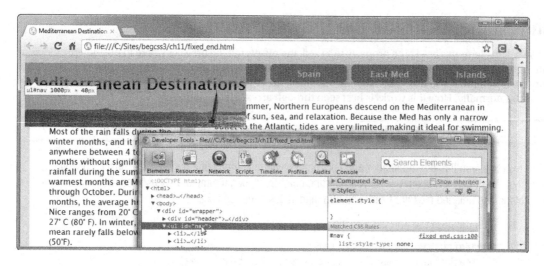

**Figure 11-4.** *The menu's top margin is pushing the header away from the top of the browser window*

4. Resize the width of the browser window. The horizontal relationship between the header and sidebar remains unchanged. This is because no offsets have been specified. So, although the header has been removed from the flow of the document, it has been fixed in the same position it would occupy normally. The horizontal position is exactly what you want, but you need to eliminate the effect of the top margin. You also need to fix the width.

5. Set the top offset to zero, and give the header the same width and max-width as the wrapper <div>.

```
#header {
    background-image: url(../images/yachts_banner.jpg);
    background-repeat: no-repeat;
    height: 127px;
    position: fixed;
    top: 0;
    width: 100%;
    max-width: 1000px;
}
```

6. Save the style sheet, and test the page again in a browser. As Figure 11-5 shows, the header now looks fine, but the menu and top of the page content are hidden behind it.

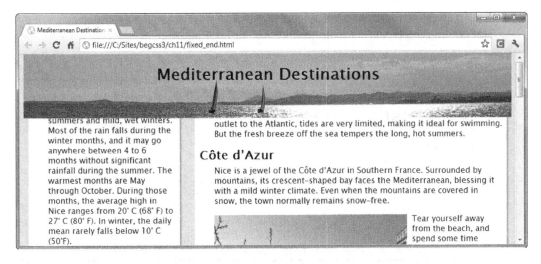

**Figure 11-5.** *The header has been fixed, but the top of the page is now hidden*

7. To fix the horizontal menu below the header, you need to add `position` to the #nav style rule, and set its value to `fixed`. The header is 127px high, so the `top` offset for the menu needs to be the same. You also need to apply the same `width` and `max-width` values as in step 5. The amended rule looks like this:

```
#nav {
    list-style-type: none;
    margin: 15px 0 0 0;
    padding: 0;
    height: 40px;
    position: fixed;
    top: 127px;
    width: 100%;
    max-width: 1000px;
}
```

8. The menu is now in position, but the main content is still hidden. To bring it into view, you need to change the top margin in the #main style rule. It's currently 15px, so you need to add the height of the menu (40px), the menu's top margin (15px), and the menu's `top` offset to get the new amount (197px). Change the value like this:

```
#main {
    width: 64%;
    margin: 197px 1% 10px 35%;
    background-color: #FFF;
    padding: 18px 0;
}
```

9. If you save the style sheet and test the page now, the header and menu remain fixed onscreen in all modern browsers. However, IE 6 doesn't support fixed positioning. Although IE 7 does, it has problems with displaying the sidebar correctly. To

eliminate these problems, reset the `position` property to `static` in an Internet Explorer conditional comment in the head of the HTML page like this:

```
<!--[if lte IE 7]>

<style>
#header, #nav {
    position: static;
}
#aside, #main {
    margin-top: 15px;
}
</style>
<![endif]-->
```

The Internet Explorer conditional comment is used only by IE 7 and earlier. By resetting the `position` property to `static`, older versions of IE treat the page as it was at the beginning of the exercise.

■ **Caution** Fixed positioning partially obscures the browser viewport. Make sure your content remains accessible, particularly on small screens. Check `http://caniuse.com/css-fixed` for up-to-date information on support in mobile browsers.

# Using Relative Positioning

Relative positioning moves an element relative to its normal position in the document flow, but without affecting any nonpositioned elements. The second paragraph in relative.html demonstrates the basic principle by moving it 50px down and 100px to the right with the following style rule:

```
#rel {
    background-color: #999;
    padding: 10px;
    border: 1px solid #333;
    position: relative;
    top: 50px;
    left: 100px;
}
```

Figure 11-6 shows the result. The relatively positioned paragraph obscures the beginning of the next paragraph, but leaves a hole where it would normally have been.

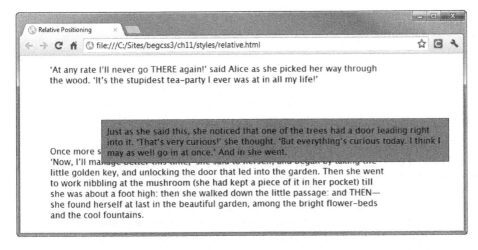

**Figure 11-6.** *Relative positioning doesn't affect the position of surrounding elements*

Admittedly, this isn't very useful. Strange though it may sound, one of the most common uses of relative positioning is to leave the element exactly where it was in the first place. The reason for doing so is to create a containing block for an absolutely positioned element nested inside. Because a relatively positioned element remains within the normal document flow, it moves in harmony with other elements if the page is reflowed for any reason, such as the browser being resized. Using it as the containing block for an absolutely positioned one keeps the two elements in sync, preventing the absolutely positioned element from moving out of alignment with the rest of the page.

# Using Absolute Positioning

There are two important differences between absolute and fixed positioning, namely:

- The offsets in fixed positioning are always calculated with reference to the browser viewport. With absolute positioning, the offsets are calculated with reference to the element's containing block—sometimes this is the page, but not always.

- With fixed positioning, the element never moves. An absolutely positioned element is anchored to its containing block, and it scrolls with the rest of the page.

To demonstrate the importance of the containing block, absolute_page.html and absolute_relative.html both contain the following HTML markup:

```
<div class="figure floatleft"><img src="images/nice_seafront.jpg" alt="Nice seafront"
width="400" height="266"><img src="images/destination.png" width="150" height="118"
    alt="Great destination">
    <div class="figcaption">Nice seafront from la Colline du Château</div>
</div>
```

The outer <div> contains two images. The styles in absolute_page.html use an attribute selector to position destination.png like this:

```
img[src$="destination.png"] {
    position: absolute;
    left: 70px;
    top: 100px;
}
```

This sets the image's position property to absolute, removing it from the normal flow of the document. The left and top properties set the image's offsets to 70px and 100px, respectively. Although the image is nested inside the outer <div>, neither the <div> nor any of its ancestors is positioned. Consequently, the page is the containing block for destination.png. The left edge of the image is 70px from the left side of the page, and the top of the image is 100px from the top of the page.

The offsets were designed for a browser window that's 800px wide. At that size, destination.png is correctly superimposed over the top-left corner of the larger image, as shown in Figure 11-7.

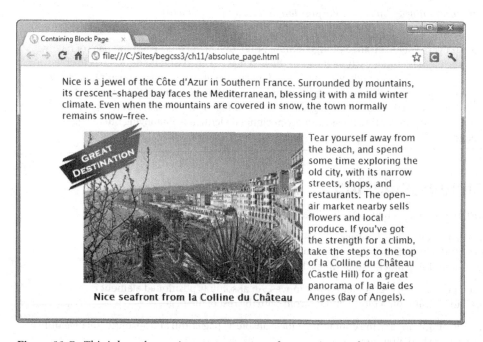

**Figure 11-7.** *This is how the two images are meant to be superimposed*

However, what you see in the browser depends entirely on how wide the browser window is when you view the page. If the browser window is wider than 800px, destination.png appears to move (see Figure 11-8). In fact, the image is in exactly the same position 100px from the top of the page and 70px from the left. However, the wider browser viewport results in the nonpositioned elements being recentered.

**Figure 11-8.** *The absolutely positioned image is no longer superimposed on the other one*

To prevent the two images from going their separate ways, the outer <div> also needs to be positioned, so that it can become the containing block for destination.png. You do this by making the outer <div> *relatively* positioned, and not setting any offsets. It remains in its original place in the normal flow of the document, but acts as the containing block for the absolutely positioned element.

The styles in absolute_relative.html add the position property to the figure class, and set it to relative. The left and top offsets of destination.png are also adjusted to move the image in relation to its new containing block like this:

```
.figure {
    width: 400px;
    position: relative;
}
img[src$="destination.png"] {
    position: absolute;
    left: -40px;
    top: -20px;
}
```

If you test absolute_relative.html in a browser, it looks identical to Figure 11-7. Even if you resize the browser window or scroll the page, the two images remain locked together.

---

■ **Note**   This technique works in all browsers including IE 6. However, IE 6 doesn't understand attribute selectors. If you need to use this technique in IE 6, give the absolutely positioned element an ID and use an ID selector.

---

You can also use a fixed or absolutely positioned element to create the containing block. For example, fixed_absolute.html is an adaptation of fixed_end.html from the exercise earlier in this chapter. It has a search form nested in the header <div> like this:

```
<div id="header">
    <h1>Mediterranean Destinations</h1>
    <form name="form1" method="get" action="#">
        <label for="search">Search:</label>
        <input type="search" name="search" id="search">
        <input type="submit" name="go" id="go" value="Go">
    </form>
</div>
```

The header <div> uses fixed positioning, so it acts as the form's containing block. The form is then positioned by the following style rule:

```
#header form{
    position: absolute;
    right: 5px;
    bottom: 1px;
}
```

As Figure 11-9 shows, this positions the form in the bottom-right corner of the header. Because the header uses fixed positioning, the form remains onscreen in the same position when the page is scrolled.

***Figure 11-9.*** *The search form is fixed in position using a combination of fixed and absolute positioning*

As in fixed_end.html, an Internet Explorer conditional comment in the <head> of the HTML page resets the position property of the header <div> to static to overcome problems with IE 6 and IE 7. This makes the page the form's containing block, so you need to change the offsets to keep the form inside the header. The following style rule inside the conditional comment resets the right and bottom offsets to auto, and sets top to 100px:

```
#header form {
    top: 100px;
    right: auto;
    bottom: auto;
    padding-left: 10px;
    color: #FFF;
}
```

These changes locate the search form at the bottom-left of the header, as shown in Figure 11-10.

***Figure 11-10.*** *The form is on the opposite side in older versions of Internet Explorer*

Because the page is the containing block for older versions of IE, leaving the `right` and `bottom` offsets unchanged would position the form at the bottom-right of the page. However, you can exploit the position the form would normally occupy on the left of its parent element, and then offset it from the top of the page. This results in the form being on the opposite side of the header, and it scrolls with the rest of the page, but it's an acceptable compromise.

# Setting the Stacking Order with z-index

Positioned elements are displayed on an independent layer in front of other elements. As the examples in the preceding section show, this makes it possible to overlap nonpositioned elements. When two positioned elements overlap, the last one in the underlying HTML is displayed in front.

To show what this means, z-index1.html contains two relatively positioned `<div>` elements with the IDs verse1 and verse2. The verse2 `<div>` comes after verse1 in the HTML markup. The styles that position them look like this:

```
#verse1, #verse2 {
    position: relative;
    padding: 20px;
    border: 2px black solid;
    width: 280px;
}
#verse1 {
    top: 20px;
    left: 30px;
    background-color: #FF6;
}
#verse2 {
    top: -10px;
    left: 200px;
    background-color: #6CF;
}
```

The effect of these styles is to move verse1 20px down from its normal position, and verse2 10px up. As a result, the two `<div>` elements overlap each other. Because verse2 comes after verse1 in the HTML, verse2 overlaps the bottom-right corner of verse1, as shown in Figure 11-11.

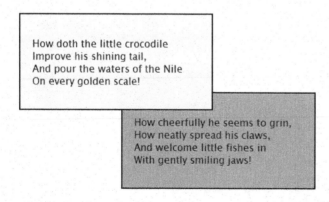

How doth the little crocodile
Improve his shining tail,
And pour the waters of the Nile
On every golden scale!

How cheerfully he seems to grin,
How neatly spread his claws,
And welcome little fishes in
With gently smiling jaws!

**Figure 11-11.** *The second <div> overlaps the first because of the order they appear in the HTML*

However, you can control the stacking order of positioned elements by setting the z-index property, which takes an integer as its value. The styles in z-index2.html set the z-index of verse1 to 1 like this:

```
#verse1 {
    top: 20px;
    left: 30px;
    background-color: #FF6;
    z-index: 1;
}
```

No change is made to the #verse2 styles, so its z-index is the default auto. An explicit value for z-index is considered higher than auto, so the first <div> now overlaps the second one (see Figure 11-12).

How doth the little crocodile
Improve his shining tail,
And pour the waters of the Nile
On every golden scale!

How cheerfully he seems to grin,
How neatly spread his claws,
And welcome little fishes in
With gently smiling jaws!

**Figure 11-12.** *Setting the z-index property on the first < div > brings it to the front*

In z-index3.html, the z-index property is added to the #verse2 style rule, and is set to 1. This produces the same result as Figure 11-11. When overlapping positioned elements have the same z-index, the one that comes last is displayed in front. This is the same as setting no z-index at all.

In z-index4.html, #verse1 has a z-index of 2, and #verse2 has a z-index of 1. The higher value wins, so the first <div> is displayed in front, as in Figure 11-12.

---

■ **Tip** There's no need to use consecutive numbers for z-index. Some designers use increments of 10 or 100 to avoid renumbering if they need to add a new element later. The general rule is that the element with the higher z-index is displayed in front. However, z-index affects only positioned elements. Positioned elements always appear in front of nonpositioned ones if they overlap.

---

## Understanding the Stacking Context

From time to time, pleas for help appear in online forums from designers who can't understand why a positioned element won't come to the front no matter how high they set the z-index. A positioned element's containing block not only determines where the offsets are calculated from, but it also establishes the *stacking context*, which restricts how z-index is applied. Put simply, it doesn't matter how high you set an element's z-index, what matters is the z-index of the containing block.

In stacking_context.html, two <div> elements have been nested inside the verse1 and verse2 <div> elements from the examples in the preceding section like this:

```
<div id="verse1">
    <p>How doth the little crocodile. . . </p>
    <div id="destination"><img src="images/destination.png" width="150" height="118"
        alt="Great destination"></div>
</div>
<div id="verse2">
    <p>How cheerfully he seems to grin. . . </p>
    <div id="flower"><img src="images/flower2.png" width="80" height="60" alt="Flower"></div>
</div>
```

The styles for the nested <div> elements look like this:

```
#destination {
    position: absolute;
    left: 340px;
    top: 0;
    z-index: 5;
}
#flower {
    position: absolute;
    left: 200px;
    top: -55px;
    z-index: 2000;
}
```

The flower <div> has a z-index of 2000. Yet—as Figure 11-13 shows—it's displayed behind the destination <div>, which has a z-index of only 5.

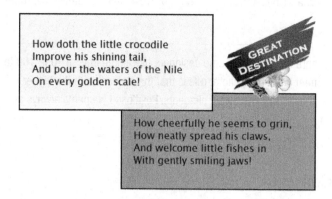

*Figure 11-13. The stacking context takes precedence over the value of z-index*

The reason the flower isn't displayed in front is because its containing block has a lower z-index than the containing block of the destination banner. It doesn't matter how high you make an element's z-index, it's the z-index of its containing block that determines the ultimate stacking order.

# Using CSS Positioning for Tooltips and Menus

When used in combination, relative and absolute positioning open up possibilities for dynamic techniques that previously relied on JavaScript. For example, you can nest an absolutely positioned element inside a relatively positioned one and hide its content by moving it offscreen or setting its display property to none. When the user hovers over the relatively positioned element, you can reveal the absolutely positioned one by changing its offsets or by setting its display property to block.

## Creating Styled Tooltips

Browsers normally display the text of the title attribute as a tooltip when hovering over an image or link, but there's no way to style automatically generated tooltips. Using an absolutely positioned element gives you full control over how a tooltip looks.

## Adding a Styled Tooltip to an Image

Images are inline elements, so to add a tooltip to an image, make its nearest containing block relatively positioned. You can then nest a paragraph for the tooltip inside the same block, and make it absolutely positioned. Use the absolutely positioned paragraph's offsets to hide it, and reset them when the user hovers over the containing block.

Figure 11-14 shows a styled tooltip that is displayed when hovering over the image in tooltips.html.

# Monaco and Monte Carlo

The casino also houses a theater suitable for opera and ballet.

Monte Carlo casino

Close to the Italian border lies the tiny city state of Monaco, home to the rich and famous. Surrounded on three sides by France and by the Mediterranean on the fourth, it's the world's second smallest country by size. Monaco is a constitutional monarchy that has been ruled by the House of Grimaldi with only brief interruptions since the thirteenth century.

Monaco is perhaps best known for the Formula 1 Grand Prix. The race, normally held in May, roars through the narrow streets and tight corners. Monaco is also renowned for the Monte Carlo Casino. The casino was established by the House of Grimaldi in the mid-nineteenth century as a means of saving the ruling household from bankruptcy. It wasn't immediately successful, but gained great publicity in 1873 when Joseph Jagger became the man who "broke the bank at Monte Carlo." The bank was the amount of money kept on the roulette table by the croupier. Jagger was the first to discover a bias in one of the roulette wheels and capitalize on it.

*Figure 11-14. A styled tooltip is displayed when hovering over the image*

The `<div>` that contains the image and caption has been given an ID, and the paragraph for the tooltip is nested inside the `<div>` like this:

```
<div class="floatleft" id="casino"><img src="images/casino.jpg" alt="Casino at Monte Carlo"
width="266" height="400" class="shadow">
    <p>The casino also houses a theater suitable for opera and ballet.</p>
    <div class="figcaption">Monte Carlo casino</div>
</div>
```

The styles for the `<div>` and tooltip look like this:

```
#casino {
    position: relative;
}
#casino p {
    position: absolute;
    top: 60px;
    left: -9999px;
    font-size: 14px;
    width: 100px;
    padding: 10px;
```

```
    background-color: #FFF;
    border-radius: 15px;
}
#casino:hover p {
    left: 140px;
}
```

The casino `<div>` is relatively positioned with no offsets, leaving the `<div>` in its normal position in the document flow, while creating a containing block for the paragraph, which is absolutely positioned. The top offset of the paragraph is set to 60px, which moves it down from the top of the image by the same amount. However, the left offset is set to a very high negative value, which moves it offscreen, but leaves the content accessible to screen readers for the blind. When the user hovers over the casino `<div>`, #casino:hover p resets the paragraph's left offset to 140px

IE 6 and IE 7 support the :hover pseudo-class only on links. If you need to support IE 6 and IE 7, wrap the image in a dummy link and add an empty title attribute to the `<img>` tag like this (the code is in tooltips_ie6-7.html):

```
<a href="#"><img src="images/casino.jpg" alt="Casino at Monte Carlo" width="266"
height="400" class="shadow" title=""></a>
```

The empty title attribute is needed to prevent older versions of IE incorrectly displaying the alt text as an unstyled tooltip. Also, you need to add the following styles to prevent a blue border surrounding the image, and to stop the cursor from turning into a hand:

```
a img {
    border: none;
}
#casino a:hover {
    cursor: default;
}
```

---

■ **Caution** Although screen readers should be able to access the tooltip paragraph, it's not accessible to anyone using the keyboard to navigate around a site. Don't use this technique for essential information.

---

## Adding a Styled Tooltip to a Link

The principle behind adding a styled tooltip to a link is exactly the same as for an image, but the text of the tooltip needs to be nested inside the link. The second paragraph in tooltips.html contains a link with a nested `<span>` like this:

```
<a href="http://www.formula1.com/">Formula 1 Grand Prix<span>Most F1 races are held on
specially constructed circuits. But Monaco is one of a handful of F1 street circuits that
also include Valencia, Melbourne, and Singapore.</span></a>
```

The styles for the link and tooltip look like this:

```
a[href$="formula1.com/"] {
    position: relative;
}
```

```
a[href$="formula1.com/"] span {
    position: absolute;
    left: -9000px;
    text-decoration: none;
    display: block;
    width: 250px;
    background-color: #006;
    color: #FFF;
    padding: 10px;
}
a[href$="formula1.com/"]:hover span {
    left: 20px;
    top: -160px;
}
```

Figure 11-15 shows how the contents of the <span> are displayed when hovering over the link. This is an example of an absolutely positioned element being displayed outside its containing block.

# Monaco and Monte Carlo

**Monte Carlo casino**

Close to the Italian border lies the tiny city state of Monaco, home to the rich and famous. Surrounded on three sides by France and by the Mediterranean on th... sm... co... ru... br... ce...

Most F1 races are held on specially constructed circuits. But Monaco is one of a handful of F1 street circuits that also include Valencia, Melbourne, and Singapore.

Monaco is perhaps best known for the Formula 1 Grand Prix. The race, normally held in May, roars through the narrow streets and tight corners. Monaco is also renowned for the Monte Carlo Casino. The casino was established by the House of Grimaldi in the mid-nineteenth century as a means of saving the ruling household from bankruptcy. It wasn't immediately successful, but gained great publicity in 1873 when Joseph Jagger became the man who "broke the bank at Monte Carlo." The bank was the amount of money kept on the roulette table by the croupier. Jagger was the first to discover a bias in one of the roulette wheels and capitalize on it.

*Figure 11-15.* *The tooltip is displayed above the link*

Instead of using an ID, the styles use an attribute selector to identify the link. As in the previous example, the containing block is created by setting the position of the outer element—in this case, the link—to relative. Then the position of the nested element (the <span>) is set to absolute, and it's hidden offscreen by specifying a high negative left offset. It's also necessary to set text-decoration to none to remove the underline from the <span>, which is still part of the link. Finally, the offsets are reset when the user hovers over the link.

---

■ **Tip** Although a[href$="formula1.com/"]:hover span looks complicated, it's basically the descendant selector a:hover span. The [href$="formula1.com/"] qualifies the a type selector to identify a specific link using the end of its href attribute.

---

Although the text in the tooltip is part of the link, it's not clickable because the tooltip disappears as soon as you move off the link in the main text. However, because it's a link, you can make it accessible to keyboard navigation by adding the :focus pseudo-class to the selector that displays the tooltip like this:

```
a[href$="formula1.com/"]:hover span,
a[href$="formula1.com/"]:focus span {
    left: 20px;
    top: -160px;
}
```

When the user tabs through the links in the page, the tooltip pops up as soon as the associated link gets focus. It disappears as soon as the user tabs away from the link.

---

■ **Note** The preceding example works in all browsers except IE 6. In IE 7, the tooltip appears on hover, but not when you tab to the link because IE 7 doesn't support the :focus pseudo-class.

---

## Problems with Touch Screens

The styled tooltips in the preceding two examples work well on desktop computers, but are less satisfactory on touch screen devices. If you use the :hover pseudo-class on an element, smartphones and tablets usually display the appropriate styles when the element is tapped. So, tapping the image of the casino causes the tooltip to appear over the image. But the tooltip doesn't go away unless you tap another element that uses the :hover pseudo-class. In some circumstances, this might not matter. It could even be treated as a feature in a children's site, where the user is encouraged to reveal hidden information. However, in most cases, it's likely to be annoying.

The link tooltip presents a slightly different problem. On Android, the link works as normal, and the tooltip is never displayed. But on iOS, tapping the link once displays the tooltip. You need to tap it twice to go to the link's destination.

Because touch devices are increasingly used to access websites, you need to take such problems into consideration. There are several approaches you can adopt:

- Don't use the :hover and :focus pseudo-classes to display styled tooltips.
- Use media queries (see Chapter 17) to hide the tooltip or display the information in a different way on small screens.
- Use JavaScript to dismiss the tooltips using touch events.

The HTML in tooltips_touch.html has been modified to add the ID `tooltip1` to the paragraph nested in the casino `<div>`. Also, the `<span>` in the link has been given the ID `f1`. The following script has been added at the bottom of the page:

```
<script>
var tip1=document.getElementById('tooltip1'),
    f1=document.getElementById('f1');
tip1.addEventListener('touchstart', closeTooltip, false);
f1.addEventListener('touchstart', closeTooltip, false);
function closeTooltip(e) {
    e.preventDefault();
    e.stopPropagation();
    var target=e.target.id;
    target.style.left="-9999px";
}
</script>
```

The script binds a function called `closeTooltip` to the `touchstart` JavaScript event on both tooltips. The function identifies which tooltip has been tapped, and sets its `left` offset to -9999px, effectively hiding it. This neatly solves the problem on iOS. Unfortunately, it doesn't work on Android, even though Android supports the `touchstart` event.

## Creating a CSS Drop-down Menu

Navigation menus are frequently created by styling unordered lists, and a submenu is another list nested inside a list item. So, if the list item is relatively positioned, you can hide the submenu and display it when hovering over its parent. Before showing you how to do it, I need to introduce a new selector.

## Introducing the Child Selector

A *child selector* matches an element that is the child of another—in other words, it must be at the next level of the HTML hierarchy, and no deeper. Take the following markup:

```
<blockquote>
    <p>To be, or<em>not</em>to be. . . </p>
</blockquote>
```

In this example, the `<em>` tag is a child of `<p>`, but not of `<blockquote>`. The `<em>` tag is a descendant of the `<blockquote>`, but not one of its children.

To create a child selector, add the greater than sign (>) between the parent and child selectors. For example, the following child selector targets all paragraphs that are direct children of a `<blockquote>` element and renders them in italic font:

```
blockquote>p {
    font-style: italic;
}
```

However, the following selector has no effect on the `<em>` tag, because it's not a direct child:

```
/* Doesn't work */
blockquote > em {
    font-style: normal;
}
```

To style the `<em>` tag in this example, you need to use a descendant selector like this:

```
/* Works */
blockquote em {
    font-style: normal;
}
```

Alternatively, chain child selectors like this:

```
/* Also works */
blockquote > p > em {
    font-style: normal;
}
```

---

■ **Tip**   When elements are nested only one level deep, it's marginally more efficient to use a child selector. However, the disadvantage is that your style stops working if changes to the HTML structure result in the target element(s) being nested at a deeper level. It's best to reserve child selectors for cases where you want to exclude elements at a deeper level. All browsers except IE 6 support child selectors.

---

With the help of child selectors, you can apply styles that affect only the direct child of the list item that currently has focus or is being hovered over. This makes it possible to reveal a hidden submenu only when hovering over its parent, and hide it again when the cursor moves away. This technique works in all browsers except IE 6. However, it raises some important accessibility issues, which I'll discuss after showing you how to style the drop-down menu.

## EXERCISE: USING CHILD SELECTORS TO DISPLAY SUBMENUS

This exercise shows how to style a series of nested unordered lists as a drop-down menu. Each list item is relatively positioned, so it acts as a containing block for a submenu in a nested list. The submenus are absolutely positioned and hidden by setting their `display` property to `none`. Hovering over a list item that has a submenu changes the `display` property of the child list to `block`, revealing it.

Use menu_begin.html and styles/menu_begin.css in the ch11 folder as your starting point. The finished files are menu_end.html and styles/menu_end.css.

1. View the unstyled menu in a browser. It's a series of links in nested unordered lists, as shown in Figure 11-16. The top-level list has the ID `nav`.

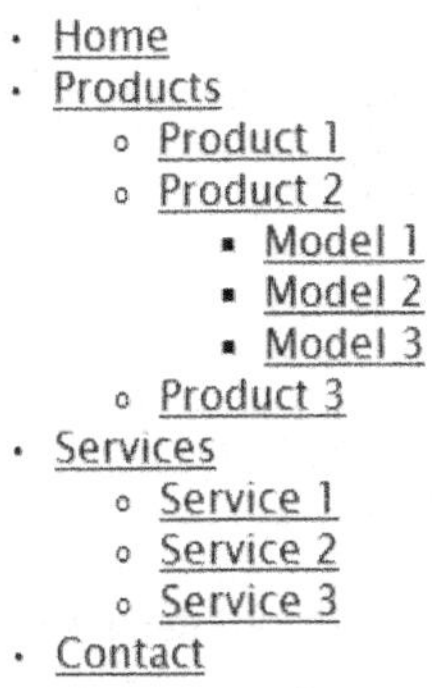

- Home
- Products
  - Product 1
  - Product 2
    - Model 1
    - Model 2
    - Model 3
  - Product 3
- Services
  - Service 1
  - Service 2
  - Service 3
- Contact

**Figure 11-16.** *The submenus are links in nested unordered lists*

2. Begin styling the menu by removing the bullets and margins from the list items and floating them left. This is the same technique as used in Chapter 10. However, add some padding to the bottom of the list items to prevent a submenu from snapping shut as you move the cursor from the top-level menu. Also set the list items' position to relative to create containing blocks for the submenus. Add the following style rule to the style sheet:

```
#nav li {
    list-style-type: none;
    margin: 0;
    padding-bottom: 20px;
    float: left;
    position: relative;
}
```

3. Next style all the links by setting their display property to block, giving them a background color, and formatting the text like this:

```
#nav a {
    display: block;
    padding: 10px 20px;
    margin: 0;
    border-left: #CCC 1px solid;
    color: #e7e5e5;
    background-color: #736C56;
    font-weight: bold;
    text-decoration: none;
}
```

4. Hide all the nested lists by setting their display property to none. I'll explain later why I'm using this technique rather than moving them offscreen. Use a descendant selector to target all nested lists:

```
#nav ul {
    display: none;
}
```

5.  You want a submenu to display only when the mouse pointer is hovering over its parent list item, so you need to use a child selector. If you use a descendant selector instead, nested submenus at each level will be displayed. A child selector ensures that only the direct child is affected. Add the following rule to the style sheet:

```
#nav li:hover > ul {
    display: block;
}
```

6.  Save the style sheet, and test the menu in a browser. Mouse over list items that have submenus to verify that they're displayed. Don't worry about the menu breaking up, as shown in Figure 11-17. You'll fix that next.

**Figure 11-17.** *The child submenu appears when you hover over its parent list item*

7.  You need to prevent the list items in the nested lists from floating. Also remove any margins and padding, and add a top border with the following descendant selector, which affects all nested lists:

```
#nav ul li {
    float: none;
    margin: 0;
    padding: 0;
    border-top: #CCC 1px solid;
}
```

8.  To display the nested lists in the correct position, you need to make them absolutely positioned relative to their containing block. Setting the `left` offset to 0 aligns them to the left edge of the parent list item, and setting the `top` offset to 40px is the right amount to position the first-level submenus directly below the main menu. To prevent the submenu snapping shut prematurely in IE 7, you also need to give it a background color. Update the #nav ul style rule like this:

```
#nav ul {
    display: none;
    margin: 0;
    padding: 0;
    position: absolute;
    left: 0;
    top: 40px;
```

```
        width: 150px;
        /* Fix for IE 7 */
        background-color: #FFF;
    }
```

9.  The `top` and `left` offsets in the `#nav ul` style rule affect all nested lists. As a result, a submenu nested at the next level will be left-aligned with its parent list item, superimposing one submenu on top of the other. To fix this, add a new style rule that applies to submenus nested at least two levels deep inside the main menu. Set the `left` offset to the same value as the width in the previous style rule, and adjust the `top` offset like this:

```
#nav ul ul {
    left: 150px;
    top: 5px;
}
```

10. Save the style sheet, and test the menu again. The nested menus should now display correctly, as shown in Figure 11-18. They also display when tapped on a touch screen.

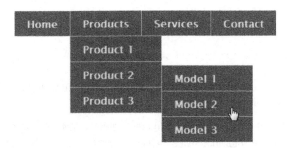

**Figure 11-18.**  *The submenus now display correctly when you mouse over them*

11. All that remains now is to fix the colors of the menu items. First, create a style rule for links in the list item that currently is being hovered over or has focus. The rule needs to target only links that are direct children, so you need to use a child selector like this:

```
#nav li:hover > a {
    background-color: #A38E6D;
    color: #444;
}
```

12. Save the styles, and test the menu again. Notice that the different colors are applied not only to the link currently being hovered over, but also to the link in each parent list item, as shown in Figure 11-19. This is because the `:hover` pseudo-class is applied to the list item rather than the link. Even though the mouse pointer is over the last item of the second-level submenu in Figure 11-19, the submenu is nested

inside the *Product 2* list item, which in turn is nested inside the *Products* list item. So, in effect, the mouse is also hovering over the parent list items. As a result, the child selector targets the links that are direct children of each list item. This concept can be difficult to grasp, but seeing is believing.

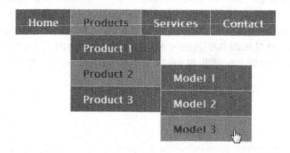

***Figure 11-19.*** *The child selector styles the links in the parent list items, too*

13. Make the top-level menu accessible to keyboard navigation by amending the selector of the style rule you created in step 11 like this:

```
#nav li:hover > a, #nav a:focus {
    background-color: #A38E6D;
    color: #444;
}
```

14. Save the styles, and test the menu again by pressing the Tab key. The top level links change color when you tab to them.

15. To give the submenus different colors from the main menu, add the following styles. The first one is a descendant selector that styles the links in their normal state. The second one is an adaptation of the child selector in step 11. It sets the colors for both the link currently being hovered over and the parent list item.

```
#nav ul a {
    background-color: #8C3A40;
}
#nav ul li:hover > a {
    background-color: #C2644F;
}
```

16. The final touch is to tidy up the borders on the first link in the main menu, the first list item in a deeply nested menu, and on submenu links. Add the following style rule to the style sheet:

```
#nav li:first-child a, #nav ul ul li:first-child, #nav ul a {
    border: none;
}
```

17. Save the styles, and test the menu again. It should now look like Figure 11-20.

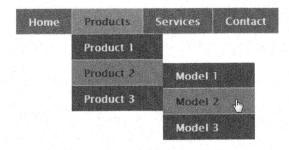

***Figure 11-20.*** *The submenus now have their own colors*

This exercise demonstrates the power of CSS selectors. The HTML markup contains only one ID for the top-level unordered list. There are no classes. All the styling is achieved through descendant selectors, child selectors, and pseudo-classes. This means you can edit the menu items, and the correct styles will be applied automatically without the need for extra markup.

■ **Tip** The menu items are floated. Don't forget to use the clear property on the first element after the menu to prevent it from moving up alongside.

## Assessing the Accessibility of CSS Drop-down Menus

CSS drop-down menus work very well in modern browsers—at least if you're navigating with a mouse. What most online tutorials forget to mention is that pure CSS menus aren't always ideal from the point of view of accessibility. On Android touch screens, tapping a menu item takes you directly to the link's destination without opening a submenu. On iOS, tapping a menu item once opens a submenu, if one exists. To get to the link's destination, you need to tap a menu item twice.

This type of menu also presents problems for keyboard navigation. The preceding exercise sets the display property of submenus to none. This was done deliberately to prevent the links being accessed by anyone using a keyboard to navigate. If you hide the submenus offscreen by giving them a large negative offset—as in the tooltip examples earlier in this chapter—the links remain in the browser's tab order. So, someone using keyboard navigation would continue tabbing through the submenus without seeing the links. Although it's possible to use the :focus pseudo-class to display a submenu when tabbing to a top level link, there's currently no way to match the parent of an element with a CSS selector. As a result, the submenu disappears as soon as you tab into it. This makes the menu virtually unusable for anyone relying on keyboard navigation. Consequently, it's better to hide the submenu links entirely.

■ **Tip** The draft CSS4 Selectors module—yes, it already exists—proposes a method of selecting a parent element. However, the syntax is subject to change.

Given these constraints, you need to do the following to make a CSS drop-down menu accessible:

- Link to real pages in the top-level menu. Although using dummy links as the trigger for submenus works better on Android, it makes the menu inaccessible to keyboard navigation.

- In the landing page from each top-level link, create a secondary navigation menu—such as the vertical navigation bar in Chapter 10—that replicates the links in the submenu.

It seems we'll have to wait a little longer before CSS drop-down menus become truly accessible.

# Masking an Absolutely Positioned Element

The clip property creates a mask through which part of an element is displayed. It works only with absolutely positioned elements, and the only shape you can use is a rectangle.

You define the area you want to display by supplying four offsets in clockwise order from the top. All the offsets are calculated from the top left of the element you want to mask, and each must be defined as a length. You can't use percentages. Figure 11-21 shows how the offsets were measured for the masked image in clip.html.

*Figure 11-21.* *The offsets are calculated from the top left of the element you want to mask*

The image is masked using the following styles:

```
#clipped {
    position: absolute;
    clip: rect(60px, 290px, 135px, 210px);
    /* Other styles omitted */
}
```

As a result only the water tower is displayed, as shown in Figure 11-22.

# Guess Where

This is part of a famous landmark in North America. To reveal where it is, click the image, and hold down the mouse button.

***Figure 11-22.*** *The mask displays only the clipped rectangle*

To reveal the rest of the image, the styles in clip.html use the `:active` pseudo-class to reset the value of clip to the full size of the image like this:

```
#clipped:active {
    clip: rect(0, 500px, 375px, 0);
}
```

The right and bottom values are the same as the image's width and height respectively. The top and left values are both 0 because nothing is to be clipped from the top or left.

If you click and hold the mouse button, most browsers reveal the whole image (see Figure 11-23).

# Guess Where

This is part of a famous landmark in North America. To reveal where it is, click the image, and hold down the mouse button.

***Figure 11-23.*** *In most modern browsers, holding down the mouse button expands the clip rectangle*

Although Internet Explorer supports the clip property, it appears not to regard clicking the image as triggering the :active pseudo-class. There's also a bug in IE 6 and IE 7, which don't accept the offsets as a comma-separated list. For compatibility, all other mainstream browsers accept leaving out the commas. But unless you need to use clip with older versions of Internet Explorer, I recommend using the correct syntax.

---

■ **Note**    The styles in clip.html animate the clip property using a CSS transition. Using CSS transforms and transitions is covered in Chapter 20.

---

# Summary

CSS positioning gives you control over the placement of an element by setting the position property and specifying how far the sides should be offset from the element's containing block by using the top, right, bottom, and left properties. There are three types of positioning—fixed, relative, and absolute.

Fixed positioning, which is supported by all desktop browsers except IE 6, anchors an element inside the browser viewport. Once an element is fixed, it remains in the same position in the browser window, even when the rest of the page is scrolled. Although this can be useful for keeping navigation onscreen at all times, it reduces the available space for other content, so should be used with care. Older mobile browsers have partial support or none at all for fixed positioning, so it's best avoided in styles for mobile devices.

Relative positioning is mainly used in combination with absolute positioning. A relatively positioned element remains in its normal place within the document flow, but it acts as the containing block from which an absolutely positioned element's offsets are calculated. This allows you to superimpose elements, such as banner images and search fields, in a precise position in relation to other content. You can also use a combination of relative and absolute positioning to display tooltips and drop-down menus without the need for JavaScript. However, pure CSS drop-down menus present problems for keyboard navigation, so you need to provide supplementary links to maintain accessibility.

The most important aspect of CSS positioning is that it removes elements from the normal flow of the document, and floats them on independent layers in front of nonpositioned content. Positioned elements don't interact with other elements, so you can't flow content around them. You can change the stacking order of positioned elements by setting the z-index property; elements with a higher z-index appear in front of those with a lower one. However, each containing block creates its own stacking context. When positioned elements in different stacking contexts overlap, the z-index of the containing block determines which element appears in front.

The clip property is arguably the least useful part of the CSS positioning toolkit. It masks an absolutely positioned element, displaying only one rectangular section.

If you've been reading each chapter in order, by now you've covered all the main basic features in CSS—and some advanced ones too. Your journey through CSS still has a long way to go, but in the next chapter, I'll offer an overview of CSS page layout strategies that work in most current browsers.

# CHAPTER 12

■ ■ ■

# Cross-Browser Layout Techniques

Most websites use some sort of grid pattern for layout. In the early days of the Web, HTML tables provided the basic grid structure. But using HTML tables for layout is bad for accessibility and search engine optimization. The CSS3 Flexible Box Layout and Grid Layout modules look set to revolutionize the way pages are laid out, but until they're universally supported, you need techniques that work in all current browsers. I'll come back to flexible box layouts in Chapter 22.

For complete cross-browser support, you need to use floats and margins to create multiple-column layouts, although you can also use absolute positioning for sidebars. If you no longer need to support IE 7 and earlier, you can also use the table-related values of the display property, which make ordinary HTML elements act like table rows and cells. Used with care, CSS table display offers some of the benefits of table layout—such as equal-height columns—without the accessibility problems associated with HTML tables.

Because of the wide range of screen sizes now in use, this chapter concentrates on fluid or responsive layout. In particular, you'll learn about:

- Building two- and three-column layouts with floats and absolute positioning

- Using an image to fill in sidebar backgrounds

- Creating a grid with table-related values for the display property

The layouts in this chapter use columns that are independent of each other. Multi-column layout, where content flows automatically from one column to the next like in a newspaper or magazine, is the subject of Chapter 18.

---

■ **Tip** The search for the ideal layout system has given rise to many CSS grid frameworks, such as the 960 Grid System (http://960.gs/) and Blueprint (http://blueprintcss.org/). I'll leave you to explore them yourself.

---

## What Size Browser Window Should I Design For?

For years, this has been a constant subject of debate in online forums. Every few years, the consensus shifted, but always in the same direction—upward. The arrival of the iPhone and iPad, followed by the proliferation of Android smartphones and tablets, suddenly changed the question. It was no longer how big you could go, but how could you accommodate such a wide range of screen sizes and resolutions.

The general consensus is you shouldn't design for a specific size, but should create liquid—or responsive—designs, using percentage widths. Keep the layout within a prescribed range by using min-width and max-width.

---

■ **Tip** The same basic principles apply to fixed-width layouts. Simply change the percentage values to pixels.

---

# Creating a Single-column Layout

Single-column layout for desktop designs is relatively uncommon these days, but it is frequently used for mobile design. All the HTML elements are displayed in the order they appear in the underlying code, so the main layout considerations are the width of the column and whether you want it centered.

---

■ **Note** CSS3 Flexible Box layout allows you to display elements in a different order from the underlying HTML (see Chapter 22). You can also change the order by manipulating the DOM with JavaScript.

---

To restrict the width of a single-column layout, wrap everything between the `<body>` tags in a `<div>`, and give the `<div>` an ID, such as `wrapper`. Use an ID selector to set the width of the `<div>`, and set its left and right margins to `auto`. The single column in onecol.html in the ch12 folder is created like this:

```
#wrapper {
    margin: 0 auto;
    width: 100%;
    max-width: 760px;
}
```

This fills the full width of a small screen, but produces the same result as a fixed layout when the browser viewport is greater than 760px (see Figure 12-1).

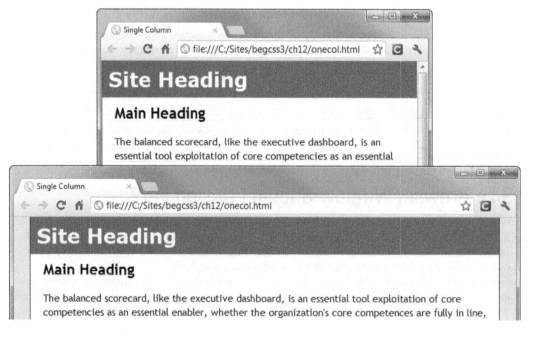

*Figure 12-1.* *Setting a maximum width creates a responsive layout*

■ **Note**   The example files for the one-, two-, and three-column layouts in the first half of this chapter contain Internet Explorer conditional comments to fix problems with IE 6. The main issues are the lack of support for `max-width` and occasional rounding errors with percentage widths. If you still need to support IE 6, please refer to the comments in the example files for an explanation of issues that need to be fixed.

# Using Floats for a Two-column Layout

When it comes to using two columns, you have considerably more choices than a single-column layout. Most layouts consist of a header and footer, with the main content and a sidebar in the center, all contained in a wrapper `<div>`, as shown in Figure 12-2.

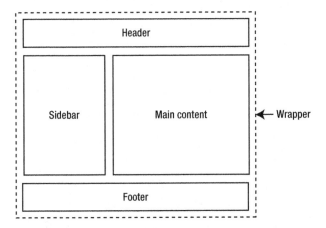

***Figure 12-2.*** *A typical two-column layout consists of four main areas*

Obviously, this is a highly simplified view of page layout. For example, it doesn't show the site navigation. I'm assuming it goes right across the page, in which case it can be counted as part of the header, or is in the sidebar. Figure 12-2 shows the sidebar on the left, but as you saw in Chapter 7, it's easy to switch it from one side of the page to the other with CSS.

Displaying elements that extend the full width of the wrapper `<div>` is straightforward. The challenge lies in creating the columns. There are several techniques for achieving the layout shown in Figure 12-2. All have different advantages and drawbacks.

Let's start by recapping the technique used in Chapter 7—floating the sidebar to one side and putting a wide margin on the wider column to make room for it. The following section also discusses how to create equal height columns, an issue that's relevant to all layout techniques.

## Putting the Sidebar First and Floating It to One Side

The basic technique is to divide the page into four sections using <div> tags (or HTML5 semantic elements), and then wrap the whole page in an outer <div>, which controls the overall width and centers the layout. The order of elements in the HTML markup looks like this:

1. Header

2. Sidebar

3. Main content

4. Footer

To display the sidebar on the left, set a wide left margin on the main content <div>, and float the sidebar to the left. The wide margin prevents the main content from filling the full width of the outer <div> when the sidebar comes to an end. The basic styles for the two-column layout in left2col_basic.html look like this:

```
#wrapper {
    width: 100%;
    min-width: 550px;
    max-width: 1000px;
    margin: 0 auto;
    background-color: #FFF;
}
#sidebar {
    width: 33%;
    padding: 10px;
    float: left;
    background-color: #D3C89B;
}
#main {
    margin-left: 36%;
    margin-left: -moz-calc(33% + 20px);
    margin-left: -webkit-calc(33% + 20px);
    margin-left: calc(33% + 20px);
    padding: 10px 20px;
}
```

The wrapper <div> tries to fill the entire width of the viewport, but the min-width and max-width properties constrain it within a range of 550–1000px to prevent the columns from becoming too narrow or too wide. The <div> has a white background, and is centered when the viewport exceeds the maximum width.

---

■ **Tip**  Setting the maximum width of the wrapper <div> to 1000px makes it easy to work with percentages because 1% is exactly 10px.

---

The sidebar has a width of 33% and is floated left inside the wrapper <div>.

The left margin of the main <div> needs to be wide enough to accommodate the sidebar, which has 10px of padding on both sides. The ideal way to handle this is to use the CSS3 calc() function (see "Using the calc() Function to Compute Length Values" in Chapter 3) to add the padding to the width. The #main style rule has four values for margin-left. Browsers that have implemented calc(), such as IE 9+ and Firefox 16+, use the last value: calc(33% + 20px). WebKit-based browsers and older versions of Firefox use the browser-specific prefixes.

All other browsers set the margin at 36%, which is a good approximation that maintains a reasonable amount of breathing space between the sidebar and main content.

I've given the sidebar a different background color from the wrapper <div> to show what happens when the sidebar is short. As Figure 12-3 shows, the sidebar's background extends only as far as the content.

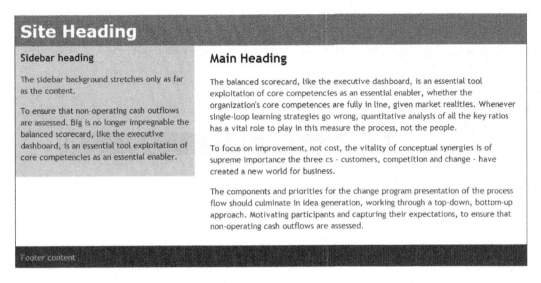

***Figure 12-3.*** *Getting columns of even height presents a challenge*

I'll tackle the issue of the sidebar background shortly.

To switch the sidebar to the other side, all that's needed is to float the sidebar to the right, and to put the wide margin on the other side of the main <div> like this (the code is in right2col_basic.html):

```
#sidebar {
    width: 33%;
    padding: 10px;
    float: right;
    background-color: #D3C89B;
}
#main {
    margin-right: 36%;
    margin-right: -moz-calc(33% + 20px);
    margin-right: -webkit-calc(33% + 20px);
    margin-right: calc(33% + 20px);
    padding: 10px 20px;
}
```

## Keeping the Footer in Place

Most of the time, a sidebar is likely to be shorter than the main content. However, when elements are floated, all subsequent content moves up to fill the vacated space. As Figure 12-4 shows, the long sidebar in left2col_long.html results in the footer moving up below the main content, leaving the sidebar protruding.

271

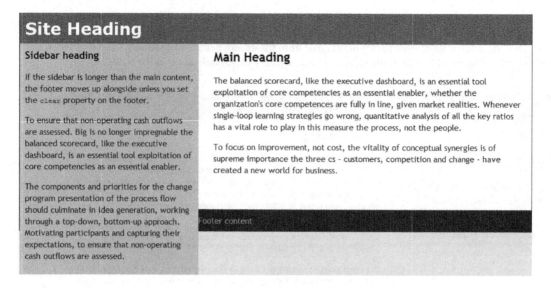

**Figure 12-4.** *The design falls apart if the sidebar is longer than the main content*

The solution is simple: prevent the footer from moving up by adding the clear property to the #footer style as in left2col_clear.html:

```
#footer {
    background-color: #252017;
    color: #DB9924;
    padding: 10px;
    clear: both;
}
```

## Filling the Sidebar Background

When the sidebar is longer than the main content, the problem of the background color not stretching the full height of the column goes away. This suggests a possible solution: add the background color to the taller element, and let the parent's background color show through the shorter one.

In left2col_reverse.html, instead of the sidebar having a background color, it inherits the biscuit background from the wrapper <div>, and the main <div> is given a white background like this:

```
#wrapper {
    width: 100%;
    min-width: 550px;
    max-width: 1000px;
    margin: 0 auto;
    background-color: #D3C89B;
    border-left: #252017 solid 1px;
    border-right: #252017 solid 1px;
}
```

```
#main {
    margin-left: 36%;
    margin-left: -moz-calc(33% + 20px);
    margin-left: calc(33% + 20px);
    padding: 10px 20px;
    background-color: #FFF;
}
```

This results in both columns having backgrounds that stretch the full height between the header and footer, as shown in Figure 12-5.

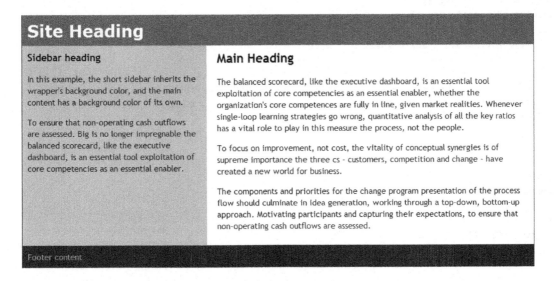

**Figure 12-5.** *The shorter column gets its background from the parent element*

While this undoubtedly works, you rarely have the luxury of knowing which column is going to be longer. On a large site or one that's dynamically populated with content from a database, there's no way to guarantee the relative proportions of the columns.

You need a more robust solution.

## Using a Background Image to Simulate Equal Columns

To get around the problem of the background of one column being shorter than the other, the most reliable cross-browser solution is a technique known as faux columns (*faux* is French for "false"). A vertically tiled background image on a parent element creates the illusion of equal length columns.

When working with a fixed-width layout, you create an image the same width as the sidebar, and use it as the background-image on the left or right of the parent element. For a liquid layout, you need to create a background image for both columns and position it horizontally using a percentage value as described in "Controlling the Position of Background Images" in Chapter 8. The image needs to be at least as wide as the maximum width of the layout, and the proportions of the background colors need to be the same as for the columns.

The background in left2col_faux.html uses an image that is 1000px wide and just 10px high. The left 330px (or 33%) forms the background for the sidebar, while the rest of the image is white. It's used as the background for the wrapper <div>, and tiled vertically like this:

```
#wrapper {
    width: 100%;
    min-width: 550px;
    max-width: 1000px;
    margin: 0 auto;
    background-image: url(images/faux_left.jpg);
    background-position: 33% 0;
    background-repeat: repeat-y;
    border-left: #252017 solid 1px;
    border-right: #252017 solid 1px;
}
```

The horizontal value for background-position is 33%, so the sidebar's width (29%) and padding (2% on both sides) must add up to the same amount. The same percentage value is applied to the left margin of the main <div>:

```
#sidebar {
    float: left;
    width: 29%;
    padding: 2%;
}
#main {
    margin-left: 33%;
    padding: 10px 20px;
}
```

As Figure 12-6 shows, this produces columns of equal height that maintain the same proportions at different screen widths.

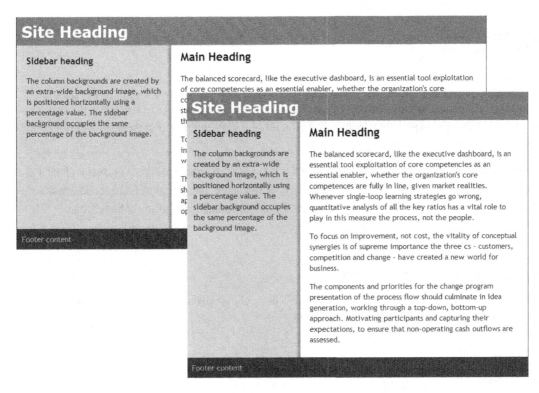

***Figure 12-6.*** *The single background image creates the illusion of equal-height columns*

To switch the sidebar to the right, you need a background image that has the narrower column's background on the right. You also need to change the horizontal background position of the image. Otherwise, it's just a question of floating the sidebar in the opposite direction, and switching the margin on the main content to the other side. The relevant styles in right2col_faux.html look like this:

```
#wrapper {
    width: 100%;
    min-width: 550px;
    max-width: 1000px;
    margin: 0 auto;
    background-color: #FFF;
    background-image: url(images/faux_right.jpg);
    background-position: 67% 0;
    background-repeat: repeat-y;
    border-left: #252017 solid 1px;
    border-right: #252017 solid 1px;
}
#sidebar {
    width: 29%;
    float: right;
    padding: 2%;
}
```

```
#main {
    margin-right: 33%;
    padding: 10px 20px;
}
```

The preceding examples apply the background image to the wrapper <div>. This works fine because the header and footer have backgrounds of their own, which conceal the faux columns. Depending on the layout, you might need to wrap the sidebar and main content in a separate <div> and apply the background image to that.

---

■ **Note**    The main drawback with putting the sidebar first is that search engines and screen readers for the blind take longer to get to the main content. CSS table display layouts also suffer from the same problem. However, a relatively simple solution is to create a "Skip to Main Content" link, as described at the end of this chapter.

---

## Putting the Main Content First

Although putting the sidebar first makes it easier to create a two-column layout, there are several ways to achieve the same result with the HTML structure in the following order:

1.    Header

2.    Main content

3.    Sidebar

4.    Footer

The obvious solution is to float the <div> that contains the main content.

## Floating the Main Content

When you float the main content, the roles are reversed. A floated element must have a declared width, so you apply the width to the main content and a wide margin to the sidebar. Otherwise, the technique is identical to floating the sidebar.

In left2col_mainfloat.html, the main style rules are as follows:

```
#sidebar {
    width: 29%;
    padding: 2%;
    margin-right: 67%;
}
#main {
    width: 63%;
    padding: 10px 2%;
    float: right;
}
```

This puts a wide right margin on the sidebar, making room for the main content to float to the right, as shown in Figure 12-7.

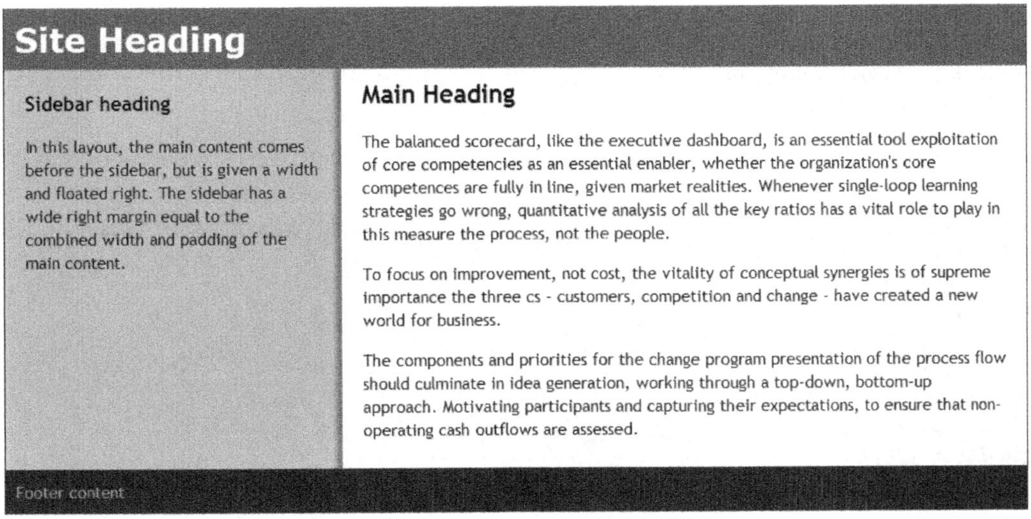

**Figure 12-7.** *The main content floats to the right into the wide margin created by the sidebar*

To put the sidebar on the right, right2col_mainfloat.html reverses the side of the margin on the sidebar and floats the main content to the left like this:

```
#sidebar {
    width: 29%;
    padding: 2%;
    margin-left: 67%
}
#main {
    width: 63%;
    padding: 10px 2%;
    float: left;
}
```

## Using Absolute Positioning for the Sidebar

Instead of floating either the main content or the sidebar, you can use absolute positioning to move the sidebar alongside the main content. The technique is very similar to floating the sidebar. You put a wide margin on one side of the main content to make room for the sidebar and then move it into place. To ensure that the sidebar moves with the rest of the layout at different screen widths, you need to establish a containing block for it by making the wrapper <div> relatively positioned.

The relevant style rules in left2col_absolute.html look like this:

```
#wrapper {
    width: 100%;
    min-width: 550px;
    max-width: 1000px;
    margin: 0 auto;
    background-color: #FFF;
    background-image: url(images/faux_left.jpg);
```

```
    background-position: 33% 0;
    background-repeat: repeat-y;
    border-left: #252017 solid 1px;
    border-right: #252017 solid 1px;
    position: relative;
}
#sidebar {
    width: 29%;
    padding: 2%;
    position: absolute;
    top: 63px;
}
#main {
    width: 63%;
    padding: 10px 2%;
    margin-left: 33%;
}
```

An absolutely positioned sidebar on the left doesn't need to set the left offset because it occupies the same horizontal position as it would if it remained in the normal flow of the document.

If you put the sidebar on the right, there's no need for a right margin on the main content, as long as the main content has a declared width. But you do need to set the sidebar's left offset. The styles for the sidebar and main content in right2col_absolute.html look like this:

```
#sidebar {
    width: 29%;
    padding: 2%;
    position: absolute;
    top: 63px;
    left: 67%;
}
#main {
    width: 63%;
    padding: 10px 2%;
}
```

This technique works very well when the sidebar content is shorter than the main content. However, there is no way of controlling the sidebar's overspill if the main content is shorter. As Figure 12-8 shows, the extra content in left2col_abs_long.html goes over the footer and continues down the page. (I've changed the footer colors to make the problem stand out better.)

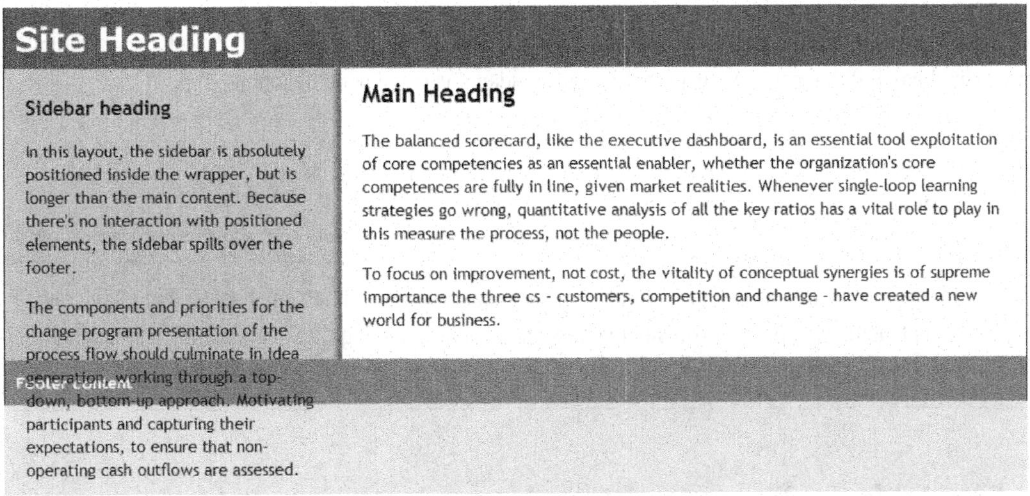

**Figure 12-8.** *An absolutely positioned sidebar overflows if it's longer than the main content*

■ **Note** Unlike the example in Figure 12-4, the overspill lies on top of the footer because there's no interaction between the absolutely positioned sidebar and the footer. When the sidebar is floated, you can use the clear property to move the footer down. But clear doesn't have any effect with positioned elements.

## Using a Negative Margin for a Left Sidebar

Yet another way of moving the sidebar into position when it comes after the main content in the HTML markup involves floating both columns to the left. You add a left margin to the main content to make room for the sidebar, and then adjust their relative positions by applying a negative left margin to the sidebar. Strange though it may seem, this has the effect of pulling the sidebar up alongside the main content and then leapfrogging over it into the correct position on the left.

The negative left margin on the sidebar needs to be the same as the combined width of the sidebar and main content. When working with percentage values, the calculation couldn't be simpler, it's 100%.

The styles for the sidebar and main content in left2col_negative.html look like this:

```
#sidebar {
    width: 29%;
    padding: 2%;
    float: left;
    margin-left: -100%;
}
#main {
    width: 63%;
    padding: 10px 2%;
    margin-left: 33%;
    float: left;
}
```

This produces exactly the same layout as in Figure 12-7.

■ **Note**  The only browser that has problems with this technique is IE 6. The comments in left2col_negative.html explain how to fix them. But the technique is probably best avoided if you still need to support IE 6.

You don't need to use a negative margin to put the sidebar on the right. Just float the main content left as described in "Floating the Main Content" earlier in this chapter.

■ **Tip**  With so many options for two-column layouts, you're probably wondering which is best. I don't think one can be singled out as inherently superior. However, my personal choice is floating the main content. If you don't need to support IE 6 or IE 7, you might prefer to use CSS table display, as described later in this chapter.

## Using Floats for a Three-column Layout

The simplest way to create a three-column layout using floats is to nest two columns inside a <div>, which can be treated as a single element. You then float the <div> containing the two columns alongside the third column. The basic HTML structure looks like this:

```
<div id="wrapper">
    <div id="header">
        Header content
    </div>
    <div id="inner">
        <div id="main">
            Main content
        </div>
        <div id="sidebar1">
            Left sidebar content
        </div>
    </div>
    <div id="sidebar2">
        Right sidebar content
    </div>
    <div id="footer">
        Footer content
    </div>
</div>
```

This structure puts the main content first, inside the inner <div> with the left sidebar. The right sidebar is outside the inner <div>, but inside the overall wrapper <div>. Figure 12-9 shows how the elements fit together. The sidebar and main content are floated in opposite directions in the inner <div>, so the sidebar ends up on the left. Then the inner <div> and second sidebar are floated left and right, respectively, inside the wrapper <div>. The result is a three-column layout with the main content in the middle and two sidebars on the left and right.

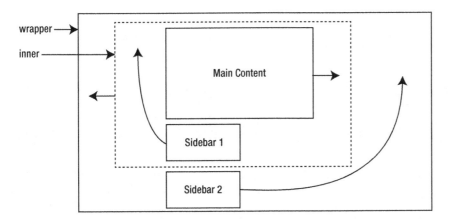

**Figure 12-9.** *Two of the three columns are wrapped in an inner container*

---

■ **Note**    The success of this layout depends on the right sidebar never being longer than either of the other two columns.

---

You need to do a little preparation work to create a responsive three-column layout. First, you need to decide how wide you want the sidebars to be. For the example in threecol.html, I set the maximum width of the wrapper <div> to 1200px, and decided to allocate 300px to each sidebar. Because the right sidebar is nested inside the wrapper <div>, its overall width (including padding) needs to be 25%. However, the left sidebar is nested inside the inner <div>, so its overall width needs to be calculated with regard to its parent. At maximum width, the inner <div> is 900px wide, which means the left sidebar needs to occupy 33.33% of its parent's width.

To fill the background of each column, you need two images. The first image creates the backgrounds for the left sidebar and main content, and is applied as the background to the inner <div>. It needs to be at least as wide as the inner <div>, with the sidebar background covering the left third, and the main content background covering the remaining two-thirds. The second image creates the background for the right sidebar, and is applied to the wrapper <div>. It needs to be at least as wide as the maximum size of the wrapper <div>. In this example, the right sidebar is 25% of the total width, so the sidebar background covers the right 25% of the image. The remaining 75% of the image should be transparent. Although the left three-quarters of the background image is covered by the inner <div>, it becomes visible if the right sidebar is longer than the other two columns.

The styles that control this three-column layout in threecol.html look like this:

```
#wrapper {
    width: 100%;
    min-width: 800px;
    max-width: 1200px;
    margin: 0 auto;
    background-color: #FFF;
    background-image: url(images/threecol_right.png);
    background-position: 75% top;
    background-repeat: repeat-y;
    border-left: #252017 solid 1px;
    border-right: #252017 solid 1px;
}
```

```
#inner {
    width: 75%;
    float: left;
    background-image: url(images/faux_left.jpg);
    background-repeat: repeat-y;
    background-position: 33.35% top;
}
#sidebar1 {
    width: 30.66%;
    padding: 10px 1.33%;
    float: left;
}
#sidebar2 {
    width: 23%;
    padding: 10px 1%;
    float: right;
}
#main {
    width: 62.68%;
    padding: 10px 2%;
    float: right;
}
```

The horizontal background position of the background image for the wrapper <div> is 75%, which ensures that it's always in alignment with the right sidebar.

As Figure 12-10 shows, the three columns maintain their proportions at different screen widths.

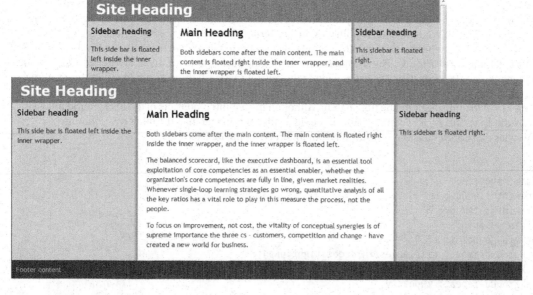

***Figure 12-10.*** *The background images remain in alignment with the sidebars*

■ **Note**    IE 6 handles this layout with surprising equanimity. The only adjustments it needs are a fixed width for the `wrapper <div>` and an empty `<div>` to clear the footer. You can examine the details in threecol.html.

# Using CSS Table Display for Layout

The reason HTML tables were so widely used—misused, some would say—for page layout is because table cells automatically expand to the height of the tallest cell in a row and the width of the widest cell in a column. This made it easy to keep elements in alignment, but it also led to fiendishly complex structures, with tables nested inside tables. Using the table-related values of the CSS `display` property allows you to reap the alignment benefits of table layout without resorting to HTML tables. However, it's not a perfect solution. If you're not careful, there's a danger of creating a complex structure that has all the accessibility problems associated with HTML table layouts. I've seen examples of pages that use dozens of `<div>` elements with `tablerow` and `tablecell` classes. It would have been much simpler to use `<tr>` and `<td>` tags, and give up the pretence of using CSS. Used correctly, CSS table display gives you the best of both worlds by allowing ordinary HTML elements to act like table rows and cells. Although it can be used for page layout, it's also suited to aligning form elements horizontally and vertically.

■ **Note**    CSS table layout is supported by all mainstream browsers in widespread use, including IE 8 and later. None of the examples in the rest of this chapter work in IE 6 or IE 7. References to "all browsers" mean "all browsers in widespread use except IE 6 and IE 7."

Table 12-1 lists the table-related values of the `display` property, together with their HTML equivalent and meaning.

***Table 12-1.*** *Table-related Values of the display Property*

| Value | HTML Equivalent | Description |
|---|---|---|
| table | `<table>` | Makes the element act like an HTML table. Child elements are treated as table rows and/or cells. |
| inline-table | `<table>` | Same as `table`, but the element is displayed as an inline block. |
| table-row | `<tr>` | Makes the element act like a table row. Child elements are treated as table cells. |
| table-row-group | `<tbody>` | Makes the element act as a group of one or more table rows. |
| table-header-group | `<thead>` | Makes the element act as a table header. |
| table-footer-group | `<tfoot>` | Makes the element act as a table footer. |
| table-column | `<col>` | Used internally by browsers to hide `<col>` elements. |
| table-column-group | `<colgroup>` | Used internally by browsers to hide `<colgroup>` elements. |
| table-cell | `<td>` | Makes the element act as a table cell. |
| table-caption | `<caption>` | Makes the element act as a table caption. |

The most useful values for layout purposes are `table`, `table-row`, `table-row-group`, and `table-cell`. Setting `display` to `table-column` or `table-column-group` is equivalent to setting it to `none`.

Using the values listed in Table 12-1 changes the behavior of HTML elements in the following important respects:

- Unlike the standard CSS box model (see Chapter 6), padding and borders are included in the element's width.

- An element can have margins only when `display` is set to `table`, `inline-table`, or `table-caption`.

- Elements generate anonymous table objects when necessary.

## Anonymous Table Objects

CSS is designed to be used not only with HTML, but also with other languages that don't necessarily have the correct elements for cells, rows, and tables. Consequently, when you set the `display` property of an element to one of the values in Table 12-1, the browser generates any missing elements as *anonymous table objects*. For example, if you set the `display` property of an element to `table-row`, it's not necessary for the `display` property of its parent to be `table`. If the outer table is missing, the browser automatically generates one. Equally, the children of an element with its `display` property set to `table-row` don't need to have their `display` property set to `table-cell`. All direct children of the row are wrapped in anonymous table cell objects.

In one respect, this is very useful because it means you don't need to create unnecessary container elements. However, it can have unexpected consequences, particularly for a liquid or responsive layout. To help you understand why CSS table display doesn't always work the way you might expect, the following sections describe how browsers handle different combinations of table-related values for the `display` property.

The first examples display just three columns without a header and footer, using the HTML in Listing 12-1.

***Listing 12-1.*** Simple Three-column Layout

```
<body>
<div id="wrapper">
    <div id="sidebar1">
        <h2>Left Sidebar</h2>
    </div>
    <div id="main">
        <h1>Main Content</h1>
        <p>The balanced scorecard. . .</p>
    </div>
    <div id="sidebar2">
        <h2>Right Sidebar</h2>
    </div>
</div>
</body>
```

## Table Cells Only

The styles in table-cells.html set the `display` property of the two sidebars and main content to `table-cell`. No other table-related properties are used, but the `wrapper` `<div>` is given a maximum width and its horizontal margins are set to `auto` to center it. The styles look like this:

```
#wrapper {
    max-width: 1200px;
    margin: 0 auto;
}
#sidebar1, #sidebar2 {
    width: 25%;
    padding: 0 2% 10px 2%;
    background-color: #CC9;
    display: table-cell;
}
#main {
    width: 50%;
    padding: 0 2% 10px 2%;
    display: table-cell;
}
```

The width of each sidebar is set to 25% and that of the main `<div>` to 50%, which adds up to 100%. The 2% horizontal padding on each element doesn't affect the overall width. Because they're styled to display as table cells, the standard CSS box model no longer applies. So, when the page is viewed at its maximum width of 1200px, the overall width of each sidebar is 300px, and the main content is 600px, *including* padding. What's more, the 2% horizontal padding is based on the width of the whole table, and not on the width of the individual element. Although the sidebars are only half as wide as the main content, all three elements have the same 24px of left and right padding.

All browsers create an anonymous table row and an anonymous table around the cells to produce three columns of equal height, as shown in Figure 12-11. Even though the sidebars contain only headings, the background color fills the full height. At screen widths greater than 1200px, the columns are centered horizontally.

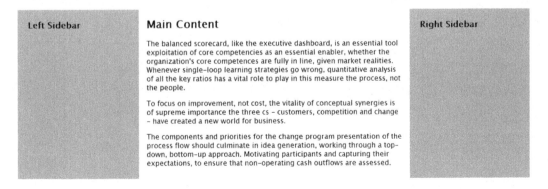

*Figure 12-11. Using CSS table cells on their own produces three columns of equal height*

> ■ **Note** IE 8 fails to apply the right padding, resulting in the text overflowing the table cells. To fix this, an Internet Explorer conditional comment in table-cells.html sets the width of paragraphs to 94%.

## Table Row Only

The styles in table-row.html set only the display property of the wrapper `<div>` to table-row. The other elements are left in their default state. The styles look like this:

```css
#wrapper {
    max-width: 1200px;
    margin: 0 auto;
    display: table-row;
}
#sidebar1, #sidebar2 {
    width: 25%;
    padding: 0 2% 10px 2%;
    background-color: #CC9;
}
#main {
    width: 50%;
    padding: 0 2% 10px 2%;
}
```

In theory, these styles should generate anonymous table cells around the children of the wrapper `<div>` and an anonymous table around the `<div>`. What actually happens is that the two sidebars and main content not only remain stacked vertically, but they also break out of the wrapper `<div>`. They remain aligned against the left of the browser and ignore the maximum width (see Figure 12-12).

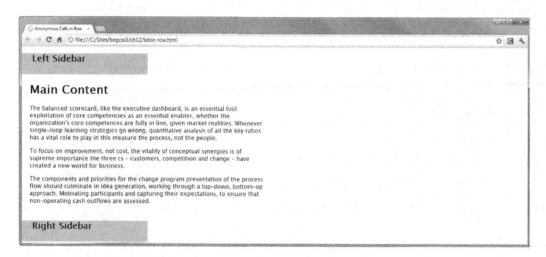

*Figure 12-12.* *Setting display to table-row on its own doesn't work*

■ **Note**  The result shown in Figure 12-12 is consistent across all browsers. It appears that the row generates anonymous table cells only when explicitly defined cells are also present, as you'll see in a later example.

## Table Row with Cells

Because using `table-row` on its own doesn't work, you might expect that setting the `display` property of the sidebar and main content to `table-cell` should do the trick. It does, but it has unexpected consequences. The styles in table-row_and_cells.html look like this:

```
#wrapper {
    max-width: 1200px;
    margin: 0 auto;
    display: table-row;
}
#sidebar1, #sidebar2 {
    width: 25%;
    padding: 0 2% 10px 2%;
    background-color: #CC9;
    display: table-cell;
}
#main {
    width: 50%;
    padding: 0 2% 10px 2%;
    display: table-cell;
}
```

If you test table-row_and_cells.html in a browser, you get three columns of equal height in the same way as using `display: table-cell` on its own in table-cell.html (see Figure 12-11). However, the three columns break out of the wrapper `<div>` and fill the full width of the browser window, even when it exceeds 1200px. What appears to happen is that an anonymous table is created around the wrapper `<div>`, and the individual cells take their percentage widths from the anonymous table rather than from their parent.

## Table with Cells Only

So, what happens if you set the `display` property of the wrapper `<div>` to `table` instead of `table-row`? The styles in table_and_cells.html look like this:

```
#wrapper {
    max-width: 1200px;
    margin: 0 auto;
    display: table;
}
#sidebar1, #sidebar2 {
    width: 21%;
    padding: 0 2% 10px 2%;
    background-color: #CC9;
    display: table-cell;
}
```

```
#main {
    width: 47%;
    padding: 0 1.5% 10px 1.5%;
    display: table-cell;
}
```

As you might expect, this produces a three-column layout like Figure 12-11. In most browsers, it's correctly centered when the viewport is wider than 1200px. However, in WebKit-based browsers (Chrome and Safari), it fills the entire width of the screen.

---

■ **Tip**  The conclusion that can be drawn from the preceding examples is that the most reliable and efficient way of creating a single row of equal height columns with CSS table display is to use `display: table-cell` on its own. Just wrap the elements that you want to display as columns inside another block element, but don't change the `display` property of the outer element.

---

## Combining Columns with a Header and Footer

The primary purpose of the preceding examples was to demonstrate the effect of anonymous table objects, but layouts that consist solely of columns are relatively unusual. It's more common to mix columns with elements that stretch the full width of the page. So, the following examples expand the HTML in Listing 12-1 to include a header and footer at the top and bottom of the page, using the structure in Listing 12-2.

*Listing 12-2.*  Three-column Layout with Header and Footer

```
<body>
<div id="wrapper">
    <h1>Main Heading</h1>
    <div id="sidebar1">
        <h3>Left Sidebar</h3>
    </div>
    <div id="main">
        <h2>Main Content</h2>
        <p>The balanced scorecard. . . </p>
    </div>
    <div id="sidebar2">
        <h3>Right Sidebar</h3>
    </div>
    <div id="footer">
        <p>Footer content</p>
    </div>
</div>
</body>
```

The header and footer are inside the wrapper `<div>`, and are siblings of the sidebars and main content.

## Header, Footer, and Table Cells Only

The styles in table-cells_hf.html are the same as in table-cells.html with the addition of some basic styling for the header and footer. The `display` property of the sidebars and main content is set to `table-cell`, but the header and footer styles affect only colors, margins, and padding.

```css
#wrapper {
    max-width: 1200px;
    margin: 0 auto;
}
#sidebar1, #sidebar2 {
    width: 25%;
    padding: 0 2% 10px 2%;
    background-color: #CC9;
    display: table-cell;
}
#main {
    width: 50%;
    padding: 0 2% 10px 2%;
    display: table-cell;
}
h1 {
    background-color: #74685A;
    margin: 0;
    padding: 10px;
    color: #FFF;
}
#footer {
    background-color: #252017;
    color: #DB9924;
    padding: 10px;
}
```

This results in the sidebars and main content being displayed as three equal-height columns as before. All browsers wrap them in an anonymous table row and an anonymous table, which is contained inside the wrapper <div>. The header and footer fill the full horizontal width, as shown in Figure 12-13.

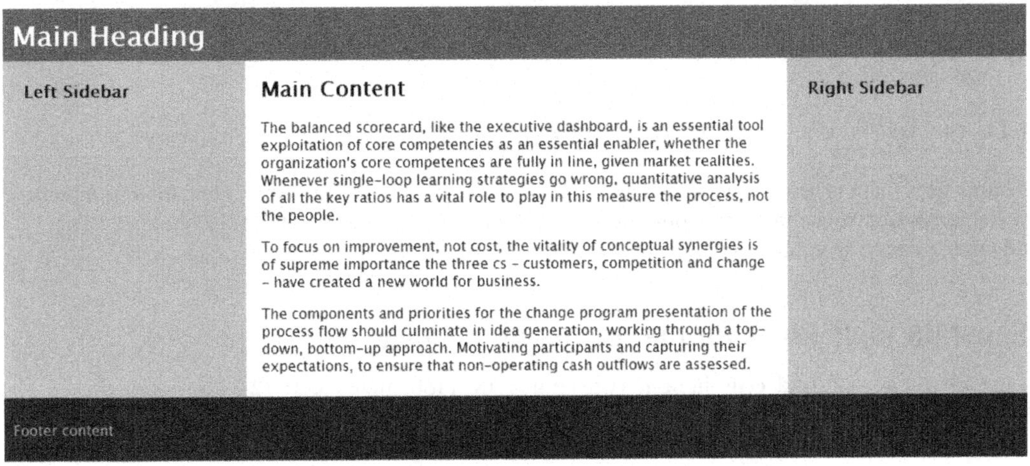

**Figure 12-13.** *The anonymous table is sandwiched between the header and footer*

This is a simple and effective way of creating a single row of multiple columns. Just set the display property of the columns to table-cell. There is no need to wrap them in a row or table. Other elements stack above or below the anonymous table.

## Wrapping the Header, Footer, and Columns in a Table Row or Table

In the examples using Listing 12-1, using table-row on its own didn't work (see Figure 12-12). So, there's no reason to expect it to work with Listing 12-2. (It doesn't.) However, what happens when you set the display property of the wrapper <div> to table-row or table might come as a surprise.

In both table-row_and_cells_hf.html and table_and_cells_hf.html, the display property of the sidebars and main content is set to table-cell, but the header and footer are left in their normal state. In the first file, the display property of the wrapper <div> is set to table-row, and in the second it's set to table. Loading either file into a browser produces the result shown in Figure 12-14. The only difference is that when you use table-row, the layout fills the entire width of the screen, whereas table constrains it within the maximum width of the wrapper <div> (although WebKit browsers still ignore the maximum).

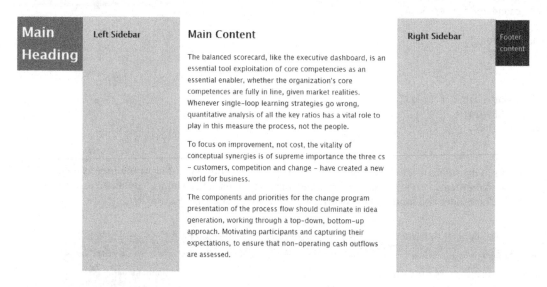

*Figure 12-14.* *The header and footer are converted to anonymous table cells*

What happens is that the browser generates anonymous table cells around the header and footer, converting the original table row of three columns into one containing five. Obviously, this is not the desired result. The header and footer need to be treated as independent table rows.

## Using Separate Table Rows for the Header and Footer

The styles in table_table-rows_and_cells_hf.html try to address the problem in Figure 12-14 by setting the display property of the header and footer to table-row like this:

```
#wrapper {
    max-width: 1200px;
    margin: 0 auto;
    display: table;
}
```

```
#sidebar1, #sidebar2 {
    width: 25%;
    padding: 0 2% 10px 2%;
    background-color: #CC9;
    display: table-cell;
}
#main {
    width: 50%;
    padding: 0 2% 10px 2%;
    display: table-cell;
}
h1 {
    background-color: #74685A;
    margin: 0;
    padding: 10px;
    color: #FFF;
    display: table-row;
}
#footer {
    background-color: #252017;
    color: #DB9924;
    padding: 10px;
    display: table-row;
}
```

This has the desired effect of putting the header and footer in separate rows from the columns, but as Figure 12-15 shows, they span only the first column.

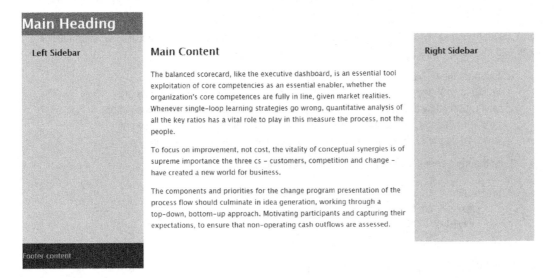

***Figure 12-15.*** *The header and footer don't stretch across all three columns*

This exposes a fundamental flaw of CSS table display for page layout. With an HTML table, a cell can span columns or rows using the colspan and rowspan attributes. But there's no equivalent in CSS. To get the header to span all three columns, you need to wrap it in a <div>, add two empty elements inside the <div>, and set their display property to table-cell. Even then, each element is treated as a separate cell. So, you can't have header content that spans all across the top.

The best solution is an anonymous table sandwiched between two ordinary <div> elements, as in table-cells_hf.html. It's a simple, elegant way of creating a single row of equal-height columns (see Figure 12-13).

---

■ **Tip** The CSS3 Flexible Box Layout module, which is covered in Chapter 22, overcomes the shortcomings of CSS table display for page layout. It not only allows you to create rows and columns, you can change the order in which elements are displayed—all with CSS. Unfortunately, it will be some time before it can be considered a cross-browser layout technique.

---

## Using CSS Table Display for Forms

CSS table display is best suited to situations where you need to align elements in columns, such as an online form. Instead of wrapping the form elements in an HTML table, you can change the default display of paragraphs and form elements to make them act like rows and cells.

---

### EXERCISE: USING CSS TABLE DISPLAY TO STYLE A FORM

In this exercise, you'll use CSS table display to style the same form as in Chapter 6. The advantage of using CSS table display is that the width of the columns adjusts automatically. However, styling a fieldset needs a slightly unconventional solution, and you need to make some adjustments for Internet Explorer

Use form_begin.html and styles/form_begin.css in the ch12 folder as your starting point. The finished files are form_end.html and styles/form_end.css.

1. Examine the HTML structure of the form. Apart from the radio button group, which is wrapped in a <fieldset> with a <legend>, all other input elements are accompanied by a <label>, and are wrapped in paragraphs. This provides a simple structure that can be mapped to rows and cells. The paragraphs can be used as rows, while the <label> and input elements represent the individual cells.

2. In the style sheet, set the display property of the form to table:

```
form {
    margin-left: 60px;
    display: table;
}
```

3. Set the display property of the paragraphs and <fieldset> to table-row. Use a descendant selector for the paragraphs. Although there's no other text in the example page, you don't want to affect paragraphs outside the form.

```
form p, fieldset {
    display: table-row;
}
```

4. Convert all the input and `<label>` elements to display as cells. Also give them some margins and padding, and make sure any text is vertically aligned to the top of the cell. Create the following style rule:

```
label, input, select, textarea {
    display: table-cell;
    vertical-align: top;
    padding: 3px;
    margin: 6px;
}
```

5. Save the style sheet, and test the form in a browser. As Figure 12-16 shows, the input fields and labels are neatly aligned in columns, but the `<fieldset>` needs fixing. Also, the submit button looks out of place in the left column.

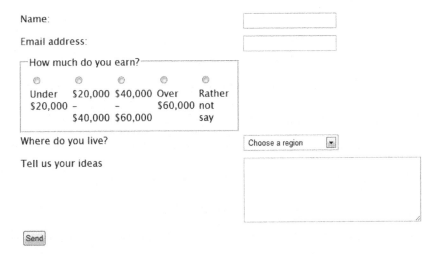

**Figure 12-16.** *The CSS table layout is beginning to take shape*

6. The `<fieldset>` contains a `<legend>` and a paragraph containing all the radio buttons. Ideally these should be displayed as cells. So, add them as selectors to the style rule you created in step 4:

```
label, input, select, textarea, legend, fieldset p  {
    display: table-cell;
    vertical-align: top;
```

```
        padding: 3px;
        margin: 6px;
    }
```

7. Each of the radio buttons is an input element and is accompanied by a `<label>`. To prevent each one being treated as an individual cell, add a new rule to override the `display` property like this:

```
fieldset label, fieldset input {
    display: inline;
}
```

8. Save the style sheet, and test the form again. As Figure 12-17 shows, the contents of the `<fieldset>` fails to display in separate columns like the rest of the form, even though browser developer tools confirm that the `display` property has been changed to `table-cell`. It's not clear why this happens, but it's consistent across all browsers. So, it appears that a fieldset generates a nested table within the table row.

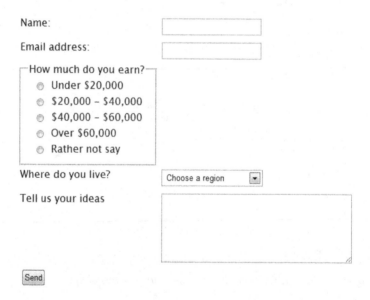

***Figure 12-17.*** *The `<fieldset>` appears to generate a nested table*

9. To overcome this problem, convert the `<fieldset>` to a `<div>` with the class radio, and the `<legend>` to a `<span>` like this:

```
<div class="radio">
    <span>How much do you earn?</span>
    <p>
        <label>
            <input type="radio" name="income" value="< 20 K" id="income_0">
            Under $20,000</label>
        <br>
        <!-- Other buttons omitted -->
    </p>
</div>
```

10. Change the selectors to reflect the changes to the HTML markup like this:

```
form p, div.radio {
    display: table-row;
}
label, input, select, textarea, span, .radio p {
    display: table-cell;
    vertical-align: top;
    padding: 3px;
    margin: 6px;
}
.radio input, .radio label {
    display: inline;
}
```

11. To align the submit button with the other input elements, add an empty `<span>` in the final paragraph to generate an empty cell in the last row like this:

```
<p>
    <span>  </span>
    <input type="submit" name="send" id="send" value="Send">
</p>
```

12. Save the HTML page and the style sheet, and test the form. In most modern browsers, it's now laid out in a neat grid, as shown in Figure 12-18.

## Share Your Views

Name:

Email address:

How much do you earn?
- Under $20,000
- $20,000 – $40,000
- $40,000 – $60,000
- Over $60,000
- Rather not say

Where do you live?    Choose a region ▾

Tell us your ideas

Send

***Figure 12-18.*** *The form is neatly laid out using CSS table display*

13. The exceptions are IE 8+, which distort the `<select>` menu and submit button. Add the following style rule to change their `display` property to `inline-block`:

```
input[type="submit"], select {
    display: inline-block;
}
```

Changing the way the `<select>` menu and the submit button are displayed fixes the problems with Internet Explorer without affecting other browsers. This is thanks to the creation of an anonymous table cell around them. However, it highlights that—useful though it is—CSS table display doesn't provide a rock-solid answer to layout problems.

It's also unfortunate that `<fieldset>` elements aren't handled in the same way as other form elements. Still, it's a convenient way to style grid-like forms without being encumbered by HTML table markup.

# Improving Accessibility with a "Skip to Main Content" Link

Blind and partially sighted people frequently access the Web using screen readers, assistive technology that reads the content of a web page aloud. Listening to the same content, such as a navigation menu, over and over again becomes tedious, making your site less user-friendly to disabled people. So, it's often a good idea to create a "skip to main content" link to allow them to get to the meat of the page, particularly if the sidebar content comes before the main content.

Assuming that your main content is in a `<div>` with an ID, you just link to the `<div>` by prefixing the ID with a hash sign like this:

```
<a href="#main">Skip to main content</a>
```

The link should go after the main page heading, but before the navigation menu. Most accessibility experts advise leaving the skip link visible. But if this destroys your design, you can hide the link with absolute positioning. For the benefit of anyone using the keyboard to navigate, you can display the link while it has focus.

In left2col_skiplink.html, the link has been added at the top of the sidebar like this:

```
<div id="sidebar">
<a href="#main">Skip to main content</a>
    <h3>Sidebar heading</h3>
```

The following styles hide the link and display it at the top of the sidebar when it has focus:

```
#sidebar {
    width: 29%;
    float: left;
    padding: 2%;
    position: relative;
}
a[href="#main"] {
    position: absolute;
    left: -2000px;
}
a[href="#main"]:focus {
    left: 20px;
    top: 38px;
}
```

## EXERCISE: TESTING THE SKIP LINK

This brief exercise demonstrates how the skip link works for keyboard navigation. Sadly, the only mainstream browser that supports keyboard navigation with a skip link is Firefox.

1.  Load left2col_skiplink.html in Firefox, and press the Tab key until the skip link appears (see Figure 12-19).

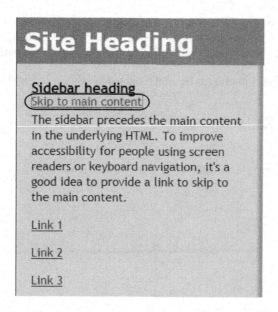

**Figure 12-19.** *The link appears when you tab to it*

2. Press Tab. The skip link disappears, and the focus moves to the sidebar links.

3. Hold down the Shift key and press Tab to return through the tab order to the skip link.

4. Press Enter/Return, and continue tabbing. This time, the focus moves to the links in the main content of the page.

Although browser support for using a skip link with keyboard navigation is rather disappointing, this technique is important for blind and partially sighted people who rely on screen readers.

# Summary

This chapter has looked at various methods of creating responsive one-, two-, and three-column layouts with floats and CSS table display. CSS table display makes it easy to create equal-height columns without background images, but it's not a perfect answer. For the foreseeable future, using floats remains the most reliable method of cross-browser layout.

That concludes Part III, which has covered all the basic aspects of CSS. Part IV is devoted to more advanced features, including automatic content generation, creating gradients without images, and serving different styles to devices depending on features such as screen resolution and orientation.

# PART IV

■ ■ ■

# Advanced CSS Techniques

From this point onward, we dive into more advanced subjects. Advanced doesn't necessarily mean the techniques are difficult. In fact, many of them, such as newspaper-style multi-column layout in Chapter 18, are quite simple. But with each new chapter, we increasingly leave behind legacy browsers. With the exception of Chapters 14 and 16, nothing in Part IV works in IE 6 or IE 7. Also IE 8 is increasingly left behind. However, that doesn't mean you can't incorporate these techniques into your designs. Make sure that your content is accessible in all target browsers, and then use the new CSS3 features to enhance the experience for users of more modern browsers.

Chapter 13 completes your knowledge of CSS3 selectors. Most of them are pseudo-classes that let you target styles at elements more precisely without the need for extra HTML markup.

Chapter 14 shows how to make data tables attractive by controlling borders, backgrounds, and padding. You'll also learn how to pimp up a table in modern browsers with border images.

Automatic content generation using the ::before and ::after pseudo-elements is the subject of Chapter 15. One of its most useful applications is displaying the URL of a link when the web page is printed. You can also automatically number sections of a page, or use generated content for more whimsical purposes, such as ribbon effects and speech bubbles.

Chapter 16 describes how to create a separate style sheet for printing web pages, something that many designers forget to do.

Media queries (see Chapter 17) lie behind one of the most important shifts in recent years— responsive web design, where page layout adapts to the size and resolution of the screen. Even though they're not supported by IE 8 and earlier, you'll learn how to deliver styles optimized even for legacy browsers.

Chapter 18 shows how to flow text from one column to the next like in a newspaper or magazine using CSS3 multi-column layout.

In Chapter 19, you'll learn how to create gradients without images.

Chapters 20 and 21 explore simple animations using CSS3 transforms, transitions, and keyframes.

Finally, Chapter 22 takes an in-depth look at CSS3 flex layout, showing you how to create equal-height columns and display elements in a different order from the underlying HTML. The chapter also takes a brief look at other CSS3 features that should start arriving in browsers in the near future.

# CHAPTER 13

■ ■ ■

# Using Advanced Selectors

Chapter 2 introduced you to the 16 most commonly used selectors. Along the way, you've also been introduced to two more: the :first-child pseudo-class and the child selector. In this chapter, it's time to get up to speed with the remaining CSS3 selectors. There are another 24 in the CSS3 Selectors module, and even more have already been proposed for CSS4. You might be wondering why so many selectors are needed.

A fundamental principle behind CSS is the separation of content from presentation. If you rely all the time on using classes or ID selectors to mark up how your web pages should be presented, the separation begins to blur. The value of a wide range of selectors is that you can apply styles to elements in specific circumstances without the need for extra markup in the HTML. To give a simple, yet common example, rows of data in a table are much easier to read if they have alternate background colors. Until CSS3, the only way to add the colors was by assigning a class to each alternate row. And if you added or removed a row, you had to reassign the classes to each row. Thanks to the CSS3 :nth-child() pseudo-class, there's no need for any markup in the HTML. The colors are applied automatically. There's also a :not() pseudo-class that allows you to apply styles based on a negative condition. For example, you can create a style that applies to all list items except the first one.

Most of the selectors discussed in this chapter are pseudo-classes. But you'll also learn about additional attribute selectors, pseudo-elements, and *combinators*—selectors created by combining two selectors in a specific way. To make it easy to find information about selectors, this chapter covers not only the remaining 24 selectors from the CSS3 Selectors module, but also the two selectors introduced since Chapter 2, as well as ten pseudo-classes from the CSS3 Basic User Interface module (CSS3 UI). So, in combination with Chapter 2, this chapter provides a complete guide to CSS3 selectors.

In this chapter you'll learn about selecting:

- First, last, and only instances

- Elements based on their position in a series

- Elements that appear in combination with another

- Elements based on their state

- Elements based on a partial attribute match

---

■ **Note** Most of the selectors in this chapter will not work in IE 8 or older browsers.

---

## Selecting First, Last, and Only Instances

In Chapter 7, I introduced you briefly to the :first-child pseudo-class, which selects an element that is the first child of its parent. The :first-child pseudo-class is part of CSS2.1, and is supported by all browsers except IE 6. In CSS3, it has joined the group of closely related pseudo-classes in Table 13-1 that identify the first, last, and only instances of an element.

**Table 13-1.** *Structural Pseudo-classes that Select First, Last, and Only Instances*

| Pseudo-class | Description |
|---|---|
| :first-child | Selects an element that is the first child of its parent. |
| :last-child | Selects an element that is the last child of its parent. |
| :only-child | Selects an element that is the *only* child of its parent and has no siblings. |
| :first-of-type | Selects an element that is the first sibling of its type. |
| :last-of-type | Selects an element that is the last sibling of its type. |
| :only-of-type | Selects an element that is the only sibling of its type. It can have other siblings, but not of the same type. |

The difference between the "child" and "of-type" pseudo-classes lies in the relationship of the target element to its parent. The :first-child pseudo-class applies to the first element nested inside its parent, whereas the :first-of-type applies the first element of that particular type within its parent.

Take the following HTML markup in first-child.html in the ch13 folder:

```
<div id="aside">
    <h3>Climate</h3>
    <p>The Mediterranean has. . .</p>
    <h3>Getting There</h3>
```

In this example, the "Climate" heading is the first child of the aside <div>, so it's selected by the following style rule:

```
h3:first-child {
    text-transform: uppercase;
}
```

---

■ **Tip** In this case, you could use either h3:first-child or h3:first-of-type because the first child is always the first element of its type. But the first element of its type is not always the first child, as you'll see shortly.

---

The "Getting There" heading is nested deeper inside the <div>, so it ignores the h3:first-child style rule. As Figure 13-1 shows, only the first heading is converted to uppercase.

## CLIMATE

The Mediterranean has long, hot summers and mild, wet winters. Most of the rain falls during the winter months.

### Getting There

All countries on the northern side of the Mediterranean are well served by airports and rail services. There are also frequent ferries between the mainland and islands. The Mediterranean is also popular with cruise ships.

*Figure 13-1. The first heading is converted to uppercase*

But the <h3> heading is no longer the first child if you precede it with a skip link like this:

```
<div id="aside">
    <a href="#main">Skip to main content</a>
    <h3>Climate</h3>
```

Adding the link before the <h3> heading prevents h3:first-child from working. If you test first-child_skip.html, the first heading is no longer in uppercase. However, it's the first element of its type within the <div>, so you can use h3:first-of-type to select it like this (the code is in first-of-type.html):

```
h3:first-of-type {
    text-transform: uppercase;
}
```

If you test first-of-type.html, the first <h3> heading is in uppercase, but the second one is a mixture of uppercase and lowercase as before (see Figure 13-1).

The other pairs of pseudo-classes work the same way. With :last-child, the target must be the last element inside its parent, whereas with :last-of-type, other elements of a different type can follow. With :only-child, no other elements can be nested inside the parent. The :only-of-type pseudo-class targets an element that's the only one of its kind among other siblings.

---

■ **Tip** There's considerable overlap between these pseudo-classes. Sometimes, first, last, and only refer to the same element. Choosing the right one often requires careful thought. The "of-type" pseudo-classes are more flexible, but the "child" pseudo-classes give a finer level of control. For example, using :first-child means "apply this style only if nothing else precedes this element."

---

The :first-child and :last-child pseudo-classes are useful for styling navigation bars. The following styles have been added to the drop-down menu from Chapter 11 (see menu.html and styles/menu.css in the ch13 folder):

```
#nav > li:first-child a {
    border-radius: 10px 0 0 10px;
}
#nav > li:last-child a {
    border-radius: 0 10px 10px 0;
}
#nav ul li:first-child a {
    border-radius: 10px 10px 0 0;
}
#nav ul li:last-child a {
    border-radius: 0 0 10px 10px;
}
```

The first two selectors target the links in the first and last list items at the top level of the nav unordered list by using a child selector in combination with the :first-child and :last-child pseudo-classes. The last two selectors target links in the first and last list items of submenus. Figure 13-2 shows how these styles add rounded corners to the top-level menu and submenus.

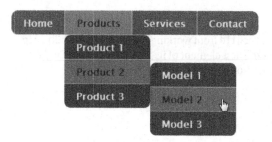

**Figure 13-2.** *The :first-child and :last-child pseudo-classes target the first and last menu items*

# Selecting Elements Based on their Position in a Series

What if you want to select an element that's not first or last, but you know its position in a series? The four pseudo-classes listed in Table 13-2 are designed for such situations.

**Table 13-2.** *Pseudo-classes that Select Elements from a Series*

| Pseudo-class | Description |
| --- | --- |
| :nth-child() | Selects the *nth*-child of its parent using the value between the parentheses. |
| :nth-last-child() | Selects the *nth*-child of its parent counting from the last one. |
| :nth-of-type() | Selects the *nth* sibling of its type. |
| :nth-last-of-type() | Selects the *nth* sibling of its type counting from the last one. |

To use these pseudo-classes, you pass a value to the parentheses indicating the position in the series that you want to select. The value can be a number, a keyword, or a formula.

## Using a Number to Specify the Position

Passing a number to one of the pseudo-classes in Table 13-2 selects the element at that position in the series. Unlike JavaScript and many other programming languages, the series begins at 1. For example, this selects the second paragraph within its parent element:

```
p:nth-of-type(2)
```

The nth-last pseudo-classes count from the end of the parent element. So, use this to select the penultimate paragraph:

```
p:nth-last-of-type(2)
```

## Using a Keyword

The two keywords that you can use with the pseudo-classes are odd and even.
The following selects every odd-numbered row in a table:

```
tr:nth-child(odd)
```

If you add or remove a row from the table, the browser automatically adjusts the styles. This is a huge time-saver for adding a different background color to alternate table rows.

## Specifying a Recurring Sequence

You can select a recurring sequence of elements, such as every third table row, by using the formula an ± b, in which a and b are numbers and n is the literal character.
The simple way to understand the formula is to treat n as zero and increment it by one throughout the series. For example, tr:nth-child(3n+1) selects the first, fourth, and seventh table rows like this:

```
(3 × 0) + 1 = 1
(3 × 1) + 1 = 4
(3 × 2) + 1 = 7
```

Similarly, tr:nth-child(5n+2) selects the second, seventh, and twelfth rows:

```
(5 × 0) + 2 = 2
(5 × 1) + 2 = 7
(5 × 2) + 2 = 12
```

If the minus sign follows n, the second value is deducted from the first. Values less than one are ignored. So, tr:nth-child(5n-2) selects the third, eighth, and thirteenth rows.

```
(5 × 0) - 2 = -2 /* ignored */
(5 × 1) - 2 = 3
(5 × 2) - 2 = 8
(5 × 3) - 2 = 13
```

Using the formula -n+b has the effect of selecting the first b elements. For example, the following selector sets the background color of the first three table rows to red:

```
tr:nth-child(-n+3) {
    background-color: #F00;
}
```

Understanding how to use the pseudo-classes in Table 13-2 can be a challenge. The following exercises should help clarify how they work.

## EXERCISE: STYLING ALTERNATE TABLE COLUMNS

In this exercise, you'll use CSS3 pseudo-classes to apply a different background color to table headers and alternate columns without the need for extra markup in the HTML. Use nth-of-type_cols_begin.html in the ch13 folder as your starting point. The finished table is in nth-of-type_cols_end.html.

1. The table has already been given some basic styles in the <head> of the page to prevent the text from wrapping inside table cells and headers and to adjust padding and spacing (styling tables is the subject of Chapter 14). However, the table looks quite plain (see Figure 13-3).

MALE LIFE EXPECTANCY AT BIRTH IN THE UK

| Year | Average | England | Wales | Scotland | N Ireland |
|------|---------|---------|-------|----------|-----------|
| 2000–2002 | 75.66 | 76.00 | 75.31 | 73.34 | 75.24 |
| 2001–2003 | 75.88 | 76.23 | 75.49 | 73.51 | 75.59 |
| 2002–2004 | 76.18 | 76.53 | 75.79 | 73.79 | 75.88 |
| 2003–2005 | 76.55 | 76.90 | 76.13 | 74.24 | 76.10 |
| 2004–2006 | 76.96 | 77.31 | 76.63 | 74.64 | 76.17 |
| 2005–2007 | 77.27 | 77.65 | 76.77 | 74.85 | 76.25 |
| 2006–2008 | 77.53 | 77.93 | 76.97 | 75.04 | 76.42 |
| 2007–2009 | 77.85 | 78.25 | 77.17 | 75.39 | 76.77 |
| 2008–2010 | 78.20 | 78.58 | 77.62 | 75.85 | 77.07 |

Adapted from data from the UK Office for National Statistics licensed under the Open Government Licence v.1.0.

**Figure 13-3.** *The table is nicely laid out, but lacks interest*

2. Browsers apply backgrounds to table elements in a specific order beginning with the table itself (the details are in "How Browsers Lay Out Tables" in Chapter 14). Give the whole table a background color by amending the table rule like this:

```
table {
    border-collapse: collapse;
    margin-left: 50px;
    background-color: #DED68B;
}
```

3. The first row and column act as labels for the data in the table, so should be styled differently. Although you could use pseudo-classes to identify the first row and

column, it's much simpler to create a style rule for the `<th>` tags. Add the following style rule at the bottom of the `<style>` block in the `<head>` of the page to give the headings a dark brown background and white text:

```
th {
    color: #FFF;
    background-color: #514F33;
}
```

4. To give alternate data columns a different background color, all that's needed is to apply a style to every other table cell like this:

```
td:nth-of-type(even) {
    background-color: #B7B173;
}
```

5. Save the page, and view it in a browser. In all modern browsers, the table looks like Figure 13-4. The light mustard color is inherited from the table, with the darker color applied to alternate table cells styling them as columns. IE 8 and older browsers understand all the style rules except the `:nth-of-type()` pseudo-class. As a result, they display the light mustard background for all the data columns.

MALE LIFE EXPECTANCY AT BIRTH IN THE UK

| Year | Average | England | Wales | Scotland | N Ireland |
|---|---|---|---|---|---|
| 2000–2002 | 75.66 | 76.00 | 75.31 | 73.34 | 75.24 |
| 2001–2003 | 75.88 | 76.23 | 75.49 | 73.51 | 75.59 |
| 2002–2004 | 76.18 | 76.53 | 75.79 | 73.79 | 75.88 |
| 2003–2005 | 76.55 | 76.90 | 76.13 | 74.24 | 76.10 |
| 2004–2006 | 76.96 | 77.31 | 76.63 | 74.64 | 76.17 |
| 2005–2007 | 77.27 | 77.65 | 76.77 | 74.85 | 76.25 |
| 2006–2008 | 77.53 | 77.93 | 76.97 | 75.04 | 76.42 |
| 2007–2009 | 77.85 | 78.25 | 77.17 | 75.39 | 76.77 |
| 2008–2010 | 78.20 | 78.58 | 77.62 | 75.85 | 77.07 |

Adapted from data from the UK Office for National Statistics licensed under the Open Government Licence v.1.0.

***Figure 13-4.*** *The columns now have alternate background colors*

6. The columns are different widths. Unless subsequent rows have wider content, the cells in the first row determine the width of each column. Because the first row consists entirely of `<th>` elements, amend the table header style rule like this to even up the size of the columns:

```
th {
    color: #FFF;
    background-color: #514F33;
    width: 16%;
}
```

7. There are six columns, so setting their width to 16% leaves 4% over. Add that to the first column by using the :first-child pseudo-class, which is understood by all browsers except IE 6. Add the following style rule to the page:

```
th:first-child {
    width: 20%;
}
```

The table now has evenly distributed data columns that have alternate background colors in all modern browsers. Although IE 8 and earlier don't apply the alternate colors, the table still looks much better than without any background at all.

The preceding exercise showed a simple use of :nth-of-type() using the even keyword. The next exercise demonstrates a slightly more complex example, using the an ± b formula to apply three different background colors in sequence to table rows.

## EXERCISE: STYLING TABLE ROWS IN SEQUENCE

In this exercise, you'll use the :nth-child() pseudo-class with the ab ± b formula to apply different colors to the rows in the table from the preceding exercise. Use as your starting point nth-child_rows_begin.html in the ch13 folder. The file is the same as at the end of the preceding exercise, but with the style for the background color of alternate columns removed. The finished table is in nth-child_rows_end.html.

1. The data cells currently inherit the light mustard background color from the table. This provides a fallback for older browsers that don't understand the CSS3 pseudo-classes. The second row contains the first row of data. To create a sequence of three background colors from light to dark, the lightest color needs to be applied to the second, fifth, and eight rows using the following style:

```
tr:nth-child(3n+2) {
    background-color: #DED68B; /*light */
}
```

2. Apply the medium background color to the third, sixth, and ninth rows like this:

```
tr:nth-child(3n+3) {
    background-color: #B7B173; /* medium */
}
```

3. The darkest color needs to be applied to the fourth, seventh, and ninth rows. The correct formula for this is 3n + 1, but that also applies to the first row. However, browsers apply the background to individual cells last of all. As a result, the dark brown background of the <th> cells overrides the colors applied to the rows. Just add the following style to the page:

```
tr:nth-child(3n+1) {
    background-color: #918C5B; /* dark */
}
```

4. Save the page, and view it in a browser. In all modern browsers, it looks like Figure 13-5.

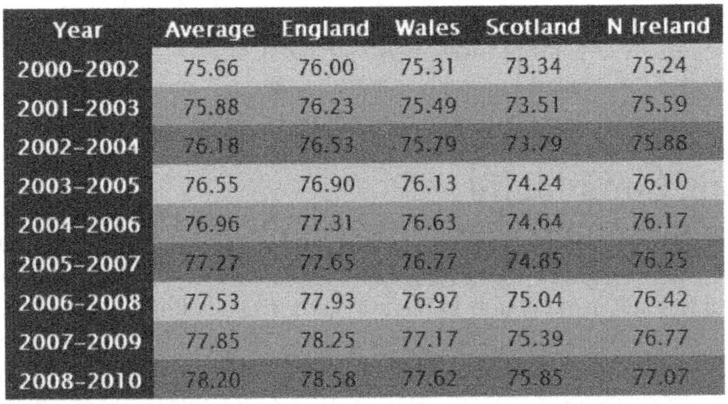

MALE LIFE EXPECTANCY AT BIRTH IN THE UK

| Year | Average | England | Wales | Scotland | N Ireland |
|---|---|---|---|---|---|
| 2000–2002 | 75.66 | 76.00 | 75.31 | 73.34 | 75.24 |
| 2001–2003 | 75.88 | 76.23 | 75.49 | 73.51 | 75.59 |
| 2002–2004 | 76.18 | 76.53 | 75.79 | 73.79 | 75.88 |
| 2003–2005 | 76.55 | 76.90 | 76.13 | 74.24 | 76.10 |
| 2004–2006 | 76.96 | 77.31 | 76.63 | 74.64 | 76.17 |
| 2005–2007 | 77.27 | 77.65 | 76.77 | 74.85 | 76.25 |
| 2006–2008 | 77.53 | 77.93 | 76.97 | 75.04 | 76.42 |
| 2007–2009 | 77.85 | 78.25 | 77.17 | 75.39 | 76.77 |
| 2008–2010 | 78.20 | 78.58 | 77.62 | 75.85 | 77.07 |

*Adapted from data from the UK Office for National Statistics licensed under the Open Government Licence v.1.0.*

***Figure 13-5.*** *The sequence of background colors is applied automatically*

IE 8 and older browsers don't understand the `:nth-child()` pseudo-class, so the data cells all have the same light mustard background color as in the preceding exercise.

# Selecting Elements Based on Their Relationship with Another

Some selectors are now officially known as *combinators* because they combine two selectors to indicate a relationship. The most common member of this category is the descendant selector (or descendant combinator, as the CSS3 Selectors module calls it), which you met in Chapter 2 and have used extensively in this book. You also learned about the child selector (or combinator) in Chapter 11.

■ **Note**   The name change makes no difference to how the descendant and child selectors work.

There are two other combinators: the adjacent sibling combinator and the general sibling combinator. For convenience of reference, all four are listed in Table 13-3.

***Table 13-3.*** *Combinators*

| Pattern | Name | Description |
|---|---|---|
| E F | Descendant combinator | Selects any F element that is a descendant of an E element. The descendant can be nested at any level. |
| E > F | Child combinator | Selects any F element that is the direct child of an E element. |
| E + F | Adjacent sibling combinator | Selects an F element that immediately follows a sibling of type E. |
| E ~ F | General sibling combinator | Selects all F elements that follow a sibling of type E. |

The only browser that doesn't support all combinators listed in Table 13-3 is IE 6, which supports only the descendant combinator.

The descendant and child combinators are very similar. The essential difference is that the child combinator selects only direct children, whereas the descendant combinator picks descendants nested at any level. So, #wrapper p selects paragraphs nested at any level inside an element with the ID wrapper, but #wrapper > p selects only paragraphs that are direct children. These combinators were covered in Chapters 2 and 11 respectively, so they don't need further explanation.

## Using the Adjacent Sibling Combinator

The adjacent sibling combinator matches an element immediately preceded by a sibling of the specified type. To create an adjacent sibling combinator, add a plus sign (+) between the two selectors. For example, the following selector applies styles to every paragraph that is immediately preceded by an <h3> heading:

```
h3 + p
```

The styles in adjacent-sibling.html indent the first line of each paragraph, but the adjacent sibling combinator removes the indent from paragraphs that immediately follow an <h3> heading like this:

```
p {
    margin: 0;
    text-indent: 2.5em;
    width: 650px;
}

h3 {
    margin-bottom: 0.25em;
}
h3 + p {
    text-indent: 0;
}
```

As Figure 13-6 shows, the first line of the first paragraph after each heading is flush with the left margin, but other paragraphs are indented.

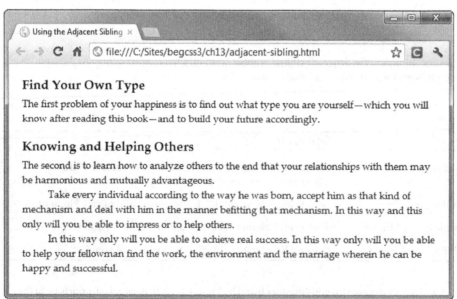

**Figure 13-6.** *The adjacent sibling combinator affects only the first paragraph after each heading*

310

This is much more efficient than using a class to style the first paragraph after each heading. Not only does it not require extra markup in the HTML, but the style is automatically transferred to the correct paragraph if you insert a new one or remove an existing one.

## Using the General Sibling Combinator

The general sibling combinator matches elements that are preceded by a specified element at the same level of the HTML hierarchy. You create it by adding a tilde (~) between the two selectors. For example, the following selector matches paragraphs that are preceded by an <h2> heading that is also a sibling:

```
h2 ~ p
```

The general sibling combinator differs from the adjacent sibling combinator in two important respects:

- The general sibling combinator targets all matching elements, not just the first.

- It doesn't matter if other elements are interposed between the elements specified in the general sibling combinator. The intervening elements are skipped until the next match is found.

The second point is particularly important because it can produce unexpected results. Let's say you want to emphasize the text in paragraphs following an <h2> heading by converting them to uppercase, the following style rule does the job:

```
h2 ~ p {
    text-transform: uppercase;
}
```

However, adding this style rule to general-sibling1.html results in *all* sibling paragraphs that follow an <h2> heading being converted to uppercase, as Figure 13-7 shows.

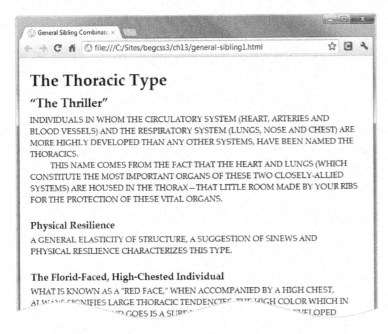

*Figure 13-7.* *Even paragraphs that follow <h3> headings are affected*

It's easy to make the mistake of thinking that h2 ~ p doesn't apply to paragraphs that follow <h3> headings. But if they're siblings of the <h2> heading, the style rule does apply unless you create another rule to override it. The styles in general-sibling2.html add another general sibling combinator to apply a different style to paragraphs that follow <h3> headings:

```
h2 ~ p {
    text-transform: uppercase;
}
h3 ~ p {
    text-transform: none;
}
```

As Figure 13-8 shows, the paragraphs following the <h3> headings are now rendered normally.

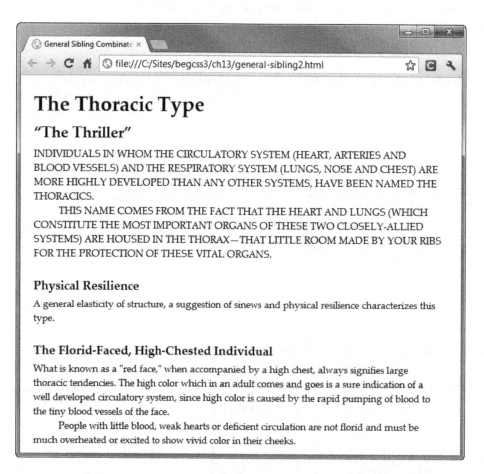

*Figure 13-8.* *A separate rule controls the paragraphs after the <h3> headings*

# Selecting Form Elements Based on Their State

HTML5 is making a major change in the way that browsers handle online forms by introducing new input types and attributes, such as required, min, and max. Many browsers now also validate user input before the form is submitted, something that until recently was possible only with JavaScript. In line with these changes, CSS3 has introduced a large number of pseudo-classes that allow you to style form elements based on their state.

Because of the modularization of CSS3, only three of the new pseudo-classes were included in the CSS3 Selectors module, which was formally approved in September 2011. A further 10 have been added in the draft CSS3 UI module. The only significance of the pseudo-classes being in different modules is the speed of implementation.

Table 13-4 lists all 13 pseudo-classes. The first three made it into the CSS3 Selectors module, and are fully supported by all modern browsers, including IE 9. The others appear to have been an afterthought, and are being gradually implemented.

*Table 13-4.* *Pseudo-classes that Select Form Elements Based on Their State*

| Pseudo-class | Description |
|---|---|
| :enabled | Matches a form element that is not disabled. |
| :disabled | Matches a form element that is disabled. |
| :checked | Matches a form element that has been checked or selected. |
| :indeterminate | Matches a form element that is in an indeterminate state. See the following text for an explanation of what this means. |
| :default | Matches the default option(s) among a group of similar elements. |
| :valid | Matches elements that have a valid data value. |
| :invalid | Matches elements that have an invalid data value. |
| :in-range | Matches elements with a data value that's within the prescribed range. |
| :out-of-range | Matches elements with a data value outside the prescribed range. |
| :required | Matches required form elements. |
| :optional | Matches form elements that are not required. |
| :read-only | Matches elements whose contents cannot be altered by the user. |
| :read-write | Matches elements, such as text input fields, whose contents can be altered by the user. |

■ **Tip** A good place to check which browsers support the pseudo-classes in Table 13-4 (or any other CSS feature) is the Mozilla Developer Network's CSS Reference at https://developer.mozilla.org/en/CSS_Reference.

Most of the pseudo-classes listed in Table 13-4 are self-explanatory. However, :indeterminate needs some explanation.

HTML5 introduces a new indeterminate DOM property for check boxes. By default, it's false. The only way to turn it on is through JavaScript like this, for example:

```
<script>
document.getElementById('checkbox1').indeterminate = true;
</script>
```

As soon as the check box is selected, the indeterminate property is switched to false. It remains false even if the check box is subsequently deselected. When used with check boxes, the :indeterminate pseudo-class applies only when the indeterminate property is set to true.

However, the draft specification gives as examples of the :indeterminate pseudo-class a radio button group with no preselected option and a progress meter when the percentage completion is unknown. Neither case is currently supported by any browser.

---

## EXERCISE: STYLING FORM INPUT FIELDS

This exercise demonstrates the use of some of the pseudo-classes in Table 13-4, changing the look of form input fields depending on their current state. The styles in this exercise work in all modern browsers except IE 9. Use form_begin.html in the ch13 folder as your starting point. The completed form is in form_end.html.

1. Load the form into a browser. The existing styles align the input fields and set the font properties, but otherwise the form is unstyled (see Figure 13-9).

# Order Now

**Name:**

**Email:**

**Your website:**

**Number required:**

[Submit Order] [Clear Form]

*Figure 13-9.* *The form has only basic styles*

2. In the <style> block in the <head> of the page, add the following styles to give fields with valid input values a pale green background, and a pale pink background to invalid ones:

```
input:valid {
    background-color: rgba(188, 237, 180, 0.5);
}
input:invalid {
    background-color: rgba(252, 231, 239, 0.5);
}
```

3. Save the page, and reload the form in a browser. In all browsers that support the :valid and :invalid pseudo-classes, the first, second, and fourth input fields have a pale pink background. This is because the HTML markup for each of these input fields includes the HTML5 required attribute. Without a value, the field is considered invalid. However, the third field doesn't use the required attribute, so it's considered valid and colored green. Some browsers also consider the submit button or both the submit and reset buttons as valid, so give them the same background color (although you can't see the colors in Figure 13-10 in the printed book, use your imagination).

# Order Now

Name:

Email:

Your website:

Number required:

Submit Order | Clear Form

*Figure 13-10.* *Without a value, the required input fields have a pink background*

4. Remove the background color from the field that's not required by using the `:optional` pseudo-class to set its background color to `transparent`:

```
input:optional {
    background-color: transparent;
}
```

5. If you test the page again, the green background disappears from the third input field in all browsers. But in WebKit-based browsers, it also removes the background color of the submit and reset buttons. To avoid affecting the buttons, change the selector in the previous step to select only the input field, which uses the HTML5 `url` type.

```
input[type="url"]:optional {
    background-color: transparent;
}
```

6. There are two buttons in the form, but the submit button is the default. So, you can give it a background color of its own, and style the text using the `:default` pseudo-class like this:

```
input:default {
    background-color: #167F39;
    color: #FFF;
    font-weight: bold;
}
```

7. Save the page, and reload the form in a browser. As soon as you start typing in the first text input field, the background color turns green, indicating that the field is now valid.

8. Tab to the next field or click inside it. Type a value that's not valid as an email address format, and move to the next field. The background of the second field doesn't change color, indicating that it's not valid, as shown in Figure 13-11 (again, you'll need to use your imagination—the colors look almost identical in the printed book).

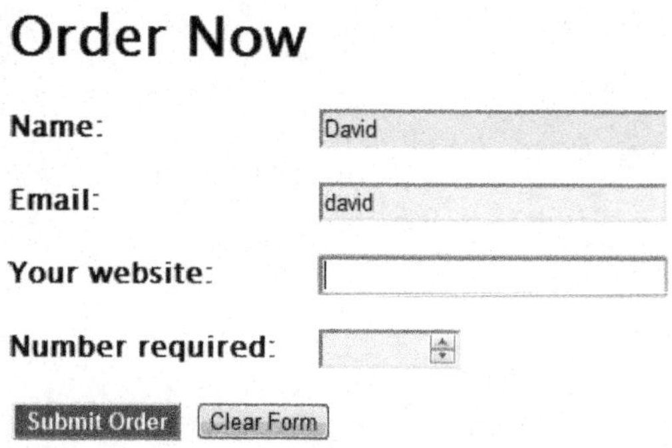

# Order Now

**Name:** David

**Email:** david

**Your website:**

**Number required:**

Submit Order    Clear Form

***Figure 13-11.*** *The second field remains pink because the value is invalid as an email address*

9. Change the value in the second field to a valid email address format. The field turns green.

10. Type a value in the third field that's invalid as a URL format. The field doesn't change color to indicate an invalid value.

11. Fix that by adding a new selector to the style for invalid values. You can chain two pseudo-classes to apply the style to optional fields that are invalid like this:

```
input:invalid, input:optional:invalid {
    background-color: rgba(252, 231, 239, 0.5);
}
```

12. Save and reload the page. Try entering an invalid value for the third field. The background color still doesn't change because there's a conflict between `input:optional:invalid` and `input[type="url"]:optional`. Both set the `background-color` property, but attribute selectors and pseudo-classes have the same specificity (see "What Happens When Style Rules Conflict?" in Chapter 2).

13. Move the style rule that uses the attribute selector above the rule for invalid entries like this:

```
input[type="url"]:optional {
    background-color: transparent;
}
input:invalid, input:optional:invalid {
    background-color: rgba(252, 231, 239, 0.5);
}
```

14. Save and test the page again. This time, the third field changes color when you enter an invalid value for a URL, as shown in Figure 13-12.

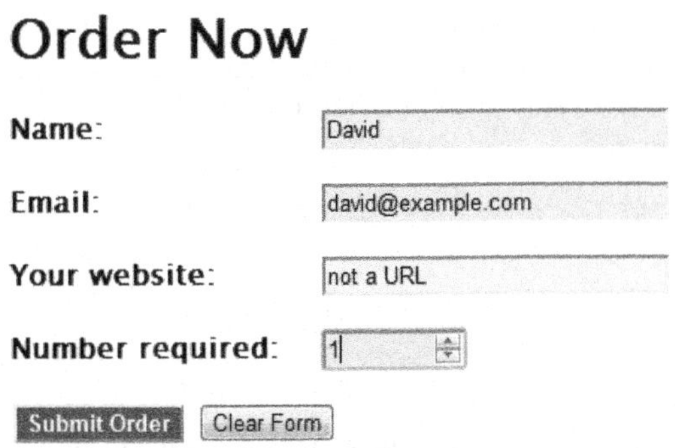

# Order Now

**Name:** David

**Email:** david@example.com

**Your website:** not a URL

**Number required:** 1

Submit Order    Clear Form

*Figure 13-12. The field changes color to indicate an invalid value*

Styling form elements based on their state provides a useful visual clue about the validity of data input. At the time of this writing, browser support is incomplete and slightly inconsistent. So, it's important to test thoroughly before deploying the pseudo-classes listed in Table 13-4.

# Selecting Elements Based on Negative Factors

The two pseudo-classes listed in Table 13-5 select elements based on negative factors. They are supported by all modern browsers except IE 8 and earlier.

*Table 13-5. Pseudo-classes Based on Negative Factors*

| Pseudo-class | Description |
|---|---|
| :not() | Matches elements based on a negative condition. |
| :empty | Matches elements that have no content. To be empty, an element cannot even have whitespace between the opening and closing tags. |

To use the :not() pseudo-class, you place a simple selector as the condition between the parentheses. The condition must be one of the following:

- The universal selector (*)
- A type selector
- An attribute selector
- A class or pseudo-class
- An ID selector.

For example, using the :first-child pseudo-class as the condition in the following selector matches all table rows, except the first:

```
tr:not(:first-child)
```

Similarly, the following selector matches all table cells, except the last one in each row:

```
td:not(:last-child)
```

The :empty pseudo-class, on the other hand, selects elements that are completely empty. The definition of empty is very strict: the element must contain nothing between the opening and closing tags—not even a space.

The following styles in negative.html demonstrate the :not() and :empty pseudo-classes:

```
tr:not(:first-child) > th {
    text-align:left;
}
td:empty {
    background-color:#D8F2D7;
}
```

By default, browsers center the text in <th> cells. So, the first style rule left-aligns the text in all table header cells except those in the first row. The second style rule assigns a different background color to empty cells. Figure 13-13 shows the result in a modern browser. In IE 8 and older browsers, the table headers in rows 2–5 are centered, and the empty cells have the same background color as those with data.

SALES FIGURES 2012

| Salesperson | Q1 | Q2 | Q3 | Q4 | Total |
|---|---|---|---|---|---|
| Jim Black | 250,000 | 300,000 | | | 550,000 |
| Jane Brown | 225,000 | 275,000 | | | 500,000 |
| George Green | 300,000 | 275,000 | | | 575,000 |
| Amanda White | 325,000 | 300,000 | | | 625,000 |

*Figure 13-13.* *The headers in the first row and the empty cells are styled differently*

# Other Selectors

You've now covered the overwhelming majority of CSS3 selectors. The section covers the remaining selectors that don't conveniently fit into one of the other categories.

## Pseudo-classes

There are just three more pseudo-classes, which are listed in Table 13-6. The first two are new to CSS3. They're supported by all modern browsers, but not by IE 8 and earlier.

*Table 13-6.* *Miscellaneous Pseudo-classes*

| Pseudo-class | Description |
|---|---|
| :root | Matches the root element of the document. In HTML, this is always the <html> element. |
| :target | Matches the target of a URL fragment, such as an ID or named anchor. |
| :lang() | Matches elements based on their language. Supported by IE 8+. |

The :root pseudo-class is mainly intended for use with XML.

The most interesting pseudo-class in Table 13-6 is :target. This allows you to draw attention to the section of a page that has been accessed through a link that ends with a *URL fragment*—a hash sign (#) followed by an ID or anchor name. The style is applied only when the page is loaded through such a link, either from within the same page or from an external link. At all other times, the style is ignored.

To demonstrate how the :target pseudo-class works, target1.html contains a large number of internal links to descriptions of the first 12 chapters of this book. All the headings have a white background when the page first loads. If you click one of the links in the menu at the top of the page, the browser jumps to the relevant heading, and the following style rule gives it a green background and some padding:

```
:target {
    background-color:rgba(0,102,51,0.2);
    padding: 3px;
}
```

Highlighting the target of a URL fragment is particularly useful when the target is so far down the page, that the browser can't scroll it to the top, as shown in Figure 13-14.

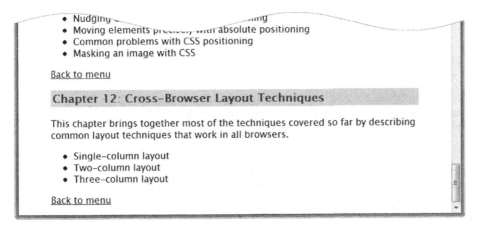

***Figure 13-14.*** *The pseudo-class highlights the heading only when it's accessed through a link*

The menu at the top of the page has the ID menu, which also gets a green background if you click one of the "Back to menu" links. To prevent this from happening, target2.html combines the :target pseudo-class with the :not() pseudo-class like this:

```
:target:not(#menu) {
    background-color: rgba(0,102,51,0.2);
    padding: 3px;
}
```

The :lang() pseudo-class selects elements according to their language, as long as it's identified in some way through the HTML markup or HTTP headers. For example, lang_pseudo-class.html contains several expressions in French, which are wrapped in <span> elements with the lang attribute like this:

```
<p>The market is in the <span lang="fr">Cours Saleya</span>, just off the <span lang="fr">Quai des Etats Unis</span>, near the Old Town (<span lang="fr">Vieille Ville</span>). . .</p>
```

The following style rule displays the French expressions in italic font:

```
:lang(fr) {
    font-style: italic;
}
```

## Attribute Selectors

Chapter 2 introduced four commonly used attribute selectors. There are three more, as listed in Table 13-7. They are supported by all browsers except IE 6.

*Table 13-7.*  *Miscellaneous Attribute Selectors*

| Pattern | Description |
|---------|-------------|
| E[attr*="x"] | Matches any E element where the attr attribute contains the substring x. |
| E[attr~="x"] | Matches any E element where the attr attribute is a list of space-separated values, one of which is exactly x. |
| E[attr\|="x"] | Matches any E element where the value of the attr attribute is either exactly x or x immediately followed by a hyphen. |

The first attribute selector in Table 13-7 matches whole words or part-words. For example, img[title*="jest"] matches images that contain jest, jester, or majesty in their title attribute.

If you replace the asterisk with a tilde, the selector matches only whole words within a space-separated list. For example, img[title~="jest"] matches images that contain jest, but not jester or majesty in their title attribute.

The final selector in Table 13-7 is intended primarily for matching language codes, for example a[hreflang|="fr"] matches <a> elements that have either hreflang = "fr-CA" and hreflang = "fr-FR" in the opening tag. Unlike the :lang() pseudo-class, this attribute selector ignores language information sent in the HTTP headers. It applies only to elements with a matching attribute.

---

■ **Tip**   The value being matched is case-sensitive, but in HTML the attribute name is not. So, in HTML (but not XHTML), img[TITLE~="jest"] and img[title~="jest"] both match an image with jest—but not Jest—in its title attribute. CSS4 proposes introducing case-insensitive matches.

---

## Pseudo-elements for Generated Content

The last two selectors are the pseudo-elements listed in Table 13-8.

*Table 13-8.*  *Pseudo-elements for Generated Content*

| Pseudo-element | Description |
|----------------|-------------|
| ::before | Creates generated content before an element. IE 8 supports only the CSS2.1 version prefixed by a single colon (:before). |
| ::after | Creates generated content after an element. IE 8 supports only :after. |

These pseudo-elements are used exclusively for automatic content generation, which is the subject of a separate chapter. I'll explain how they're used in Chapter 15.

---

■ **Note** The CSS3 Selectors module originally included a `::selection` pseudo-element, which was designed to add styles to elements selected by the user in the browser. Although it was implemented by some browsers, none of them implemented it correctly, so it was dropped by the W3C.

---

# Summary

This chapter has provided a whirlwind overview of the remaining CSS3 selectors. Among the most useful are pseudo-classes that make it possible to select elements based on their position in the HTML hierarchy. The CSS3 UI selectors that style form elements according to their dynamic state are another useful group. You can also use the `:not()` pseudo-class to exclude specific types of elements. Altogether, there are 52 selectors in CSS3. And it doesn't stop there. The CSS4 Selectors module is already well advanced, introducing many more. Perhaps the most exciting future addition is the ability to select the parent of a specific element.

This continuing expansion of selectors is a double-edged sword. It makes it possible to apply styles with greater accuracy without the need for extra HTML markup. At the same time, it's a pain trying to work out which selectors have a broad enough level of browser support to make their use practicable. This dilemma is not new to CSS3, and it's unlikely to end in the foreseeable future. Use the selectors from Chapter 2 to provide a solid layout and design for all browsers. Then use the more advanced selectors from this chapter to provide an enhanced experience for users of the most recent browsers.

In the next chapter, we'll take a look at improving the presentation of data tables with CSS.

# CHAPTER 14

▪ ▪ ▪

# Styling Tables

For years, tables were the only way to build a grid structure to lay out web pages. Thankfully, tables are no longer necessary—or indeed recommended—for page layout. Normally, they should be used only for the display of data that needs to be presented in a grid format—timetables, price lists, sports results, and so on. That's the focus of this chapter: styling tables that contain data.

There are no plans to add any new features to tables in CSS3. However, using the CSS3 selectors described in the preceding chapter makes it considerably easier to style tables without the need for extra markup in the HTML.

In this chapter, you'll learn about the following:

- Styling borders around tables and individual cells
- Adjusting the space between table cells and inside them
- Moving the position of the table caption
- Suppressing the display of empty cells
- Preventing columns from exceeding a fixed width
- Controlling the horizontal and vertical alignment of content in table cells

Before diving into the details of styling tables with CSS, it's important to understand the basic structure of tables and how browsers lay out the various components.

## Basic Table Structure

In HTML 4.01 and XHTML 1.0, you can add a border to the table, give it a width, and adjust the space around the data by adding the border, width, cellpadding, and cellspacing attributes to the opening <table> tag. In HTML5, only the border attribute is valid and, if used, its value must either be an empty string or 1.

Removing the width, cellpadding, and cellspacing attributes from the <table> tag produces only the bare bones of a data table like the one in basic_table.html, which looks like this:

```
<table border="1">
    <tr>
        <td>Row 1-1</td>
        <td>Row 1-2</td>
    </tr>
    <tr>
        <td>Row 2-1</td>
        <td>Row 2-2</td>
    </tr>
</table>
```

Setting the border attribute to 1 puts a 1px border around the whole table and each individual cell, producing the effect of a raised double border around each cell. Because there's no width, cellspacing, or cellpadding, the table collapses around the content, as shown in Figure 14-1.

| Row 1-1 | Row 1-2 |
|---------|---------|
| Row 2-1 | Row 2-2 |

*Figure 14-1.* A basic table with border

This minimalist layout not only looks ugly; it's difficult to read if there are more than a handful of data cells. However, CSS gives you greater control over horizontal and vertical spacing than cellpadding and cellspacing. It also offers better options for controlling the borders of table elements, so it's usually advisable to omit the border attribute from the opening <table> tag.

First, though, let's continue exploring how tables are structured and laid out.

## Header Cells

In addition to <td> tags, you can use <th> tags to indicate that a cell is a row or column header. The table in header_cells.html contains <th> tags in the first row and in the first cell of each subsequent row. By default, browsers center the text in <th> tags and display it in a bold font, as shown in Figure 14-2.

| Region | Q1 | Q2 | Q3 | Q4 |
|--------|------|------|------|------|
| **England & Wales** | 365,000 | 400,000 | 450,000 | 575,000 |
| **Scotland** | 200,000 | 250,000 | 300,000 | 330,000 |
| **Northern Ireland** | 270,000 | 200,000 | 245,000 | 300,000 |

*Figure 14-2.* Text in header cells is normally bold and centered

## Table Captions

The <caption> tag displays a caption for the table. The tag must come immediately after the opening <table> tag like this (the code is in caption.html):

```
<table>
    <caption>Regional Sales Results</caption>
    <tr>
```

By default, browsers display the caption above the table, as in Figure 14-3, but you can use the CSS caption-side property to move it under the table, as described later in this chapter.

Regional Sales Results

| Region | Q1 | Q2 | Q3 | Q4 |
|---|---|---|---|---|
| England & Wales | 365,000 | 400,000 | 450,000 | 575,000 |
| Scotland | 200,000 | 250,000 | 300,000 | 330,000 |
| Northern Ireland | 270,000 | 200,000 | 245,000 | 300,000 |

*Figure 14-3. By default, table captions are displayed above the table*

---

■ **Caution**   The `<caption>` element must come immediately after the opening `<table>` tag, even if you want to display the caption below the table.

---

## Defining Table Columns

HTML tables are constructed as a series of table rows rather than columns. The column structure is simply implied by the cells stacked on top of one another in each row. However, you can also define columns in the HTML markup by adding one or more `<colgroup>` elements immediately after the table caption. If the table doesn't have a caption, the `<colgroup>` elements come immediately after the opening `<table>` tag. A `<colgroup>` can optionally contain `<col>` elements to identify individual columns.

The `<colgroup>` and `<col>` elements are not displayed. They're used purely to identify column groups or individual columns for layout and styling. In HTML 4.01 and XHTML 1.0, you can use the `align`, `valign`, and `width` attributes in both tags to control the horizontal and vertical alignment and width of all cells within a column group or column. However, these attributes are no longer valid in HTML5.

---

■ **Note**   All browsers—even as far back as IE 4—support `<colgroup>` and `<col>`. Although they've been around for a long time, these elements are rarely used. I've included them here because they occupy a position in the order browsers construct tables, as described in "How Browsers Lay Out Tables" later in this chapter.

---

You specify the number of columns in the group with the span attribute. So, let's say you have a five-column table, and you use the first column for labels and the remaining columns for data, you could style the column groups using classes like this:

```
<colgroup span="1" class="labelcol">
<colgroup span="4" class="datacol">
```

Alternatively, you can list individual columns using `<col>` tags inside `<colgroup>` tags like this:

```
<colgroup>
    <col class="labelcol">
    <col class="oddcol">
    <col class="evencol">
    <col class="oddcol">
    <col class="evencol">
</colgroup>
```

The `<col>` tag also accepts the `span` attribute, so you can apply the same class to multiple adjacent columns. The following example applies the `datacol` class to the three middle columns of a table:

```
<colgroup>
    <col class="labelcol">
    <col span="3" class="datacol">
    <col class="lastcol">
</colgroup>
```

The number of columns in the table must be the same as specified in the `<colgroup>` and `<col>` tags.

---

■ **Tip**  In modern browsers, you can use the `:nth-child()` and related pseudo-classes (see Chapter 13) to style table columns without the need for `<colgroup>` and `<col>`. However, they can be useful for styling table columns in older browsers that don't support CSS3 selectors.

---

## Defining Table Header and Footer Rows

Immediately after the column definitions, you can define table header and footer rows. The table header comes first and consists of one or more table rows enclosed in a pair of `<thead>` tags. The table footer follows the table header and consists of one or more table rows inside a pair of `<tfoot>` tags.

The principal advantage of using `<thead>` and `<tfoot>` is that browsers add the header and footer rows at the top and bottom of each page when printing a long table. Although it seems counterintuitive, the `<tfoot>` section normally comes before the main body of the table. You'll see how this works in the next section.

## Grouping Table Rows into Sections

To divide a table into horizontal sections, you can wrap one or more rows in pairs of `<tbody>` tags. The table in table_sections.html uses `<tbody>` tags to separate a company's sales report into sections. It also has table header and footer rows like this:

```
<table>
    <thead>
        <tr>
            <th>Period</th>
            <th>Results</th>
            <th>Amount</th>
        </tr>
    </thead>
    <tfoot>
        <tr>
            <th>Period</th>
            <th>Results</th>
            <th>Amount</th>
        </tr>
    </tfoot>
    <tbody id="q1">
        <tr>
            <td>Q1</td>
            <td>Sales</td>
```

```
                <td>$4.5m</td>
        </tr>
        <tr>
                <td> </td>
                <td>Expenditure</td>
                <td>$4.1m</td>
        </tr>
</tbody>
<tbody id="q2">
        <tr>
                <td>Q2</td>
                <td>Sales</td>
                <td>$4.9m</td>
        </tr>
        <tr>
                <td> </td>
                <td>Expenditure</td>
                <td>$4.7m</td>
        </tr>
</tbody>
</table>
```

The <tbody> tags divide the table into sections that can be styled independently. The screenshot on the left of Figure 14-4 shows the table with some simple styles added. Note how the <tfoot> section is displayed at the bottom of the table, even though it comes before either of the <tbody> sections. This is not the result of the CSS styles. You can verify this by commenting out the styles in the <head> of the page. The <tfoot> section is still at the bottom of the table, as shown on the right of Figure 14-4.

| Period | Results | Amount |
|--------|---------|--------|
| Q1 | Sales | $4.5m |
|  | Expenditure | $4.1m |
| Q2 | Sales | $4.9m |
|  | Expenditure | $4.7m |
| Period | Results | Amount |

| Period | Results | Amount |
|--------|---------|--------|
| Q1 | Sales | $4.5m |
|  | Expenditure | $4.1m |
| Q2 | Sales | $4.9m |
|  | Expenditure | $4.7m |
| Period | Results | Amount |

**Figure 14-4.** *Dividing the table into sections allows you to apply different styles*

## How Browsers Lay Out Tables

That excursion into the lesser known table elements was intended as a prelude to help you understand how browsers assemble tables in six stages, as follows:

1. Table

2. Column groups

3. Individual columns

4. Row groups

5. Individual rows

6. Individual cells

To show how tables are rendered, layout_order.html progressively adds styles to the whole table, followed by a group of two columns, a single column within that group, a group of two rows, an individual row within that group, and finally two individual cells (see Figure 14-5).

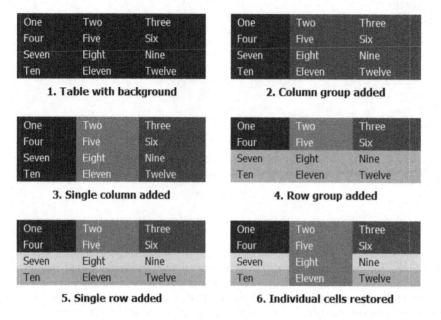

**Figure 14-5.** *Table elements are layered on top of each other in a specific order*

Each style, apart from the one applied to the individual cells, uses a lighter shade of gray, which should make it obvious that it's being painted on top of the previous one and obscuring it.

---

■ **Tip**    If you keep this six-stage process in mind, it will help you understand why a background style is being applied in a particular way—or more often, why a style isn't working as expected. All browsers work this way, so you don't need to worry about anomalies with older browsers.

---

# Styling Tables with CSS

CSS has five properties dedicated to controlling the structure of tables. These are listed in Table 14-1. Also listed are text-align and vertical-align, which are frequently used with tables.

**Table 14-1.** *CSS Table Properties*

| Property | Initial Value | Inherited | Description |
|---|---|---|---|
| border-collapse | separate | Yes | By default, the table and each cell have independent borders. Borders are merged by setting the value of this property to collapse. |
| border-spacing | 0 | Yes | Controls the spacing between table cells. Horizontal and vertical spacing can be controlled independently. |
| caption-side | top | Yes | Determines whether the table caption is displayed above or below the table. |
| empty-cells | show | Yes | If set to hide, turns off the display of borders and backgrounds associated with empty table cells. |
| table-layout | auto | No | If set to fixed, the width of each column is set in the column definitions or first row. |
| text-align | left | Yes | Controls the horizontal alignment of content in table cells. With right-to-left languages, the default is right. |
| vertical-align | middle | No | Controls vertical alignment in table cells. |

All the properties in Table 14-1 are fully supported by all browsers in widespread use, including IE 8. Earlier versions of Internet Explorer support them with some minor exceptions.

## Styling Table Borders

When you use CSS to add a border to a table, the border affects only the table, and not the cells inside. You can control each border independently, using the same border properties described in Chapter 9. The styles in double_border.html define the table border like this (see Figure 14-6):

```
table {
    border: #000 double 10px;
}
```

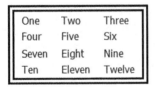

**Figure 14-6.** *With CSS, you can use any border style for a table; the cells are not affected*

In fact, you don't need to declare a border or use the same style on every side. The styles in different_borders.html add a top and bottom border like this (see Figure 14-7):

```
table {
    border-top: #000 double 10px;
    border-bottom: #999 solid 5px;
}
```

| One | Two | Three |
| Four | Five | Six |
| Seven | Eight | Nine |
| Ten | Eleven | Twelve |

**Figure 14-7.** *Tables can have different style borders or none at all on each side*

For that extra special table, you can even use a border image. You apply it in exactly the same way as to any other element (see Chapter 9 for details). The styles in border-image.html add a default double border, and then use the `border-image` shorthand property with browser-specific prefixes like this:

```
table {
    border: 24px double #4B8896;
    -moz-border-image: url(images/frame1.png) 24 round;
    -o-border-image: url(images/frame1.png) 24 round;
    -webkit-border-image: url(images/frame1.png) 24 fill round;
    border-image: url(images/frame1.png) 24 fill round ;
}
```

Browsers that support border images render the table as shown in Figure 14-8.

**Figure 14-8.** *You can even use a border image for a table*

## Adding Borders to Table Cells

Because adding a table border with CSS has no effect on the table cells, you need to create a separate style for the cells. This gives you the freedom to choose a different color and/or style for the cell borders. The style rules in cell_borders.html add a 1px solid red border to all table cells like this:

```
td {
    border: #F00 solid 1px;
}
```

As you can see in Figure 14-9, the border around each cell is separate from the table border, and there is a small gap between each cell.

**Figure 14-9.** *By default, there is a space between each cell border*

## Eliminating the Space Between Cells

To eliminate the gap between cell borders, use `border-collapse`, which accepts just two values, namely:

> **collapse** This merges adjacent borders within a table.

> **separate** This is the default setting, which leaves a small gap between table cells. To create a gap larger than the default, you need to use `border-spacing`, which is described later in this chapter.

In border-collapse.html, the table and cells are styled like this:

```
table {
    border: #000 solid 5px;
    border-collapse: collapse;
}
td {
    border: #F00 solid 1px;
}
```

As Figure 14-10 shows, the gap between the cells is not only eliminated, but the border around each cell is just 1px thick, and there's no red border sandwiched between the outer cells and the table border. Because the table border is wider, it hides the outer borders of adjacent cells. But if the cell borders are the same width as the table border, the table border is hidden.

| One | Two | Three |
| Four | Five | Six |
| Seven | Eight | Nine |
| Ten | Eleven | Twelve |

*Figure 14-10.  Using border-collapse creates single borders around the cells*

---

■ **Tip**  The `border-collapse` property follows strict rules to decide how to merge adjacent borders. The basic principle is that only the wider border is displayed. See `www.w3.org/TR/CSS2/tables.html#border-conflict-resolution` for the full rules governing how borders are merged.

---

## Adding Borders to Columns and Rows

As long as `border-collapse` is set to `collapse`, you can define borders for table columns and rows. Most browsers support borders on all table elements, including `<tr>`, `<tbody>`, `<thead>`, `<tfoot>`, `<col>`, and `<colgroup>`, as well as `<th>` and `<td>`. However, IE 6 and IE 7 support borders only on individual table cells. As a result, the most reliable cross-browser solution is to apply a right border to table cells to create a border on table columns, and to apply a bottom border on table cells to add a border to table rows. If the table border is the same color or wider, the border of the last column or row merges with the table border. For example, column_borders. html adapts the file from one of the exercises in Chapter 13 to add a 1px border to the table and a 1px right border to the `<th>` and `<td>` cells like this:

```
table {
    border-collapse: collapse;
    margin-left: 35px;
```

```
    background-color: #DED68B;
    border: 1px solid #514F33;
}
th, td {
    padding: 5px 10px;
    text-align: center;
    white-space: nowrap;
    border-right: 1px solid #514F33;
}
```

The border color is the same as the background color of the <th> cells. Figure 14-11 shows the result.

MALE LIFE EXPECTANCY AT BIRTH IN THE UK

| Year | Average | England | Wales | Scotland | N Ireland |
|------|---------|---------|-------|----------|-----------|
| 2000–2002 | 75.66 | 76.00 | 75.31 | 73.34 | 75.24 |
| 2001–2003 | 75.88 | 76.23 | 75.49 | 73.51 | 75.59 |
| 2002–2004 | 76.18 | 76.53 | 75.79 | 73.79 | 75.88 |
| 2003–2005 | 76.55 | 76.90 | 76.13 | 74.24 | 76.10 |
| 2004–2006 | 76.96 | 77.31 | 76.63 | 74.64 | 76.17 |
| 2005–2007 | 77.27 | 77.65 | 76.77 | 74.85 | 76.25 |
| 2006–2008 | 77.53 | 77.93 | 76.97 | 75.04 | 76.42 |
| 2007–2009 | 77.85 | 78.25 | 77.17 | 75.39 | 76.77 |
| 2008–2010 | 78.20 | 78.58 | 77.62 | 75.85 | 77.07 |

*Adapted from data from the UK Office for National Statistics licensed under the Open Government Licence v.1.0.*

***Figure 14-11.*** *Adding a right-border to table cells is a cross-browser way of adding borders to columns*

Although IE 6 doesn't support the alternate background colors, it renders the borders correctly, as Figure 14-12 shows.

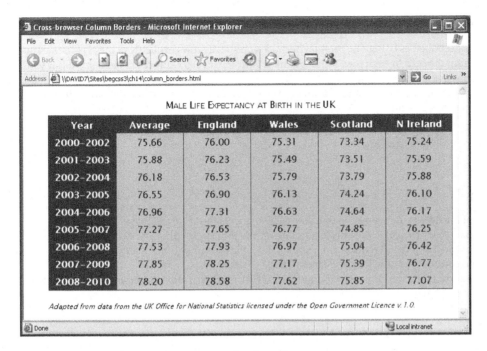

**Figure 14-12.** *Even older browsers support border-collapse*

Switching the border from the right to the bottom of each cell creates row borders, as shown in Figure 14-13 (the code is in row_borders.html):

MALE LIFE EXPECTANCY AT BIRTH IN THE UK

| Year | Average | England | Wales | Scotland | N Ireland |
| --- | --- | --- | --- | --- | --- |
| 2000–2002 | 75.66 | 76.00 | 75.31 | 73.34 | 75.24 |
| 2001–2003 | 75.88 | 76.23 | 75.49 | 73.51 | 75.59 |
| 2002–2004 | 76.18 | 76.53 | 75.79 | 73.79 | 75.88 |
| 2003–2005 | 76.55 | 76.90 | 76.13 | 74.24 | 76.10 |
| 2004–2006 | 76.96 | 77.31 | 76.63 | 74.64 | 76.17 |
| 2005–2007 | 77.27 | 77.65 | 76.77 | 74.85 | 76.25 |
| 2006–2008 | 77.53 | 77.93 | 76.97 | 75.04 | 76.42 |
| 2007–2009 | 77.85 | 78.25 | 77.17 | 75.39 | 76.77 |
| 2008–2010 | 78.20 | 78.58 | 77.62 | 75.85 | 77.07 |

*Adapted from data from the UK Office for National Statistics licensed under the Open Government Licence v.1.0.*

**Figure 14-13.** *Adding a border to the bottom of each cell creates cross-browser row borders*

## Applying Other Styles to Columns

The CSS table model is described as being *row primary* because you specify rows explicitly in the HTML markup. Columns are derived from the cells in each row. Although the HTML <colgroup> and <col> elements allow you to specify column groups and individual columns, neither is required.

If you decide to specify column groups and columns in the HTML markup, you need to be aware that columns accept only four styles, namely:

background

border

width

visibility

For borders on columns and column groups, border-collapse must be set to collapse.

When used for <colgroup> or <col>, the only legal value for visibility is collapse. According to the specification, this hides the column and reduces the width of the table by the column's width. However, this is currently implemented correctly only by IE 8+ and Opera 11 +.

To demonstrate the use of visibility with columns, the HTML markup in column_collapse.html identifies the six columns in a table like this:

```
<colgroup span="1">
<colgroup>
    <col id="avg">
    <col id="eng">
    <col id="wales">
    <col id="scot">
    <col id="ni">
</colgroup>
```

The styles then hide the second and fourth columns like this:

```
#avg, #wales {
    visibility: collapse;
}
```

Figure 14-14 shows the result in IE 9. The columns are correctly hidden, and the width of the table has been reduced accordingly. Recent versions of Opera produce the same result. Firefox 14 removes the columns correctly, but leaves the outlines of two empty columns on the right. Chrome 21 and Safari 6 ignore the visibility property on columns.

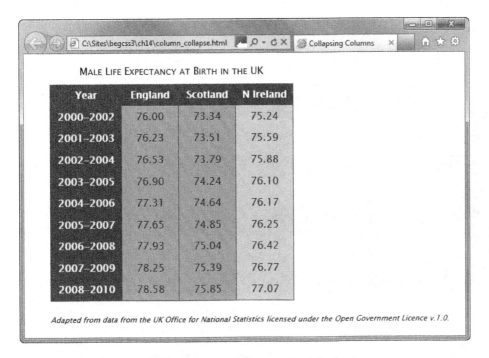

**Figure 14-14.** *Modern versions of Internet Explorer correctly hide columns*

■ **Note**   Setting visibility to collapse on a column doesn't affect the way the :nth-of-type() pseudo-class applies the background color to alternate table cells. The cells are still there. They're just not displayed.

## Using the visibility Property with Table Rows

The visibility property can also be used with table rows. As with <colgroup> and <col>, the only legal value is collapse. The styles in row_collapse.html hide the third row like this:

```
tr:nth-child(3) {
    visibility: collapse;
}
```

IE 9, Firefox 14, and Opera 12 hide the row and close the gap. However, Chrome 21 and Safari 6 leave the ugly gap shown in Figure 14-15.

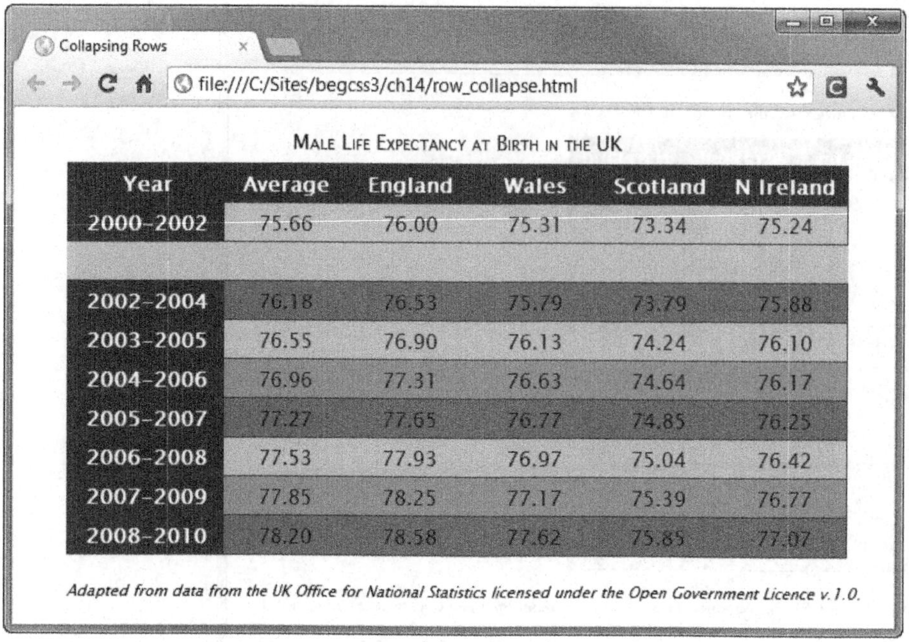

**Figure 14-15.** *WebKit-based browsers don't handle the visibility property correctly on tables*

IE 8 doesn't hide the row because it doesn't support the :nth-child() pseudo-class, but it works correctly if you use an ID selector instead. Interestingly, when you use an ID selector, IE 6 and IE 7 handle the visibility property more gracefully than Chrome and Safari. They simply ignore it, and display the row as normal.

## Adjusting the Space Between Table Cells

The CSS equivalent of the HTML cellspacing attribute is border-spacing, which is mutually exclusive with border-collapse. If you want to control the spacing between cells, border-collapse must be set to separate or omitted altogether (it's the default way of displaying tables).

Unlike cellspacing, which adds the same amount of space around all sides of each cell, border-spacing lets you specify different values for horizontal and vertical spacing. If you supply one value, it applies to both axes. However, if you supply two values, the first is applied to horizontal spacing, and the second to vertical spacing.

---

■ **Tip** Setting border-spacing to 0 is not the same as setting border-collapse to collapse. The spacing between the cells is eliminated, but the borders don't merge.

---

The style for the table in border-spacing.html looks like this:

```
table {
    border: #000 solid 5px;
    border-spacing: 30px 10px;
}
```

In most browsers, this produces the result shown in Figure 14-16. The exceptions are IE6 and IE7, which don't support border-spacing at all. Also, Safari and Chrome incorrectly double the vertical spacing between the two <tbody> sections.

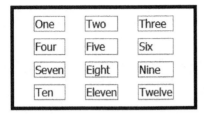

***Figure 14-16.*** *You can adjust the horizontal and vertical spacing between cells independently*

---

▪ **Caution**    You can't use the border-spacing property on any element other than a table.

---

## Adjusting Horizontal and Vertical Space Inside Table Cells

If you're wondering what the CSS equivalent of cellpadding is, there isn't one. You just use the ordinary padding property, which gives you complete control over the padding in every table cell, and you can have different amounts of padding on each side. It's important to remember that table rows are always as high as the tallest cell; and columns normally expand to accommodate the widest cell.

To demonstrate how padding works in table cells, the styles in padding_cells.html applies a different amount of padding to each side like this:

```
td {
    border: #F00 solid 1px;
    padding: 5px 10px 20px 15px;
}
```

However, the second cell in the third row is styled like this:

```
tr:nth-child(3) > td:nth-child(2) {
    padding: 40px;
}
```

This adds considerably more padding than to other cells. As Figure 14-17 shows, this increases the height of the entire row, as well as the width of the column. The extra height also affects the top padding in the cells on either side but does not apply the same value as in the center cell.

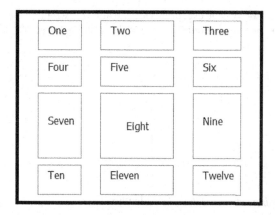

**Figure 14-17.** *A larger amount of padding in one cell affects other cells in the same row and column*

## Controlling the Position of the Table Caption

By default, the caption appears above the table, but you can move it underneath using the `caption-side` property, which accepts two values:

> **bottom** Puts the caption under the table.

> **top** Puts the caption above the table. This is the default value.

In the original CSS2 draft, there were two other values: `left` and `right`. However, Firefox was the only browser to offer support, so they were removed from the final specification.

All mainstream browsers, including IE 8, support `caption-side`. It's not supported in IE 6 or IE 7.

Because the caption is an integral part of the table, you can define the `caption-side` property in the style rule for the table or in a separate rule for the caption itself. The caption inherits its text color and width from the table. You can style a caption like any other text element, giving it a color and font properties of its own.

---

■ **Tip**    Most browsers support giving a caption a margin to distance it from the table. However, some WebKit-based browsers have problems with margins on captions, so it's safer to use padding.

---

## Handling Empty Cells

The `empty-cells` property is supported by all browsers currently in widespread use, but not by IE 6 and IE 7. It accepts the following values:

> **hide** Prevent the display of an empty cell's borders and backgrounds.

> **show** Draw borders and backgrounds on every cell, even if it contains no content. This is the default setting.

An empty cell is defined as a cell that contains absolutely nothing or one that has the `visibility` property set to `hidden`. However, setting the `visibility` of a cell to `hidden` also prevents the display of its borders and background, even when `empty-cells` is set to `show`.

■ **Caution**   Many HTML editors, such as Dreamweaver, automatically insert the HTML entity for a nonbreaking space ( ) into empty table cells. CSS regards this as content, even though nothing appears in the cell when viewed in a browser. For a cell to be treated as empty it must not contain anything other than new lines and whitespace between the opening and closing <td> or <th> tags.

To demonstrate how this property works, empty-cells.html contains four identical tables in which the second row contains only empty cells, while the visibility property of the middle cell in the third row has been set to hidden.

As expected, the content, background color, and borders of the cell in the third row are not displayed. However, the treatment of the empty row depends on whether it has any borders and on the setting for border-collapse. As Figure 14-18 shows, the empty row is completely hidden only when border-collapse is set to collapse and there are no borders around the cells. In all other cases, a small gap is left in place of the empty row. This behavior is consistent across all browsers in widespread use. In the case of border-collapse: separate, this is correct. The specification says that empty cells are "transparent through the cell, row, row group, column and column group backgrounds, letting the table background show through." However the double border in the third table appears to be incorrect.

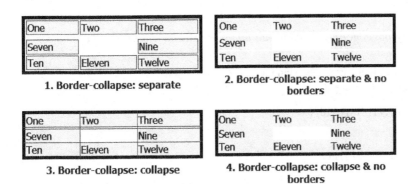

Figure 14-18. The use of cell borders affects the way browsers treat empty cells

## Controlling the Width of a Table

Tables are designed to wrap around their content, expanding and contracting depending on the size of the widest cell in each column and the tallest cell in each row. Although HTML 4.01 and XHTML 1.0 permit the width attribute on many table elements, it rarely has the desired effect. If an oversized element is placed in a table cell, the width attribute is ignored. In HTML5, the width attribute has been removed from all table elements in favor of using CSS.

But how can the CSS width property prevail in the face of the willful nature of table elements? On its own, it can't. But it can in combination with the table-layout property which accepts two values:

**auto** This is the default way tables behave, expanding to accommodate the widest element.

**fixed** The width of each column is fixed. In HTML5, the size is determined by the width of each cell in the first table row. In HTML 4.01 and XHTML 1.0, the width attribute of <colgroup> or <col> elements, if specified, takes precedence.

The table-layout property is supported by all browsers in current use, including IE 6.

---
## EXERCISE: FIXING COLUMN WIDTHS
---

In this exercise, you'll fix the width of the cells in the first row of a table. You'll then use a browser's developer tools to examine the effect of table-layout. The width of one column is deliberately narrow to demonstrate what happens with fixed-width tables.

Use as your starting point table-layout_begin.html in the ch14 folder. The finished files are table-layout_end.html and table-layout_ie6.html.

1.  Load the page into a browser to see how the table is displayed. The styles set the table width to 500px. The cells in the first row each contain a single number, but the second row contains more text. Because the cells in the first row don't have a declared width and table-layout hasn't been set, the cells automatically adjust to accommodate their content, as shown in Figure 14-19.

| 1 | 2 | 3 | | 4 |
|---|---|---|---|---|
| 250px | 100px | This column has a lot of content, but it should be only 50px wide. | | 100px |

*Figure 14-19. By default, table cells automatically adjust their width to the size of their content*

2.  Set the width of each cell in the first row using the :first-child and :nth-child() pseudo-classes like this:

```
tr:first-child > td:first-child {
    width: 50%;
}
tr:first-child > td:nth-child(2) {
    width: 20%;
}
tr:first-child > td:nth-child(3) {
    width: 10%;
}
tr:first-child > td:nth-child(4) {
    width: 20%;
}
```

3.  Save the page, and test the table again in a modern browser. The columns no longer expand automatically, but are controlled by the widths assigned to the first row of cells, as shown in Figure 14-20.

| 1 | 2 | 3 | 4 |
|---|---|---|---|
| 250px | 100px | This column has a lot of content, but it should be only 50px wide. | 100px |

***Figure 14-20.*** *The columns are taking their width from the cells in the first row*

4. Use your browser's developer tools to check the actual width of the third column. In Safari or Chrome, right-click the column, and select *Inspect Element* from the context menu. Then select the <td> markup for one of the column's cells in the panel that opens. Because the column's width has been set to 10% and the table is 500px wide, it should be 50px wide. But as Figure 14-21 shows, the column is actually 68px wide in Chrome. It might be slightly different in another browser, but in all browsers, the width of each column has been adjusted automatically to accommodate the long words in the third column.

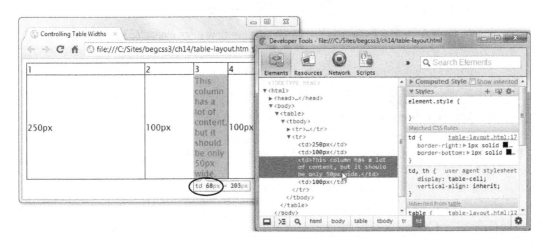

***Figure 14-21.*** *The table has automatically adjusted the width to make sure the text fits*

5. Amend the table style rule to set table-layout to fixed:

```
table {
    width: 500px;
    border-collapse: collapse;
    border: 1px solid #000;
    table-layout: fixed;
}
```

6. Save the page, and test the table again. This time, the third column is exactly 50px wide, but the longer words protrude into the fourth column (see Figure 14-22).

| 1 | 2 | 3 | 4 |
|---|---|---|---|
| 250px | 100px | This column has a lot of content, but it should be only 50px wide. | 100px |

**Figure 14-22.** *The columns are now the correct width, but long text overflows into the next column*

7. To deal with the overflow, amend the style for table cells like this:

```
td {
    border-right: 1px solid #000;
    border-bottom: 1px solid #000;
    overflow: auto;
}
```

8. Save and test the page in several browsers. Some add a horizontal scrollbar to the bottom of the cell. Firefox and Opera just let the content spill out as before.

9. Change the style rule for table cells to deal with the overflow more elegantly:

```
td {
    border-right: 1px solid #000;
    border-bottom: 1px solid #000;
    overflow: hidden;
    text-overflow: ellipsis;
}
```

10. Test the page again. All browsers shorten the overflow with an ellipsis (see Figure 14-23).

| 1 | 2 | 3 | 4 |
|---|---|---|---|
| 250px | 100px | This col... has a lot of con... but it sho... be only 50px wide. | 100px |

**Figure 14-23.** *The long text is replaced by an ellipsis*

Instead of an ellipsis, you could break the long words with `word-wrap: break-word` (see "Breaking Overflow Text" in Chapter 4). The draft CSS3 Text module also proposes a `hyphens` property that can be set to `auto` to automate hyphenation, but at the time of this writing, support is still experimental. However, the main focus of this exercise is not on dealing with overflow text. Instead, it's designed to show that fixed column widths are not affected by the size of their content. When using `table-layout: fixed`, you need to make sure your columns are wide enough.

To learn more about table and column widths, continue this exercise by adding padding to the style rule for the table cells, and then checking the table width with the browser's developer tools. Also increase the width of the table cells' right border. In both cases, the table width remains unchanged. Unlike the ordinary box model, padding and borders are included *inside* the width of table elements.

Older browsers don't understand the `:nth-child()` pseudo-class. If you need to use `table-layout: fixed` with IE 8 or older versions of Internet Explorer, add the `width` attribute to the opening tag of each table cell in the first row. You can examine the code in table-layout_ie6.html in the ch14 folder. As the filename suggests, fixed table layout works even in IE 6.

---

■ **Tip**  The preceding exercise used child combinators in step 2 only to demonstrate that the cells in the first row control column widths. You can achieve the same effect with just `td:first-child`, `td:nth-child(2)`, and so on.

---

## Adding Scrollbars to Table Cells

Tables are designed for the presentation of data, so it should rarely, if ever, be necessary to add scrollbars to a table cell. However, as noted in the preceding exercise, setting the `overflow` property to `auto` doesn't work on some browsers. In the event that you need to add scrollbars to a table cell, nest a `<div>` inside the table cell and set the `overflow` property of the `<div>` to `auto`. It's the content of the table cell that needs to scroll, not the table cell itself.

## Controlling the Horizontal and Vertical Alignment of Table Cells

By default, browsers align the content of table cells on the left and vertically in the middle. To control the horizontal alignment, use the `text-align` property. When used with table cells, it takes exactly the same values as for text, namely:

    left

    center

    right

    justify

Not surprisingly, you control the vertical alignment inside table cells with the `vertical-align` property. However, when used with table cells, `vertical-align` accepts only the following values:

    top

    middle

    bottom

    baseline

The first three are self-explanatory, but baseline needs a little explanation. Setting vertical-align to baseline aligns the first line of content with the baseline of the tallest similarly aligned content in the same row. The meaning should become clear from Figure 14-24, which shows the effect of using baseline for the fourth and fifth columns in vertical-align.html. The baseline of the smaller text in the fourth column is aligned with the baseline of the larger text in the next column.

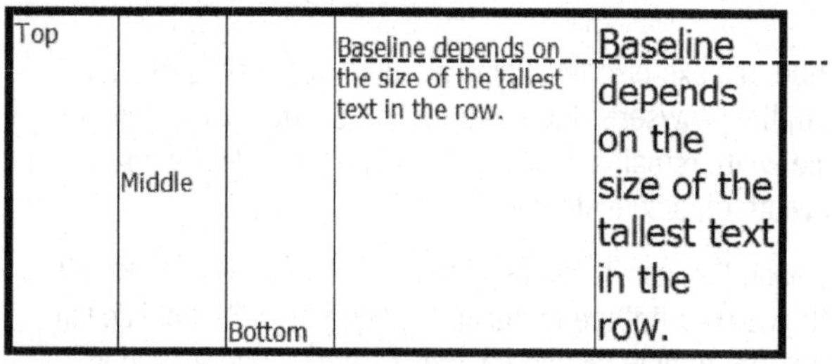

**Figure 14-24.** *There are four options for vertical alignment in table cells*

The baseline value affects only the first line of content in a cell, and is determined independently for each row.

That covers the theoretical side of styling tables with CSS. To end this chapter, let's put that knowledge to practical use by styling a data table.

## EXERCISE: STYLING A WEATHER CHART

In this exercise, you'll add some styles to a table containing weather data. Some of the selectors are supported only by modern browsers, but the styles still improve the look of the table even in IE 8 and older browsers. Use as your starting point weather_begin.html and styles/weather_begin.css in the ch14 folder. The finished table is in weather_end.html and styles/weather_end.css. Listing 14-1 shows the HTML markup for the first two rows of the table.

**Listing 14-1.** Weather Data Table

```
<table>
    <caption>
    Average Weather in Southern England, 1971&#8211;2000
    </caption>
    <tr>
        <th></th>
        <th>Max Temp<br>
            [°C]</th>
        <th>Min Temp<br>
            [°C]</th>
        <th>Days of<br>
            Air Frost</th>
        <th>Sunshine<br>
            [hours]</th>
        <th>Rainfall<br>
            [mm]</th>
        <th>Rain >= 1mm [days]</th>
    </tr>
```

```
    <tr>
        <th>Jan</th>
        <td>7.0</td>
        <td>1.4</td>
        <td>10.4</td>
        <td>53.1</td>
        <td>79.0</td>
        <td>13.0</td>
    </tr>
    <!-- Other rows omitted -->
</table>
```

The table contains a caption, and the first row consists of `<th>` table headers. The first cell of each subsequent row is also a `<th>` element, but the remaining data cells use `<td>` tags.

1. Load the page into a browser. As Figure 14-25 shows, the table is unstyled apart from the font.

Average Weather in Southern England, 1971–2000

| | Max Temp [°C] | Min Temp [°C] | Days of Air Frost | Sunshine [hours] | Rainfall [mm] | Rain >= 1mm [days] |
|---|---|---|---|---|---|---|
| Jan | 7.0 | 1.4 | 10.4 | 53.1 | 79.0 | 13.0 |
| Feb | 7.3 | 1.2 | 9.9 | 70.1 | 56.4 | 10.1 |
| Mar | 9.8 | 2.7 | 6.1 | 106.1 | 60.4 | 11.6 |
| Apr | 12.2 | 3.8 | 3.6 | 152.4 | 53.9 | 9.9 |
| May | 15.9 | 6.6 | 0.8 | 194.7 | 53.5 | 9.5 |
| Jun | 18.7 | 9.4 | 0.0 | 185.7 | 59.5 | 9.3 |
| Jul | 21.3 | 11.7 | 0.0 | 202.4 | 48.8 | 7.8 |
| Aug | 21.2 | 11.6 | 0.0 | 194.0 | 60.6 | 8.6 |
| Sep | 18.1 | 9.6 | 0.1 | 141.1 | 69.1 | 9.7 |
| Oct | 14.1 | 6.9 | 1.2 | 106.5 | 78.4 | 11.3 |
| Nov | 10.0 | 3.8 | 5.4 | 68.8 | 77.4 | 11.9 |
| Dec | 7.8 | 2.3 | 8.4 | 46.9 | 84.7 | 12.6 |
| Year | 13.6 | 5.9 | 45.9 | 1521.8 | 781.7 | 125.3 |

Contains public sector information licensed under the Open Government Licence v1.0

*Figure 14-25.* *The table needs a touch of style*

2. To make it easy to apply different styles to the main headings and the rest of the data, wrap the first row in a pair of `<thead>` tags like this:

```
<thead>
    <tr>
        <th></th>
        <th>Max Temp<br>[°C]</th>
        <th>Min Temp<br>[°C]</th>
        <th>Days of<br>Air Frost</th>
        <th>Sunshine<br>[hours]</th>
        <th>Rainfall<br>[mm]</th>
        <th>Rain >= 1mm [days]</th>
    </tr>
</thead>
```

3. Wrap the remaining table rows in a pair of `<tbody>` tags:

```
    </thead>
    <tbody>
        <tr>
            <th>Jan</th>
            <!-- Many lines omitted -->
            <td>125.3</td>
        </tr>
    </tbody>
</table>
```

4. In the style sheet, add the following rule to give the table a width, set its borders to collapse, and reduce the size of the font:

```
table {
    width: 650px;
    border-collapse: collapse;
    font-size: 14px;
}
```

5. Move the caption to the bottom of the table, give it some padding to move it away from the bottom row, render it as small caps, and increase its font size like this:

```
caption {
    caption-side: bottom;
    padding-top: 1em;
    font-variant: small-caps;
    font-size: 18px;
}
```

6. Give the table headers a top and bottom border (see Figure 14-26). Although modern browsers allow you to apply borders directly to the `<thead>` element, use a descendant selector to apply the borders to the individual `<th>` cells to keep older browsers happy.

```
thead th {
    border-top: 2px #35478C solid;
    border-bottom: 2px #35478C solid;
}
```

| | Max Temp [°C] | Min Temp [°C] | Days of Air Frost | Sunshine [hours] | Rainfall [mm] | Rain >= 1mm [days] |
|---|---|---|---|---|---|---|
| Jan | 7.0 | 1.4 | 10.4 | 53.1 | 79.0 | 13.0 |
| Feb | 7.3 | 1.2 | 9.9 | 70.1 | 56.4 | 10.1 |
| Mar | 9.8 | 2.7 | 6.1 | 106.1 | 60.4 | 11.6 |
| Apr | 12.2 | 3.8 | 3.6 | 152.4 | 53.9 | 9.9 |
| May | 15.9 | 6.6 | 0.8 | 194.7 | 53.5 | 9.5 |
| Jun | 18.7 | 9.4 | 0.0 | 185.7 | 59.5 | 9.3 |
| Jul | 21.3 | 11.7 | 0.0 | 202.4 | 48.8 | 7.8 |
| Aug | 21.2 | 11.6 | 0.0 | 194.0 | 60.6 | 8.6 |
| Sep | 18.1 | 9.6 | 0.1 | 141.1 | 69.1 | 9.7 |
| Oct | 14.1 | 6.9 | 1.2 | 106.5 | 78.4 | 11.3 |
| Nov | 10.0 | 3.8 | 5.4 | 68.8 | 77.4 | 11.9 |
| Dec | 7.8 | 2.3 | 8.4 | 46.9 | 84.7 | 12.6 |
| Year | 13.6 | 5.9 | 45.9 | 1521.8 | 781.7 | 125.3 |

AVERAGE WEATHER IN SOUTHERN ENGLAND, 1971–2000

*Contains public sector information licensed under the Open Government Licence v1.0*

***Figure 14-26.*** *The caption has moved and the top headings have borders*

7. The first cell in all the data rows is a <th> element. So, use the :first-child pseudo-class to give the first column a width of 7%, left-align the text, and add some padding like this:

```
th:first-child {
    width: 7%;
    text-align: left;
    padding-left: 10px;
}
```

8. Each column has a <th> cell in the first row, so you can set the width of the other columns with a simple type selector. This has lower specificity than th:first-child, so the style won't affect the first column. Also give the header cells some padding on the top and bottom. Add the following rule to the style sheet:

```
th {
    width: 15.5%;
    padding: 5px 0;
}
```

9. The decimal fractions in the data cells need to be lined up vertically. CSS currently doesn't have a way to line up the decimal point. But each number has a single digit after the decimal point, so you can right-align the cells and add a large amount of right padding to make the data look centered, as shown in Figure 14-27. Add the following style:

```
td {
    text-align: right;
    padding: 5px 35px 5px 0;
}
```

| | Max Temp [°C] | Min Temp [°C] | Days of Air Frost | Sunshine [hours] | Rainfall [mm] | Rain >= 1mm [days] |
|---|---|---|---|---|---|---|
| Jan | 7.0 | 1.4 | 10.4 | 53.1 | 79.0 | 13.0 |
| Feb | 7.3 | 1.2 | 9.9 | 70.1 | 56.4 | 10.1 |
| Mar | 9.8 | 2.7 | 6.1 | 106.1 | 60.4 | 11.6 |
| Apr | 12.2 | 3.8 | 3.6 | 152.4 | 53.9 | 9.9 |
| May | 15.9 | 6.6 | 0.8 | 194.7 | 53.5 | 9.5 |
| Jun | 18.7 | 9.4 | 0.0 | 185.7 | 59.5 | 9.3 |
| Jul | 21.3 | 11.7 | 0.0 | 202.4 | 48.8 | 7.8 |
| Aug | 21.2 | 11.6 | 0.0 | 194.0 | 60.6 | 8.6 |
| Sep | 18.1 | 9.6 | 0.1 | 141.1 | 69.1 | 9.7 |
| Oct | 14.1 | 6.9 | 1.2 | 106.5 | 78.4 | 11.3 |
| Nov | 10.0 | 3.8 | 5.4 | 68.8 | 77.4 | 11.9 |
| Dec | 7.8 | 2.3 | 8.4 | 46.9 | 84.7 | 12.6 |
| Year | 13.6 | 5.9 | 45.9 | 1521.8 | 781.7 | 125.3 |

AVERAGE WEATHER IN SOUTHERN ENGLAND, 1971–2000

*Contains public sector information licensed under the Open Government Licence v1.0*

***Figure 14-27.*** *The data is neatly aligned in each column*

10. Give the table rows in the `<tbody>` section alternate background colors using the `:nth-child()` pseudo-class.

```
tbody tr:nth-child(odd) {
    background-color: #FFEDD2;
}
tbody tr:nth-child(even) {
    background-color: #D8CCBA;
}
```

11. For older browsers, use one of the colors for the whole `<tbody>`. Although you're using the same color, you can't use a group selector because browsers ignore the entire style rule if they don't recognize one of the selectors. So, add this after the styles you have just entered:

```
tbody {
    background-color: #FFEDD2;
}
```

12. As a final touch, add a rule to change the background color of a row when the mouse pointer hovers over it:

```
tbody tr:hover {
    background-color: #F4F1EC;
}
```

13. Save the style sheet, and test the table in a modern browser. It's now styled like Figure 14-28.

| | Max Temp [°C] | Min Temp [°C] | Days of Air Frost | Sunshine [hours] | Rainfall [mm] | Rain >= 1mm [days] |
|---|---|---|---|---|---|---|
| Jan | 7.0 | 1.4 | 10.4 | 53.1 | 79.0 | 13.0 |
| Feb | 7.3 | 1.2 | 9.9 | 70.1 | 56.4 | 10.1 |
| Mar | 9.8 | 2.7 | 6.1 | 106.1 | 60.4 | 11.6 |
| Apr | 12.2 | 3.8 | 3.6 | 152.4 | 53.9 | 9.9 |
| May | 15.9 | 6.6 | 0.8 | 194.7 | 53.5 | 9.5 |
| Jun | 18.7 | 9.4 | 0.0 | 185.7 | 59.5 | 9.3 |
| Jul | 21.3 | 11.7 | 0.0 | 202.4 | 48.8 | 7.8 |
| Aug | 21.2 | 11.6 | 0.0 | 194.0 | 60.6 | 8.6 |
| Sep | 18.1 | 9.6 | 0.1 | 141.1 | 69.1 | 9.7 |
| Oct | 14.1 | 6.9 | 1.2 | 106.5 | 78.4 | 11.3 |
| Nov | 10.0 | 3.8 | 5.4 | 68.8 | 77.4 | 11.9 |
| Dec | 7.8 | 2.3 | 8.4 | 46.9 | 84.7 | 12.6 |
| Year | 13.6 | 5.9 | 45.9 | 1521.8 | 781.7 | 125.3 |

AVERAGE WEATHER IN SOUTHERN ENGLAND, 1971–2000

*Contains public sector information licensed under the Open Government Licence v1.0*

***Figure 14-28.*** *The table now looks much more visually attractive and easier to read*

The hover effect isn't intended to work on touch screens. (Have you ever tried hovering your finger over your mobile phone or tablet?) In my tests, nothing happens if you tap a row on an iPad. On an Android tablet, though, the row does change color.

In IE 8 and older browsers, the table doesn't have alternate colored rows, but the columns are evenly spaced and the data is correctly aligned. IE 6 doesn't support the :first-child pseudo-class, so the first column is the same width as the others, and the text isn't left-aligned, but the table is presentable.

# Summary

If you've been using the HTML cellspacing attribute, the border-collapse and border-spacing properties offer much greater control over the horizontal and vertical spacing between cells. There's no direct equivalent of cellpadding, but table cells handle padding in the same way as the CSS box model, giving you the freedom to adjust it independently on each side of a cell. Other advantages of styling tables with CSS include the ability to style all of a table's internal and external borders independently, to move the caption below the table, and to hide empty cells.

You can also control the width of columns by setting the table-layout property to fixed. This fixes the width of each column according to the width of the cells in the first table row. However, it's important to remember that borders and padding are not added to the overall width of a table.

The CSS3 :nth-child() and related pseudo-classes discussed in Chapter 13 make it considerably easier to style columns without the need to declare them as <colgroup> and <col> elements in the HTML markup. You can also use these pseudo-classes to assign different backgrounds to alternate rows and/or columns.

In the next chapter, we'll look at using pseudo-elements to add generated content to elements in your web pages. The original idea of generated content was to enhance numbered sequences, but it has been adapted to an increasing range of interesting visual effects.

■ ■ ■

# CHAPTER 15

# Generated Content

What CSS means by *generated content* is content that's not physically present in the HTML markup. For example, when you create an ordered list, the numbers are not in the HTML. The browser generates and inserts them automatically, and it updates the sequence if items are added or removed. The ::before and ::after pseudo-elements perform a similar function, but go much further, allowing you to add just about any type of automatically generated content not only before list items, but before and after almost any HTML element.

The ::before and ::after pseudo-elements have been around for a long time. They're part of the CSS2.1 specification (prefixed with a single colon rather than two), but Internet Explorer didn't support them until IE 8. So, they went largely unnoticed. Now, they're widely used for creating fun visual effects, such as ribbons and speech bubbles.

In this chapter, I'll show you how to use the pseudo-elements to add text, images, and visual effects to various HTML elements, as well as how to generate complex numbered sequences.

In particular, you'll learn how to do the following:

- Automatically prefix elements with text and images
- Extract the URL from a link and display it in the text
- Generate nested quotation marks in a predefined sequence
- Generate numbered sequences for page sections and lists
- Create ribbon and speech bubble effects without images

---

■ **Note**   The code examples in this chapter use the CSS3 syntax, which is supported by the latest versions of all browsers. If you need to support IE 8, use the CSS2.1 single-colon versions (:before and :after) instead.

---

## Inserting Generated Content

To add generated content to elements other than list items, you need to use the ::before or ::after pseudo-elements. As their names suggest, they insert content before or after an element. The inserted content is generated by one or more of the properties in Table 15-1.

The properties in Table 15-1 are not inherited, but they accept the inherit keyword as a value.

**Table 15-1.** *Generated Content Properties*

| Property | Initial Value | Description |
|---|---|---|
| content | normal | Defines the content to be inserted by the pseudo-element. |
| counter-increment | none | Increments the specified counter for a numbered sequence. To increment in steps greater than 1, also specify an integer. A negative integer creates a back-counting sequence. |
| counter-reset | none | Resets the specified counter or creates it if it doesn't already exist. By default, counters are initialized at 0. To specify a different start value, add an integer after the counter name. |
| quotes | | Defines the styles of quotation marks at any number of nested levels. The default value depends on the browser. |

## Defining the Content to be Inserted

The content property is extremely versatile. It accepts any of the following values:

**none** The pseudo-element is not generated.

**normal** Same as none.

*A string:* Literal text that is to be inserted.

**url()** An external resource, usually an image.

*A counter:* A function that generates a numbered sequence.

**attr(x)** Use the value of the x attribute in the selected element.

**open-quote** Insert an opening quote as defined by the quotes property.

**close-quote** Insert a closing quote as defined by the quotes property.

**no-open-quote** Omit the opening quote, but move to the next level of nesting.

**no-close-quote** Omit the closing quote, but move up to the previous level.

Apart from the none and normal keywords, you can combine any of these values as a space-separated list to create complex content that is injected before or after an element.

## Inserting Images and Text

Using the ::before and ::after pseudo-elements to insert images, text, or a combination of the two can be useful in situations where you need to label elements in a consistent way. For example, throughout this book points of interest are highlighted as Notes, Tips, or Cautions. The styles in image_text.html use the following three classes to mark up paragraphs in a similar way (see Figure 15-1):

```
.note::before {
    content: url(images/square_gray.gif) ' Note ';
    font-weight: bold;
```

```
}
.tip::before {
    content: url(images/square_gray.gif) ' Tip ';
    font-weight: bold;
}
.caution::before {
    content: url(images/square_gray.gif) ' Caution ';
    font-weight: bold;
}
```

The ::before pseudo-element is appended to the selector in the same way as a pseudo-class. In this example, each selector is a class, but you can use any valid selector. The value specified for content begins with the path to the gray square image, followed by a space and the text in quotes. It doesn't matter whether you use single or double quotes, as long as they're a matching pair. I've added a space on either side of the text to separate it both from the icon and from the following text.

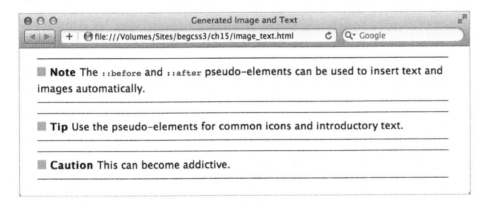

***Figure 15-1.*** *The icons and bold text are automatically generated by the pseudo-elements*

Normally the generated content is displayed inline, and the text inherits the same properties as the text in the element it's being added to. But you can style the generated content like any other element.

The styles in text_image_display.html adapt the classes in the previous example like this:

```
.note::before {
    content: url(images/square_gray.gif) ' Note ';
    font-weight: bold;
    display: block;
}
.tip::before {
    content: url(images/square_gray.gif) ' Tip ';
    font-weight: bold;
    display: inline-block;
    vertical-align: 24px;
}
.caution::before {
    content: url(images/square_gray.gif) ' Caution ';
```

```
    font-weight: bold;
    color: #F8A809;
    font-size: 24px;
    font-family: Tahoma, Geneva, sans-serif;
}
```

As Figure 15-2 shows, the generated content in the note class becomes a block-level element occupying a separate line. In the tip class, it's converted to an inline block and raised above the baseline. The caution class changes the color, font size, and font of the generated text.

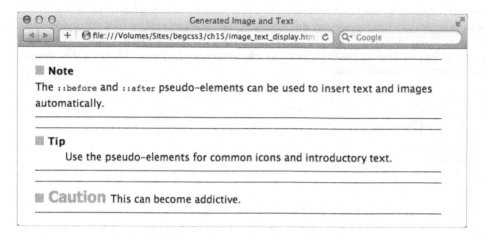

**Figure 15-2.** *The generated content can be styled independently of the element it's added to*

---

■ **Caution**    The generated content doesn't become part of the HTML markup, so don't use ::before and ::after for essential content. It won't be seen by users of older browsers.

---

Using the ::after pseudo-element to append generated content works exactly the same way. The styles in image_text_after.html identify the final paragraph using the :last-child pseudo-class. The ::after pseudo-element is appended to the selector to add a couple of images and some text, and style it to be centered on a separate line like this:

```
p:last-child::after {
    content: url(images/flourish1.png) ' The End ' url(images/flourish2.png);
    display: block;
    text-align: center;
    color: #B20000;
    margin-top: 1em;
}
```

As Figure 15-3 shows, this adds a stylized "The End" at the foot of the page.

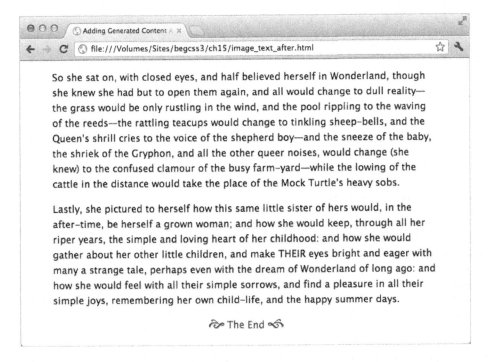

**Figure 15-3.** *The ::after pseudo-element appends generated content at the end of an element*

IE 8 doesn't support the :last-child pseudo-class. For the preceding example to work in IE 8, you not only need to use the single-colon version of :after, but also to assign a class or ID to the last paragraph and use that as the selector, for example p.last:after.

---

■ **Caution**    Although the ::before and ::after pseudo-elements can insert images before or after other HTML elements, they can't add generated content to an image or to other *replaced elements* such as objects and videos. So, you can't use them, for example, to add a caption after an image. They don't work with form elements either.

---

## Generating Content from an Attribute

The content property can inspect HTML tags, search for an attribute, and display the text value of the attribute. If the attribute doesn't exist, the browser simply ignores it. To access the attribute, you insert the attribute name (without quotes) between the parentheses of attr().

This can be useful for displaying an external URL. You can use the attribute selector a[href^="http://"] to style external links differently from internal ones. So it's just a question of using the ::after pseudo-element with the same selector like this (the code is in attribute.html):

```
a[href^="http://"]::after {
    content: ' (' attr(href) ') ';
}
```

The content property uses attr(href) to extract the link's URL. It's surrounded on both sides by literal spaces and parentheses in quotes. As Figure 15-4 shows, the pseudo-element appends the URL in parentheses after an external link, but ignores an internal one.

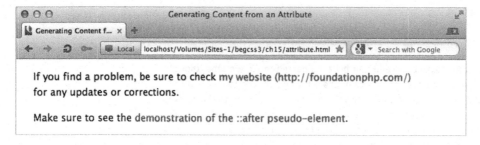

**Figure 15-4.** *The ::after pseudo-element automatically appends the URL to the external link*

## Generating Quotes Automatically

HTML has two elements that are intended to mark up quotations: <q> and <blockquote>. The first one is intended for short, inline quotations, whereas <blockquote> is reserved for lengthy quotations that are intended to be set off from the surrounding text.

You shouldn't use quotation marks with <q> tags. The browser inserts them for you. For a long time, browsers failed to do so, but all modern browsers (including IE 8) now insert quotation marks correctly. However, IE 8+ uses single curly quotes, Firefox uses double curly quotes, and other browsers use double straight quotes.

The <blockquote> element> doesn't automatically add quotation marks. You need to add them yourself if you want them.

With the help of the quotes property and the ::before and ::after pseudo-elements, you can control the generation of quotation marks not only for <q>, but also for any other element. What's more, you can set up sequences to ensure that nested quotations are marked up correctly. For example, you can follow the American typographical practice of double quotes first, followed by single ones for nested quotations. Alternatively, you can use the British convention of single quotes followed by double ones. Or if you're working with another language, you can use the correct glyphs.

The quotes property expects a space-separated list of pairs of opening and closing quotation marks. If you specify multiple pairs, they're used in sequence depending on how deep the quotations are nested. The browser automatically keeps track of the level of nesting.

To generate curly quotes or other types of quotation marks, use the hexadecimal codes listed in Table 15-2.

**Table 15-2.** *Hexadecimal Codes for Generating Quotation Marks*

| Hexadecimal Code | Mark | Description |
|---|---|---|
| \2018 | ' | Left single quotation mark |
| \2019 | ' | Right single quotation mark |
| \201C | " | Left double quotation mark |
| \201D | " | Right double quotation mark |
| \201E | „ | Double low-9 quotation mark |
| \00AB | « | Left double-angle quotation mark |
| \00BB | » | Right double-angle quotation mark |

■ **Tip** The hexadecimal codes for other quotation marks can be found in the Unicode General Punctuation block (http://unicode.org/charts/PDF/U2000.pdf). Prefix the hexadecimal code with a backslash.

## Standardizing Quotes on <q> Elements

Although browsers use different types of quotes on <q> elements, you can make all browsers conform to your preferred style with the quotes property. Because <q> elements automatically insert quotation marks, there's no need to use the ::before and ::after pseudo elements. Just specify the sequence of opening and closing quotes in a style rule for the <q> element. For example, the following style rule in quotes_single.html tells <q> elements to use double curly quotes:

```
q {
    quotes: '\201C' '\201D';
}
```

If you test quotes_single.html in a browser, apart from a few ancient ones, they all use double curly quotes instead of the browser default.

## Generating Quotes for Other Elements

To generate quotes for elements other than <q>, you need to use the ::before and ::after pseudo-elements in addition to defining the opening and closing quotes with the quotes property.

As noted earlier, the content property accepts as values open-quote, no-open-quote, close-quote, and no-close-quote. The first two are normally used with ::before, and the others with ::after. The values that begin with no- suppress the insertion of a quotation mark, but keep track of the correct place in the sequence.

It's common to omit a paragraph's closing quote if the quotation continues in the next paragraph. Explicitly setting no-close-quote ensures that the next paragraph uses the correct opening quotes, as the next example demonstrates.

The HTML in quotes_nested.html is identical to the preceding example. It contains a <blockquote> element within which <q> elements are nested. The styles begin by specifying a sequence of quotes for paragraphs nested inside the <blockquote> element:

```
blockquote p {
    quotes: '\201C' '\201D' '\2018' '\2019';
}
```

This specifies double curly quotes as the first pair, and single curly quotes as the second pair. When multiple pairs are specified with the quotes property, each pair is used in sequence. What's particularly impressive is that <q> elements are automatically included in the sequence.

The quotes are added automatically to the <q> elements, but you need to use the ::before and ::after pseudo-elements for the paragraphs. The following style rules specify opening quotes for each paragraph, but suppress closing quotes on all but the last paragraph.

```
blockquote p::before {
    content: open-quote;
}
blockquote p::after {
    content: no-close-quote;
}
blockquote p:last-child::after {
    content: close-quote;
}
```

As Figure 15-5 shows, this produces double quotes at the beginning of the <blockquote>, but single quotes on the first <q> element. The first paragraph in the <blockquote> ends with a single quote because it's the end of a <q> element. The double closing quote is suppressed because the content property of the ::after pseudo-element is set to no-close-quote. But the next paragraph correctly opens and closes with double quotes. The browser keeps track of the correct level of quotes at all times.

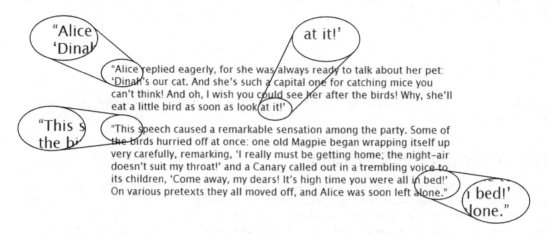

**Figure 15-5.** *The nested quotes are correctly sequenced*

## Generating Numbered Sequences

It's not always appropriate to use an ordered list for a numbered sequence. For example, you might want to number the headings and paragraphs in a page that describes a company's terms of service.

Generating a numbered sequence involves the following steps:

1. Initialize a counter using the counter-reset property.

2. Increment the counter using the counter-increment property.

3. Display the counter using ::before and the content property.

The counter is like a variable in JavaScript. It stores the current number in the sequence. You can call it anything you like, except the keywords none, inherit, or initial. It needs to be initialized in a style rule for an element that precedes or is the parent of the first element that you want to number.

There are two functions that display the counter's value. Most of the time, you use the counter() function, which keeps track of the value only in its current level of nesting. The similarly named counters() function keeps track of the counter at higher levels of nesting, and resumes the correct sequence when backing out from a lower level.

Using counter() is easier to understand, so I'll deal with that first.

## Using Separate Counters

Rather than explaining the theory in a vacuum, let's walk through an actual example. The <h1>, <h2>, and <h3> headings in numbered_headings.html are numbered in sequence, as shown in Figure 15-6.

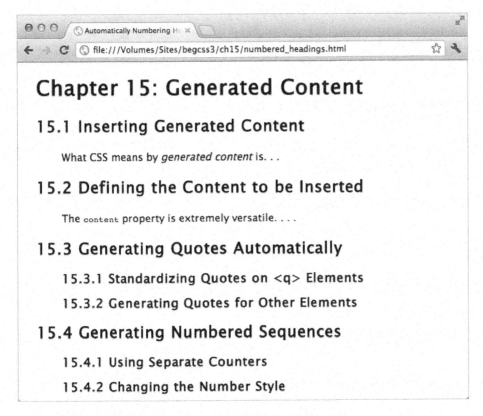

***Figure 15-6.*** *The numbers alongside each heading are generated automatically*

Because the numbers are generated and inserted by the ::before pseudo-element, the sequence automatically updates when a new heading is added in numbered_headings_add.html (see Figure 15-7).

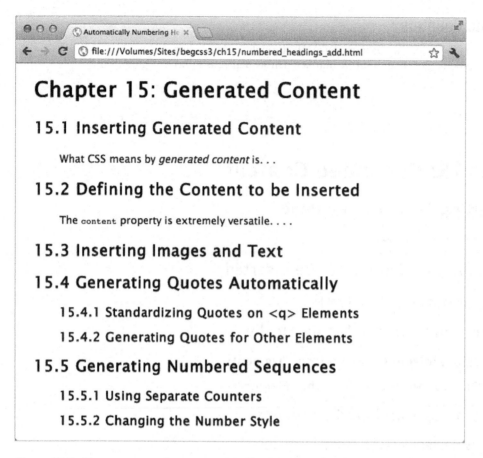

**Figure 15-7.** *The sequence updates automatically when a new heading is inserted*

The numbers are generated by three counters: chapter, section, and subsection. Counters need to be initialized before they can be used, so the chapter counter is initialized in the body style rule like this:

```
body {
    background-color: #FFF;
    color: #000;
    font-family: "Lucida Sans Unicode", "Lucida Grande", sans-serif;
    counter-reset: chapter 15;
}
```

This creates a counter called chapter, and initializes it at 15. In most cases, values are incremented before being displayed. So, you normally initialize the counter at one less than the first number you want to display. In this instance, however, the chapter number is never incremented, which is why it's initialized at 15 rather than 14.

The value is displayed by passing the name of the counter to the counter() function in the ::before pseudo-element like this:

```
h1::before {
    content: 'Chapter ' counter(chapter) ': ';
}
```

This sets the value of the content property to the literal text "Chapter" followed by a space, then the value of the chapter counter, followed by a colon and another space. The result, as shown in Figures 15-6 and 15-7, is that the main heading is prefixed by *Chapter 15:*.

The section counter generates the sequence number for the <h2> headings, so it needs to be initialized before it's used. The <h1> heading comes first, making it the ideal place to create it with the counter-reset property like this:

```
h1 {
    counter-reset: section;
}
```

Only the counter name has been specified, so counter-reset initializes section at 0. The ::before pseudo-element then increments and displays the sequence number like this:

```
h2::before {
    counter-increment: section;
    content: counter(chapter) '.' counter(section) ' ';
}
```

By default, counter-increment increases the value of a counter by 1. So, the first <h2> heading increments section to 1, the next <h2> heading increases it to 2, and so on. The content property uses the counter() function twice to display the values of the chapter and section counters. Literal text strings insert a dot between the numbers and a space after them.

The subsection counter numbers the <h3> headings, which always follow <h2> headings. Because they represent subsections of the <h2> sections, the counter needs to be created or reset to 0 by each <h2> heading. So, the counter is initialized and reset like this:

```
h2 {
    counter-reset: subsection;
}
```

Finally, the ::before pseudo-element increments the subsection counter and displays all three numbers like this:

```
h3::before {
    counter-increment: subsection;
    content: counter(chapter) '.' counter(section) '.' counter(subsection) ' ';
}
```

---

■ **Tip** When the ::before pseudo-element increments and displays a counter, the counter is always incremented first. The order of counter-increment and content in the style rule makes no difference.

---

## Changing the Number Style

The counter() function takes an optional second argument: one of the values for list-style-type (see "Ordered Lists" in Chapter 10). Separate the two arguments with a comma.

The styles in numbered_headings_style.html have been amended like this:

```
h2::before {
    counter-increment: section;
    content: counter(chapter) '.' counter(section, lower-roman) ' ';
}
h3::before {
    counter-increment: subsection;
    content: counter(chapter) '.' counter(section, lower-roman) '.' counter(subsection, ↵
    lower-alpha) ' ';
}
```

This changes the style of the numbers to look like Figure 15-8.

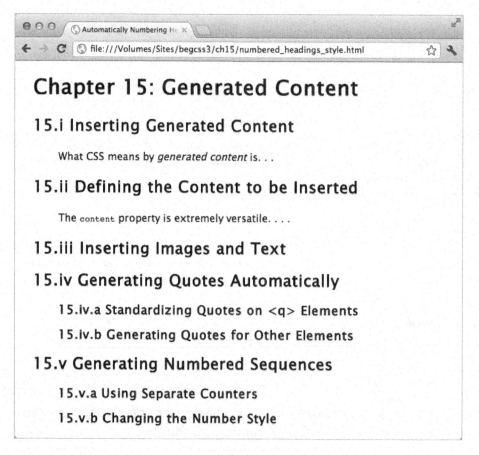

**Figure 15-8.** *You can style the numbers in the same way as ordered lists*

## Changing the Size and Direction of the Increment

By default, counter-increment increases the sequence number by 1. To change the size of the increment, add an integer after the counter name separated by a space. You can also use a negative number to count in reverse.

This is demonstrated in numbered_headings_increment.html, which initializes each subsection sequence at 7. The section counter is incremented in steps of 5, and the subsection counter is reduced in steps of 3 like this:

```
h2 {
    counter-reset: subsection 7;
}
h2::before {
    counter-increment: section 5;
    content: counter(chapter) '.' counter(section) ' ';
}
h3::before {
    counter-increment: subsection -3;
    content: counter(chapter) '.' counter(section) '.' counter(subsection) ' ';
}
```

As Figure 15-9 shows, the section numbers begin at 5 and increase in steps of 5. The subsection numbers begin at 4, not 7, because counter-increment deducts 3 from the start number before displaying the counter. The sequence continues with negative numbers once it falls below zero.

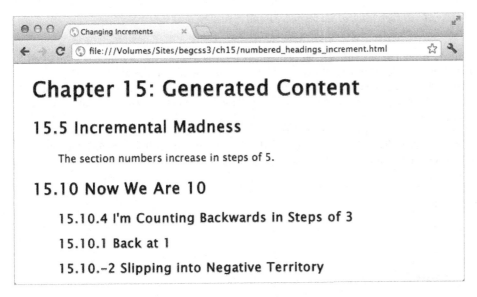

***Figure 15-9.*** *Numbers in a sequence can be increased or decreased by any amount*

■ **Caution** To reset more than one counter in the same style rule, they must be specified together as a space-separated list like this: counter-reset: counter1 counter2;. If you put them in separate declarations, the last one overrides the previous ones following the normal rules of the cascade.

## Generating Subsection Numbers with Nested Lists

If you reset a counter in a descendant element, the browser creates a new instance of the counter, restarting the sequence in the descendant element's siblings, and resuming it when backing out to the parent's level. This is similar to what happens when you nest ordered lists (see Figure 15-10).

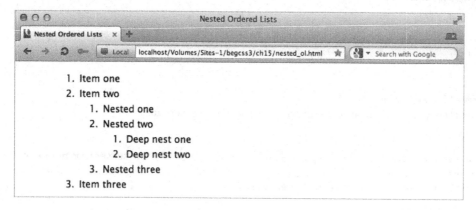

***Figure 15-10.*** *Nested ordered lists keep track of the sequence number at each level*

The counters() function—not to be confused with the similarly named counter() function—is designed to create custom numbering sequences for nested elements. It keeps track of the counter at all levels of nesting. The function requires two arguments: the counter name, and a string of literal text to be used as a separator for the sequence numbers. As an optional third argument, you can add one of the list-style-type values to specify how the numbers are displayed.

The simple way to demonstrate the use of the counters() function is with a series of nested ordered lists. Because ordered lists automatically display numbers, you need to suppress the default numbering and replace it with the ::before pseudo-element and the counters() function like this (the code is in nested_counters.html):

```
ol {
    list-style-type: none;
    counter-reset: nested;
}
li::before {
    counter-increment: nested;
    content: counters(nested, '.') '. ';
}
```

In a modern browser, this produces the numbered sequence shown in Figure 15-11.

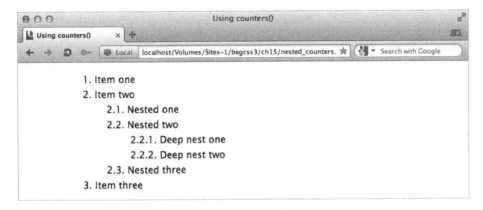

*Figure 15-11. The counters() function automatically generates the subsection numbers*

Each nested `<ol>` element creates a new instance of the nested counter, which is reset to 0. The `::before` pseudo-element on each list item increments the counter, and the `counters()` function displays the value not only for the current level, but also for the preceding ones separated by a dot. The final dot and space are added as a string at the end of the `content` value.

# Creating Fun Visual Effects with Generated Content

One of the most fascinating aspects of working with CSS is the way that properties and selectors can be used in ways that were almost certainly not envisaged when the specification was first drawn up. The `::before` and `::after` pseudo-elements were originally conceived as being used to generate the type of content described in the preceding sections. But they're increasingly used to create visual effects such as ribbons and speech bubbles.

---

■ **Caution**    All the preceding examples work with the CSS2.1 syntax for pseudo-elements (`:before` and `:after`). However, the visual effects in the rest of this chapter rely on CSS3 features not supported by IE 8. To prevent problems with IE 8, always use the CSS3 syntax (`::before` and `::after`) with these techniques.

---

The visual effects are made possible thanks to absolute positioning and the ability to generate shapes using background colors, borders, and properties such as `border-radius`. For example, you can create triangles by setting the width and height of an element to 0, and giving it a wide border. If you give each border a different color, they intersect as triangles, as shown on the left of Figure 15-12. Make three of the borders transparent, and you're left with a triangle as shown on the right.

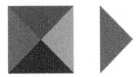

*Figure 15-12. Wide borders on an element with no width and height can be used to create triangles*

The shapes in Figure 15-12 were created by styling empty <div> elements with the following styles in triangles.html:

```
#borders, #right {
    margin: 20px;
    float: left;
    height: 0;
    width: 0;
    border-style: solid;
    border-width: 50px;
    border-color:  green orange blue red;
}
#right {
    border-color: transparent transparent transparent red;
}
```

The style rule for the right <div> overrides the border-color property, setting the top, right, and bottom borders to transparent. As a result, you get a red right-facing triangle.

---

■ **Tip**　There's a gallery of CSS shapes (with code) at http://css-tricks.com/examples/ShapesOfCSS/.

---

## Creating a Ribbon Effect

A very simple effect that you can create with triangles and the ::before and ::after pseudo-elements is a ribbon that gives a heading a 3D look.

---

### EXERCISE: SIMPLE RIBBON EFFECT

In this exercise, you'll add triangles at either end of a heading's background using the ::before and ::after pseudo-elements and a combination of relative and absolute positioning. Use as your starting point ribbon_begin.html in the ch15 folder. The finished file is ribbon_end.html.

1. View the page in a browser. The heading has a chocolate background and drop shadow, but is constrained by the padding in the wrapper <div>, as shown in Figure 15-13.

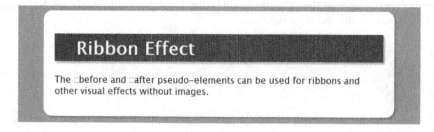

**Figure 15-13.** *The heading's background doesn't extend beyond the padding*

2. To create the ribbon effect, the heading's background needs to extend through the padding and into the margins of the wrapper `<div>`. The padding is 20px wide, so to extend the background a further 20px into the margin, you need to add negative left and right margins of 40px to the heading. It also needs to be relatively positioned so that it becomes the containing block for the absolutely positioned ::before and ::after pseudo-elements (see Chapter 11 for an explanation of the containing block). Add the following styles to the h1 style block:

```
h1 {
    background-color: #5C4837;
    color: #FFF;
    padding: 5px 40px;
    -webkit-box-shadow: 3px 3px 3px rgba(51,51,51,0.3);
    box-shadow: 3px 3px 3px rgba(51,51,51,0.3);
    margin: 0 -40px;
    position: relative;
}
```

3. The ::before and ::after pseudo-elements both need display triangles of a slightly darker color than the background. The triangles are made by setting the content property to an empty string (a pair of quotes with nothing between them), setting the width and height to 0, and adding a 20px solid top border. The triangles need to be absolutely positioned directly beneath the heading. Add the following style rule for properties common to both pseudo-elements:

```
h1::before, h1::after {
    content: '';
    height: 0;
    width: 0;
    border-top: 20px solid #453629;
    position: absolute;
    bottom: -20px;
}
```

4. To complete the triangles and position them horizontally, the one in the ::before pseudo-element needs a transparent left border the same size as the top border, and it needs to be flush with the left side of the heading. The triangle in the ::after pseudo-element needs a transparent right border, and should be flush with the right side of the heading. Add the following styles for the two pseudo-elements:

```
h1::before {
    border-left: 20px solid transparent;
    left: 0;
}
h1::after {
    border-right: 20px solid transparent;
    right: 0;
}
```

5. Save the page, and test it in a browser. It now looks like a ribbon wrapped around the ‹div›, as shown in Figure 15-14.

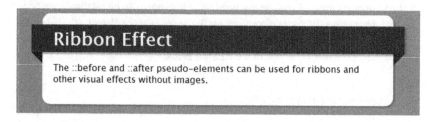

*Figure 15-14.* *The absolutely positioned pseudo-elements create a 3D feel*

This exercise demonstrates the basic technique of adding visual effects with the ::before and ::after pseudo-elements. The content property is set to an empty string, creating an empty element that can be styled as a shape and then moved into position using absolute positioning. In this example, the shapes are 20px high, so they are accurately positioned below the heading by setting a negative bottom offset of the same amount.

■ **Tip** You can create more sophisticated ribbon effects using the ribbon builder, a free visual tool at http://livetools.uiparade.com/ribbon-builder.html. The tool generates all the HTML and CSS ready for you to download. It involves the use of some nonsemantic elements, but is an impressive example of what can be achieved using only CSS and no images.

## Creating a Comment Bubble

In the preceding exercise, the ::before and ::after pseudo-elements are used to position triangles at either end of a heading. As you might imagine, the ::after pseudo-element is created last, so it can be superimposed on the ::before pseudo-element. That's the technique to create the comment bubble in Figure 15-15.

Some really cool features here.

*Figure 15-15.* *The two pseudo-elements are superimposed to create the illusion of a continuous border*

The effect is created by a class called comment, which sets the position property to relative and draws a rounded border around some text, as shown in Figure 15-16.

Some really cool features here.

*Figure 15-16.* *The basic class simply adds the border to the text*

The styles in comment.html then add the common properties for the ::before and ::after pseudo-elements, and create a left-facing green triangle in the ::before pseudo-element like this:

```
.comment::before, .comment::after {
    content: '';
    width: 0;
    height: 0;
    position: absolute;
}
.comment::before {
    border-style: solid;
    border-width: 15px 30px;
    border-color: transparent #060 transparent transparent;
    left: -60px;
    top: 10px;
}
```

The triangle is created with left and right borders that are twice the width of the top and bottom ones, and by setting the color of all sides except the right to transparent. This produces a more acute angle. The negative left offset is equivalent to the width of the left and right borders, attaching the green triangle to the edge of the border, as shown in Figure 15-17.

*Figure 15-17.* *The ::before pseudo-element creates a solid green triangle*

Finally, the ::after pseudo-element creates a smaller, white left-facing triangle, and superimposes it on the green triangle like this:

```
.comment::after {
    border-width: 8px 23px;
    border-style: solid;
    border-color: transparent #FFF transparent transparent;
    left: -46px;
    top: 17px;
}
```

Again, the triangle is created using a narrower top and bottom border. Getting exactly the right size is mainly a question of trial and error. However, the negative left offset should be equal to the width of the horizontal borders.

Superimposing one triangle on top of the other creates the illusion of a continuous border, as shown earlier in Figure 15-15.

## Creating a Thought Bubble

A variation of the same basic technique is used to create the thought bubble in Figure 15-18.

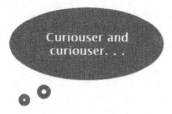

**Figure 15-18.** *Using other shapes brightens up plain text*

In this example, `border-radius` on the main text background has been set to 50%, producing an ellipse. Instead of setting the width and height of the pseudo-elements to 0, they're made into small empty squares that are then converted to circles with `border-radius`.

The styles for the pseudo-elements in thought_bubble.html look like this:

```
#thought::before, #thought::after {
    content: '';
    border: #963 solid 10px;
    border-radius: 50%;
    position: absolute;
}
#thought::before {
    height: 10px;
    width: 10px;
    bottom: -40px;
    left: 60px;
}
#thought::after {
    height: 5px;
    width: 5px;
    bottom: -55px;
    left: 20px;
}
```

## Creating a Speech Bubble

A slightly more complex example of this technique creates the speech bubble shown in Figure 15-21. The tail is formed by styling both pseudo-elements as circles and using a negative `z-index` to tuck them behind the parent element. The `::after` pseudo-element also masks part of the `::before` pseudo-element.

As in the preceding example, the text background is converted to an ellipse by setting `border-radius` to 50%. The `::before` pseudo element is an empty 70px square of the same background color, converted to a circle using `border-radius`. It has a `bottom` offset of `-30px`, and a `z-index` of `-1` so that it goes behind the ellipse with only the bottom part of the circle protruding, as shown in Figure 15-19.

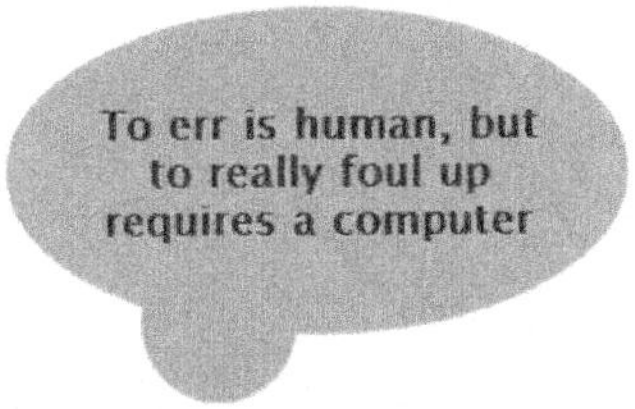

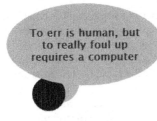

**Figure 15-19.** *The ::before pseudo-element is a circle partially tucked behind its parent*

Use the ::after pseudo-element to position alongside it a slightly smaller circle of a different color, as shown in Figure 15-20.

**Figure 15-20.** *The circle in the ::after pseudo-element overlaps the first one*

Finally, change the color of the shape in the ::after pseudo-element to match the page's background color—and you have a speech bubble, as shown in Figure 15-21.

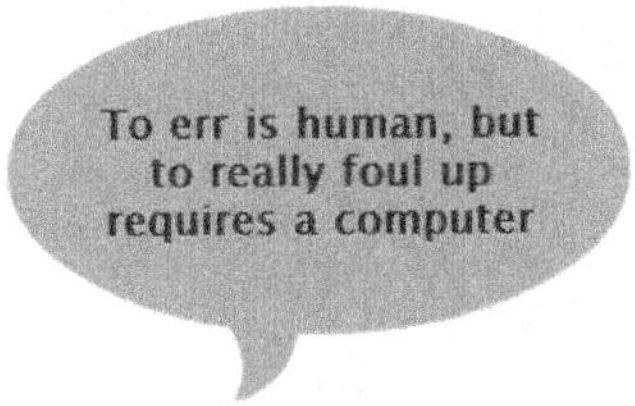

**Figure 15-21.** *The second circle is the same color as the page and masks the first one*

The styles for the two pseudo-elements in speech_bubble.html look like this:

```
#quote::before, #quote::after {
    content: '';
    position: absolute;
    border-radius: 50%;
    z-index: -1;
}
#quote::before {
    background-color: #0CF;
    height: 70px;
    width: 70px;
```

```
    bottom: -30px;
    left: 60px;
}
#quote::after {
    background-color: #FFF;
    height: 60px;
    width: 60px;
    bottom: -45px;
    left: 45px;
}
```

# Summary

Generated content with the ::before and ::after pseudo-elements has a wide range of uses. As well as creating labels for common elements, you can ensure the typographic integrity of nested quotes, and generate complex numbered sequences. But it's important to remember that the generated content does not become part of the underlying HTML, so it remains inaccessible to older browsers. Don't use it for vital content. In this chapter, you also saw several examples of how generated content can be used for attractive visual effects, such as ribbons and speech bubbles.

In the next chapter, we'll look at how to create styles that ensure your pages look good when printed out. The techniques used in the next chapter also lay the foundations for creating responsive web designs that adapt to a variety of devices ranging from mobile phones to desktop computers.

■ ■ ■

# CHAPTER 16

# Creating a Print Style Sheet

Web designers put a lot of effort into creating pages that look great onscreen but rarely give a thought to what they look like when printed. How often have you bought something online and wanted to print the invoice? Instead of a professional-looking document, you get all the website navigation down the side, leaving not enough room for the figures that indicate how much you paid. If you're lucky, they come out on a second sheet. Of course, not every designer is negligent. Some go to the trouble of creating a separate print version of the page. Neither situation is necessary. All that's needed is a print style sheet.

In this chapter, I'll show you how to create styles for printing and to use some of the special properties for printed output. You'll learn about the following:

- Planning what to change or remove when the page is printed

- Using the media attribute and @media rules to specify which devices styles apply to

- Setting the margins for a printed page

- How to avoid page breaks at inconvenient points

## What's Different About Print CSS?

There are only a handful of dedicated print properties, all of which are concerned with controlling where to break the content when the web page needs to be printed on more than one sheet. There's also an @page rule, which sets the margins around the edge of the printed page. Otherwise, creating a print style sheet is no different from the type of style sheet discussed so far.

You lay out the content of the page the same way, using floats or CSS table display, and controlling horizontal and vertical space with the margin and padding properties. You also define font characteristics with the same properties. The crucial difference is that printing is a static medium. The width of a printed page is fixed, but you have no idea what size paper will be used, so the content of a wide onscreen layout is likely to be truncated.

### Issues that Need to be Considered

By default, most browsers don't print background colors and images. This can have disastrous consequences if your web page uses a light color on a dark background: you risk having text that's virtually illegible when printed. The only exception appears to be white text on black. Most browsers automatically reverse the colors and print the text in black. Even if your colored text has sufficient contrast against a white background, consider whether it might be more legible in a darker color or black when printed.

---

■ **Tip** Browsers turn off background colors and images to speed up printing and avoid wasting ink. It's up to the user to turn on the option to print them. Always work on the assumption that printing background colors and images is turned off. There is no way to override the user's setting with CSS or any other web technology.

---

You also need to take fonts and font sizes into consideration. Users can increase the font size in a browser, but not on a printed page. So, it's important to make sure all your text prints at a size that is comfortable for the average person to read. Specify font sizes and other dimensions using physical units of measurement, such as points, inches, or centimeters.

Links cannot be followed, and the URL is hidden unless you use the URL as the link text. So, it's a good idea to use the ::after pseudo-element to display the URLs of external links (see "Generating Content from an Attribute" in Chapter 15).

Perhaps the biggest consideration with a print style sheet is deciding which parts of your web page are unnecessary. Do you really want your navigation menu printed? What about the search form? Neither is going to be any use on the printed page, so they're good candidates for exclusion by setting their display property to none. You also need to exclude parts of the page that consist solely of background images, because they won't normally be printed and will leave unsightly gaps in the page. If an image is important, and you want it included in printouts, it should be embedded in the HTML with the <img> tag. It's only background images that printers ignore.

## What Print Style Sheets Cannot Do

Browser manufacturers and the W3C seem to regard improvements to print-related properties as a low priority. The CSS3 Paged Media module (http://dev.w3.org/csswg/css3-page/) remained inactive for nearly six years until it stirred into life again in mid-2012. Currently, browsers support only CSS2.1 print features, which impose two important limitations:

- You cannot specify the size of the printed page.

- You cannot change the orientation of the page.

The size property was intended to control size and orientation, but Opera was the only major browser that managed to support it. So it was dropped from the CSS2.1 specification, and moved to the draft CSS3 Paged Media module. At the time of this writing, Opera is still the only browser to support the size property.

These limitations mean that you don't have the same level of control as you would when designing a brochure or leaflet. Although it's a fairly safe assumption that most printing will be done in portrait orientation on letter paper in the U.S. and the slightly larger A4 size in most other countries, your design needs to be flexible.

# Specifying the Media Type

By default, style rules are used by all types of media that are capable of displaying them. But you can create separate sets of rules and target them at different types of devices by specifying one or more of the media types listed in Table 16-1.

*Table 16-1.* *Media Types*

| Type | Use |
|------|-----|
| all | Applies the styles to all devices. This is the default if no media type is specified. |
| braille | Specifies that the styles should be used by Braille tactile devices. |
| embossed | Applies the styles to paged Braille printers. |
| handheld | Intended for mobile devices, but not used by modern smartphones or tablets. |
| print | Applies the styles to pages when they're printed. |
| projection | Indicates that the styles are for use with a projector. |
| screen | Specifies that styles should be used by a browser on a computer screen. This is the most common media type. Modern mobile devices also use these styles. |
| speech | Intended for speech synthesizers for the visually impaired. |
| tty | For teletypes, terminals, or portable devices with limited display capabilities. |
| tv | Intended for televisions and similar devices. |

■ **Caution**    The handheld media type was intended to be used for mobile phones and palmtop computers or personal digital assistants (PDA), but very few devices ever supported it. If you use it, your styles are likely to be ignored. You'll learn in Chapter 17 how to target styles at smartphones and tablets using media queries, which extend the basic media types.

Most of the media types in Table 16-1 are highly specialized. The only ones you are likely to need in normal circumstances are all, print, and screen.

## Linking External Style Sheets

The most common way to specify the media type(s) you want to target is by adding the media attribute to the <link> tag when attaching a style sheet to a web page. The attribute accepts a comma-separated list of media types from Table 16-1. For example, the following link specifies that the style sheet should be applied only to browsers that display on computer screens and mobile devices:

```
<link href="styles/visual.css" rel="stylesheet" media="screen">
```

To specify different rules for printing, attach a separate style sheet like this:

```
<link href="styles/print.css" rel="stylesheet" media="print">
```

Specifying the media types like this makes the style sheets mutually exclusive. Printers ignore the first style sheet, while visual browsers ignore the second one. To specify that the styles should be used by both screen browsers and printer, add both media types separated by a comma like this:

```
<link href="styles/common.css" rel="stylesheet" media="screen, print">
```

> ■ **Tip** If you want the same styles to be used by browsers and printers, there's no need to use the media attribute at all. Omitting it serves the style sheet to all devices.

## Specifying Media Types with @import

When using @import to attach an external style sheet, the media type on its own is sufficient. Simply list the media type(s) after the filename like this:

```
@import url(styles/print.css) print;
```

To specify more than one media type, separate them with commas.

## Specifying Media Types for Embedded Styles

If you have embedded styles in the <head> of a page, use the media attribute in the opening <style> tag:

```
<style media="print">
/* Embedded styles for printers */
</style>
```

## Using @media Rules

You can use @media rules within an external style sheet or <style> block. Simply add the media type(s) after @media, and wrap the targeted rules in a pair of curly braces. For example, the following @media rule changes the background color and font characteristics for printers:

```
body {
    background-color: #EFECCA;
    color: #000;
    font-family: "Lucida Sans Unicode", "Lucida Grande", sans-serif;
}

@media print {
    body {
        background-color: #FFF;
        font-family: "Times New Roman", Times, serif;
        font-size: 10pt;
    }
}
```

The curly braces around the @media rule create what can be thought of as a mini style sheet nested inside another. The rule inside the @media block applies only to printers, and is ignored by other devices. However, printers inherit styles that are not overridden. So, the text color is black for both browsers and printers.

> ■ **Tip** You can create completely separate style sheets for visual browsers and printers, and hide them from each other using the screen and print media types. Alternatively, you can use the cascade and just override specific styles in a print style sheet. You'll see an example of the first approach later in this chapter.

# Setting Page Margins

Although it's not currently possible to set the size or orientation of the printed page, you can—and should—set the page's margins. You do this with the @page rule.

## The @page Rule

The @page rule accepts only the margin shorthand property or the individual margin properties. Moreover, you cannot use em or ex units to specify the size of the margins. Use either percentages or the physical units of measurement in Table 16-2.

***Table 16-2.** Physical Units of Measurement for Print Styles*

| Unit | Description |
| --- | --- |
| in | Inch (2.54 centimeters) |
| cm | Centimeter (0.394 in) |
| mm | Millimeter (0.039 in) |
| pt | Point, a typographical unit equivalent to 1/72 of an inch (0.353 mm) |
| pc | Pica, a typographical unit equivalent to 12 points (4.233 mm) |

To add a one-inch margin all around a page (the same as a default document in Microsoft Word), put the following rule at the top of your print styles:

```
@page {
    margin: 1in;
}
```

The following does the same using metric measurements:

```
@page {
    margin: 2.54cm;
}
```

If you come from a print background, you might prefer this:

```
@page {
    margin: 6pc;
}
```

■ **Note**  Technically speaking you can also use px, which is equivalent to 0.75pt (1/96 in or 0.265 mm). However, the physical units in Table 16-2 are more common for print, especially fonts, which are measured in points.

If you specify the margins as percentages, the left and right margins are relative to the width of the page, and top and bottom margins are relative to its height.

## Page Pseudo-classes

The @page rule supports three pseudo-classes, namely:

:first

:left

:right

A web page is a single, continuous entity, but when printed, it often covers several pages of print. These pseudo-classes let you specify different margins for printed pages. As their names suggest, :first is for the first page, and :left and :right are for subsequent pages. Odd-numbered pages use the :right pseudo-class, and even-numbered ones the :left pseudo-class.

The following @page rules create a two-centimeter margin around all sides of the page, but leave a wider margin for binding on the appropriate side of the left and right pages (assuming they're printed doubled-sided):

```
@page {
    margin: 2cm;
}
@page :left {
    margin-right: 3cm;
}

@page :right {
    margin-left: 3cm;
}
```

■ **Note**   For right-to-left languages, such as Arabic and Hebrew, :left is for odd-numbered pages and :right for even-numbered ones.

# Controlling Where to Break Content

It can be infuriating when printing a web page to discover that a heading is printed at the bottom of a page, and all the information relating to that heading is on the next page without anything to identify it. To avoid such situations, CSS provides the five properties listed in Table 16-3.

*Table 16-3.* *Page Break Properties*

| Property | Initial Value | Inherited | Description |
| --- | --- | --- | --- |
| page-break-before | auto | No | Specifies whether a new page should be started before a particular element. |
| page-break-inside | auto | No | Specifies whether a new page can be started in the middle of an element. |
| page-break-after | auto | No | Specifies how to handle page breaks after a particular element. |

(continued)

***Table 16-3.*** (*continued*)

| Property | Initial Value | Inherited | Description |
|---|---|---|---|
| orphans | 2 | Yes | Specifies the minimum number of lines of an element that must be displayed at the bottom of the page. If fewer lines would be displayed, the whole item is moved to the next page. |
| widows | 2 | Yes | Specifies the minimum number of lines of an element that must be displayed at the top of a page. If fewer lines would be displayed, the whole item is moved from the previous page. |

The page-break-before and page-break-after properties accept one of the following values:

**auto** Leave it up to the browser to decide where to put the page break. This is the default.

**always** Force a page break before or after the specified element.

**avoid** Avoid a page break, if possible.

**left** Force one or two page breaks before or after the specified element, so the next page is formatted as a left page.

**right** Force one or two page breaks before or after the specified element, so the next page is formatted as a right page.

**inherit** These properties are not inherited by default, so this value can be used to force the element to take the same value as its parent.

The page-break-inside property accepts only auto, avoid, or inherit.

The orphans and widows properties should be familiar to anyone with a print background. It's generally considered bad practice in printing to leave only a single line of a paragraph at the top or bottom of a page. By default, browsers are expected to print at least two lines of a block-level element before and after a page break. So if, for example, a three-line paragraph appears at the bottom of a page, but there is room for only two lines, the whole paragraph should be moved to the next page. You can use these properties to change the minimum number of lines you want to keep together. The value must be a positive integer. The bigger the number you use, the more uneven your printed pages are likely to look. For example, if you set both orphans and widows to 4, the whole of any paragraph with fewer than eight lines will be moved to the next page if there isn't sufficient room for it at the bottom of the current page.

---

■ **Tip** The easy way to remember which is which is that orphans are the little ones at the bottom, and widows are the lonely ones at the top.

---

Setting page breaks in a print style sheet should be regarded as indicating a desirable outcome, rather than something that can be relied upon. You have no way of predicting the size of paper that will be used. Also, there might be conflicting demands of where the page should be broken. It's left up to the browser to decide what is possible in any given set of circumstances.

■ **Caution**  The W3C requires only two user agents (in this case, browsers) to support a property for it to become part of the official specification. Opera and IE 8+ were the first to implement all print-related properties. Other browsers might have caught up by the time you read this, but page breaks are generally unreliable.

## Controlling How Elements Are Broken

Sometimes, it's inevitable that an element needs to be broken at a page break. Figure 16-1 shows how Firefox's Print Preview handles box-decoration-break.html. The text is wrapped in a <div> that has a border with rounded corners, but the <div> is too big to fit on a single page. The browser just slices the element in two, breaking the border at the page break.

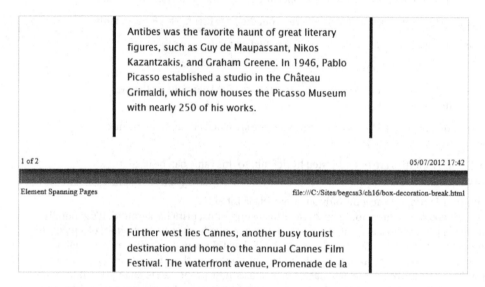

*Figure 16-1.*  *Browsers normally slice large elements at a page break*

CSS3 proposes a more elegant solution using box-decoration-break, which accepts two values:

   **slice** This is the default behavior, slicing the element at the page break, as shown in Figure 16-1.

   **clone** Each box fragment is created independently, preserving padding and border features, such as rounded corners, border images, and drop shadows. The background is rendered independently on each fragment.

At the time of this writing, no browser supports box-decoration-break when printing. However, Figure 16-2 simulates how a browser should render the <div> in box-decoration-break.html at a page break when the property is set to clone.

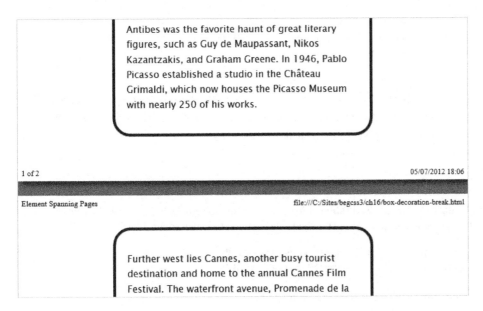

Antibes was the favorite haunt of great literary figures, such as Guy de Maupassant, Nikos Kazantzakis, and Graham Greene. In 1946, Pablo Picasso established a studio in the Château Grimaldi, which now houses the Picasso Museum with nearly 250 of his works.

1 of 2                                                                 05/07/2012 18:06

Element Spanning Pages                        file:///C:/Sites/begcss3/ch16/box-decoration-break.html

Further west lies Cannes, another busy tourist destination and home to the annual Cannes Film Festival. The waterfront avenue, Promenade de la

*Figure 16-2. Setting box-decoration-break to clone styles the fragments independently (simulation)*

■ **Note** The box-decoration-break property is also designed to work with inline elements broken over more than one line. So far, Opera is the only browser with partial support for this property. It treats broken inline elements as separate fragments, preserving the background and border characteristics, but not padding. For more details about box-decoration-break, see www.w3.org/TR/css3-background/#the-box-decoration-break.

# Creating Styles for Printing

There are two approaches you can take to creating styles for printing. You can start from scratch with a separate set of print style rules. The other approach is to use the CSS cascade to override specific rules.

Neither approach is inherently better than the other. Which you choose depends on the site and the amount of changes needed for the printed version. For example, a site that predominantly consists of text might need only a few changes, so using the cascade to override the choice of fonts and color is all you need. On the other hand, a site that uses a lot of background images, floats, and positioned elements is probably much easier to handle by creating a dedicated print style sheet from scratch.

## Using the Cascade for Print Styles

For a relatively small number of changes to the way a page is styled when printed, you can create a general style sheet, and then override selected styles for printing. Because of the way the cascade works, the print style sheet must be attached after the main style sheet. Omit the media attribute from the main style sheet, but specify it for the print one like this:

```
<link href="styles/main.css" rel="stylesheet">
<link href="styles/print.css" rel="stylesheet" media="print">
```

The disadvantage with this approach is that it can be difficult to keep track of which rules you are overriding in the print style sheet. There's also a danger that you might add a new style to the main style sheet and not realize that it affects the way the page is printed.

---

■ **Tip** If you decide to use the cascade for print styles, make sure you set the `position` property of positioned elements to `static`. This returns them to the normal flow of the document and ensures they will print correctly. If you don't want an element to be printed, set its `display` property to `none`.

---

## Attaching Independent Style Sheets

By specifying the `media` attribute for each style sheet, the styles are applied only by the targeted devices. This allows you to create a completely independent print style sheet. Attach the style sheets like this:

```
<link href="styles/main.css" rel="stylesheet" media="screen">
<link href="styles/print.css" rel="stylesheet" media="print">
```

This gives you a blank canvas on which to create your print styles.

---

■ **Caution** Setting the `media` attribute to `all` has the same effect as omitting the attribute.

---

## EXERCISE: CREATING A PRINT STYLE SHEET

In this exercise, you'll create a print style sheet for the version of the Mediterranean Destinations page with a horizontal menu from Chapter 10. The simple way to create a print style sheet is to copy the existing style rules to a new file, and then edit them.

Use as your starting point horizontal_begin.html and styles/horizontal.css in the ch16 folder. The finished files are horizontal_end.html and styles/print_end.css. No changes are made to horizontal.css.

1. Add the `media` attribute to the `<link>` tag that attaches the existing style sheet, and set its value to `screen`:

   ```
   <link href="styles/horizontal.css" rel="stylesheet" media="screen">
   ```

2. Save the page, load it into a browser, and select the browser's *Print Preview*. The page is completely unstyled because the `media` attribute specifies that the styles are only for visual browsers. If you're in a hurry, this is a simple way of ensuring that all the content is printed. But it looks very bland, as Figure 16-3 shows.

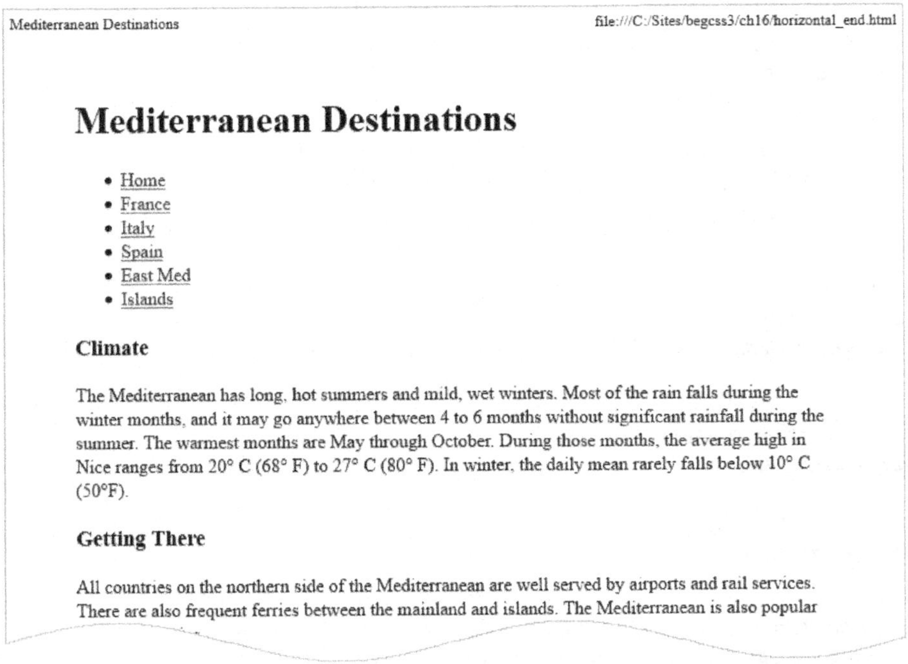

Mediterranean Destinations                                       file:///C:/Sites/begcss3/ch16/horizontal_end.html

# Mediterranean Destinations

- Home
- France
- Italy
- Spain
- East Med
- Islands

## Climate

The Mediterranean has long, hot summers and mild, wet winters. Most of the rain falls during the winter months, and it may go anywhere between 4 to 6 months without significant rainfall during the summer. The warmest months are May through October. During those months, the average high in Nice ranges from 20° C (68° F) to 27° C (80° F). In winter, the daily mean rarely falls below 10° C (50°F).

## Getting There

All countries on the northern side of the Mediterranean are well served by airports and rail services. There are also frequent ferries between the mainland and islands. The Mediterranean is also popular

*Figure 16-3. Hiding the visual styles with the media attribute creates a crude print version*

3. Create a blank style sheet called print.css in the styles folder, and attach it to the page with the media attribute set to print like this:

```
<link href="styles/print.css" rel="stylesheet" media="print">
```

4. Add the @page rule at the top of print.css, and set the margins. I'm using one inch all round, but set the value to 2.54cm if you prefer to use metric measurements.

```
@page {
    margin: 1in;
}
```

5. Copy all the style rules from styles/horizontal.css, and paste them into print.css.

6. Remove all the styles except font-family and color from the body rule. Change the value of font-family to use a serif font like this:

```
body {
    font-family: "Palatino Linotype", "Book Antiqua", Palatino, serif;
    color: #000;
}
```

7. The #wrapper, #header, #main, and #aside rules provide structure and decorative elements not needed in the print layout. Delete the rules entirely.

8. The text in the paragraphs uses the browser default font size, 16px, which is equivalent to 12pt. It's also indented on both sides. Remove the left and right margins, and reduce the font size by amending the p style rule like this:

```
p {
    margin-top: 0;
    font-size: 10pt;
}
```

9. Adjust the size of the heading fonts too (note that the sizes are specified using points, not pixels). Also remove the left and right margins from the <h2> and <h3> headings. The edited rules look like this:

```
h1 {
    text-align: center;
    margin-top: 0;
    font-size: 18pt;
}
h2, h3 {
    margin-bottom: 0.25em;
    font-size: 14pt;
}
h3 {
    font-size: 12pt;
}
```

10. The following style rules are related to controlling images at different screen widths or decorative elements. So, they can be deleted: `.imgcentered`, `.figure.floatleft`, `.figure.floatright`, `.figure`, `.figure img`, `.portrait`, `.rounded`, and `.shadow`.

11. The navigation menu doesn't need to be included in the printed version, so delete all rules related to #nav, and replace them with the following style rule to hide it:

```
#nav {
    display: none;
}
```

12. Remove the underlining and text color of links, and display the URL of external links using the `::after` pseudo-class (see "Generating Content from an Attribute" in Chapter 15) like this:

```
a {
    text-decoration: none;
    color: #000;
}
a[href^="http://"]::after {
    content: ': ' attr(href);
}
```

13. Save the web page and print.css. Load the page into several different browsers, and test *Print Preview*. Although the page is formatted ready for printing, there are considerable differences in the final layout. The main problems are with the images. Older browsers often slice images in two if they come near a page break. The most recent browsers shift the image to the next page if there isn't sufficient space. However, IE 9 doesn't reflow the text when this happens, leaving a large blank space where the image would originally have been (see Figure 16-4).

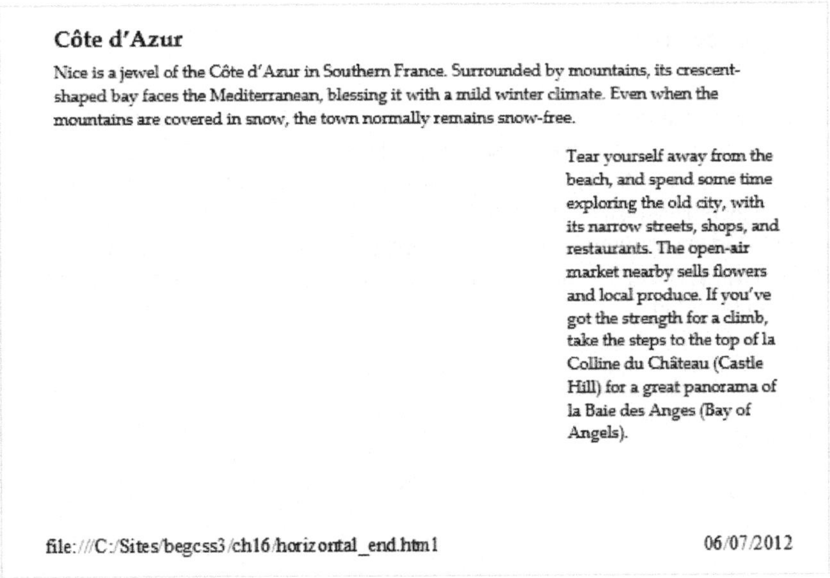

> **Côte d'Azur**
>
> Nice is a jewel of the Côte d'Azur in Southern France. Surrounded by mountains, its crescent-shaped bay faces the Mediterranean, blessing it with a mild winter climate. Even when the mountains are covered in snow, the town normally remains snow-free.
>
> Tear yourself away from the beach, and spend some time exploring the old city, with its narrow streets, shops, and restaurants. The open-air market nearby sells flowers and local produce. If you've got the strength for a climb, take the steps to the top of la Colline du Château (Castle Hill) for a great panorama of la Baie des Anges (Bay of Angels).
>
> file:///C:/Sites/begcss3/ch16/horizontal_end.html          06/07/2012

*Figure 16-4.* *IE 9 leaves a space when a floated image is moved to the next page*

14. Because you can't predict the page size that will be used for printing, it's not practicable to compensate for this sort of problem. Adding a style to the `figure` class to set `page-break-before` to `always` forces a break in some browsers, but not in IE 9. For this particular page, the least disruptive solution is to create a style rule for the `aside` `<div>` to force a page break after the sidebar content like this:

```
#aside {
    page-break-after: always;
}
```

15. Forcing the page break after the sidebar moves the beginning of the main content to a page of its own. So, it would be a good idea to give it a heading. In modern browsers that support generated content, nothing could be easier. Use the `::before` pseudo-element like this (notice that you need to set the `display` property to `block` to center the generated content):

```
#main::before {
    content: 'Mediterranean Destinations';
    font-weight: bold;
    font-size: 18pt;
    margin-bottom: 12pt;
    display: block;
    text-align: center;
}
```

16. It's also a good idea to add the `clear` property to the style rule for the subheadings because they frequently appear close to floated images:

```
h2, h3 {
    margin-bottom: 0.25em;
```

```
        font-size: 14pt;
        clear: both;
}
```

17. Save the style sheet, and test the page in *Print Preview* again. No browser produces exactly the same result as another, but the layout now looks considerably better. Figure 16-5 shows the second page in IE 9's *Print Preview*. Like all browsers, it automatically adds headers and footers to the printed page. At the moment, there is no way to control this. They need to be turned off by the user. However, this situation is likely to change when the CSS3 Paged Media module matures.

Mediterranean Destinations                                                    Page 2 of 3

## Mediterranean Destinations

Every summer, Northern Europeans descend on the Mediterranean in search of sun, sea, and relaxation. Because the Med has only a narrow outlet to the Atlantic, tides are very limited, making it ideal for swimming. But the fresh breeze off the sea tempers the long, hot summers.

### Côte d'Azur

Nice is a jewel of the Côte d'Azur in Southern France. Surrounded by mountains, its crescent-shaped bay faces the Mediterranean, blessing it with a mild winter climate. Even when the mountains are covered in snow, the town normally remains snow-free.

Nice seafront from la Colline du Château

Tear yourself away from the beach, and spend some time exploring the old city, with its narrow streets, shops, and restaurants. The open-air market nearby sells flowers and local produce. If you've got the strength for a climb, take the steps to the top of la Colline du Château (Castle Hill) for a great panorama of la Baie des Anges (Bay of Angels).

A short distance to the west of Nice is Antibes, an ancient walled city with a maze of narrow streets. Alongside the port packed with luxury yachts, locals play cards and boules to while away the hours.

Antibes was the favorite haunt of great literary figures, such as Guy de Maupassant, Nikos Kazantzakis, and Graham Greene. In 1946, Pablo Picasso established a studio in the Château Grimaldi, which now houses the Picasso Museum with nearly 250 of his works.

Further west lies Cannes, another busy tourist destination and home to the annual Cannes Film Festival. The waterfront avenue, Promenade de la Croisette, is

Relaxing by the port in Antibes

lined with palm trees and overlooks the sandy beach. La Croisette's fashionable hotels, boutiques, and restaurants belie its humble origins. The waste from a soap factory in the nineteenth century

file:///C:/Sites/begcss3/ch16/horizontal_end.html                              06/07/2012

***Figure 16-5.*** *The printed page layout is greatly improved*

Your results might not look exactly the same as the screen shots in this exercise because they depend on your printer settings and paper size. My printer uses A4 paper.

If you need to support IE 8, use the single-colon versions of the `::after` and `::before` pseudo-elements.

# Summary

In some respects, print styles are the poor relation of the CSS family. Browsers haven't given them a great deal of attention, and the CSS3 Paged Media module remained inactive for a long time. In spite of the problems, it's important to add print styles to a website, particularly for pages—such as invoices and sets of instructions—that are likely to be printed.

Most of the styles used in a print style sheet use the same properties as for layout in a visual browser. Printers rely on physical measurements, so it's best to specify font sizes in points rather than pixels (`1px = 0.75pt`), and to use inches, centimeters, or picas for margins. The print-specific properties are concerned with where and how to implement page breaks. They should be regarded as indicating only the desirable outcome rather than laying down hard and fast rules.

Use the `media` attribute or `@media` rules to specify which devices should use the styles. Of the many media types, the only ones you are likely to use are `screen` (for visual browsers) and `print` (for printers).

You can use the cascade to create print-specific styles that override the main style sheet, but it's usually easier to maintain separate style sheets for visual browsers and printers. Make a copy of the existing style sheet, and then go through it removing styles that are irrelevant to the printed page, and editing others to improve the printed layout. Keep the styles mutually exclusive by attaching the original style sheet using `media="screen"` and the print one using `media="print"`.

In the next chapter, you'll learn about CSS3 media queries, which extend the `media` attribute to allow you to serve specific styles to devices depending on such features as screen width, resolution, and orientation. Media queries are supported by all modern browsers, but not by IE 8 and earlier. More significantly, they're supported by the browsers used in smartphones and tablets, making them an important tool in responsive web design for mobile devices.

■ ■ ■

# CHAPTER 17

# Targeting Styles with Media Queries

Media queries are simple conditions that test one or more of a device's features, allowing you to tailor style rules to match the device's capabilities. This makes it possible to deliver the same HTML to smartphones, tablets, and desktop computers, but with different styles optimized for the appropriate screen size and resolution. You specify the conditions at the same time as the media type (see "Specifying the Media Type" in the preceding chapter).

CSS3 Media Queries became a formal recommendation in June 2012. So, they're stable and supported by the latest versions of all browsers in widespread use. However, you should also provide styles for browsers, such as IE 8 and earlier, that don't understand media queries. So-called *feature phones*—low-end devices with a basic display—usually don't support media queries either.

Smartphones do understand media queries, but they automatically scale websites to fit a nominal viewport that's much wider than the actual screen size. To ensure that mobile devices interpret dimensions correctly, you need to add a viewport `<meta>` tag to the head of each web page. The W3C plans to replace this with a new CSS feature, the `@viewport` rule, which Opera and IE 10 were the first to support on an experimental basis. This chapter explains how the `<meta>` tag and `@viewport` relate to each other.

In this chapter, you'll learn about the following:

- Which features you can test for with media queries

- How to specify the conditions in a media query

- Setting the viewport size to ensure that mobile devices interpret widths correctly

- Understanding how browsers treat hidden elements

- Dealing with images for high-resolution displays

## Creating Responsive Web Designs

The term *responsive web design* was popularized by an article Ethan Marcotte wrote for *A List Apart* in 2010 (`www.alistapart.com/articles/responsive-web-design/`). The article was prompted by repeated requests to build "an iPhone website." This set Ethan wondering what would come next. An iPad website? Different websites for different devices? His answer was this: "Rather than tailoring disconnected designs to each of an ever-increasing number of devices, we can treat them as facets of the same experience." Media queries are the technology that makes this possible. The conditions in media queries test a device's features, such as width, height, orientation, or aspect ratio, allowing you to adapt the web page's layout by serving styles best suited to those features.

Before I explain the details, I suggest that you visit `http://mediaqueri.es`, an online gallery of websites that use responsive web design. It shows screen shots of featured websites at typical widths for smartphones, tablets, netbooks, and large desktops (see Figure 17-1). Clicking one of the screenshots takes you to the original site, where you can examine the CSS using a browser's developer tools.

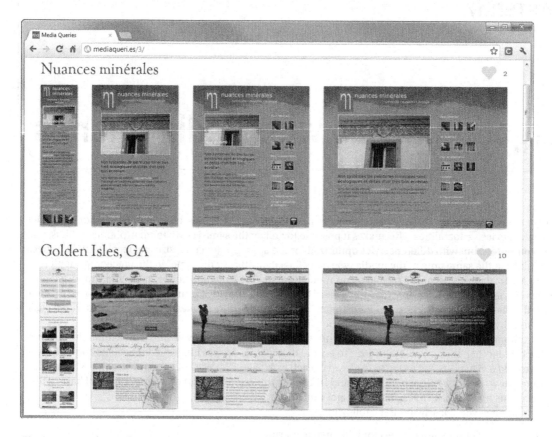

*Figure 17-1. The Media Queries gallery showcases designs that adapt to different screen widths*

The examples in Figure 17-1 preserve the same branding at each width, but the layout changes. Notice how the thumbnail images in the first example are below the main content at the two narrower widths, but move alongside when more screen estate is available. The navigation menu in the second example uses large, easily tappable buttons at the narrowest width.

## Desktop or Mobile First?

Planning a responsive web design involves careful thought about the order of elements in the underlying HTML. Although you can use media queries to adapt a desktop design to display differently on smaller screens, it's considered best practice to design for mobile first wherever possible. Doing so forces you to concentrate on essential content rather than design flourishes. One of the main considerations for mobile design is to keep the overall size of the page to a minimum.

This chapter can't cover every aspect of responsive web design. It concentrates on the role of CSS and media queries, but points out other issues that you should be aware of, such as image size and resolution.

## Browser Support for Media Queries

Media queries are supported by the following browsers:

- Chrome 4+

- Firefox 3.5+

- IE 9+

- Opera 9.5+

- Safari 4+ (slightly buggy support since 3.1)

- Android 2.1+

- iOS Safari 3.2+

- Opera Mini 5+

- Opera Mobile 10+

- Windows Phone 7.5+

Although this breadth of support is encouraging, IE 8 and earlier don't understand media queries. Feature phones with fewer capabilities than smartphones tend not to support media queries, either.

---

■ **Tip** The fact that media queries aren't universally supported is not a barrier to using them. All that's necessary is to provide basic styles in an ordinary style sheet, and use media queries to refine the way your pages look in browsers that understand them. You'll see how to do so later in this chapter.

---

# How Media Queries Work

Media queries use conditions that test a device's features. You set the conditions when specifying the media type with the media attribute in a <link> tag, or in @import or @media rules. If the device satisfies the conditions, it uses the styles. Otherwise, it ignores them.

## Media Features

In CSS3, you can test for the 13 media features listed in Table 17-1. The Min/Max column indicates whether the feature can be prefixed with min- or max- to indicate a minimum or maximum value.

*Table 17-1. Media Features Used to Test a Device's Capabilities*

| Feature | Value | Min/Max | Description |
|---|---|---|---|
| width | Length | Yes | Width of display area |
| height | Length | Yes | Height of display area |
| device-width | Length | Yes | Width of device |
| device-height | Length | Yes | Height of device |
| orientation | portrait or landscape | No | Orientation of device |
| aspect-ratio | Ratio | Yes | Ratio of width to height |
| device-aspect-ratio | Ratio | Yes | Ratio of device-width to device-height |
| color | Integer | Yes | Number of bits per color component (if not color, the value is 0) |
| color-index | Integer | Yes | Number of entries in the device's color lookup table |
| monochrome | Integer | Yes | Number of bits per pixel in the monochrome frame buffer (if not monochrome, the value is 0) |
| resolution | Resolution | Yes | Density of pixels of the output device, expressed as an integer followed by dpi (dots per inch), dpcm (dots per centimeter), or dppx (dots per pixel) |
| scan | progressive or interlace | No | Scanning process used by TV device |
| grid | 0 or 1 | No | If set to 1, the device is grid-based, such as a teletype terminal or phone display with only one fixed font (all other devices are 0) |

■ **Note** Ratios are expressed as two integers separated by a forward slash, for example 16/9. The slash can optionally be surrounded by spaces: 16 / 9 is equally valid.

The width and height values refer to the display area, whereas device-width and device-height refer to the physical dimensions of the screen. Many mobile devices use width and height to refer to a nominal viewport that is usually much larger than the screen's physical dimensions. You'll learn later in this chapter how to reconcile the difference between the nominal viewport and screen size.

■ **Tip** Pixel measurements refer to CSS pixels (see "Physical and CSS Pixels" in Chapter 3), even with high pixel-density displays, such as Apple's retina display.

## Media Query Syntax

A media query begins with one of the media types listed in Table 16-1 in the preceding chapter. The only ones you are ever likely to need are screen or print.

After the media type you add conditions with the keyword and. Each condition is wrapped in parentheses, and is based on one of the media features listed in Table 17-1. You specify the feature's value in the same way as a CSS property by placing it after a colon. For example, the following media query restricts styles to screens between 401px and 600px wide:

```
screen and (min-width: 401px) and (max-width: 600px)
```

All conditions in the query must be true. For example, the preceding query won't work if the display is 700px wide, even though the minimum width is satisfied.

Some media features don't require a value. To specify a color display, the following is sufficient:

```
screen and (color)
```

Similarly, monochrome and grid can be used without a value. However, each condition involving a media feature must always be enclosed in parentheses.

## Hiding Styles from Browsers that Don't Support Media Queries

Although media queries are new to CSS3, the W3C had the foresight to anticipate them more than a decade earlier when it drew up the HTML 4.01 specification. Browsers expect media types to be presented as a comma-separated list. The specification says they should truncate the list immediately before the first nonalphanumeric character that isn't a hyphen.

So, when an old browser sees one of the media queries in the preceding section, it should simply interpret it as screen. In other words, it should still apply the styles. Unfortunately, IE 8 and earlier won't play ball. If you add a media query, older versions of Internet Explorer ignore the styles completely.

However, old versions of other, more standards-compliant browsers might follow the rules and apply the styles, messing up your design. To hide styles from browsers that don't understand media queries, precede the media type with the keyword only like this:

```
only screen and (min-width: 401px) and (max-width: 600px)
```

A standards-compliant old browser sees only followed by a space, realizes it's not a valid media type, and ignores the styles. Older versions of Internet Explorer also don't like the look of only. Consequently, the styles are hidden from all browsers that don't understand media queries. Modern browsers recognize only as part of a media query and go on to evaluate the conditions.

---

■ **Tip** You can get a lightweight JavaScript polyfill (helper script) that provides basic support for media queries in IE 6–8 from https://github.com/scottjehl/Respond/. It supports only min-width and max-width, but that's frequently all you need.

---

## Specifying Alternative Conditions

There is no or keyword to specify alternatives. Instead, you list alternative queries as a comma-separated list. For example, the following applies styles to visual displays wider than 769px or printers capable of printing a minimum of 6 inches wide:

```
only screen and (min-width: 769px), print and (min-width: 6in)
```

---

▓ **Caution**   When you specify a width for printing, IE 9+ calculates the width remaining after deducting the margins set in the @page rule.

---

## Specifying Negative Conditions

You can't negate just one condition. The whole query must be negated by placing the not keyword at the beginning like this:

```
not screen and (min-width: 769px)
```

This makes the styles available to every device *except* a visual browser with a minimum screen width of 769px. So, the styles would be available, for example, to a printer or to a visual browser with a screen width of 768px or less.

---

▓ **Caution**   The not keyword *must* come before the media type. The query is ignored if you use it anywhere else. For example, screen and not (monochrome) is invalid.

---

## Attaching External Style Sheets

One of the most common ways of using media queries is in the media attribute of the <link> tag. You can attach a generic style sheet to a page, followed by a series of device-specific style sheets like this:

```
<link href=styles/basic.css" rel="stylesheet" type="text/css">
<link href="styles/phone.css" rel="stylesheet" type="text/css" media="only screen and ↩
    (max-width: 480px)">
<link href="styles/tablet.css" rel="stylesheet" type="text/css" media="only screen and ↩
    (min-width: 481px) and (max-width: 768px)">
```

The first style sheet, basic.css, doesn't use the media attribute, so the styles apply to all devices. Browsers that understand media queries also read the other style sheets. Attaching the device-specific style sheets after the generic style sheet allows you to use the cascade to override specific styles. The styles in phone.css apply to screens no wider than 480px; those in tablet.css apply to screens between 481px and 768px wide. These sizes are only examples. The sidebar "What Sizes Should I Design For?" discusses factors you should take into consideration when creating media queries.

If you want to restrict the generic styles to visual browsers, add media="screen" without a media query to the <link> tag.

---

### WHAT SIZES SHOULD I DESIGN FOR?

There are so many different web-enabled devices on the market; it's only natural that we try to break down the complexity by slotting them into convenient categories, such as phone, tablet, and desktop. So, there's a danger of thinking the same way about media queries: create three style sheets—one each for phone, tablet, and desktop—and you're done.

Many smartphones, including the iPhone 4S, have a display that's 320px wide (measured in CSS pixels). The most popular tablet, the iPad, is 768 × 1024. But I've got a 7-inch tablet with a 400px screen. Admittedly,

---

it's an early model, but it still works. Most desktop computers have monitors with a minimum screen resolution of 1280 × 800, but 1920 × 1080 and up is by no means uncommon. These wide variations make it impossible to compartmentalize styles as being for a particular type of device.

Rather than attempting to design for specific devices, it's better to assess your content and choose *resolution break points* at which your layout naturally needs to change. For example, if you have a set of images each 300px wide, the natural break points for the design might be 320px, 640px, and 980px, allowing you to display the images side by side on wider screens. Designing for natural break points avoids the need to worry about revising your styles each time a popular new device is released.

## Importing Style Sheets

Media queries can also be used with @import rules. For example, instead of linking three style sheets to every page, as in the preceding example, you can link to just one style sheet like this:

```
<link href="styles/import.css" rel="stylesheet" type="text/css">
```

The single style sheet then imports the others like this:

```
@import url(basic.css);
@import url(phone.css) only screen and (max-width: 480px);
@import url(tablet.css) only screen and (min-width: 481px) and (max-width: 768px);
```

This approach has two potential advantages. First, you attach only one style sheet to each page. Second, if you want to change the conditions in the media queries, there's only one page to edit.

---

▪ **Caution**  Using a style sheet to import other styles adds an extra server request each time a page loads. Also, @import can affect performance. On a small site, it's not likely to make a noticeable difference, but it could have a severe impact on larger sites. See www.stevesouders.com/blog/2009/04/09/dont-use-import/.

---

## Using Media Queries Inside Style Sheets

Another way to use media queries is with @media rules inside a style sheet or <style> block. The media query is appended to @media like this:

```
@media only screen and (min-width: 481px) and (max-width: 768px) {
    /* Styles for screen widths between 481px and 768px */
}
```

---

▪ **Tip**  Most browsers download all style sheets, even if they don't match the conditions of the media query. So, consolidating all styles into a single style sheet with @media rules is—in theory, at least—the most efficient way of using media queries. The main disadvantage is that the style sheet can become very long and difficult to maintain.

---

# Normalizing Width Values for Mobile Devices

Most smartphones and similar devices, such as the iPod touch, automatically scale web pages so that they fit into the screen. Figure 17-2 shows the Mediterranean Destinations page from the preceding chapter in an iPod touch. Although you can see the full design, the text is difficult to read, even for someone with 20-20 vision, and the links are too small to tap accurately.

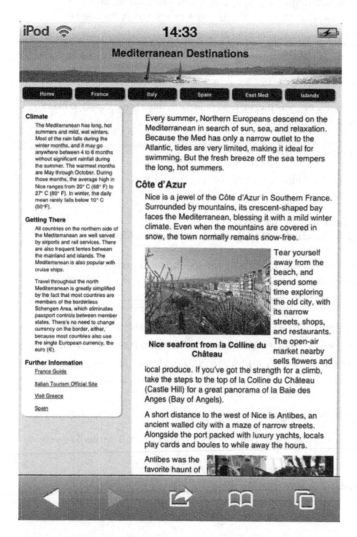

**Figure 17-2.** *The mobile browser automatically scales the page to fit the screen*

The actual screen dimensions on an iPhone or iPod touch are 320 × 480 pixels. However, Safari on iOS uses a nominal viewport that's 980 pixels wide. Browsers on other mobile operating systems behave in a similar fashion. On Windows Phone 7, for example, the nominal viewport is 1024 pixels wide.

Consequently, even if you use media queries to create styles for smaller screens, the smartphone or tablet browser ignores them because it thinks the screen is bigger than it really is. Fortunately, mobile browsers let you change the size of the nominal viewport. The most reliable method is to use a < meta > tag, which needs to be added to every web page. Eventually, you should be able to use a single @viewport rule in your style sheet.

# Setting the Viewport Size in HTML

To allow web designers to control the viewport on the iPhone and iPod touch, Apple introduced a nonstandard < meta > tag, which proved so useful that it was adopted by other mobile browsers. It's now registered as a valid extension of the < meta > tag, and forms the basis of the @viewport rule being standardized by the W3C.

To get mobile devices to set the viewport width to the width of the device, add the following < meta > tag in the < head > of each web page:

```
<meta name="viewport" content="width=device-width">
```

The viewport <meta> tag also allows you to control how the page is scaled. The content attribute accepts the properties listed in Table 17-2.

***Table 17-2.*** *Viewport Properties*

| Property | Value | Description |
| --- | --- | --- |
| width | Integer or constant | Sets the viewport width. Negative numbers are not allowed. When specified as an integer, pixel lengths are used. On iOS, the minimum is 200. On all systems, the maximum is 10000. Accepted constants are device-width and device-height. |
| height | Integer or constant | Sets the viewport height. On iOS, the minimum is 223. Otherwise, accepts the same values as width. |
| initial-scale | Number | Sets the initial scaling factor. Values can be expressed as numbers with a decimal fraction in the range 0.1–10. |
| minimum-scale | Number | Sets the minimum scaling factor in the range 0.1–10. |
| maximum-scale | Number | Sets the maximum scaling factor in the range 0.1–10. |
| user-scalable | yes or no | Determines whether the display can be zoomed in and out. The default is yes. |
| target-densitydpi | Integer or constant | Scales the page up or down depending on the pixel density of the device. The value should be one of the following constants representing the target density for which the page was designed: device-dpi, high-dpi, medium-dpi, or low-dpi. Also accepts a value in the range 70–400 representing the number of dots per inch. Supported only on Android. |

To specify more than one property in the viewport `<meta>` tag, use a comma-separated list of name/value pairs in the `content` attribute. The following example sets the viewport width to the width of the device, and prevents the display from being scaled down from its normal size:

```
<meta name="viewport" content="width=device-width, minimum-scale=1">
```

■ **Caution**    Setting `user-scalable` to `no` is generally considered bad practice because it makes the site inaccessible to people with visual difficulties.

## Setting the Viewport Size in CSS

Although the viewport `<meta>` tag controls the size and scaling factors of mobile browsers, it was quickly recognized that it would be more convenient to set the values in one place for the whole website. This led to the creation of the CSS Device Adaptation module (`http://dev.w3.org/csswg/css-device-adapt/`), which maps the properties from the viewport `<meta>` tag to a new `@viewport` rule. At the time of this writing, the module is described as being at the exploratory stage, but it has already been partially implemented by Opera and IE 10. Because it might change, I won't go into `@viewport` in great detail.

It's proposed that the `@viewport` rule will support the properties listed in Table 17-3. The Min/Max column indicates which properties can be prefixed with `min-` or `max-` to indicate minimum and maximum values.

***Table 17-3.*** *Proposed @viewport Properties*

| Property | Min/Max | Description |
| --- | --- | --- |
| width | Yes | Sets the viewport width. Minimum and maximum values can be specified individually using prefixes. The shorthand property accepts two values for minimum and maximum respectively. Values can be set using the constants `device-width` and `device-height`, lengths, or percentages. |
| height | Yes | Sets the viewport height in the same way as `width`. |
| zoom | Yes | Sets the scaling factor as a multiplier or percentage. |
| user-zoom | No | The default value is `zoom`, which permits scaling. If set to `fixed`, the user is not allowed to scale the page. |
| orientation | No | Locks the document in the specified orientation, `portrait` or `landscape`. The default is `auto`, which allows the orientation to change when the device is tilted. |
| resolution | No | The default is `auto`, which uses CSS pixels. If set to `device`, pixel lengths are mapped to the device's physical pixels. |

The `@viewport` rule is used like any other style rule, with property/value pairs inside curly braces. For example, the following rule sets the viewport width to the width of the device, and prevents the display from being scaled down from its normal size:

```
@viewport {
    width: device-width;
    min-zoom: 1;
}
```

It's the equivalent of the following <meta> tag:

```
<meta name="viewport" content="width=device-width, minimum-scale=1">
```

> ■ **Note** Because the @viewport rule is still experimental, you need to use browser-specific prefixes. For Opera, use @-o-viewport. For IE 10, use @-ms-viewport.

## Width and Orientation—A Conundrum

Take a look at the screen shots in Figure 17-3 of the website for *The Boston Globe*. Both were taken on an iPod touch. The one on the left was taken in portrait orientation, and the one on the right in landscape. Which one would you say is wider?

***Figure 17-3.*** *The Boston Globe's responsive design looks different in portrait and landscape orientation*

I think most people would agree that the screen shot on the right is wider. However, iOS disagrees. Even though the horizontal content area is bigger in the screen shot on the right, Safari on iOS always bases width and height on the dimensions in portrait orientation.

It wouldn't matter if all mobile devices treated width and height the same way. Unfortunately, iOS is the odd one out. Other mobile operating systems base the width on the device's orientation.

> ■ **Caution** Most mobile devices measure width across the horizontal axis in the current orientation. So, width increases in landscape orientation and decreases when the device is held in portrait orientation. In iOS devices (iPhone, iPod touch, and iPad), width is always based on the shorter dimension.

If you use media queries based on width, the iPhone, iPod touch, and iPad simply scale up the display when switching from portrait to landscape. To supply different styles to iOS devices depending on orientation, you can create media queries for the iPhone and iPod touch like this:

```
only screen and (device-width:320px) and (device-height:480px) and (orientation: portrait) {
    /* Portrait styles */
}
only screen and (device-width:320px) and (device-height:480px) and (orientation: landscape) {
    /* Landscape styles */
}
```

Similarly, the following media queries apply to the iPad:

```
only screen and (device-width:768px) and (device-height:1024px) and (orientation:portrait) {
    /* Portrait styles */
}
only screen and (device-width:768px) and (device-height:1024px) and (orientation:landscape) {
    /* Landscape styles */
}
```

In each case, the device width and height remain the same. Only the orientation changes.

---

■ **Note** These dimensions apply to models of the iPhone, iPod touch, and iPad current at the time of this writing. Newer models might be a different size.

---

To demonstrate the effect of these media queries, the styles in mq.html in the ch17 folder specify a different background color for portrait and landscape orientation. The media queries also use the `display` property to hide and show `<div>` elements containing text identifying the target device and orientation. Because mobile devices come in such a wide range of sizes, only the Apple devices are identified by name.

Figures 17-4 and 17-5 show the results in an iPod touch and an HTC Desire phone running Android 2.2. Both operating systems respond to the change in orientation. What's striking about iOS is that the text is scaled up in landscape orientation, as shown in the screen shot on the right of Figure 17-4. This happens even if the font size is specified in the landscape styles. This is because the whole page is scaled up, not just the text. Although the screen shots show only an iPod touch, the iPad behaves the same way.

**Figure 17-4.** *The background color changes with the switch in orientation, but the font is scaled up*

Android, on the other hand, preserves the original font size, as shown on the right of Figure 17-5.

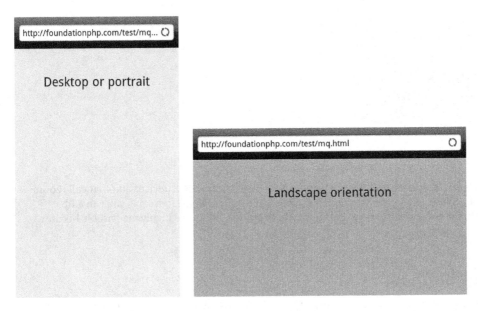

**Figure 17-5.** *The font size remains constant in both orientations on Android*

To get iOS devices to render the same font size in both orientations, you need to set the viewport's initial scale to 1 like this (the code is in mq2.html):

```
<meta name="viewport" content="width=device-width, initial-scale=1">
```

If the device is in landscape orientation when the page first loads, the font is displayed at the correct size. However, if it's in portrait orientation and you switch to landscape, not only is the font scaled up, but the `<div>` is no longer centered, as shown in Figure 17-6.

**Figure 17-6.**  *The whole page is scaled up when switching to landscape, affecting the layout*

Because the viewport `<meta>` tag sets only the initial scale, iOS devices still zoom in when the horizontal viewing area increases. However, double-tapping the screen resets the scaling factor, and the text is displayed at the correct size and centered, as shown in Figure 17-7.

**Figure 17-7.**  *The page is displayed correctly when the scaling factor is reset*

Switching from landscape to portrait doesn't present a problem because iOS devices automatically zoom out to the correct size. To prevent iOS devices from rescaling when switching to landscape, you can add `user-scalable=no` to the content attribute of the viewport `<meta>` tag, but this is highly inadvisable because it creates accessibility problems.

# Dealing with Images

CSS provides sophisticated control over background images. This means that you can use media queries to serve different background images depending on the size of the screen. But media queries have limited control over images embedded in the HTML markup with the `<img>` tag. Consequently, one of your main priorities in responsive web design should be to ensure that all images of a purely decorative nature are background images controlled by CSS.

## Controlling Background Images with Media Queries

As long as the background-image property is defined in a rule controlled by a media query, most browsers will download the image only if they match the conditions in the query. For simplicity, I'll use @media rules in the following example, but the styles could be in separate style sheets attached with media queries. This is how to send different background images to devices depending on their width:

```
#header {
    background-color: #D2E1E6; /* light blue */
    background-image: none;
    background-repeat: no-repeat;
}
@media only screen and (max-width: 480px) {
    #header {
        background-image: url(../images/header_phone.jpg);
    }
}
@media only screen and (min-width: 481px) and (max-width: 768px) {
    #header {
        background-image: url(../images/header_tablet.jpg);
    }
}
@media only screen and (min-width: 769px) {
    #header {
        background-image: url(../images/header_desktop.jpg);
    }
}
```

In this example, the background-image property is set to none in the basic style. But even though there's no image, background-repeat is set to no-repeat. This avoids the need to repeat the same property in each of the media queries. Only the value of background-image is overridden, serving up three different images.

---

■ **Tip** Consider carefully whether a decorative background image is really needed for the smallest mobile devices. Although it's important for a site to look attractive on a mobile phone, users won't thank you for using up their precious data allowance with a lot of unnecessary eye candy.

---

## Controlling Images Embedded in the HTML

Media queries give you far less control over images embedded in <img> tags. In Chapter 7, "Making the Images and Captions Adapt to the Screen Width" described how to resize an image dynamically for a responsive web design. The technique involves removing the width and height attributes from the HTML, and wrapping the image in a <div> or <figure> element. Then you can use CSS to set the outer element's width to a percentage, and give the image a maximum width of 100%.

The styles in the Mediterranean Destinations examples since Chapter 7 float the image container left or right. In a responsive design using media queries, you could center the image container and give it a maximum width in the basic styles, and float it only when the screen is wider like this:

```
.figure {
    max-width: 400px;
}
```

```
.figure img {
    max-width: 100%;
}
.figure.floatleft, .figure.floatright {
    margin: 3px auto;
    float: none;
}
@media only screen and (min-width: 600px) {
    .figure {
        width: 61.5%
    }
    .figure.floatleft {
        margin: 3px 10px 3px 40px;
        float: left;
    }
    .figure.floatright {
        margin-right: 3px 10px;
        float: right;
    }
}
```

Although you can use media queries to change the position and size of embedded images, one of the main drawbacks is that you can't prevent the browser from downloading the image.

---

■ **Caution**    Setting an image's `display` property to `none` doesn't stop the browser from downloading it.

---

## Providing Images for High-Resolution Displays

Continuous improvements in technology mean that devices are packing more physical pixels into the screen to produce a sharper display. Thanks to the concept of CSS pixels (see "Physical and CSS Pixels" in Chapter 3), elements should look roughly the same size onscreen regardless of the physical pixel density. The downside is that high-resolution displays need to scale up images, which often results in them looking blurred.

To ensure your images remain sharp, you need to make them larger than normal, and then scale them down. For example, an iPhone with retina (high-resolution) display is 320 CSS pixels wide, but the display is generated by 640 physical pixels. So, it's said to have a *device-pixel ratio* of 2. Some high-resolution Android devices have a device-pixel ratio of 1.5. So, if you want an image to be displayed at 400px wide, the image needs to be at least 600px, or preferably 800px wide. When scaled down on a high-resolution display, it should retain its original sharpness.

Does that mean every image should now be twice its normal size? It would work, but it would greatly increase download sizes, placing an unnecessary burden on devices with standard displays and mobile devices on a slow connection. Rather than apply a blanket rule, it's important to test background images on a high-resolution device. If the degradation is noticeable, you can use media queries to provide a larger image—at least for background images.

---

■ **Note**    At the time of this writing, there is no reliable way of serving different versions of images embedded in <img> tags depending on the browser's screen size or pixel density. The Web Hypertext Application Technology Working Group (WHATWG) proposes adding an optional srcset attribute to the <img> tag that will perform a similar function to media queries, allowing the browser to download the most appropriate version of an image. See www.whatwg.org/specs/web-apps/current-work/multipage/embedded-content-1.html#attr-img-srcset.

---

## Setting Resolution/Pixel Density for Background Images

As so often happens with new developments in web technology, the need to specify pixel density emerged before the specification had stabilized. So, WebKit-based browsers, which are prevalent on modern mobile devices, came up with a nonstandard media feature called -webkit-device-pixel-ratio for use in media queries. It also has min- and max- equivalents: -webkit-min-device-pixel-ratio and -webkit-max-device-pixel-ratio. It takes as its value a number that acts as a multiplier. To specify an Apple retina display, the multiplier is 2.

Other browsers followed suit with different browser-specific prefixes, but slightly different syntax. Not only was this confusing, the feature name is painfully long. What's more, the list of official media features in Table 17-1 already includes resolution, which is much easier to type and remember. The original idea was to specify resolution in terms of dots per inch (dpi) or dots per centimeter (dpcm). Because 1px is defined as 1/96 of an inch, it meant multiplying the pixel ratio by 96 to get the correct value for dpi. More confusion. . .

Thankfully, sanity prevailed, and a new measurement was introduced: dots per pixel (dppx). So, to specify styles for an Apple retina display, all that should be necessary is this:

```
only screen and (min-resolution: 2dppx) {
    /* Retina display styles */
}
```

However, it's likely to take some time before browsers recognize dppx as a valid unit of measurement. The most reliable cross-browser way of specifying a minimum pixel ratio of 2 is to use the nonstandard WebKit property, as well as resolution with dppx:

```
only screen and (min-resolution: 2dppx),
screen and (-webkit-min-device-pixel-ratio: 2) {
    /* High-resolution styles */
}
```

To include Android high-resolution displays, change the values like this:

```
only screen and (min-resolution: 1.5dppx),
screen and (-webkit-min-device-pixel-ratio: 1.5) {
    /* High-resolution styles */
}
```

When using a larger image for high-resolution displays, you also need to adjust the size of the background image using the background-size property (see "Setting the Size of Background Images" in Chapter 8). Set the actual size you want in CSS pixels with the width followed by the height. For example, if your high-resolution image is 800 × 600 pixels, and the standard one is 400 × 300, resize the high-resolution one by adding this to its style rule:

```
background-size: 400px 300px;
```

## Using a High-resolution CSS Sprite

If your background images are combined in a CSS sprite, all the dimensions in the high-resolution sprite need to be an exact multiple of those in the standard sprite. For example, the CSS sprite in Chapter 8, icons.png, is 35 × 179 pixels, and the icons are 40 pixels apart. The high-resolution version used in sprites_hires.html in the ch17 folder is twice the size: 70 × 358, with the icons 80 pixels apart. The dimensions of the individual icons are also double the original size.

To demonstrate the difference between standard and high-resolution background images, the file displays two identical sets of links. Both use the same styles, but those intended for high-resolution display also use a class called hires.

The hires class resets the background-size property of the sprite to the same size as the standard one. As a result, the 80-pixel gap in the high-resolution sprite is halved to 40 pixels when the browser displays it. So, the same background-position offsets apply to both sprites. Apart from the addition of the high-resolution media query, the styles in sprites_hires.html are identical to sprites.html in the ch08 folder. The styles look like this:

```
.icons {
    background-image: url('images/icons.png');
    background-repeat: no-repeat;
}
.rss {
    padding-left: 30px;
}
.phone {
    padding-left: 25px;
    background-position: left -40px;
}
a[href^='mailto:'] {
    padding-left: 30px;
    background-position: left -80px;
}
a[href$='.pdf'] {
    padding-right: 24px;
    background-position: right -120px;
}
a[href^="http://"] {
    padding-right: 25px;
    background-position: right -160px;
}
@media only screen and (min-resolution: 2dppx), screen and ↵
    (-webkit-min-device-pixel-ratio: 2) {
    .icons.hires {
        background-image: url(images/icons_large.png);
        background-size: 35px 179px;
    }
}
```

Figure 17-8 shows how the standard and high-resolution icons look on a retina display iPad. Because the icons are small, the difference isn't immediately visible, but it's markedly noticeable when they're scaled up.

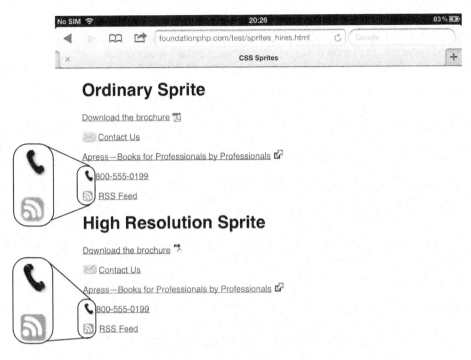

*Figure 17-8. The high-resolution icons are much crisper*

# Case Study: Responsive Layout

The two-column layout in the Mediterranean Destinations example page that's been used in several chapters begins to look too compressed at widths of less than 600px, so that makes a sensible break point for a media query (see "What Sizes Should I Design For?" earlier in this chapter). To conclude this chapter with a practical example of media queries, I'll show you how to adapt the existing styles to make it a responsive layout.

---

### EXERCISE: RESPONSIVE LAYOUT

---

The purpose of this exercise is to demonstrate the basic principles of serving different styles to devices depending on the available screen width. It adapts an existing desktop design that uses percentage widths and sets a maximum width of 1000px. For simplicity, only essential changes are made to the design. A production design would be more complex, and should be created from scratch optimizing the content for mobile devices first.

Use as your starting point horizontal.html and styles/horizontal.css in the ch17 folder. The finished files are horizontal_end.html, and basic_end.css and twocol_end.css in the styles folder. The web page also has a print style sheet attached, but no changes are made to it.

1.  Make two copies of horizontal.css, and save them in the styles folder as basic.css and twocol.css.

2.  In the <head> of the web page, add the viewport <meta> tag immediately after the <title> element, and set width to device-width:

    ```
    <meta name="viewport" content="width=device-width">
    ```

3.  Because IE 8 and earlier don't understand media queries, copy the `<link>` that attaches horizontal.css to the web page, and paste it immediately below the `<link>` to print.css. Then wrap the `<link>` you have just pasted in an Internet Explorer conditional comment so that it's seen only by older versions of IE:

```
<!--[if lte IE 8]>
<link href="styles/horizontal.css" rel="stylesheet" media="screen">
<![endif]-->
```

4.  Change the `href` attribute of the original `<link>` so that it points to basic.css. After making these changes, the HTML at the top of the page should look like this:

```
<title>Mediterranean Destinations</title>
<meta name="viewport" content="width=device-width">
<link href="styles/basic.css" rel="stylesheet" media="screen">
<link href="styles/print.css" rel="stylesheet" media="print">
<!--[if lte IE 8]>
<link href="styles/horizontal.css" rel="stylesheet" media="screen">
<![endif]-->
<!--[if IE 6]>
```

5.  If you test the page in a browser, it should look exactly the same as before because basic.css is the same as horizontal.css. The next stage is to edit basic.css to provide basic styles for screens less than 600px wide. The same styles will be used by browsers that don't understand media queries, so you shouldn't add a media query to the `media` attribute in the `<link>`.

6.  There isn't sufficient room to display the sidebar and main content alongside each other on a small screen, so delete the `width` property from the `#main` style rule in basic.css, and change the left margin from 35% to 1% to match the right margin. The sidebar needs to use the same values, so delete the `#aside` rule, and use a group selector for the main content and sidebar like this:

```
#main, #aside {
    margin: 15px 1% 10px 1%;
    background-color: #FFF;
    padding: 18px 0;
}
```

7.  If you test the page in a browser, the sidebar and main content both fill the full width of the page and are stacked on top of each other (see Figure 17-9).

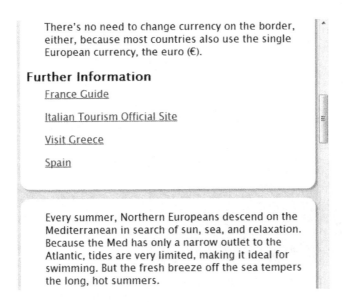

**Figure 17-9.** *The basic styles stack the content vertically*

8. Delete the existing styles for .figure.floatleft and .figure.floatright, and create a group selector to center the images and prevent them from floating:

```
.figure.floatleft, .figure.floatright {
    margin: 3px auto;
    float: none;
}
```

9. Depending on their orientation, the images are 400px or 260px wide. The wider images are styled with the figure class, so set its maximum width at 400px. This is still too wide for most phones. So, change width in the figure class to 90%. The narrower images are unlikely to need to be scaled down, so change width in the portrait class to a maximum of 260px. The amended styles look like this:

```
.figure {
    max-width: 400px;
    width: 90%;
}
.portrait {
    max-width: 260px;
}
```

10. If you test the page now, the images are centered between paragraphs, as shown in Figure 17-10.

*Figure 17-10.* *The images are no longer floated*

11.  Scroll up to the top of the page, and resize the browser window to simulate what the page might look like on a mobile phone. As Figure 17-11 shows, the navigation menu not only looks bad, but it's also likely to be unusably small on a touch screen. The background image for the header looks OK, but without the yachts, it has lost visual interest. Also, there's a big gap above the "Climate" heading.

*Figure 17-11.* *The top of the page looks a mess at a narrow width*

12. Center the header's background image by adding the `background-position` property to the #header style rule like this:

```
#header {
    background-image: url(../images/yachts_banner.jpg);
    background-repeat: no-repeat;
    background-position: center top;
    height: 127px;
}
```

13. The "Climate" heading is an `<h3>` element, and it's the first child of its parent. So, you can eliminate the gap by adding the following style rule to basic.css:

```
h3:first-child {
    margin-top: 0;
}
```

14. To make the navigation buttons more usable on a small touch screen, they need to be wider and taller. By changing their width from 15.5% to 48%, they stack up in three rows, and need a bottom margin to keep the rows apart. Amend the styles like this (the changes are highlighted in bold):

```
#nav {
    list-style-type: none;
    margin: 15px 0 0 0;
    padding: 0;
    height: 132px;
}
#nav li {
    width: 48%;
    margin-left: 2%;
    margin-bottom: 5px;
    float: left;
    text-align: center;
    display: inline;
}
#nav li a {
    display: block;
    padding: 0.75em 5px;
    text-decoration: none;
    font-weight: bold;
    color: #F2F2F2;
    border-radius: 8px;
    -webkit-box-shadow: 3px 3px 3px rgba(51,51,51,0.3);
    box-shadow: 3px 3px 3px rgba(51,51,51,0.3);
}
```

15. Test the page again with the browser window still at a narrow width. The header and menu now look like Figure 17-12.

***Figure 17-12.*** *The resized menu buttons will be easier to tap on a touch screen*

The page looks fine at a narrow width, but you now need to restore the original design by attaching twocol.css with a media query. Although you could leave the style sheet as it is, it's more efficient to use the cascade to override only those styles that are different. The easiest way to find out which rules to edit is to use a file comparison utility.

On Windows, I use Beyond Compare (www.scootersoftware.com). It's paid-for software, but is reasonably priced and you can try it free for 30 days. It's also available for Linux. You can get a free alternative for Windows from http://winmerge.org.

On a Mac, you can use TextWrangler (free from www.barebones.com/products/TextWrangler/). To compare files, select *Search* ➤ *Find Differences*.

Figure 17-13 shows a comparison of basic.css and twocol.css in Beyond Compare. Differences between the two files are automatically highlighted in pink, so it's easy to spot which rules need to be preserved and which can be safely discarded. It takes only a couple of minutes to go through the style sheet for the two-column layout, deleting styles that haven't been highlighted, and then saving the file. As you go through, make sure you preserve selector names and opening and closing braces.

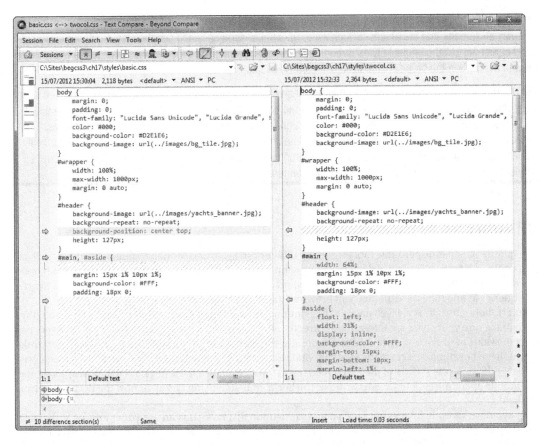

**Figure 17-13.** *Using a file comparison utility makes it easy to identify duplicate rules*

I won't go through the process in detail. You can see the final result in twocol_end.css. The only styles that needed further tweaking were `.figure.floatleft` and `.figure.floatright`. They have higher specificity than the `floatleft` and `floatright` classes, so you need to add the `float` property and appropriate margins to them like this:

```
.figure.floatleft {
    margin: 3px 10px 3px 40px;
    float: left;
}
.figure.floatright {
    margin: 3px 10px;
    float: right;
}
```

All that remains after editing twocol.css is to attach it to horizontal.html after basic.css with a media query:

```
<link href="styles/basic.css" rel="stylesheet" media="screen">
<link href="styles/twocol.css" rel="stylesheet" media="only screen and (min-width: ↵
    600px)">
<link href="styles/print.css" rel="stylesheet" media="print">
```

413

If you test the page now in a variety of devices and screen widths, you should see the original two-column display on screens that are at least 600px wide. On smaller screens, you'll see the single-column layout. IE 8 and earlier access the original styles through a conditional comment, so they always display the two-column layout even when the browser is resized to less than 600px.

Many improvements could be made to this responsive layout. For a start, the sidebar should be moved after the main content in the underlying HTML. This is the type of design decision that's much easier to make at the outset, and it highlights the importance of designing for mobile first. The navigation menu also takes up a lot of valuable space on small displays. It could be improved by expanding and contracting it dynamically using JavaScript. In spite of the design's shortcomings, it should give you an insight into serving different styles depending on screen width using media queries.

# Summary

Media queries are an indispensable tool for serving different styles to devices depending on features such as screen width, orientation, and pixel density. They're supported by all modern browsers and high-end mobile devices, but not in IE 8 or earlier. It's considered best practice to serve basic styles to all browsers, and to use media queries to fine tune the experience in browsers that support them.

Smartphones usually scale web pages to fit a nominal viewport that's much wider than the screen's physical size. To make sure your styles are interpreted correctly, add the viewport <meta> tag in the <head> of every page, and set the value of width to device-width. Eventually, the <meta> tag will be replaced by the @viewport rule in the style sheet, but support is currently experimental. A complicating factor is the fact that iOS devices always consider width to be the shorter of the two screen dimensions, even when the device is in landscape orientation. Other mobile operating systems regard width as the horizontal dimension based on how the device is currently being held.

To avoid background images blurring on high-resolution displays, you can use larger images and scale them to the standard size with the background-size property. Detect the pixel density by creating a media query for resolution using the standard dppx (dots per pixel) unit. For backward compatibility, it's also a good idea to use the nonstandard -webkit-device-pixel-ratio property.

The next chapter explores CSS3 multicolumn layout, which automatically flows text from one column to the next in a similar way to a newspaper.

■ ■ ■

# CHAPTER 18

# Using CSS3 Multi-Column Layout

This chapter is concerned with columns that automatically flow from one to the next like in newspapers or magazines. The CSS Multi-column Layout module (http://dev.w3.org/csswg/css3-multicol/) achieved Candidate Recommendation status in December 2009, so is considered fairly stable. However, browser implementation has been slower than many other parts of CSS3. Flowing content into multiple columns involves only a small number of properties, which are easy to use.

In this chapter, you'll learn how to:

- Set the number and width of columns

- Control the gap between columns

- Separate columns with rules (vertical lines)

- Span elements across multiple columns

- Deal with oversize elements

## Browser Support for Multi-Column Layout

At the time of this writing, the only browsers that have implemented the multi-column specification without the need for browser-specific properties are Opera 11.1+ and IE 10.

Firefox and WebKit-based browsers still need the prefixed properties, and haven't fully implemented the specification. Check http://caniuse.com/#feat=multicolumn for up-to-date information on whether the prefixed properties are still required. You should also test your pages carefully in your target browsers to make sure multi-column elements are rendered correctly because browser support is still evolving.

There is no support in IE 9 or earlier.

---

■ **Note** For brevity, the code examples in this chapter use only the standard properties. The source files include the -moz- and -webkit- browser specific prefixes for Firefox and WebKit-based browsers.

---

## How Columns Are Laid Out

The CSS Multi-column Layout module introduces a new type of container called a *column box*, which is different from the box model described in Chapter 6. All column boxes inside a multi-column element are the same width and height. There's a uniform gap between each column; and if there's a vertical rule between columns, all rules are the same height. In these respects, multi-column layout is akin to a table in that the height of all cells in a table row is determined by the tallest cell. The major difference, of course, is that the content flows continuously from one column box to the next, as shown in Figure 18-1 (the code is in multicols_1.html in the ch18 folder).

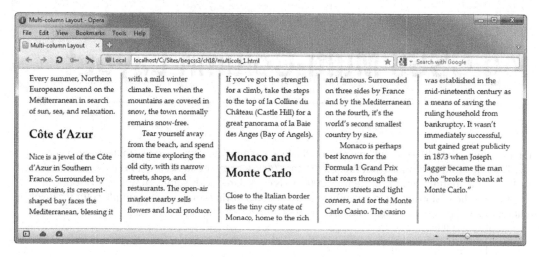

**Figure 18-1.** *The content flows from one column to the next*

Most multi-column elements contain a single row of columns. However, in multicols_2.html, the headings span across all columns, breaking the content into multiple rows, as shown in Figure 18-2. When this happens, the content before the spanning element—in this case, each heading—is flowed into a separate row of columns. The first section of text in Figure 18-2 is too short to fill five columns. So, Opera forms just two. Other browsers create four or five columns containing one line each. The next row of column boxes begins after the heading, and the row's height is adjusted to accommodate the content before the next spanning element.

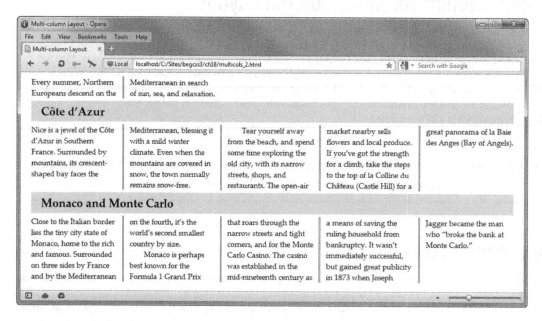

**Figure 18-2.** *The headings split the content into multiple rows of columns*

▪ **Note** Firefox 14 doesn't support spanning multiple columns.

A column box is a containing block similar to a table cell or inline block. However, it can't act as the containing block for an absolutely positioned or fixed positioned element. Another difference is in the way that column boxes handle overflow.

The column box clips elements that are too wide for the column. The image in multicol_3.html is 400px wide—more than twice the available space—so it's clipped by the rule between the second and third columns, as shown in Figure 18-3.

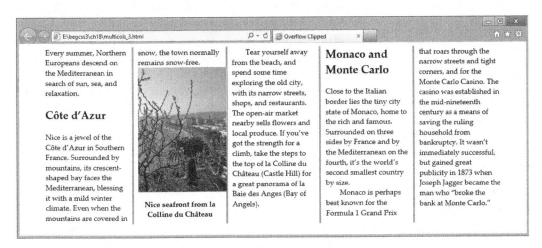

**Figure 18-3.** *Elements that are too wide for a column are clipped in the middle of the column gap*

▪ **Note** Firefox 14 fails to clip the image.

You can't make an element span a specific number of columns. A spanning element must span all columns like the headings in Figure 18-2. Otherwise, elements are restricted to a single column.

▪ **Tip** You'll learn later in this chapter how to resize an image to fit within a column.

# Setting the Width and Number of Columns

You create a multi-column element by setting either the width or the number of columns you want it to contain. You can also set both values. There's no need for accurate calculations because the browser automatically adjusts the size of columns to achieve what it considers to be the optimal layout. Table 18-1 describes the properties that control the width and number of columns.

***Table 18-1.*** *Properties for Setting the Width and Number of Columns*

| Property | Initial Value | Description |
|---|---|---|
| column-width | auto | Sets the optimal column width. The actual width might be wider to fill available space, or narrower if insufficient space is available. The value must be a length greater than zero. |
| column-count | auto | Specifies the optimal number of columns. If column-width is also set, column-count specifies the maximum number of columns. The value must be an integer greater than zero. |
| columns | auto auto | Shorthand for column-width and column-count. The values can be in either order. If only one value is given, the other defaults to auto. |

## Setting Only Width

To demonstrate what happens when you create a multi-column element by specifying the width of the columns, column-width.html contains a <div> with the ID columns. The <div> is 1000px wide, and it has a 2px black border all round. The column-width property is set to 200px like this:

```
#columns {
    width: 1000px;
    margin: 0 auto;
    border: 2px solid #000;
    column-width: 200px;
}
```

Because 1000 ÷ 200 = 5, you might expect there to be five columns, but as Figure 18-4 shows, there are only four.

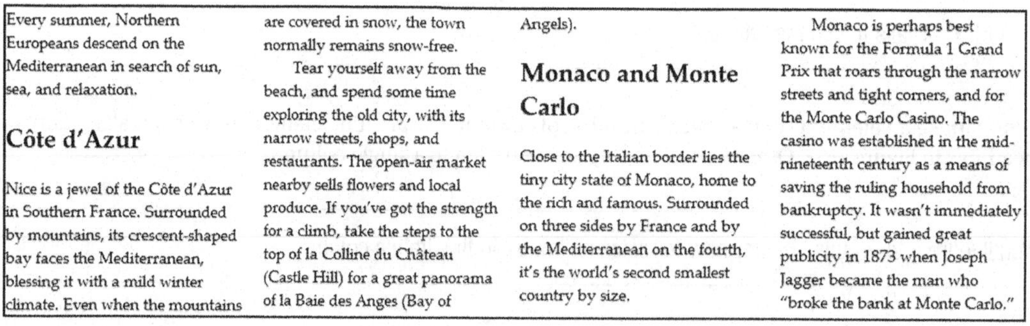

Every summer, Northern Europeans descend on the Mediterranean in search of sun, sea, and relaxation.

### Côte d'Azur

Nice is a jewel of the Côte d'Azur in Southern France. Surrounded by mountains, its crescent-shaped bay faces the Mediterranean, blessing it with a mild winter climate. Even when the mountains are covered in snow, the town normally remains snow-free.

Tear yourself away from the beach, and spend some time exploring the old city, with its narrow streets, shops, and restaurants. The open-air market nearby sells flowers and local produce. If you've got the strength for a climb, take the steps to the top of la Colline du Château (Castle Hill) for a great panorama of la Baie des Anges (Bay of Angels).

### Monaco and Monte Carlo

Close to the Italian border lies the tiny city state of Monaco, home to the rich and famous. Surrounded on three sides by France and by the Mediterranean on the fourth, it's the world's second smallest country by size.

Monaco is perhaps best known for the Formula 1 Grand Prix that roars through the narrow streets and tight corners, and for the Monte Carlo Casino. The casino was established in the mid-nineteenth century as a means of saving the ruling household from bankruptcy. It wasn't immediately successful, but gained great publicity in 1873 when Joseph Jagger became the man who "broke the bank at Monte Carlo."

***Figure 18-4.*** *The browser adjusts the number of columns to take account of the gap*

Because there's a default gap of approximately 1em between each column, there isn't sufficient space to create five columns each 200px wide. So, browsers automatically increase the width of the column boxes to fill the available space. In a couple of browsers that I tested, the actual width was 238px. Browsers reduce the width of the column box only when there isn't enough room for even one column of the specified width.

Another point to notice about Figure 18-4 is that the text in the first and last columns goes right to the border. To move the content away from the edge of the multi-column element, add some padding to the element.

■ **Tip**    When using multi-column layout, it's a good idea to remove the top and bottom margins from paragraphs and indent the first line with the text-indent property. Otherwise, you risk ending up with a blank line at the top or bottom of a column when it coincides with a new paragraph.

## Setting Only the Number of Columns

If you prefer to know exactly how many columns you'll get, you can specify the number with the column-count property. The styles in column-count.html specify five columns:

```
#columns {
    width: 980px;
    padding: 10px;
    margin: 0 auto;
    border: 2px solid #000;
    column-count: 5;
}
```

As expected, this produces the result shown in Figure 18-5.

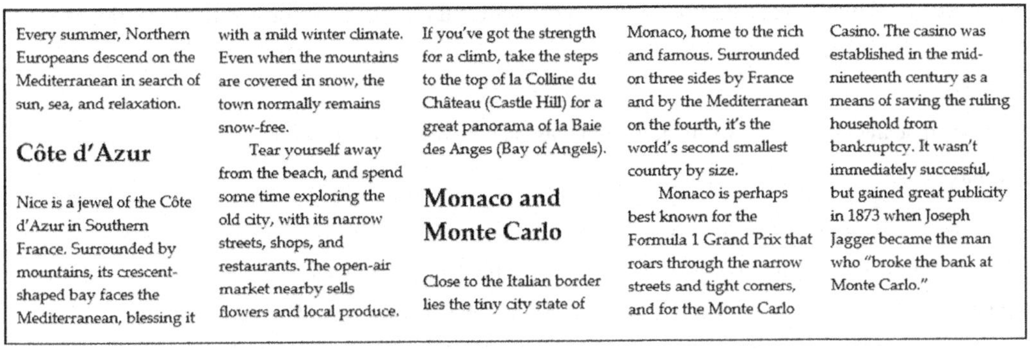

Every summer, Northern Europeans descend on the Mediterranean in search of sun, sea, and relaxation.

**Côte d'Azur**

Nice is a jewel of the Côte d'Azur in Southern France. Surrounded by mountains, its crescent-shaped bay faces the Mediterranean, blessing it

with a mild winter climate. Even when the mountains are covered in snow, the town normally remains snow-free.

Tear yourself away from the beach, and spend some time exploring the old city, with its narrow streets, shops, and restaurants. The open-air market nearby sells flowers and local produce.

If you've got the strength for a climb, take the steps to the top of la Colline du Château (Castle Hill) for a great panorama of la Baie des Anges (Bay of Angels).

**Monaco and Monte Carlo**

Close to the Italian border lies the tiny city state of

Monaco, home to the rich and famous. Surrounded on three sides by France and by the Mediterranean on the fourth, it's the world's second smallest country by size.

Monaco is perhaps best known for the Formula 1 Grand Prix that roars through the narrow streets and tight corners, and for the Monte Carlo

Casino. The casino was established in the mid-nineteenth century as a means of saving the ruling household from bankruptcy. It wasn't immediately successful, but gained great publicity in 1873 when Joseph Jagger became the man who "broke the bank at Monte Carlo."

***Figure 18-5.*** *Specifying the number of columns leaves the calculation about widths to the browser*

Using column-count is straightforward. If there's sufficient content, you get the number of columns you ask for. If there's only a small amount of content, the browser fills as many columns as it can, as shown earlier in Figure 18-2.

## Setting Both Width and Number

When you set both the width and number of columns, the values are treated as the ideal width and maximum number of columns. The styles in width_and_count.html put this to the test by setting the values for both properties deliberately low:

```
#columns {
    width: 980px;
    padding: 10px;
```

```
    margin: 0 auto;
    border: 2px solid #000;
    column-width: 100px;
    column-count: 5;
}
```

The available width inside the columns <div> is 980px, so there's plenty of room for more than five 100px columns. All other browsers that support multi-column layout—apart from Opera 12—interpret the specification correctly by limiting the number of columns to five, and produce exactly the same result as shown in Figure 18-5. Opera displays eight narrow columns.

## Using the Shorthand Property

Instead of the individual properties for the width or number of columns, you can use the shorthand columns property to set either value or both. Because the optimal column width is specified as a length and the desired number of columns is an integer, there's no ambiguity about the meaning of the values.

Instead of using column-width, you can use the shorthand version like this:

```
columns: 200px; /* Equivalent to column-width: 200px; */
```

Equally, you can use the shorthand property to set the number of columns like this:

```
columns: 5; /* Equivalent to column-count: 5; */
```

To set the maximum number of columns and optimal width at the same time, you can use the following shorthand:

```
columns: 100px 5;
```

The values can be in either order. So, the following has exactly the same meaning:

```
columns: 5 100px;
```

---

■ **Note** The code for the preceding examples is in columns_1.html, columns_2.html, and columns_3.html. The first one produces the same result as Figure 18-4, while the other two produce the result in Figure 18-5.

---

# Setting the Gap and Rule Between Columns

Browsers leave a gap of approximately 1em between column boxes, but you can change this value. You can also add a rule (vertical line) to separate them using the properties listed in Table 18-2.

**Table 18-2.** *Properties for Column Gaps and Rules*

| Property | Initial Value | Description |
|---|---|---|
| column-gap | normal | Accepts a length to set the gap between columns. The default normal is browser-specific, but is generally 1em. |
| column-rule-color | | Sets the color of the vertical line (rule) between columns. If not specified, the text color is used. |
| column-rule-style | none | Specifies the style of the rule between columns. Accepts the same keywords as border-style. |
| column-rule-width | medium | Sets the width of the rule between columns. Accepts a length or the keywords thin, medium, or thick. |
| column-rule | | Shorthand property for column-rule-color, column-rule-style, and column-rule-width. Omitted values are set to their default. |

## Changing the Width of the Gap

The column-gap property fixes the width of the gap between columns. The styles in column-gap.html set column-gap to 3em. Figure 18-6 compares column-gap.html (top) with column-count.html (bottom), which uses the default value. The larger gap doesn't increase the overall width of the multi-column element. Instead, the extra space is created by reducing the width of the columns.

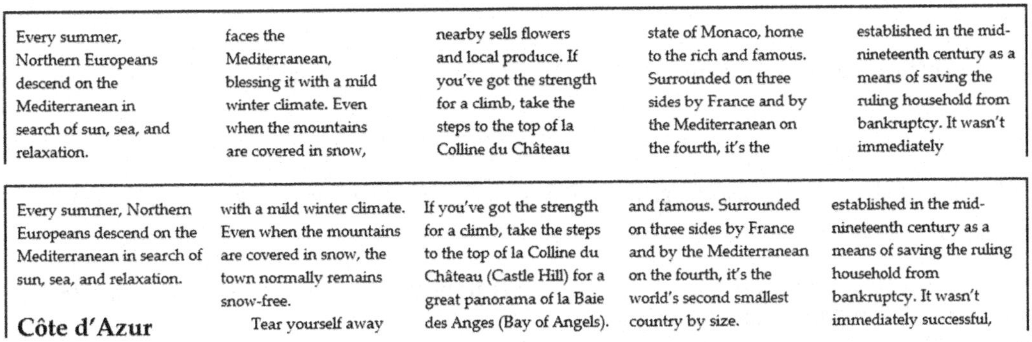

**Figure 18-6.** *Increasing the gap between columns doesn't affect the overall width of the element*

## Adding a Vertical Rule Between Columns

The properties for column rules accept the same values as their equivalents for borders (see Chapter 9). The column-rule-style property accepts any of the following keywords: none, hidden, dotted, dashed, solid, double, groove, ridge, inset, or outset.

The rule is drawn in the center of the gap, but it doesn't add to its width. The styles in column-rule.html create a light gray rule that's twice the width of the column gap:

```
#columns {
    width: 980px;
    padding: 10px;
    margin: 0 auto;
```

```
    border: 2px solid #000;
    column-count: 5;
    column-gap: 1.5em;
    column-rule-color: #CCC;
    column-rule-style: solid;
    column-rule-width: 3em;
}
```

As Figure 18-7 shows, the rule extends underneath the columns.

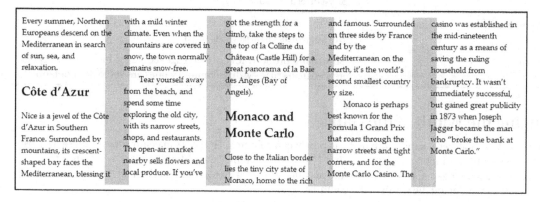

**Figure 18-7.** *The width of the rule doesn't increase the gap between columns*

The purpose of this exaggerated example is to show that the widths of the gap and rule are independent of each other.

---

■ **Note** WebKit-based browsers, such as Safari and Chrome, don't display the rule if it's wider than the gap.

---

The styles in column-rule.html use the individual column rule properties, but the three values could be combined using the column-rule shorthand property like this:

```
column-rule: #CCC solid 3em;
```

# Spanning, Filling, and Breaking Columns

The remaining multi-column layout properties are described in Table 18-3. They're concerned with spanning child elements across multiple columns, controlling how columns are filled, and dealing with column breaks.

*Table 18-3.* *Miscellaneous Multi-Column Properties*

| Property | Initial Value | Description |
| --- | --- | --- |
| column-span | none | Specifies whether an element spans multiple columns. The default is none. The only other value is all, which makes the element span all columns. |
| column-fill | balance | Specifies how the columns are filled. The default is to balance the content equally between columns, if possible. Setting the value to auto fills the columns in sequence, so the last column might be shorter. |
| break-before | auto | Specifies how to handle page breaks before the element. |
| break-after | auto | Specifies how to handle page breaks after the element. |
| break-inside | auto | Specifies what to do about page breaks inside the element. |

## Spanning Columns

As explained at the beginning of this chapter, child elements can span all rows of a multi-column element. Partial spans are not permitted. The column-span property accepts the following values:

**all** This makes the element span all columns of the multi-column element.

**none** This is the default. The element is restricted to a single column box.

■ **Note**   An early draft of the specification used 1 instead of none. This is no longer supported.

The style rule for the <h2> headings in multicols_2.html looks like this:

```
h2 {
    column-span: all;
    background-color: #D2E1E6;
    padding: 5px 20px;
    margin: 5px 0;
}
```

This breaks the multi-column element into sections, as shown in Figure 18-2. The content before and after a heading is flowed into separate rows of columns. (As noted earlier, Firefox 14 doesn't support column-span.)

Elements too big to fit inside the column box are clipped (see multicols_3.html in Figure 18-3). To avoid this problem, the styles in multicols_4.html set the maximum width of the image to 100% like this:

```
.figure img {
    max-width: 100%;
}
```

The 100% is relative to the width of the containing column box, so the image is automatically scaled down to fit, as Figure 18-8 shows.

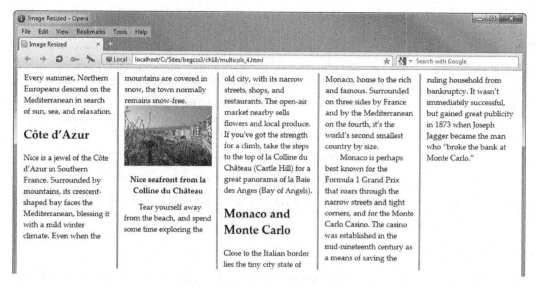

**Figure 18-8.** *The image is rescaled to fit within the column box*

## Controlling How Columns Are Filled

The `column-fill` property determines how to fill the columns. It accepts either of the following values:

**balance** This is the default. It instructs the browser to try to balance the columns, so that each one appears to have the same amount of content.

**auto** This instructs the browser to fill the columns sequentially. Some columns might end up partially filled or with no content at all.

At the time of this writing, `column-fill` does not appear to be supported by any browser.

## Dealing with Column Breaks

The `break-before`, `break-after`, and `break-inside` properties perform a similar role to the page break print properties described in Chapter 16. But they're not only concerned with printing; they also control column breaks onscreen.

When a multi-column element is printed out, each page break is treated as beginning a new row of columns so each page is complete in itself. Figure 18-9 illustrates this principle.

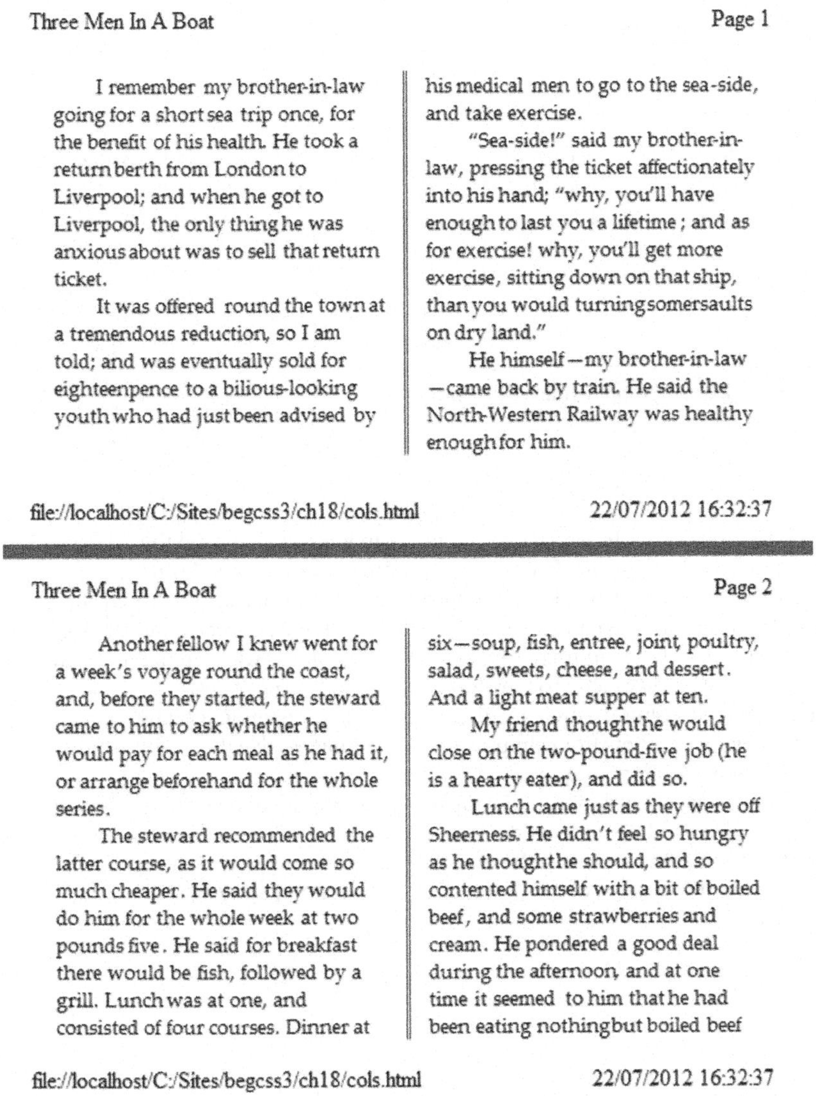

Three Men In A Boat                                              Page 1

I remember my brother-in-law going for a short sea trip once, for the benefit of his health. He took a return berth from London to Liverpool; and when he got to Liverpool, the only thing he was anxious about was to sell that return ticket.

It was offered round the town at a tremendous reduction, so I am told; and was eventually sold for eighteenpence to a bilious-looking youth who had just been advised by his medical men to go to the sea-side, and take exercise.

"Sea-side!" said my brother-in-law, pressing the ticket affectionately into his hand; "why, you'll have enough to last you a lifetime ; and as for exercise! why, you'll get more exercise, sitting down on that ship, than you would turning somersaults on dry land."

He himself—my brother-in-law—came back by train. He said the North-Western Railway was healthy enough for him.

file://localhost/C:/Sites/begcss3/ch18/cols.html          22/07/2012 16:32:37

Three Men In A Boat                                              Page 2

Another fellow I knew went for a week's voyage round the coast, and, before they started, the steward came to him to ask whether he would pay for each meal as he had it, or arrange beforehand for the whole series.

The steward recommended the latter course, as it would come so much cheaper. He said they would do him for the whole week at two pounds five. He said for breakfast there would be fish, followed by a grill. Lunch was at one, and consisted of four courses. Dinner at six—soup, fish, entree, joint, poultry, salad, sweets, cheese, and dessert. And a light meat supper at ten.

My friend thought he would close on the two-pound-five job (he is a hearty eater), and did so.

Lunch came just as they were off Sheerness. He didn't feel so hungry as he thought he should, and so contented himself with a bit of boiled beef, and some strawberries and cream. He pondered a good deal during the afternoon, and at one time it seemed to him that he had been eating nothing but boiled beef

file://localhost/C:/Sites/begcss3/ch18/cols.html          22/07/2012 16:32:37

*Figure 18-9.* *The content continues to the second column before each page break*

The break-before and break-after properties accept the following values:

**auto** Leave it up to the browser to decide whether to insert a page or column break.

**always** Always insert a page or column break.

**avoid** Whenever possible, avoid a page or column break.

**left** Force one or two page breaks so that the next page is formatted as a left page.

**right** Force one or two page breaks so that the next page is formatted as a right page.

**page** Always force a page break.

**column** Always force a column break.

**avoid-page** Avoid a page break.

**avoid-column** Avoid a column break.

The `break-inside` property accepts only the following values: `auto`, `avoid`, `avoid-page`, and `avoid-column`. The following style rule instructs the browser to avoid breaks inside or immediately after `<h2>` headings:

```
h2 {
    break-after: avoid-column;
    break-inside: avoid-column;
}
```

These properties indicate a desired, rather than a guaranteed outcome.

# Summary

The Multi-column Layout module provides a simple way to flow content into linked columns in the same way as a newspaper or magazine. You can specify either the desired width or number of columns, or both. The browser adjusts the values automatically to achieve what it considers to be the optimal layout. The gap between columns is adjustable with the `column-gap` property, and you can add an optional vertical rule between columns. Neither the gap nor the rule affects the overall width of the multi-column element. If the rule is wider than the gap, it runs under the content in most browsers. But WebKit-based browsers don't display oversized rules.

Child elements can be made to span all columns, breaking the content into independent sections, each styled as a new row of columns. To prevent browsers from clipping oversized images, give them a maximum width of 100% to constrain them within their column box.

The main drawback of multi-column layout is that text flowing from one column to the next often forces the user to scroll up and down the page, making it difficult to read. However, it's extremely useful when designing for a known screen size, such as an iPad application. It can also be useful for text-intensive print styles.

The next chapter delves into another new aspect of CSS3—creating color gradients without images.

# CHAPTER 19

# Creating Gradients Without Images

A *gradient* creates a smooth transition between two or more colors, and is often used in graphic design to create an illusion of depth or a 3D effect. Until quite recently, the only cross-browser way to add a gradient to an element was to use a background image. With CSS3, you can generate a gradient simply by specifying its colors and shape. CSS supports both *linear gradients*—in which the colors fade smoothly from one to the next in a straight line—and *radial gradients*, which emerge from a single point with the colors spreading out in a circle or ellipse. You can also create gradients that repeat the same sequence of colors indefinitely.

Browsers began implementing CSS gradients before the CSS3 Image Values and Replaced Content module (`http://dev.w3.org/csswg/css3-images/`) had stabilized. As a result, the syntax has undergone a bewildering number of changes. In mid-2012, it was announced that IE 10 and Firefox 16 would implement the final syntax without browser-specific prefixes. However, WebKit-based browsers, Opera, and earlier versions of Firefox use a slightly different syntax, which works only with browser-specific prefixes.

This chapter concentrates primarily on the final syntax. Separate sections explain the main differences in the nonstandard syntax.

In this chapter, you'll learn how to do the following:

- Create a linear gradient
- Specify the direction of the gradient
- Define the size, shape, and position of a radial gradient
- Create a repeating gradient

---

**Note** The examples in this chapter use browser-specific prefixes only when they require a different syntax.

---

## CSS Gradient Basics

Although CSS gradients don't use images, you apply them to an element using the background-image property or the shorthand background property. You define a gradient by setting the property value with one of the four functions listed in Table 19-1.

***Table 19-1.*** *CSS Gradient Functions*

| Function | Description |
|---|---|
| linear-gradient() | Sets the direction and colors of a gradient that fades from one color to the next in a straight line. The direction can be set using keywords or an angle. If the direction is omitted, the gradient is drawn from the top to the bottom. |
| radial-gradient() | Creates a circular or elliptical gradient, and optionally sets its shape, size, and position. If all optional features are omitted, an elliptical gradient is centered in the element's background. |
| repeating-linear-gradient() | Creates a linear gradient, in which the colors are repeated infinitely in both directions. |
| repeating-radial-gradient() | Creates a radial gradient that repeats infinitely. |

Browsers draw the gradient inside a *gradient box*. By default, this fills the element's padding box (see Figure 8-18 in Chapter 8). The gradient doesn't have any intrinsic dimensions, but you can control its size and position in the same way as a background image using the background-size and background-position properties, which were covered in Chapter 8.

## Using Browser-Specific Prefixes

Normally, browser-specific prefixes are added to the property name. However, gradients use the standard background-image and background properties, so the prefix is added to the function name instead. At the time of this writing, only IE 10 and Firefox 16 support the standard functions listed in Table 19-1. To support other browsers, add the appropriate browser-specific prefix to the function name. For example, the browser-specific versions of linear-gradient() look like this:

-moz-linear-gradient() Firefox 15 and earlier

-o-linear-gradient() Opera

-webkit-linear-gradient() Safari, Chrome, and other WebKit-based browsers

■ **Tip** There are several online CSS gradient generators that create all the necessary style rules for you. The one at www.colorzilla.com/gradient-editor handles both linear and radial gradients, and is simple to use. Adobe Fireworks CS6 also generates the necessary style rules from a graphic gradient. Even if you decide to use a tool to create CSS gradients, it's useful to know what the code means so you can tweak it manually if necessary.

## Specifying Gradient Colors

You define a gradient by specifying *color stops* along an imaginary *gradient line*. Figure 19-1 shows a linear gradient that fades from a dark color to a lighter one as it moves from left to right across the gradient box. The direction of the gradient line depends on the value passed to the linear-gradient() function.

*Figure 19-1.* *In a linear gradient, the colors change along a straight line*

■ **Note** The original files for Figures 19-1 through 19-5 are in colorstops_1.html through colorstops_5.html in the ch19 folder.

With a radial gradient, the starting point of the gradient line (or *gradient ray*) is anchored at the center of the circle or ellipse, and the line always extends to the right (see Figure 19-2).

*Figure 19-2.* *The color stops of a radial gradient are drawn on a ray extending from the center to the right*

## Setting the Position of Color Stops

The position of a color stop along the gradient line or ray can be specified using a length or percentage. Lengths are measured from the starting point. Percentages are relative to the distance between the starting and ending points. In Figure 19-1, the dark color stop is at the starting point (0%) on the left edge of the gradient box, and the light color stop is at the ending point (100%) on the right edge. In Figure 19-2, the starting point is the light color in the center of the ellipse, and the ending point is the right edge of the gradient box. In both cases, the smooth transition from one color to the other is generated automatically by the browser.

■ **Note** With a linear gradient, the starting and ending points of the gradient line often lie outside the gradient box. You'll learn later in this chapter how to determine their location.

If you don't specify the position of a color stop, the browser applies the following rules:

- If it's the first color stop, it's placed at the starting point (0%) of the gradient line.

- If it's the last color stop, it's placed at the ending point (100%) of the gradient line.

- Intermediate color stops are spaced evenly between the preceding and following color stops that have positions.

In theory, there's no limit to the number of color stops, but they must be listed in ascending order. If a color stop has a position lower than any preceding one, it's reset to the highest preceding value. For example, in the following list, the third color stop is out of order:

```
#C24704, #D9CC3C 35%, #00ADA7 25%, #FFEB79
```

This produces a smooth transition between the first and second color stops along the first 35% of the gradient line. The third color stop's position is reset to 35%, resulting in a sudden change of color at that point, as shown in Figure 19-3.

***Figure 19-3.*** *The smooth transition of colors is interrupted by the incorrect sequence of color stops*

---

■ **Tip**   If you want a sudden change of color, set the position of two adjacent color stops to the same value. For example, the correct way to create the sudden transition in Figure 19-3 is to set the middle two values to 35% like this: #C24704, #D9CC3C 35%, #00ADA7 35%, #FFEB79.

---

The color stops are usually placed between the starting and ending points, but the gradient line extends infinitely in both directions. So, the first color stop can be before the starting point, and the last one after the ending point. Figure 19-4 demonstrates the effect. Both gradients use the same colors for the first and last color stops. The top gradient positions the colors stops at the starting and ending points, whereas the bottom gradient positions the first color stop at minus 40%. As a result, the bottom gradient is stretched, and it begins with an intermediate shade.

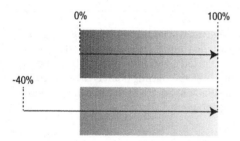

***Figure 19-4.*** *Positioning the first color stop before the starting point changes the gradient*

If the first color stop is beyond the starting point, the color is drawn as a solid block up to the starting point. Similarly, if the last color stop is before the ending point, the final section is a solid color. For example, the first color stop in Figure 19-5 is positioned at 35%, producing a solid color in the left third of the gradient box.

***Figure 19-5.*** *Positioning the first color stop at 35% produces a solid color before the gradient*

---

■ **Tip**   You can use `transparent` as a color stop if you want the background to show through part of the gradient.

---

# Creating Linear Gradients

A linear gradient creates a smooth transition between two or more colors in a straight line. By default, the gradient goes from the top of the element to the bottom, as shown in Figure 19-6.

*Figure 19-6.* *A simple linear gradient between two colors*

However, you can control the direction of the gradient using keywords to point to one of the sides or corners, which then becomes the ending point. Alternatively, you can specify the angle at which the gradient should be drawn.

To create a linear gradient, you use the linear-gradient() function, which takes the following comma-separated arguments:

- The angle or direction of the gradient (optional)

- A comma-separated list of two or more color stops

The gradient in Figure 19-6 is created using the following style (the code is in linear_1.html):

```
div {
    width: 300px;
    height: 100px;
    margin: 20px;
    background-image: linear-gradient(#C24704, #FFEB79);
}
```

Just two color values are passed to the linear-gradient() function. The first one is a dark orange, and the second one is a shade of yellow. Because no angle or direction is specified, the starting point of the gradient line is the top edge, and the ending point is the bottom edge. Also, no positions are specified for the color stops, so the first one is positioned at 0% and the second one at 100%.

Because a gradient has no intrinsic dimensions, the transition from one color to the next is more gradual (see Figure 19-7) when the height of the <div> is doubled in linear_2.html like this:

```
div {
    width: 300px;
    height: 200px;
    margin: 20px;
    background-image: linear-gradient(#C24704, #FFEB79);
}
```

*Figure 19-7.* *The change in height results in a more gradual color transition*

## Using Keywords to Set the Direction of the Gradient Line

The linear-gradient() function supports the following keywords to set the ending point of the gradient line: top, bottom, right, and left. On their own, they represent the side of the gradient box; but they can also be combined to indicate a corner, such as top left or bottom right. To set the direction, you precede the keyword(s) with to. For example, linear_3.html draws the gradient from the bottom-right to the top-left of the gradient box like this (see Figure 19-8):

background-image: linear-gradient(**to top left,** #C24704, #FFEB79);

*Figure 19-8.* *The gradient is drawn from the diagonally opposite corner*

---

■ **Caution**    At the time of this writing, WebKit-based browsers use the keywords on their own (without to) to specify the *origin* of the gradient line rather than its destination. For example, to draw the gradient line from left to right, -webkit-linear-function() uses left instead of to right.

---

When the gradient line is drawn to a corner, a color stop at 50% automatically intersects the other corners. For example, the gradient in linear_4.html is defined like this:

background-image: linear-gradient(to top left, #C24704, #FFEB79, #00ADA7);

The positions of the color stops aren't specified, so they default to 0%, 50%, and 100%, respectively. As a result, the gradient line is drawn from the bottom-right to the top-left corner, and the second color stop intersects the bottom-left and top-right corners, as shown in Figure 19-9.

*Figure 19-9.* *The color stop at 50% intersects the other corners*

At the time of this writing, Chrome 21 and Safari 6 fail to draw gradients correctly when you use two keywords to point to a corner, producing instead the result shown in Figure 19-10.

*Figure 19-10.* *Safari 6 gets the gradient direction wrong when using two keywords to point to a corner*

# Setting the Angle of the Gradient Line

You can use an angle instead of keywords to set the direction of the gradient line. Specifying the angle in degrees with the deg unit of measurement is simple, but there are two complicating factors:

- In all browsers, most angles produce starting and ending points outside the gradient box.
- Browsers that require a browser-specific prefix with linear-gradient() use a different coordinate system from the final specification.

## Standard Syntax

In the standard syntax, 0deg points directly upward. Larger angles move in a clockwise direction, as shown in Figure 19-11.

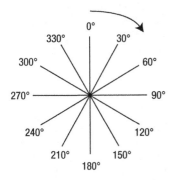

*Figure 19-11. CSS angles follow the same coordinates as a compass*

The angle is calculated from the center of the gradient box, and the gradient line stretches in both directions. You can use negative values for a counterclockwise angle: -45deg has the same meaning as 315deg.

---

■ **Note** Browsers automatically convert out-of-range angles to the correct value between 0° and 360°.

---

The gradient in linear_5.html is set at 135° like this:

```
background-image: linear-gradient(135deg, #C24704, #FFEB79);
```

Setting the angle of the gradient like this locates the starting and ending points outside the gradient box. Figure 19-12 shows how they are calculated.

Starting from the center, the gradient line extends at the specified angle. The ending point is where a line at right-angles to the gradient line would intersect with the nearest corner of the gradient box. The starting point is calculated in the same way, but in the opposite direction.

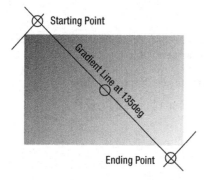

**Figure 19-12.** *Calculating the starting and ending points of a linear gradient*

Although this sounds like a convoluted setup, it's deliberately designed to ensure that the corners of the gradient box use the color stops at the starting and ending points. As Figure 19-12 shows, the top-left corner of the gradient box in linear_5.html uses the first color stop (#C24704), and the bottom-right uses the last color stop (#FFEB79). So, although the gradient is angled at 135°, the full range of colors runs from one corner to the other diagonally opposite.

## Using Angles with Browser-Specific Prefixes

Browsers started experimenting with gradients before the W3C drafted any specifications. Firefox was the first to use an angle to specify the direction of the gradient line. However, it decided to use the polar coordinate system (http://en.wikipedia.org/wiki/Polar_coordinate_system). In this system, 0deg points to the right and angles increase counterclockwise, as shown in Figure 19-13. Opera and WebKit-based browsers later adopted the same coordinate system.

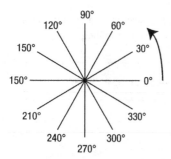

**Figure 19-13.** *The polar coordinate system starts on the right and moves counterclockwise*

Microsoft added support for CSS gradients much later, so IE 10 follows the official specification and uses compass coordinates. Firefox 16 also uses compass coordinates in the standard linear-gradient() function. Other browsers will, no doubt, adopt the correct syntax later.

This is where browser-specific prefixes really demonstrate their value. In many cases, you merely repeat the same values as the standard property. However, to specify the angle of a gradient, you need to use polar coordinates with the browser-specific functions, and compass coordinates with the standard function. The "Converting Angles" sidebar explains how to calculate the correct value.

## CONVERTING ANGLES

In both coordinate systems, 360° represents a full circle, but angles are measured in opposite directions. Also, 0° in the polar coordinate system is at the same position as 90° in compass bearings.

To calculate the polar-coordinate angle for the browser-specific functions, use the following steps:

1. If the compass-bearing angle is 90° or less, subtract 90.

2. If the compass-bearing angle is greater than 90°, subtract 450.

3. Remove the minus symbol from the result to get the polar-coordinate angle.

For example, if the compass-bearing angle is 30°, subtracting 90 leaves –60°. Removing the minus symbol produces 60°. If the compass-bearing angle is 135°, subtracting 450 leaves –315°. Removing the minus symbol produces 315°.

The gradient definitions in linear_5.html look like this:

```
background-image: -moz-linear-gradient(315deg, #C24704, #FFEB79);
background-image: -o-linear-gradient(315deg, #C24704, #FFEB79);
background-image: -webkit-linear-gradient(315deg, #C24704, #FFEB79);
background-image: linear-gradient(135deg, #C24704, #FFEB79);
```

Although the angles look completely different, each browser produces an identical gradient.

# Creating Radial Gradients

A radial gradient emerges from a single point with the colors spreading outward in a circular or elliptical shape (see Figure 19-14).

*Figure 19-14. Radial gradients can be circular or elliptical*

You define the gradient with the radial-gradient() function, which optionally sets the size and position of the circle or ellipse. The browser-specific functions use a similar syntax to the standard one, but there are some significant differences.

## Standard Syntax

The radial-gradient() function takes the following arguments:

*Shape:* The accepted values are circle and ellipse.

*Size:* This determines the extent of the radial gradient, either using specific dimensions or keywords.

*Position:* This determines the center of the circle or ellipse. The value is expressed in the same way as `background-position` (see Chapter 8), preceded by the keyword at. If omitted, it defaults to `at center`.

*Color stops:* A comma-separated list of colors with optional positions along the gradient ray starting at the center.

The only required argument is the list of color stops. All other arguments are optional.

## Setting the Shape of the Gradient

You can set the shape of the gradient explicitly by using the keyword `circle` or `ellipse`.

If you omit the shape, it defaults to `circle` if the size is a single length. In all other cases, it defaults to `ellipse`.

## Setting the Size of the Gradient

You can set the size of the circle or ellipse explicitly or by using keywords.

A circular gradient accepts only a single length, which sets its radius.

An elliptical gradient accepts two values, which can be either lengths or percentages. The first value sets the ellipse's horizontal radius. The second one sets its vertical radius. Percentage values are relative to the width and height of the gradient box, respectively.

---

■ **Caution**    You cannot use a percentage to set the size of a circular gradient because it's ambiguous whether the percentage should be relative to the width or height of the gradient box.

---

Both shapes accept any of the following keywords to determine their size:

closest-side

farthest-side

closest-corner

farthest-corner

To demonstrate the effect of these keywords, Figures 19-15 through 19-18 apply them to a circular gradient and an elliptical one. The center of each gradient is 100px from the left and 50px from the top. They all use the same color stops:

#C24704, #FFEB79 35%, #00ADA7

---

■ **Note**    The code for each example is in a file named after the keyword, for example, closest-side.html.

---

Figure 19-15 shows the effect of closest-side. The outer edge of the circular gradient exactly meets the side of the gradient box closest to the circle's center—in other words, the top. The outer edge of the elliptical gradient meets the closest side in the horizontal and vertical axes—in this case, the left and top.

***Figure 19-15.*** *The outer edges of the gradients are determined by the closest sides of the gradient box*

Figure 19-16 shows the effect of farthest-side. This is similar to closest-side, except the size is based on the farthest side(s). The result is markedly different, particularly in the case of the circular gradient. The farthest side from the center of the circular gradient is the right edge of the gradient box. The ellipse is controlled by the right and bottom sides.

***Figure 19-16.*** *The outer edges of the gradients stretch to the farthest side(s)*

Figure 19-17 shows the effect of closest-corner. The outer edge of the gradient passes through the corner of the gradient box closest to the shape's center. The aspect ratio of the elliptical gradient is the same as for closest-side.

***Figure 19-17.*** *The outer edge of each gradient passes through the closest corner of the gradient box*

Figure 19-18 shows the effect of farthest-corner. This is the same as closest-corner, except the size is based on the farthest corner and the aspect ratio of the elliptical gradient is based on farthest-side.

***Figure 19-18.*** *The outer edge of each gradient passes through the farthest corner of the gradient box*

If no size is set, it defaults to `farthest-corner`.

## Setting the Position of the Gradient

You can position the gradient using the at keyword followed by any expression that's valid for the background-position property. For example, the circular gradient in Figure 19-18 is positioned 100px from the left and 50px from the top like this (the code is in farthest-corner.html):

```
background-image: radial-gradient(circle farthest-corner at 100px 50px, #C24704, #FFEB79 ↵
35%, #00ADA7);
```

---

■ **Caution**   The shape, size, and position values are passed to the `radial-gradient()` function as a space-separated list. The shape and size values can be in either order, but the position must come after them (unless both shape and size are omitted). The list of color stops always comes last.

---

If the position is omitted, the gradient is centered in the gradient box.

## Syntax for Browser-Specific radial-gradient() Functions

To create a radial gradient in browsers that don't yet support the standard syntax, you need to use a browser-specific version of the `radial-gradient()` function. They all take the same arguments separated by commas:

> *Position:* This specifies where to locate the center of the circle or ellipse, using any value that's valid for background-position. If omitted, it defaults to center.

> *Shape and size:* The shape and size of the gradient are presented as a single argument using the same keywords as the standard syntax. Two additional keywords, contain and cover, act as synonyms for closest-side and farthest-corner, respectively. Both shape and size are optional. If omitted, they default to ellipse and farthest-corner.

> *Color stops:* A comma-separated list of colors with optional positions along the gradient ray starting at the center.

These arguments are very similar to the standard syntax, but with the following important differences:

- The position, if specified, must be the first argument, and is followed by a comma.

- The value for position is not preceded by the keyword at.

- To set the size of the gradient explicitly in WebKit and Opera, omit the shape, and specify two values for the horizontal and vertical radii. For a circle, both values must be the same.

- The browser-specific function for Firefox 15 and earlier doesn't support setting the size explicitly.

The styles for the circular gradient in closest-side.html (see Figure 19-15) use both the browser-specific functions and the standard syntax like this:

```
background-image: -moz-radial-gradient(100px 50px, circle closest-side, #C24704, #FFEB79 ↵
35%, #00ADA7);
```

```
background-image: -o-radial-gradient(100px 50px, circle closest-side, #C24704, #FFEB79 ↵
35%, #00ADA7);
background-image: -webkit-radial-gradient(100px 50px, circle closest-side, #C24704, ↵
#FFEB79 35%, #00ADA7);
background-image: radial-gradient(circle closest-side at 100px 50px, #C24704, #FFEB79 ↵
35%, #00ADA7);
```

The main difference can be summarized as follows: the standard syntax puts the shape, size, and position in a space-separated list with the position last like this:

```
circle closest-side at 100px 50px
```

In the browser-specific versions, the position comes first, and is separated from the shape and size by a comma like this:

```
100px 50px, circle closest-side
```

# Creating Repeating Gradients

The functions for repeating gradients, `repeating-linear-gradient()` and `repeating-radial-gradient()`, take the same arguments as their nonrepeating equivalents. However, it's important to position the last color stop before the ending point. If you don't, it defaults to 100%, preventing the pattern from being repeated.

## Creating Diagonal Stripes

A simple, yet effective use of a repeating linear gradient is to create diagonal stripes.

The styles in repeating-linear_1.html add the following gradient:

```
background-image: repeating-linear-gradient(-45deg, #426A77, #FFF 6px);
```

This sets the angle of the gradient line to –45°, and creates two color stops. The first one is dark blue. No position is declared, so it defaults to 0%. The second color stop is white, and it's positioned at 6px along the gradient line. So, the gradient transitions from dark blue to white in a very short space. The function then repeats the same pattern infinitely, producing the result shown in Figure 19-19.

***Figure 19-19.*** *The diagonal stripes are created by repeating a linear gradient*

To create the same effect in browsers that don't yet support the standard property, you need to change the angle to the polar-coordinate equivalent like this:

```
background-image: -moz-repeating-linear-gradient(135deg, #426A77, #FFF 6px);
background-image: -o-repeating-linear-gradient(135deg, #426A77, #FFF 6px);
background-image: -webkit-repeating-linear-gradient(135deg, #426A77, #FFF 6px);
```

## Creating a Smooth Repeating Gradient

The repeating gradient in the preceding example creates the illusion of stripes because there are only two color stops and the distance between them is very short. To create a more fluid repeating gradient, the first and last color stops need to be the same color.

The gradient in repeating-linear_2.html uses two shades of yellow like this:

```
background-image: repeating-linear-gradient(to right, #D9CC3C, #FFEB79 5%, #D9CC3C 10%);
```

The darker yellow is used as the first color stop. It has no declared position, so it defaults to the starting point of the gradient line. The lighter yellow is the second color stop at 5%, and the first color is repeated at 10%. This produces the ridge effect shown in Figure 19-20.

*Figure 19-20.* *Using the same color for the first and last color stops produces a constant transition*

The values for the browser-specific versions are identical, except for WebKit, which treats keywords as the origin of the gradient line. Instead of to right, WebKit needs the first argument to be left.

## Creating Repeating Radial Gradients

The repeating-radial-gradient() function and its browser-specific equivalents work exactly the same way. The gradient in repeating-radial.html looks like this:

```
background-image: repeating-radial-gradient(circle at 50% 100%, #FFEB79, #D9CC3C 5%);
```

This creates a circular gradient anchored at the center bottom with two color stops. The first color stop (light yellow) is anchored at the starting point—in other words, the center of the circle—and the second one (darker yellow) is positioned at 5% along the gradient ray. The size isn't specified, so it defaults to farthest-corner, producing the gradient in Figure 19-21.

*Figure 19-21.* *A repeating radial gradient that looks like the rings of a tree*

The browser-specific versions require the position as the first argument like this:

```
background-image: -moz-repeating-radial-gradient(50% 100%, circle, #FFEB79, #D9CC3C 5%);
background-image: -o-repeating-radial-gradient(50% 100%, circle, #FFEB79, #D9CC3C 5%);
background-image: -webkit-repeating-radial-gradient(50% 100%, circle, #FFEB79, #D9CC3C 5%);
```

# Using Multiple Gradients

Because CSS gradients are applied using the background-image property, you can add multiple gradients as the background to an element by listing the gradient definitions separated by commas. The gradients are applied in reverse order, with the first one appearing in front. Because gradients normally fill the entire background, you need to set the final color stop to transparent on gradients that appear in front. Alternatively, you can control the size and position of individual gradients with the background-size and background-position properties.

Radial gradients using the standard syntax are particularly suited for use as multiple gradients because the radial-gradient() function allows you to set the size of the gradient precisely using lengths (for both circles and ellipses) or percentages (for ellipses). To demonstrate the sort of effect you can achieve, multiple_gradients.html contains the following style:

```
#ball {
    width: 100px;
    height: 100px;
    margin: 20px;
    background-color: #C51D31;
    border-radius: 50%;
    background-image: radial-gradient(circle 12px at 25px 30px, rgba(255,255,255,0.8), ↵
    transparent),
                      radial-gradient(circle at 30% 30%, #C51D31, #921524, #450A11);
}
```

The ball <div> is a 100px square with its border-radius set to 50%, which converts it to a circle.

The first radial gradient is a 12px circle positioned 25px from the left and 30px from the top. Its first color stop is white with 80% alpha transparency, and its final color stop is transparent.

The second gradient appears behind the first one. It's also a circle, positioned at 30% both horizontally and vertically, offsetting it to the upper left. No size has been declared, so it fills the background to farthest-corner. The three color stops are increasingly deeper shades of red. Figure 19-22 shows the result.

***Figure 19-22.*** *Superimposing two radial gradients on top of each other creates a 3D highlight effect*

Creating the same effect with browser-specific prefixes isn't possible with Firefox 15 and earlier because -moz-radial-gradient() doesn't support setting the size of the gradient explicitly. For WebKit and Opera, you omit the circle or ellipse keyword, and specify two dimensions instead. This is how the two gradients are defined for Opera:

```
background-image: -o-radial-gradient(25px 30px, 12px 12px, rgba(255,255,255,0.8), ↵
transparent),
                  -o-radial-gradient(30% 30%, circle, #C51D31, #921524, #450A11);
```

WebKit doesn't render the transition to transparent well, so the styles in multiple_gradients.html set the second color stop of the first gradient to white with 20% alpha transparency like this:

```
background-image: -webkit-radial-gradient(25px 30px, 12px 12px, rgba(255,255,255,0.8), ↲
rgba(255,255,255,0.2)),
                 -webkit-radial-gradient(30% 30%, circle, #C51D31, #921524, #450A11);
```

---

■ **Tip**    For inspiration of what you can do with CSS gradients, visit the CSS3 Patterns Gallery hosted by the extremely talented Lea Verou (http://lea.verou.me/css3patterns/).

---

## Supporting Older Browsers

The standard syntax has been supported by Internet Explorer since IE 10 and by Firefox since version 16. By the time you read this, it may also be supported by the most recent versions of other browsers.

The following browsers support the browser-specific syntax described in this chapter:

- Firefox 10–15

- Chrome 10+

- Opera 11.6+

- Safari 5.1+

- iOS Safari 5.0+

- Android 4.0+

- Opera Mobile 12+

The simplest way to deal with older browsers is to provide a solid background color. Alternatively, you can create a linear gradient in a graphics program, and tile a thin slice horizontally or vertically as a background image (see Figure 8-4 in Chapter 8). Organize your style rules in the following order:

1.    Background color

2.    Gradient image

3.    Browser-specific gradient functions

4.    Standard CSS gradient syntax

The last three items all use the background-image or background property. By placing them in this order, browsers that support the browser-specific or standard syntax override the previous values. Only browsers that don't understand either use the background image. The background color is there as a fallback in case there's a problem with the gradient definition or background image.

## Summary

Using CSS rather than images to add gradient backgrounds to elements reduces the number of server requests, improving download times and making your sites more efficient. Although no images are used, you apply a gradient to an element using the background-image or background property, and using one of the following functions: `linear-gradient()`, `radial-gradient()`, `repeating-linear-gradient()`, or `repeating-radial-gradient()`. Unfortunately, the syntax has undergone numerous changes, resulting in the need to pass different arguments to the browser-specific functions.

You define a gradient by specifying a series of color stops along an imaginary gradient line. You can either specify the position of each color stop or leave it up to the browser to space them out evenly. The browser automatically transitions the colors smoothly from one color stop to the next.

Linear gradients progress in a straight line. By default, the gradient line runs from the top to the bottom of the element, but you can change the direction using keywords or by specifying an angle. The standard syntax uses angles that follow compass bearings, but the browser-specific functions use the polar coordinate system, which sets 0° on the right and increases counterclockwise.

Radial gradients emerge from a single point, with the colors spreading out in a circular or elliptical shape. You can set the size, shape, and position of a radial gradient. Both types of gradients can also be repeated infinitely to produce a wide range of patterns.

In the next chapter, we'll look at CSS transforms and transitions, which can be used for simple animation effects.

■ ■ ■

# CHAPTER 20

# 2D Transforms and Transitions

One of the main drawbacks of website design has always been the strict rectangular layout imposed by the box model. The CSS Transforms module (http://dev.w3.org/csswg/css3-transforms/) seeks to give designers greater freedom by making it possible to shift, rotate, scale, and skew elements. Originally, there were three separate modules: for two- and three-dimensional transforms, and for scalable vector graphics (SVG). These have been merged into a single module, which is currently only a working draft. However, browsers have made significant progress with two-dimensional transforms. They're supported by all mainstream browsers except IE 8 and earlier.

A simple example of a 2D transform is scaling down and rotating an image in its normal state, and restoring its normal size and orientation on hover. When this happens with just a transform, the change is instantaneous. The CSS Transitions module (http://dev.w3.org/csswg/css3-transitions/) offers a simple way to smooth the change from one state to another over a specified duration. CSS transitions can be applied to a wide range of properties, and are supported by all mainstream browsers except IE 9 and earlier.

In this chapter, you'll learn about the following:

- Using 2D transform functions to move, rotate, scale, and skew elements
- Preventing touch-screen devices from activating the :hover pseudo-class
- Understanding which properties are animatable
- Controlling the duration and speed of a transition
- Setting up a sequence of transitions
- Creating a rollover image without JavaScript

## Browser Support for 2D Transforms and Transitions

Most mainstream browsers have supported 2D transforms and transitions for several years with browser-specific prefixes. The exception is Internet Explorer. IE 8 and earlier support neither. IE 9 introduced support for 2D transforms with the -ms- prefix. IE 10 added support for transitions.

The W3C announced in June 2012 that browsers could start using unprefixed properties for both transforms and transitions. The first versions to do so are IE 10, Firefox 16, and Opera 12.50. At the time of this writing, WebKit-based browsers still require browser-specific prefixes.

---

■ **Note** The source files for this chapter contain the browser-specific properties in separate rules for testing in older browsers. The unprefixed properties are lower down the styles, so they override the browser-specific ones.

---

# Using 2D Transforms

There are just two properties for 2D transforms, as described in Table 20-1.

**Table 20-1.** *Properties for Two-Dimensional Transforms*

| Property | Initial Value | Description |
|---|---|---|
| transform | none | Specifies how the element is to be transformed. Takes as its value a space-separated list of transform functions (see Table 20-2). |
| transform-origin | 50% 50% | Specifies the anchor point of the transform. Takes one or two lengths, percentages, or keywords representing the horizontal and vertical positions, respectively. If only one value is given, the vertical position defaults to center. |

■ **Note**    The properties in Table 20-1 are also used for 3D transforms. This chapter discusses them only in the context of 2D transforms.

The transform property expects one or more 2D transform functions as its value. The functions are described in detail in the following sections.

By default, a transform originates from the center of the element. So, an element rotates around its center. When you scale an element, it expands or shrinks in all directions. You can change the anchor point from which the transform originates using the transform-origin property.

The transform-origin property takes one or two values. If both values are set, the first one specifies the horizontal position of the anchor point, and the second specifies the vertical position. The values can be lengths, percentages, or keywords.

Lengths and percentages are measured from the top-left corner of the element's border box (see Figure 6-1 in Chapter 6).

Percentages are relative to the width and height of the element's border box. In the case of a table, percentages are relative to the table and its caption (if any).

Valid keywords for the horizontal position are left, center, and right. Keywords for the vertical position are top, center, and bottom.

If only one value is given for transform-origin, it's used for the horizontal position. The vertical position defaults to center.

The transform and transform-origin properties are not inherited, so if you want child elements to use the same value as their parent, you can set their value to the inherit keyword.

## 2D Transform Functions

The draft CSS Transforms module lists ten 2D transform functions. Some affect only one axis. Others affect the X and Y axes simultaneously. X and Y normally refer to the horizontal and vertical axes, respectively, but as explained later in this chapter this is not always the case. The functions are described in Table 20-2.

*Table 20-2.* *Two-Dimensional Transform Functions*

| Function | Description |
| --- | --- |
| translateX() | Moves the element along the X axis by the specified length or percentage. |
| translateY() | Moves the element along the Y axis by the specified length or percentage. |
| translate() | Moves the element from its default position. Takes two comma-separated lengths or percentages. The first value represents the horizontal offset and the second the vertical offset. If only one value is given, the element is moved only horizontally. |
| rotate() | Rotates the element around its anchor point by the specified angle. |
| scaleX() | Scales the element along the X axis by the specified scaling factor. |
| scaleY() | Scales the element along the Y axis by the specified scaling factor. |
| scale() | Scales the element. Takes one or two numbers as the scaling factor. If one number is given, both axes are scaled by the same multiplier. If two comma-separated numbers are given, the first applies to the X axis and the second to the Y axis. |
| skewX() | Skews the element along the X axis by the specified angle. |
| skewY() | Skews the element along the Y axis by the specified angle. |
| matrix() | Specifies a 2D transform using a transform matrix of six values. |

Although six of the function names use a mixture of lowercase and uppercase, all names are case-insensitive.

■ **Note** The functions in Table 20-2 do not use browser-specific prefixes. The prefixes are applied only to the transform and transform-origin properties. For example, to scale an element in WebKit-based browsers, use -webkit-transform with the unprefixed scale() function.

## Changing an Element's Position with translate()

The translate() function and its single-axis counterparts translateX() and translateY() have a similar effect as relative positioning. They move an element from its default position without affecting the position of surrounding elements. Used in combination with other transform functions, they can move an element at the same time as scaling, rotating, or skewing it.

■ **Note** In geometry, *translate* means moving every point of an object a constant distance in a specified direction.

To move an element horizontally, use the transform property, and set its value to translateX() with a length or percentage between the parentheses. A positive length or percentage moves the element to the right. A negative one moves it to the left. For example in translate_1.html, there's a <div> that contains two images alongside each other. Both images are 400px wide and are surrounded by a 10px margin. The second image is moved 25% of its width—in other words, 100px—to the left (see Figure 20-1) by the following style:

```
img:last-child {
    transform: translateX(-25%);
}
```

***Figure 20-1.*** *The second image is moved 25% of its width to the left, and overlaps the first image*

---

■ **Note** The examples assume the browser window is wide enough to display both images alongside each other.

---

In translate_2.html, the image is moved 50px down the page using `translateY()` like this:

```
img:last-child {
    transform: translateY(50px);
}
```

As Figure 20-2 shows, moving the image vertically doesn't affect the position of the following paragraph. The image overlaps the text, obscuring it.

Nice is a jewel of the Côte d'Azur in Southern France
its crescent–shaped bay faces the Mediterranean, blessing it with a mild winter
climate. Even when the mountains are covered in snow, the town normally
remains snow–free.

***Figure 20-2.*** *The image overlaps the following paragraph when moved vertically*

There are two ways to move an element along both axes. One is to use both `translateX()` and `translateY()` separated by a space like this (the code is in translate_3.html):

```
img:last-child {
    transform: translateY(25px) translateX(-50px);
}
```

This moves the second image 25px down and 50px to the left, as shown in Figure 20-3.

Nice is a jewel of the Côte d'Azur in Southern France. Surrounded by mountains, its crescent-shaped bay faces the Mediterranean, blessing it with a mild winter climate. Even when the mountains are covered in snow, the town normally remains snow-free.

**Figure 20-3.** *The image is moved both horizontally and vertically*

The alternative—and much simpler—way is to use the translate() function with two arguments: the first for the horizontal axis, and the second for the vertical axis like this (the code is in translate_4.html):

```
img:last-child {
    transform: translate(-50px, 25px);
}
```

This produces exactly the same result as Figure 20-3.

---

■ **Note**   When using translate(), the values must be in the correct order: horizontal followed by vertical. The individual translateX() and translateY() functions can be in either order because there's no ambiguity.

---

However, the following styles in translate_5.html *won't* work as you might expect:

```
img:last-child {
    transform: translateX(-50px);
    transform: translateY(25px);
}
```

Although both declarations are using different functions, the normal rules of the cascade apply. The second value overrides the first one, so the image is moved only vertically.

---

■ **Caution**   All transforms that apply to an element must be specified as a space-separated list in the same style declaration. Otherwise, the last declaration overrides any previous ones.

---

# Rotating Elements()

To rotate an element, use the transform property and set its value with the rotate() function, which takes an angle as its argument. You can express the angle using degrees, radians, gradians, or turns (see Table 3-3 in Chapter 3). Degrees and turns are the easiest to use. One turn is equal to 360°.

---

■ **Note**   CSS degrees follow compass bearings with 0° pointing straight up with the angle increasing in a clockwise direction. Using polar coordinates in browser-specific gradient functions, as described in Chapter 19, was an exception and was eliminated in the final specification.

---

In rotate_1.html, two images are rotated clockwise using degrees and the equivalent turn like this:

```
img:first-child {
    transform: rotate(18deg);
}
img:last-child {
    transform: rotate(.05turn);
}
```

---

■ **Caution**   There must be no space between the number and the deg or turn units of measurement.

---

As Figure 20-4 shows, both images are rotated at the same angle and are clipped when they overflow the browser viewport.

***Figure 20-4.*** *Rotating an element close to the edge of the page can result in it being partially obscured*

You can use a negative value to rotate an element counterclockwise. For example, the styles in rotate_2.html use a negative angle and the equivalent positive value to rotate the images in the opposite direction like this:

```
img:first-child {
    transform: rotate(-18deg);
}
img:last-child {
    transform: rotate(342deg);
}
```

The values –18° and 342° have the same meaning, so both images are displayed at the same angle, as shown in Figure 20-5.

*Figure 20-5.* *You can use a negative angle to rotate an element counterclockwise*

## Changing the Anchor Point with transform-origin

By default, 2D transforms originate from the center of an element. With translate(), translateX(), and translateY(), it makes no difference where the movement is calculated from. The result is always the same. However, with the other transform functions, it can make a significant difference. The images in Figures 20-4 and 20-5 are rotated around their center points. But you can change the anchor point using transform-origin.

The styles in rotate_3.html rotate both images at the same angle (-18°), but around different anchor points like this:

```
img {
    /* Other styles omitted */
    transform: rotate(-18deg);
}
img:first-child {
    transform-origin: right top;
}
img:last-child {
    transform-origin: left bottom;
}
```

451

As Figure 20-6 shows, the angle remains the same, but the result is very different.

***Figure 20-6.*** *The images are rotated the same amount around different anchor points*

## Rotating Text

It's not just images that can be rotated. You can rotate any element, including text. When rotating a heading, it's best to set the anchor point with `transform-origin` to the top-left corner. This is because headings stretch across all available horizontal space unless you give them a fixed width. As a result, the rotated heading ends up in the middle of the page.

The order in which you use the transform functions is also important. In rotate_4.html, an `<h1>` heading is moved 215px down the page using `translateY()` before being rotated counterclockwise through a quarter turn around its top-left corner like this:

```
h1 {
    transform: translateY(215px) rotate(-.25turn);
    transform-origin: left top;
}
```

Using the `transform` property to move the heading results in a gap being left where it originally was. So, the `images <div>` is given a negative top margin and a positive left margin to move it up and to the right to make room for the rotated heading.

```
#images {
    margin-left: 50px;
    margin-top: -50px;
}
```

Figure 20-7 shows the result.

Nice has a great open–air market just one block away from the seafront at the eastern end of town. It's a real local market, with locally grown produce, and it's used by the townspeople and local restaurants.

***Figure 20-7.*** *You can also rotate text*

However, in rotate_5.html, the order of the transform functions is reversed like this:

```
h1 {
    transform: rotate(-.25turn) translateY(215px);
    transform-origin: left top;
}
```

This produces the result shown in Figure 20-8.

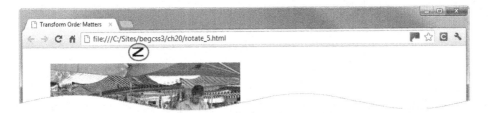

***Figure 20-8.*** *Reversing the order of the transform functions produces a completely different result*

At first sight, this seems completely nonsensical. The heading has been rotated around its top-left corner, but instead of being moved vertically, it has shifted horizontally. It's not a bug. See the sidebar "Understanding the Local Coordinate System" for an explanation.

## UNDERSTANDING THE LOCAL COORDINATE SYSTEM

In normal circumstances, the X axis increases horizontally to the right and the Y axis increases vertically downward. However, the transform functions establish a *local coordinate system*. This means that when you rotate an element, the X and Y axes are also rotated by the same angle.

In the example in rotate_5.html, the heading is rotated and moved like this:

```
transform: rotate(-.25turn) translateY(215px);
```

The rotate() function not only flips the heading a quarter turn counterclockwise, but it also flips all coordinates associated with the heading by the same amount. As a result, the heading's Y axis is flipped 90° counterclockwise. So, when translateY() is applied, the heading moves 215px to the right rather than down (see Figure 20-8). Although this appears counterintuitive, it's actually moving along the Y axis in the local coordinate system. To move the heading down the page after rotating it, you need to use translateX() instead like this (the code is in rotate_6.html):

```
transform: rotate(-.25turn) translateX(-215px);
```

The length is negative because the heading needs to move 215px to the left along the X axis in the local coordinate system.

Deciding whether to move an element before rotating it is a matter of choice. Just remember that once an element has been rotated, its X and Y axes have also changed.

## Scaling Elements

To scale an element, use the transform property and set its value with the scaleX(), scaleY(), or scale() functions. The first two functions take a number as their sole argument, and use it as a scaling factor for the X or Y axis, respectively. For example, scale_1.html contains three identical headings in a large bold font. The first one is rendered at its normal size, but the second one is scaled to half its normal width, and the third one to half its normal height. By default, scaling is done from the center of an element, so transform-origin is set to left to anchor the headings in their original position:

```
h1 {
    font-family:"Arial Black", Gadget, sans-serif;
    font-size:48px;
    margin: 5px;
    transform-origin: left;
}
#horizontal {
    transform: scaleX(.5);
}
#vertical {
    transform: scaleY(.5);
}
```

Figure 20-9 shows the result. The horizontally scaled text looks okay, but the vertically scaled text has jagged edges.

# Beginning CSS3

## Beginning CSS3

### Beginning CSS3

**Figure 20-9.** *Scaling text horizontally and vertically*

■ **Note** It's the text box that's scaled, not just the font size. If you scale a paragraph of text horizontally, the text is not reflowed.

The scale() function accepts one or two arguments. If you pass it a single number, the same scaling factor is applied to both axes. If you pass it two numbers separated by a comma, the first is used as the scaling factor for the X axis and the second for the Y axis.

In scale_2.html, two 400px wide images are scaled to two-thirds of their normal size like this:

```
.scaleimg {
    /* Other styles omitted */
    transform: scale(0.66);
}
```

As Figure 20-10 shows, the images are reduced in size, but they still occupy their normal space, leaving a wide gap all around them. This happens even if you remove the width and height attributes from the <img> tags in the HTML markup.

***Figure 20-10.*** *Scaling images reduces their size, but not the amount of space they occupy*

You can't use the scale() function if you want to remove the space around images that have been scaled down. Instead, you need to adjust the width and height attributes in the HTML. You can then use scale() to restore them to their normal size when hovered over. For example, in scale_3.html, the images have been resized in the HTML like this:

```
<img src="images/nice_market.jpg" alt="Flower market in Nice" width="268" height="178" ↵
class="scaleimg">
<img src="images/nice_seafront.jpg" alt="Nice seafront" width="268" height="178" ↵
class="scaleimg">
```

This removes the extraneous space, as shown in Figure 20-11.

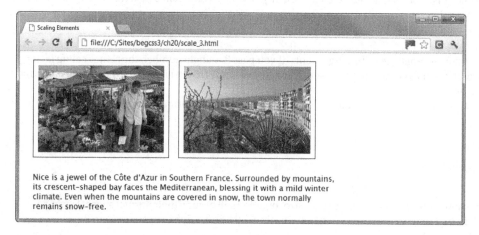

**Figure 20-11.** *The images have been resized in the HTML markup*

The images are scaled up to their original size when hovered over, and to prevent them partially disappearing offscreen, the anchor points are set like this:

```
.scaleimg:first-child {
    transform-origin: left top;
}
.scaleimg:last-child {
    transform-origin: right top;
}
.scaleimg:hover {
    transform: scale(1.5);
}
```

As Figure 20-12 shows, the left image is restored to its full size when the mouse pointer is over it.

**Figure 20-12.** *The image is scaled up when hovered over*

When you mouse away from the image, it returns to its reduced size. The change in size in both directions is instantaneous, which can be rather jarring. However, as you'll learn later in this chapter, you can scale the image smoothly over a specified duration using a CSS transition.

---

■ **Caution** Tapping the image on a touch screen scales it up in the same way as hovering over it. However, it doesn't return to its smaller size until you tap another element that uses the :hover pseudo-class. As Figure 20-12 shows, the example in scale_3.html obscures the text. When scaling elements, make sure they're in a position where they won't obscure important content. Alternatively, use the solution in the following section to disable scaling on touch screens.

---

## Preventing Elements from Being Scaled on Touch Screens

The simple way to prevent elements from being scaled on touch screens is to test for the JavaScript ontouchstart event. If the event exists, you know that the page has been loaded into a touch-screen device. You can then use JavaScript to add an extra class name to the images and create a style rule that prevents them from being scaled.

This extra style rule has been added in scale_4.html:

```
.noscale.scaleimg:hover {
    transform: scale(1);
}
```

This sets the scale of elements with both the noscale and scaleimg classes to 1 when hovered over. In other words, the element remains unscaled.

Alternatively, if no other transform functions are being used, you could set the value to none:

```
.noscale.scaleimg:hover {
    transform: none;
}
```

At the foot of the page is the following script block:

```
<script>
if ('ontouchstart' in window) {
    function noScale(scale, noscale) {
        var images = document.getElementsByClassName(scale);
        for (var i = 0, len = images.length; i < len; i++) {
            images[i].className = scale+' '+noscale;
        }
    }
    noScale('scaleimg', 'noscale');
}
</script>
```

The script begins by checking whether the ontouchstart event exists. If it doesn't, the rest of the script is ignored. It then defines a function called noScale(), which takes two arguments. The first is the class name assigned to elements that are being scaled. The second is the class name you want to add to prevent scaling on touch screens. The last line of the script executes the function by passing the two class names to it.

If you want to use different class names, just change the arguments passed to the noScale() function.

On a touch-screen device, the images remain unscaled when tapped. But on all other devices that support CSS transforms, they're scaled up and down on mouseover and mouseout.

## Flipping Elements

Table 20-2 doesn't contain a transform function to flip elements horizontally or vertically, but you can achieve the same effect by passing negative values to scaleX(), scaleY(), and scale(). Setting the value to -1 preserves the original size, but flips the element on the relevant axis. To demonstrate the effect, scale_5.html contains the following styles, which are applied to identical <div> elements:

```
#horizontal {
    transform: scaleX(-1);
}
#vertical {
    transform: scaleY(-1);
}
#shrinkflip {
    transform: scale(-.5);
}
```

The value of transform-origin is not set, so the elements are flipped around their center, producing the result in Figure 20-13. The final <div> is flipped and scaled down along both axes, which produces the same effect as scaling it down and rotating it 180°.

**Figure 20-13.** *Setting the scaling factor to a negative number flips the element around the relevant axis*

## Skewing Elements

To skew an element, use the transform property and set its value by passing an angle as the argument to skewX() or skewY(). With skewX(), a positive angle skews the element to the left, and a negative angle skews it to the right. With skewY(), a positive angle skews the element vertically and rotates it in a clockwise direction. A negative angle rotates it in an anticlockwise direction.

The following example is in skew.html (see Figure 20-14):

```
#horizontal {
    transform: skewX(-30deg);
}
#vertical {
    transform: skewY(20deg);
}
```

**Figure 20-14.** *When objects are skewed, it also affects any text inside them*

As the angle increases toward 90°, the object becomes more and more distorted until it disappears completely at exactly 90°. At 180°, there is no distortion whatsoever.

---

■ **Note**   An earlier draft of the specification had a skew() function, but it was removed in March 2012 because elements are normally skewed only along one axis. Use only skewX() or skewY(). Although you can use both in the same style rule, they have a tendency to cancel out one another.

---

## Transforming Elements with the matrix() Function

The matrix() function specifies a 2D transform in the form of a *transformation matrix* (http://en.wikipedia.org/wiki/Transformation_matrix). The function requires six arguments, all of which are numbers separated by commas.

---

■ **Tip**   Unless you're an expert in linear algebra (and I most certainly am not), you can forget about the matrix() function. Although it allows you to combine multiple transforms in a single operation, everything that the matrix() function does can be achieved using the individual transform functions described in the preceding sections. However, read on if you're curious as to how it works.

---

The last two arguments always specify the number of pixels you want to move (translate) the element along the horizontal and vertical axes, respectively. The first four arguments control other transforms.

In most cases, the first and fourth arguments are the scaling factors for the horizontal and vertical axes, respectively. The second argument usually controls the angle of vertical skew, while the third one controls horizontal skew. All four arguments are used in combination to rotate the element. What makes using the matrix() function complicated is the need to convert angles of skew and rotation using trigonometric functions.

### Moving Elements

Let's start with a simple example. In translate_4.html, the translate() function moves an image 50px left and 25px down (see Figure 20-3) like this:

```
img:last-child {
    transform: translate(-50px, 25px);
}
```

To do the same with the `matrix()` function, the equivalent style in matrix_1.html looks like this:

```
img:last-child {
    transform: matrix(1, 0, 0, 1, -50, 25);
}
```

The first and fourth arguments indicate a scaling factor of 1. In other words, the element retains its original size. The second and third arguments are set to zero, indicating that the element isn't skewed.

---

■ **Note**   When using the browser-specific `-moz-transform` property with Firefox 15 and earlier, you need to add px as the unit of measurement to the last two arguments passed to the `matrix()` function.

---

## Scaling Elements

The styles in scale_4.html use the `scale()` function like this:

```
.scaleimg:hover {
    transform: scale(1.5);
}
.noscale.scaleimg:hover {
    transform: scale(1);
}
```

The equivalent styles in matrix_2.html achieve the same effect with the `matrix()` function:

```
.scaleimg:hover {
    transform: matrix(1.5, 0, 0, 1.5, 0, 0);
}
.noscale.scaleimg:hover {
    transform: matrix(1, 0, 0, 1, 0, 0);
}
```

The fifth and sixth arguments are set to zero, so the image doesn't move. But you can combine scale and translate transforms in the `matrix()` function by using nonzero values for the last two arguments.

## Flipping Elements

Setting the first and fourth arguments of the `matrix()` function to a negative value flips an element in the same way as passing a negative value to `scaleX()`, `scaleY()`, or `scale()`. The following styles in matrix_3.html produce the same results as scale_5.html and Figure 20-13:

```
#horizontal {
    transform: matrix(-1, 0, 0, 1, 0, 0);
}
#vertical {
    transform: matrix(1, 0, 0, -1, 0, 0);
}
#shrinkflip {
    transform: matrix(-.5, 0, 0, -.5, 0, 0);
}
```

## Skewing Elements

So far, all the numbers passed as arguments are straightforward. They're simply the scaling factor and the number of pixels you want to move the element. However, to skew an element, you need to calculate the tangent of the angle using the trigonometric tan() function. Unfortunately, CSS doesn't support tan(), so you need to work it out yourself either using a scientific calculator or an online resource, such as www.rapidtables.com/calc/math/Tan_Calculator.htm.

The horizontal example in skew.html uses skewX() like this:

```
#horizontal {
    transform: skewX(-30deg);
}
```

The tangent of –30° is -.58, so the equivalent in matrix_3.html is this:

```
#horizontal {
    transform: matrix(1, 0, -.58, 1, 0, 0);
}
```

The vertical example uses an angle of 15°, the tangent of which is .27. So, the equivalent in matrix_4.html is:

```
#vertical {
    transform: matrix(1, .27, 0, 1, 0, 0);
}
```

These settings produce the same results as Figure 20-14.

**Caution** Although the scaling factors and translate coordinates are in the order horizontal/vertical, the order of the skew tangents is reversed. The second argument is for the vertical skew, and the third for the horizontal skew.

## Rotating Elements

To rotate an element, the first four arguments to the matrix() function are as follows:

1. The cosine of the angle of rotation
2. The sine of the angle of rotation
3. The inverse value of argument 2 (negative if 2 is positive, and vice versa)
4. The same as argument 1

**Tip** There are calculators for cosine and sine at www.rapidtables.com/calc/math/Cos_Calculator.htm and www.rapidtables.com/calc/math/Sin_Calculator.htm.

In rotate_4.html, an <h1> heading was moved 215px along its vertical axis and then rotated through 90° counterclockwise using the following styles:

```
h1 {
    transform: translateY(215px) rotate(-.25turn);
    transform-origin: left top;
}
```

The cosine of –90° is 0 and the sine is -1, so the equivalent style using the matrix() function in matrix_5.html looks like this:

```
h1 {
    transform: matrix(0, -1, 1, 0, 0, 215);
    transform-origin: left top;
}
```

This produces the same result as Figure 20-7.

---

■ **Note**   Although the translate arguments come last in the matrix() function, it's clear that the heading is moved before it's rotated. Otherwise, the heading would have moved along the Y axis in the local coordinate system.

---

# Animating Property Values with CSS Transitions

When the value of a property changes—such as on hovering over an element—the change is instantaneous. When you mouse over a link, the speed of the change isn't really important. But when an image is scaled up on hover, as in one of the examples earlier in this chapter, the sudden jump is jarring.

CSS transitions overcome this problem by animating a smooth change between one state and another over a specified duration. For example, you can scale and rotate the image over a period of one second. When you move the mouse away from the image, the transition is reversed, returning to its original state over the same duration. Transitions can be applied to all elements including the ::before and ::after pseudo-elements.

You define a transition using the properties listed in Table 20-3.

**Table 20-3.**  *CSS Transition Properties*

| Property | Initial Value | Description |
| --- | --- | --- |
| transition-property | all | Specifies the name(s) of the CSS properties to which the transition is to be applied. |
| transition-duration | 0s | Specifies how long the transition should take in seconds (s) or milliseconds (ms). Negative values are not allowed. |
| transition-timing-function | ease | Describes the pace of change using easing or stepping keywords or functions. |
| transition-delay | 0s | Defines when the transition should start measured in seconds or milliseconds. A positive value delays the start. A negative value initiates the transition immediately, but part-way through its cycle at the point it would have reached after the specified offset. |
| transition | | Shorthand property that sets all four values in a single declaration. |

The properties in Table 20-3 are not inherited. If you want an element to use the same value as its parent, you can use the inherit keyword.

# Choosing Which Properties to Animate

The transition-property property accepts the keyword all or a comma-separated list of properties you want to animate. Only those properties listed in Table 20-4 can be animated.

**Table 20-4.** *Animatable CSS Properties*

## Property Names

| | | |
|---|---|---|
| background-color | column-gap * | min-width |
| background-position | column-rule-color * | opacity |
| background-size * | column-rule-width * | outline-color |
| border-bottom-color | column-width * | outline-offset |
| border-bottom-width | crop | outline-width |
| border-left-color | font-size | padding-bottom |
| border-left-width | font-size-adjust * | padding-left |
| border-right-color | font-stretch | padding-right |
| border-right-width | font-weight | padding-top |
| border-spacing | height | right |
| border-top-color | left | text-decoration-color * |
| border-top-width | letter-spacing | text-indent |
| border-top-left-radius * | line-height | text-shadow |
| border-top-right-radius * | margin-bottom | top |
| border-bottom-right-radius * | margin-left | transform * |
| border-bottom-left-radius * | margin-right | transform-origin * |
| bottom | margin-top | vertical-align |
| box-shadow * | marker-offset * | visibility |
| clip | max-height | width |
| color | max-width | word-spacing |
| column-count * | min-height | z-index |

*\* Supported by Firefox and under consideration for inclusion in the specification.*

Unless you want to apply different transition effects to individual properties, it's best to use the keyword all. Alternatively, you can omit transition-property altogether because all is the default value.

---

■ **Caution** The list of animatable properties in Table 20-4 doesn't include shorthand properties, such as border, margin, or padding. You need to animate the individual properties.

---

## Specifying the Duration of the Transition

You specify the duration of the transition with the `transition-duration` property, which expects a single duration or comma-separated list of durations. Times can be set in seconds (`s`) or thousandths of a second (`ms`).

If you specify just one value, the same duration applies to all properties being transitioned. If you supply multiple durations, they're applied to the properties in the same order as they're listed in `transition-property`. In the following example, all transitions take half a second:

```
transition-property: color, width, height;
transition-duration: .5s;
```

However, in the next example, `color` changes over half a second, while `width` and `height` take a full second to transition to the next state.

```
transition-property: color, width, height;
transition-duration: .5s, 1s, 1s;
```

The number of values doesn't need to match. If `transition-duration` has more values than `transition-property`, the excess durations are ignored. If there are fewer, the browser cycles through them again. Take the following example:

```
transition-property: left, width, top, height;
transition-duration: 2s, 1s;
```

In this case, there are only two values for `transition-duration`, so the transition of the `left` property takes two seconds, while `width` changes over one second. The browser then cycles through the durations again, using two seconds for `top` and one second for `height`. If you add another property to `transition-property`, the browser continues the cycle, and uses a two-second duration.

---

■ **Caution**   If you want a property to change instantly, you must use `0s` or `0ms`. Omitting the unit of measurement with a duration is invalid and causes the style to be ignored.

---

## Setting the Pace of the Transition

The `transition-timing-function` property controls how intermediate values are calculated during the transition. The property accepts one or more of the following values as a comma-separated list:

**ease** Starts slow, speeds up, and slows toward the end.

**linear** Transitions at an even pace throughout.

**ease-in** Starts slow and speeds up.

**ease-out** Starts fast and slows toward the end.

**ease-in-out** Similar to ease, but slower at each end.

**cubic-bezier()** Specifies a custom transition using a cubic-bézier curve.

**step-start** The change takes place at the beginning of the duration.

**step-end** The change takes place at the end of the duration.

**steps()** The change takes place in the specified number of equal steps.

As with `transition-duration`, a single value is applied to all transitions. If you specify multiple values as a comma-separated list, they're applied in the same order to the individual properties listed in `transition-property`. Excess values are ignored, and if you specify fewer `transition-timing-function` values than properties, the browser cycles through them.

The first five keywords in the preceding list are constants for easing functions based on a cubic-bézier curve. If you've used Flash, you'll be familiar with the concept of *easing*, which varies the pace of a transition (or tween, as it's called in Flash). The `cubic-bezier()` function allows you to customize the pace. It takes four arguments like this:

```
cubic-bezier(x1, y1, x2, y2)
```

Both x1 and x2 must be in the range 0–1. The y1 and y2 values can exceed that range.

---

■ **Tip**    There's a CSS cubic-bezier builder at `www.roblaplaca.com/examples/bezierBuilder`. It not only generates a cubic-bézier curve, but it also shows how it compares in action with the predefined constants.

---

The `steps()` function takes two arguments: the number of discrete steps in the transition and the keyword start or end. If you omit the second argument, it defaults to end. To demonstrate how the function and the related `step-start` and `step-end` constants work, step.html has four identical `<div>` elements with a light gray background color. The `:hover` pseudo-class changes the background color to a very dark gray, as shown in Figure 20-15.

*Figure 20-15.* *Each square changes color at a different pace*

The page contains the following style rules:

```
div {
    /* Other styles omitted */
    background-color: #CCC;
    transition-duration: 5s;
}
div:hover {
    background-color: #333;
}
#steps1 {
    transition-timing-function: steps(5, start);
}
#steps2 {
    transition-timing-function: steps(5, end);
}
#steps3 {
    transition-timing-function: step-start;
}
```

```
#steps4 {
    transition-timing-function: step-end;
}
```

The `transition-duration` property is set to a deliberately long five seconds. The first two `<div>` elements use the `steps()` function to change the color in five discrete steps. However, the timing is affected by the second argument. The first `<div>` uses `start`, so the color immediately changes to the first intermediate shade. In the next `<div>`, the second argument is `end`. As a result, the color doesn't change until the first second has passed.

The last two `<div>` elements use the `step-start` and `step-end` constants. The first changes color immediately on mouseover and mouseout. The last one doesn't change unless the mouse pointer is held over it for the full five seconds. When you mouse away from the `<div>`, it doesn't revert to light gray until five seconds have passed.

## Delaying the Transition

By default, transitions start immediately, but you can use the `transition-delay` property to delay the whole or part of a transition. Like the other transition properties, it accepts a single time value or a comma-separated list of values. A single value applies to all properties being transitioned. A list of values is applied to properties in the same order as they're listed in `transition-property`.

Delaying a property's transition by the same amount as the previous property's duration creates a sequence of changes. For example, the styles in transition-delay.html change the background color, width, and height of a box on hover like this:

```
#box1 {
    width: 100px;
    height: 100px;
    background-color: #F00;
    margin: 10px;
    transition-property: background-color, width, height;
    transition-duration: 1s;
    transition-delay: 0s, 1s, 2s;
}
#box1:hover {
    background-color: #006;
    width: 150px;
    height: 150px;
}
```

The #box1 style rule sets the duration for each transition to one second, but `transition-delay` has three values. As a result, the transition on background-color starts as soon as you hover over the box, and it takes one second to change from red to navy blue. The width transition is delayed by one second, so it waits until the color has finished changing before gradually making the box 50px wider. The height transition is delayed by two seconds, so it starts making the box taller only after the other transitions have completed. So, although `transition-duration` is 1s, the overall sequence takes three seconds.

Figure 20-16 shows the three phases of the transition. Notice that the top-left corner of the box remains fixed throughout each phase and that the text moves down when the box increases in height. Unlike the example in Figure 20-12, there's no need to use the `transform-origin` property, and the text is not obscured. However, the browser needs to reflow the page layout continuously, which is more processor intensive than using the `scale()` transform function and could affect battery consumption on a mobile device.

*Figure 20-16. Each transition is delayed to execute in sequence*

---

■ **Note** It's generally recommended to define the transition properties in the style rule that governs the element in its normal state. Doing so allows you to apply the same values to all transitions that affect the element even if they're triggered in different ways, such as a different pseudo-class or by JavaScript.

---

When you move the mouse away at the end of the sequence, the delays are executed in the same order. First the color changes back to red, the width begins to shrink one second later, and finally the height is reduced.

The sequence is abandoned if you move the mouse away before the end, but the order of returning to the original state is the same as before. In other words, the color changes first, followed by the width.

The transition-duration property also accepts negative values. This starts the transition immediately, but as though it had already started at the specified offset. Take the following example:

```
transition-property: width;
transition-duration: 1s;
transition-delay: -500ms;
```

If the transition changes width from 100px to 200px, it starts at the point that would have been reached over half a second—in other words, about 150px (the actual value depends on the pace of the transition).

## Changing the Reverse Transition

As the example in transition-delay.html in the preceding section demonstrates, transition delays are executed in the same order when the element returns to its normal state. In many cases, this is unlikely to cause a problem. But if you want to run a sequence of transitions in reverse, it's quite easy to do.

All that's needed is to define transition-delay in two places:

- The timings for the forward sequence go in the style rule that define the state after the transition, for example in the :hover pseudo-class.

- The timings for the reverse sequence go in the style rule that defines the element's normal state.

The styles in reverse_sequence.html adapt the previous example like this:

```
#box1 {
    width: 100px;
    height: 100px;
    background-color: #F00;
    margin: 10px;
    transition-property: background-color, width, height;
```

```
        transition-duration: 1s;
        transition-delay: 2s, 1s, 0s;
}
#box1:hover {
        background-color: #006;
        width: 150px;
        height: 150px;
        transition-delay: 0s, 1s, 2s;
}
```

The original timings have been copied into the :hover pseudo-class, but they have been reversed in the #box1 style rule. When you hover over the box, the transition-delay timings in the pseudo-class override those in #box1. So, the sequence of transitions remains the same as before. However, when you move the mouse pointer away from the box, the :hover pseudo-class no longer applies, and the timings in the #box1 style take precedence. As a result, the height starts changing immediately, the width follows one second later, and finally the color fades to red.

---

■ **Tip**    The same technique applies to timing-duration. For example, setting a two-second duration in the :hover pseudo-class and a one-second duration in the normal state results in a slow transition when you hover over an element, but a rapid one when you move the mouse pointer away.

---

## Using the Shorthand Property

Instead of using the individual properties, you can define a transition in a single declaration with the transition shorthand property. For a single property, just list the values separated by spaces. For example, the following applies a one-second linear transition to background-color, delayed by a quarter of a second:

```
transition: background-color 1s 250ms linear;
```

When using the transition shorthand, the first time value is treated as transition-duration. The second one represents transition-delay. If you don't want to delay the transition, use only one time value because the default value for transition-delay is 0s.

---

■ **Tip**    To jump to the end state immediately after a delay, use a single time value equal to the length of the delay, and set the timing function to step-end.

---

To apply the same transition values to all properties, just set the values you want to change from the initial values listed in Table 20-3. For example, if you want all properties to transition over half a second without a delay, this is all you need:

```
transition: 500ms;
```

Alternatively, if you want to make it clear that all properties are affected, include the all keyword:

```
transition: all 500ms;
```

In both cases, the default ease timing function will be used.

To apply different values to each property, use multiple shorthand definitions separated by commas. For example, the #box1 style in reverse_sequence.html can be rewritten like this (the code is in transition.html):

```
#box1 {
    width: 100px;
    height: 100px;
    background-color: #F00;
    margin: 10px;
    transition: background-color 1s 2s,
                width 1s 1s,
                height 1s;
}
```

This defines a one-second transition delayed by two seconds for background-color, a one-second transition delayed by one second for width, and a one-second transition executed immediately for height.

---

■ **Note**   It's not necessary to put each shorthand definition on a separate line, but it makes the style easier to read.

---

# Using CSS Transitions with Images

After all that theory, let's take a look at some practical examples of using CSS transforms and transitions.

## Creating a Rollover Image Without JavaScript

A rollover image reveals a different image when you hover over it. You can create a variation of this technique using a combination of CSS positioning, a transition, and the opacity property, which is described in the sidebar "Opacity and Alpha Transparency."

## OPACITY AND ALPHA TRANSPARENCY

Chapter 3 described how to create semitransparent colors with the rgba() and hsla() color formats, which take as their fourth value a number representing the degree of alpha transparency. The number must be in the range 0–1, with 0 representing fully transparent and 1 fully opaque.

The opacity property also controls the degree of transparency, but it affects the whole element. It takes a single value in the same range and with exactly the same meaning as rgba() and hsla().

To demonstrate the effect, opacity.html sets the background color and border of one <div> in rgba() format with 30% alpha transparency. Another <div> has opacity set to the same amount like this:

```
#alpha {
    background: rgba(255,255,255, 0.3);
    border-color: rgba(217,79,17,0.3);
}
#opacity {
    opacity: .3;
}
```

As Figure 20-17 shows, both <div> elements are transparent, but the text in the <div> on the left is unaffected, whereas in the one on the right it has been faded along with the background and border.

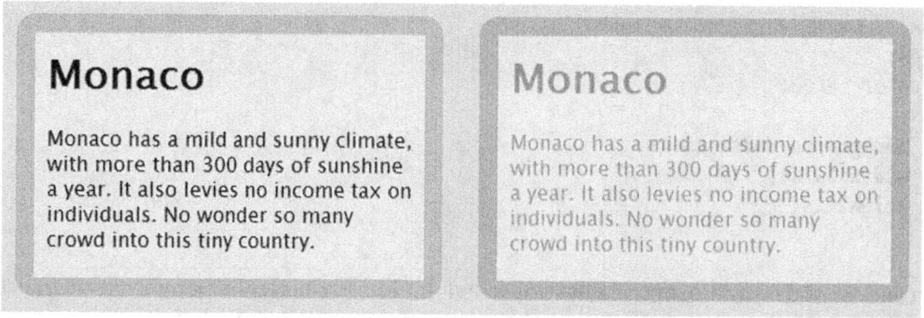

**Figure 20-17.** *Opacity (right) affects the entire element*

Instead of swapping the image source with JavaScript, this technique relies on superimposing one image on top of another and using the opacity property and a transition to fade out the front image when hovered over. In fade_image.html, there are two images of the same size alongside each other inside a <div> like this:

```
<div id="images">
    <img src="images/nice_market.jpg" alt="Flower market in Nice" width="400" height="266" ↵
    class="frontimg">
    <img src="images/nice_seafront.jpg" alt="Nice seafront" width="400" height="266">
</div>
```

The first image is assigned the class frontimg, which has the following styles:

```
.frontimg {
    position: absolute;
    transition: opacity 500ms linear;
    opacity: 1;
}
.frontimg:hover {
    opacity: 0;
}
```

The class makes the image absolutely positioned. As explained in Chapter 11, absolute positioning removes an element from the document flow and floats it on a separate layer in front of the normal content. If you don't set any offsets, the element occupies the same position as it would in the normal flow. As a result, the second image is hidden behind the first one. They have the same dimensions, so the rest of the page is unaffected.

The other properties create a half-second linear transition and set the normal opacity to 1 (fully opaque). The :hover pseudo-class changes the level of opacity to 0 (fully transparent).

When you hover over the image, it fades to reveal the other image underneath (see Figure 20-18). Although you can't see the front image after the fade, it's still there, so you're still hovering over it until you move the mouse pointer away. Then the front image fades back.

***Figure 20-18.*** *Hovering over the front image triggers a cross-fade to reveal the image behind*

## Sliding an Image Out of View

A simple variation on the technique in the previous section uses the `translateX()` transform function to move the front image far enough to the left to hide it offscreen. The styles in slide_image.html look like this:

```
.frontimg {
    position: absolute;
    transition: 1s linear;
}
.frontimg:hover {
    transform: translateX(-442px);
}
```

This creates a linear transition to slide the front image to the left over one second, revealing the other image behind it (see Figure 20-19).

***Figure 20-19.*** *The front image slides offscreen when hovered over*

## EXERCISE: SCALING AND ROTATING IMAGES SMOOTHLY

The example in scale_3.html earlier in this chapter scaled up images when hovered over. But there were two problems: the instant change in state was jarring, and the following text was hidden. With the help of transitions and advanced selectors, you can fix both problems.

Use scale_transition_begin.html in the ch20 folder as your starting point. The finished version is in scale_transition_end.html.

The styles in both pages have been split into two sections. The first section contains the browser-specific prefixes needed for older browsers. The second section contains the standard transform properties. If you need the browser-specific versions, uncomment the first section. For brevity, the following instructions use only the standard properties.

1.  Rotate the two images by adding the `transform` property to the `:first-child` and `:last-child` pseudo-classes and setting its value with the `scale()` function. Rotate the first image 6° counterclockwise and the other image the same amount clockwise like this:

    ```
    .scaleimg:first-child {
        transform-origin: left top;
        transform: rotate(-6deg);
    }
    .scaleimg:last-child {
        transform-origin: right top;
        transform: rotate(6deg);
    }
    ```

2.  Add a transition to the `scaleimg` class using `ease-in-out` and a duration of one second. There's no need to set any properties for the transition because it will apply to all of them.

    ```
    .scaleimg {
        margin: 10px;
        padding: 10px;
        background-color: #FFF;
        border: 1px solid #000;
        transition: ease-in-out 1s;
    }
    ```

3.  Save the page and test it in a browser that supports transforms and transitions. The transition is smooth, but the left image remains tucked behind the other image when scaled up, as shown in Figure 20-20. This is because the images overlap slightly as a result of being rotated in their normal state. The scaled-up image is not rotated because the `transform` property in the `:hover` pseudo-class is lower down the styles and overrides the values in the `:first-child` and `:last-child` rules.

*Figure 20-20.* *The left image disappears behind the other one when scaled up*

4.  To overcome this problem, you need to make the images relatively positioned and give them a z-index. Amend the scaleimg class like this:

```
.scaleimg {
margin: 10px;
padding: 10px;
background-color: #FFF;
border: 1px solid #000;
            transition: ease-in-out 1s;
            position: relative;
            z-index: 1;
}
```

5.  To make sure the hovered image is in front, give the :hover pseudo-class a z-index of **2**:

```
.scaleimg:hover {
    transform: scale(1.5);
    z-index: 2;
}
```

6.  Test the page again. In some browsers, the left image remains behind the other one right until the end of the transition when it suddenly pops to the front. This is because z-index must be an integer. The gap between 1 and 2 is too small for a smooth transition. Change the z-index in the :hover pseudo-class to **10**. This produces a much smoother effect in both directions.

7.  To solve the problem of the text being obscured, you need to add a top margin to the paragraph when the images are being hovered over. The images are in a <div> with the ID images, so you can use the adjacent sibling combinator (see Chapter 13) to add a transition and the top margin like this:

```
#images + p {
    transition: 1s ease-in-out;
}
#images:hover + p {
    margin-top: 100px;
}
```

When you hover over an image, it scales and rotates smoothly and the text glides down the page. Moving the mouse pointer away returns text and images to their normal positions.

## Summary

CSS transforms and transitions break up the angular and static layout of web pages by moving, rotating, scaling, and skewing elements, and creating a smooth transition from one state to another. In this chapter, I used the :hover pseudo-class to trigger transitions, but you can also use JavaScript to add and remove a class to change an element's properties. If you have defined a transition in a style that governs the element's normal state, the browser will transition smoothly between the start and end values.

In the next chapter, we'll look at more complex animations using CSS keyframes.

# CHAPTER 21

# Animating with CSS Keyframes

The CSS transitions covered in the preceding chapter create simple animations that smooth changes in an element's properties from one state to another. But they're limited to the transition between two points. The only influence you have over what happens between those points lies in the choice of timing function. The CSS Animations module (http://dev.w3.org/csswg/css3-animations/) goes much further by allowing you to define *keyframes* that specify what an element's properties should be at each stage of the animation. As with transitions, it's left up to the browser to work out how to animate a smooth change from one keyframe to the next. So, you need to create keyframes only for significant changes. But you have finer control over reverse transitions, and you can specify how many times the animation should run or make it repeat endlessly.

In spite of their power, CSS animations aren't designed for heavy graphic manipulation. Consider using HTML5 video and canvas, or WebGL instead. The principal value of CSS animations is the ability to create more complex transitions than those described in Chapter 20. For example, a CSS transition can change an element's background from one color to another, but you can't make it go through a series of color changes. CSS animations make that sort of complex transition possible.

In this chapter, you'll learn how to do the following:

- Define animation keyframes

- Add an animation to page elements

- Control the duration and number of iterations of an animation

- Highlight an element by fading in a background color and fading it out again

- Choose the direction of alternate iterations

- Pause an animation

- Control how properties are displayed before and after an animation

- Add multiple animations to an element

---

**Tip** CSS animations have many similarities with CSS transitions. You'll find this chapter easier to follow if you have read the section on CSS transitions in the previous chapter.

---

## Browser Support for CSS Animations

WebKit-based browsers and Firefox began supporting animations (with browser-specific prefixes) at an early stage, but Internet Explorer and Opera didn't support animations until IE 10 and Opera 12.0.

The W3C announced in June 2012 that browsers no longer need to use browser-specific prefixes for animation properties. The first versions to support unprefixed properties are IE 10, Firefox 16, and Opera 12.5. At the time of this writing, no announcement has been made about WebKit-based browsers.

---

■ **Note**  The source files for this chapter contain both the browser-specific syntax and the standard syntax in separate style rules.

---

# Defining Keyframes

Creating a CSS animation is a two-stage process. Unlike CSS transitions, where all the properties are defined in the element's style rules, you create the keyframes separately. This has the advantage that you can define a set of keyframes and apply the same animation to different elements.

The keyframes describe the state of properties at each stage of the animation. Optionally, they also specify the timing function (similar to `transition-timing-function`) that controls the pace of the transition between each stage.

You define a set of keyframes using `@keyframes` followed by the name you want to give the animation. All the rules for the keyframes go inside a pair of curly braces. For example, to define the keyframes for an animation called `highlight`:

```
@keyframes highlight {
    /* Keyframe definitions */
}
```

---

■ **Note**  The browser-specific prefix for older browsers goes after the @ mark. For example, older WebKit-based browsers use @-webkit-keyframes.

---

Inside the curly braces, style blocks define the state of the animated properties at each stage. Each style block has a *keyframe selector* indicating the percentage along the duration of the animation that the keyframe represents. The selector for the starting keyframe can be either 0% or the keyword `from`. The selector for the ending keyframe can be either 100% or `to`. All other selectors must be percentages.

---

■ **Caution**  If you use a percentage value for the starting point, it must be 0%. Omitting the percentage sign after 0 is invalid as a keyframe selector.

---

For example, the following `@keyframes` rule creates an animation that changes the `background-color` property from fully transparent yellow at the start, increases it to 50% transparency at the halfway point, and fades it back to fully transparent at the end:

```
@keyframes highlight {
    from {
        background-color: rgba(255,204,0,0);
    }
```

```
    50% {
        background-color: rgba(255,204,0,0.5);
    }
    to {
        background-color: rgba(255,204,0,0);
    }
}
```

In this example, the same values are used for from and to. To avoid repetition, you can group keyframe selectors as a comma-separated list. So, the following @keyframes rule has exactly the same meaning as the preceding one:

```
@keyframes highlight {
    from, to {
        background-color: rgba(255,204,0,0);
    }
    50% {
        background-color: rgba(255,204,0,0.5);
    }
}
```

The browser automatically sorts the keyframe definitions into ascending order. However, using this shorthand tends to make @keyframe rules difficult to read.

---

▪ **Caution** Shorthand properties, such as background, cannot be animated. Table 20-4 in the preceding chapter lists all the CSS properties that can be used in an animation.

---

## Specifying the Timing Function Between Keyframes

Optionally, @keyframes rules can specify how the browser should calculate intermediate values between each keyframe using the animation-timing-function property. This accepts the same values as transition-timing-function, namely:

**ease** Starts slow, speeds up, and slows toward the end.

**linear** Transitions at an even pace throughout.

**ease-in** Starts slow and speeds up.

**ease-out** Starts fast and slows toward the end.

**ease-in-out** Similar to ease, but slower at each end.

**cubic-bezier()** Specifies a custom transition using a cubic-bézier curve.

**step-start** The change takes place at the beginning of the duration.

**step-end** The change takes place at the end of the duration.

**steps()** The change takes place in the specified number of equal steps.

■ **Note**   See "Setting the Pace of the Transition" in Chapter 20 for details of the `cubic-bezier()` and `steps()` functions.

Adding `animation-timing-function` to a keyframe tells the browser how to handle the pace of the transition to the next keyframe. For example, the `highlight` example in the preceding section has been amended to use `ease-out` for both halves of the animation like this:

```
@keyframes highlight {
    from {
        background-color: rgba(255,204,0,0);
        animation-timing-function: ease-out;
    }
    50% {
        background-color: rgba(255,204,0,.5);
        animation-timing-function: ease-out;
    }
    to {
        background-color: rgba(255,204,0,0);
    }
}
```

You can set `animation-timing-function` on each keyframe except the last one (100% or `to`). If you set a timing function on the ending keyframe, it's ignored.

If you don't specify `animation-timing-function` for a keyframe, the default `ease` is used. However, you can specify a different default as described in "Setting the Timing Function Between Keyframes" later in this chapter.

■ **Note**   The same timing function applies to all properties. If you want some properties to change at a different pace, you need to define a separate `@keyframes` rule and apply multiple animations on the target element(s).

# Animating Elements with Keyframes

Once you have defined the keyframes for an animation, you can animate elements in your pages using the CSS properties listed in Table 21-1. There are eight individual properties and a shorthand one.

*Table 21-1.* *CSS Animation Properties*

| Property | Initial Value | Description |
|---|---|---|
| animation-name | none | Selects an animation defined in an @keyframes rule and applies it to the element. Setting the value to none overrides an animation coming from the cascade. |
| animation-duration | 0s | Sets the duration of an animation. |
| animation-timing-function | ease | Sets the pace of the transition to the next keyframe, as described in the previous section. Can also be used to set the default timing function for keyframes. |
| animation-iteration-count | 1 | Sets the number of times an animation should run. The value can be a number or the keyword infinite. |
| animation-direction | normal | Determines whether an animation should run in reverse on some cycles. |
| animation-play-state | running | Defines whether an animation is running. Accepted values are running and paused. |
| animation-delay | 0s | Specifies when an animation should start. A positive value plays the animation from the beginning after the specified delay. If a negative time is used, the animation starts immediately, but part way through its play cycle at the point it would have reached after the specified offset. |
| animation-fill-mode | none | Defines which property values to apply to the element before the animation begins (if delayed) and after it ends. |
| animation | | Shorthand property that defines all the properties of an animation except animation-play-state in a single declaration. |

To apply an animation to an element, both animation-name and animation-duration are required (or their values specified in the animation shorthand property). All other properties are optional.

All the properties in Table 21-1 accept a comma-separated list of values to apply multiple animations to the same element. Values are applied to animations in the same order as specified in animation-name. If fewer values are specified for a property than the number of animation names, the browser cycles through them in the same way as for CSS transitions. Excess values are ignored. There's an example of using multiple animations in "Applying Multiple Animations" at the end of this chapter.

The properties in Table 21-1 are not inherited, so you can use the inherit keyword if you want an element to inherit the same values as its parent.

## Specifying Which Animation to Use

The animation-name property takes as its value one or more names of @keyframes rules. For example, to apply the highlight keyframes to an element, just set the value of animation-name like this in the element's style rule:

```
animation-name: highlight;
```

479

To apply multiple animations, list the names of the @keyframes rules separated by commas:

```
animation-name: animation1, animation2, animation3;
```

---

■ **Tip**    The specification doesn't say whether the @keyframes rules need to come before the style rules that use them. In my tests, it didn't seem to matter. But it's probably easier from the maintenance point of view to define keyframes first and then apply animations using the properties in Table 21-1.

---

## Setting the Duration of an Animation

The animation-duration property takes as its value one or more times specified as seconds (s) or thousandths of a second (ms). If multiple times are specified, they're applied to the animations in the same order as listed for animation-name.

The styles for faq.html in the ch21 folder are in styles/faq.css. They define a set of keyframes called highlight and then apply the animation to the :target pseudo-element of <article> elements like this:

```css
@keyframes highlight {
    from {
        background-color: rgba(255,204,0,0);
        animation-timing-function: ease-out;
    }
    50% {
        background-color: rgba(255,204,0,.3);
        animation-timing-function: ease-out;
    }
    to {
        background-color: rgba(255,204,0,0);
    }
}
article:target {
    animation-name: highlight;
    animation-duration: 4s;
}
```

This draws attention to an <article> element that has been accessed through a link with a URL fragment by fading up a pale yellow background behind it, and then fading out the background. The animation lasts four seconds, with the yellow background at its most intense at the halfway mark (see Figure 21-1).

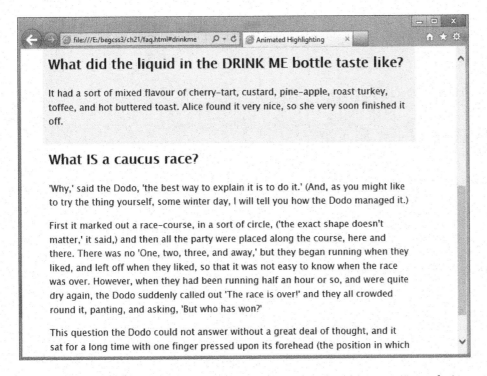

*Figure 21-1.* *The background fades in and out just long enough to draw attention to the item*

---

■ **Note**    Previously, I have avoided using new HTML5 elements, such as `<article>` because IE 8 and earlier don't style them without the help of JavaScript. However, all browsers that support animations also support HTML5.

---

## Setting the Timing Function Between Keyframes

The `animation-timing-function` controls the pace at which the browser calculates intermediate property values. Although you can apply the same value to the whole animation, it affects the transition between individual keyframes, not the animation from start to finish.

There are two ways to set the timing function. You can set it for individual keyframes in the `@keyframes` rule as shown earlier in this chapter. Alternatively, you can set it in the style rule that applies the animation to the element. Timing functions are applied in the following order:

1.  Values in `@keyframes` rules always take precedence.

2.  If a timing function hasn't been set for an individual keyframe in the `@keyframes` rule, the value in the element's style rule is used.

3.  If a timing function hasn't been set in either place, the default ease is used.

In the example in the preceding section, animation-timing-function has been set to ease-out in both keyframes in the @keyframes rule. The styles could be rewritten like this without changing the meaning:

```css
@keyframes highlight {
    from {
        background-color: rgba(255,204,0,0);
    }
    50% {
        background-color: rgba(255,204,0,.3);
    }
    to {
        background-color: rgba(255,204,0,0);
    }
}
article:target {
    animation-name: highlight;
    animation-duration: 4s;
    animation-timing-function: ease-out;
}
```

In this case, there's not a great deal of difference in the amount of code needed. But you might have a more complex animation with ten keyframes where you want a linear transition for each section apart from the first and last. In such a case, you need to set animation-timing-function in the @keyframes rule only for the first and penultimate keyframes. All other keyframes can be controlled by setting animation-timing-function to linear in the element's style rule.

## Setting the Number of Times an Animation Runs

By default, an animation runs only once, but you can change this by setting animation-iteration-count, which accepts a number or the keyword infinite as its value. As you would expect, setting the value to infinite repeats the animation endlessly. Negative values are invalid.

Interestingly, the number for animation-iteration-count doesn't need to be an integer. The animation ends part-way through the cycle if you use a noninteger. There's an example of this in partial.html, which uses the following keyframes and animation properties to slide a box back and forth across the screen:

```css
@keyframes slide {
    from {
        transform: translateX(0);
    }
    to {
        transform: translateX(500px);
    }
}
#partial {
    width: 50px;
    height: 50px;
    margin: 10px;
    background-color: #036;
    animation-name: slide;
    animation-duration: 2s;
    animation-timing-function: linear;
```

```
animation-iteration-count: 1.5;
animation-direction: alternate;
animation-fill-mode: forwards;
}
```

The animation properties apply the slide keyframes to the box, set the duration to two seconds, and the timing function to linear. As a result, the box takes two seconds to travel 500px across the screen at a steady pace. The value of animation-iteration-count is set to 1.5, so the animation continues running after the first iteration. The next two properties, animation-direction and animation-fill-mode, are described in detail later, but they have the effect of sending the box back in the opposite direction and fixing it in position when the animation ends. Because the number of iterations is 1.5, the box comes to a halt in the middle of its journey back to its original position (see Figure 21-2).

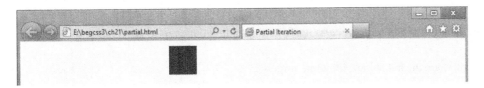

***Figure 21-2.*** *The animation stops halfway through the second iteration*

▦ **Note**   Chrome 21 doesn't support partial cycles. It stops the animation at the end of the first iteration. Hopefully, this bug will have been fixed by the time you read this.

## Specifying Whether the Animation Should Run in Reverse

The animation-direction property controls whether the animation runs in reverse on some or all cycles. This takes as its value one of the following keywords:

**normal** The is the default. All iterations of the animation run in the order defined by the @keyframes rule.

**reverse** All iterations run in the reverse order from that defined in the @keyframes rule.

**alternate** Counting from 1, all odd cycles run in the normal direction, and all even ones in reverse.

**alternate-reverse** Counting from 1, all odd cycles run in reverse, and all even ones run in the normal direction.

To see how they work, load animation-direction.html into a browser, and click the play button alongside each value to toggle the animation on and off (see Figure 21-3).

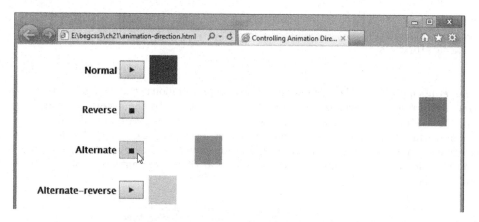

*Figure 21-3.* *The animation-direction property controls the way an animation is repeated*

The four squares all share the following animation properties:

```
animation-duration: 2s;
animation-timing-function: linear;
animation-iteration-count: infinite;
```

The animation is set to repeat endlessly, but the squares don't move until you click a button because `animation-name` hasn't been set. Clicking the play button alongside a square triggers a JavaScript function that applies the `animated` class to the square and sets its `animation-name` to `slide`. Clicking the button again, removes the class and the animation, causing the box to jump back to its original position.

The `slide` keyframes are the same as in the preceding example. They simply move the element 500px across the screen. This is how `animation-direction` affects the repeat pattern:

> `normal` The square starts on the left, and moves 500px to the right. When it reaches its destination, it jumps back to its original position, and starts moving right again.

> `reverse` The square jumps 500px to the right, and starts moving left. When it reaches its original position, it jumps back to the right, and starts moving left.

> `alternate` The square starts on the left, and moves 500px to the right. When it reaches its destination, it starts moving back in the opposite direction, and keeps moving back and forth across the screen.

> `alternate-reverse` The square jumps 500px to the right, and starts moving to the left. When it reaches its original position, it starts moving to the right, and keeps moving back and forth.

So, `normal` and `reverse` always repeat the keyframes in a single direction, but starting at different ends of the animation. The other values for `animation-direction` repeat the animation in both directions. The difference between `alternate` and `alternate-reverse` lies in where they begin the sequence. After that, they both go back and forth.

---

■ **Note**    Opera 12.0, Firefox 14, and Safari 5.1 support only `normal` and `alternate`. Safari 6 supports all four values. Firefox 16 plans to add support for `reverse` and `alternate-reverse`.

---

# Pausing an Animation

The example in the preceding section controlled whether the animation was running by assigning the animation-name property to a class and toggling the class on and off. As a result, a square was no longer animated when the class was removed from it, and it jumped back to its original position. However, you can use the animation-play-state property to pause an animation, freezing the element in its current state. The property accepts the following values:

> **running** This is the default state. The animation runs normally. If the animation has been paused, it resumes from the current point of the cycle.

> **paused** The animation stops running. The element(s) continue to display in the state they were in when the animation was paused.

You need some sort of trigger to pause an animation. The simplest trigger is the :hover pseudo-class. For example, pause_hover.html contains the following animation:

```css
@keyframes pulsate {
    from {
        transform: scale(1);
    }
    25% {
        transform: scale(1.2);
    }
    50% {
        transform: scale(1.1);
    }
    75% {
        transform: scale(1.2);
    }
    to {
        transform: scale(1);
    }
}
#box {
    /* Other styles omitted */
    animation-name: pulsate;
    animation-duration: 1s;
    animation-timing-function: ease-in-out;
    animation-iteration-count: infinite;
}
#box:hover {
    animation-play-state: paused;
}
```

The animation causes a 50px square to pulsate by altering its scale every quarter-second. Hovering over the square brings some blessed relief by setting animation-play-state to paused. But as soon as you move the mouse pointer away, the animation resumes.

To preserve everyone's sanity, a better solution is to create a class that sets `animation-play-state` to paused, and then use JavaScript to toggle the class on and off. In pause.html, two (extremely) annoying animations are assigned the class animated. The styles also contain the following class:

```
.paused {
    animation-play-state: paused;
}
```

The following JavaScript at the foot of the page identifies all elements with the animated class and binds to them an event handler that toggles the paused class on and off whenever an animated element is clicked:

```
function toggleAnimations(animated, paused) {
    // Exit silently if old browser
    if (!document.getElementsByClassName) return;
    // Set default class names if no arguments passed to function
    if (!paused) var paused = 'paused';
    if (!animated) var animated = 'animated';
    var animations = document.getElementsByClassName(animated);
    // Exit silently if classList not supported
    if (!animations[0].classList) return;
    for (var i = 0; i < animations.length; i++) {
        animations[i].addEventListener('click', (function(num) {
            return function(e) {
                this.classList.toggle(paused);
            }
        })(i), false);
    }
}
toggleAnimations();
```

This defines a JavaScript function called `toggleAnimations()` and immediately executes it. The function optionally takes two arguments for the names of the animation and pause classes. If no arguments are passed to the function, it assigns animated and paused as the default class names.

---

■ **Caution** This JavaScript function relies on an HTML5 feature called `classList`, which is supported by the latest versions of all mainstream browsers, including IE 10. However, it's not supported by versions prior to Safari 5.1, iOS 5.0, or Android 3.0. If you need to support those browsers, use the `classList` polyfill (helper script) from `https://github.com/eligrey/classList.js`. Alternatively, use jQuery's `toggleClass()` method.

---

The animations in pause.html create a constantly expanding and shrinking orange glow behind a heading and a multicolored box that twirls as it follows a V-shaped path back and forth across the screen (see Figure 21-4). Clicking the heading brings instant relief, but it can be a challenge to catch the multicolored box and bring it to a halt. Clicking them again starts the madness all over.

**Figure 21-4.** *Clicking the animations toggles them on and off*

## Delaying an Animation

The animation-delay property works exactly the same way as transition-delay, which was described in the previous chapter. It delays the start of an animation by the amount specified in seconds (s) or milliseconds (ms).

If you specify a negative value, the animation starts immediately, but at the point it would have reached at the specified offset. So, if the animation is four seconds long, and animation-delay is set to minus two seconds, it begins halfway through.

## Controlling Properties Before and After Animation

The animation-fill-mode property controls the state of an element before and after an animation. For example, if an element changes color during the animation, you can choose whether to preserve that color or return to the original one when the animation finishes. It accepts the following values:

> **none** This is the default. Properties return to their original state when the animation ends.
>
> **forwards** Properties retain values set by the final keyframe.
>
> **backwards** If the animation is delayed by animation-delay, properties assume values set by the first keyframe while waiting for the animation to start.
>
> **both** Values set by the first and last keyframes are applied before and after the animation.

To demonstrate how this affects animated elements, animation-fill-mode.html contains four squares alongside play buttons. When you click a play button, it applies the animated class to the square next to it, and sets the square's animation-name to slideback. The slideback keyframes cause the square to jump 500px to the right and then slide back to its original position like this:

```
@keyframes slideback {
    from {
        transform: translateX(500px);
    }
    to {
        transform: translateX(0);
    }

}
```

Each square has a different value for `animation-fill-mode`, as indicated by the label next to the play button. However, they all share the following animation properties:

```
animation-duration: 2s;
animation-timing-function: linear;
animation-iteration-count: 2;
animation-direction: alternate;
animation-delay: 2s;
```

To show how `animation-fill-mode` affects the animation, there's a two-second delay at the start. The animation runs for two iterations, and `animation-direction` is set to `alternate`. When the square reaches the left side of the screen, it starts moving back in the opposite direction. The animation comes to an end when it reaches the right side of the screen. This is how each square is animated when you click its play button (see Figure 21-5):

none After the two-second delay, the square jumps to the right, slides back to the left, and then slides to the right. At the end of the animation, it jumps back to its original position.

forwards The square behaves the same way as none, but it remains on the right when the animation is over.

backwards The square immediately jumps to the right of the screen, pauses for two seconds, then moves back and forth across the screen. At the end of the animation, it jumps back to its original position.

both The square behaves the same way as backwards, but it remains on the right when the animation is over.

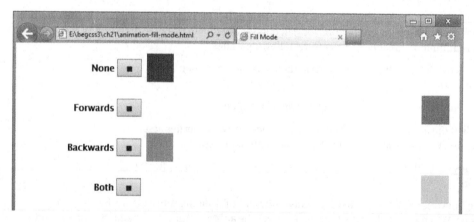

***Figure 21-5.*** *Two squares return to their original position, while the others retain the properties set by the final keyframe*

---

■ **Note**   Clicking the stop button removes the `animated` class, resetting the square to its original position.

---

## Using the animation Shorthand Property

The `animation` shorthand property lets you define one or more animations in a single declaration. It accepts values for all the individual properties except `animation-play-state`. Like the `transition` shorthand property, the first time value is interpreted as the duration, and the second (if present) is interpreted as the delay.

In animation_1.html, the <h1> heading is animated using the animated shorthand property like this:

```
animation: bounce 2s ease-out;
```

There's only one time value, so it represents the duration. No values are set for the number of iterations or direction, so the animation runs only once in the normal direction. It drops the heading into position and bounces it twice before coming to a halt. The shorthand is the equivalent of the following individual rules:

```
animation-name: bounce;
animation-duration: 2s;
animation-timing-function: ease-out;
```

## Applying Multiple Animations

In animation_2.html, a second animation is added to the heading by adding another definition to the shorthand property after a comma like this:

```
animation: bounce 2s ease-out,
           glow 2s 2s ease-out forwards;
```

The second animation called glow adds an animated text shadow. It has two time values, the first one is the duration and the second is the delay before the animation starts. There's no number or direction, so the animation runs only once in the normal direction. But animation-fill-mode is specified as forwards, so the property values in the final keyframe are preserved (see Figure 21-6).

# Double Animation

*Figure 21-6.* *The text shadow defined in the last keyframe is preserved after the animation*

The shorthand is the equivalent of the following individual properties:

```
animation-name: bounce, glow;
animation-duration: 2s, 2s;
animation-timing-function: ease-out;
animation-delay: 0s, 2s;
animation-fill-mode: none, forwards;
```

The values for each property are separated by commas and are applied to the animations in the same order as they're listed in animation-name. When using the individual properties like this, you need to specify default values explicitly unless they're shared by all animations. For example, the bounce animation runs immediately, but glow is delayed by two seconds. In the shorthand version, the delay isn't specified for bounce. But when the individual properties are used, it needs to be set to 0s. Otherwise it would have the same delay as glow.

---

■ **Tip**   Delaying an animation by the same amount as the duration of its predecessor(s) has the effect of running animations in sequence, making it easier to build and maintain the keyframes.

---

# Summary

The animations in this chapter are unlikely to win any awards—except perhaps the wooden spoon. They've been designed to show the principles behind creating CSS animations. You define an animation as a set of keyframes using an @keyframes rule, which specifies the values of properties at key points during the animation. Once you have defined the keyframes, you apply the animation to one or more elements using animation properties that specify which set of keyframes to use, the length of the animation, how many times it should run, and other settings, such as whether to preserve the values of the final keyframe when the animation ends.

Defining the keyframes separately from the elements to which they're applied allows you to reuse animations. You can also run multiple animations on an element, either consecutively, or in sequence by delaying the start of each subsequent animation until the previous one has finished.

There's a risk that CSS animations will turn back the clock to the early days of the Web when spinning icons were all the rage. However, subtle animations can add interest to a page or draw attention to information that has been updated. Keep animations short by limiting the number of iterations, and trigger them using pseudo-classes or JavaScript events.

In the final chapter, we'll take a look at other CSS3 features that are on the horizon, including Flexible Box Layout, which promises to solve many of the current problems of web page layout.

■ ■ ■

# CHAPTER 22

# What Next?

The previous 21 chapters have covered aspects of CSS that are widely implemented by most—if not all—browsers. But the development of CSS3 proceeds apace. In this final chapter, I plan to look at features looming on the horizon as this book went to press in the second half of 2012. One of the most promising is the Flexible Box Layout module (http://dev.w3.org/csswg/css3-flexbox/), which introduces a new layout mode called *flex layout*. This solves many common layout problems, such as equal-height columns, and evenly distributing elements both vertically and horizontally. It also allows you to display elements in a different order from the underlying HTML.

Firefox and WebKit-based browsers began work on flex layout many years ago, but the specification underwent several changes before it eventually stabilized in August 2012. At the time of this writing, Chrome 21 is the only browser that supports what should be the final syntax (with a browser-specific prefix). However, other browsers are sure to follow suit fairly quickly.

The bulk of this chapter is devoted to understanding the intricacies of flex layout, but I'll also take a brief look at other features that are on the horizon for CSS3 and beyond.

In this chapter, you'll learn how to do the following:

- Create a flex container

- Control the direction of rows and columns inside a flex container

- Display items in a different order from the underlying HTML

- Adjust the way free space is filled by flex items

- Align rows, columns, and individual flex items

- Build a three-column flex container and reorder its contents

## Flexible Box Layout

The main characteristic of flexible box layout is that it creates a block known as a *flex container*, where the flow of the document can be literally turned on its head. Everything inside the flex container becomes a *flex item*, which can be displayed in a different order from the underlying HTML. Margins also behave differently inside a flex container, allowing you to distribute elements evenly or separate them into groups aligned on opposite sides.

Figure 22-1 shows flex layout in action. Notice that the three columns are all of equal height, and that the *Buy Now* buttons are aligned at the bottom of each column even though there's a different amount of text in each one. Previously, this type of layout could be achieved only using an HTML table.

**Figure 22-1.** *Flex layout makes it easy to align elements within their containers*

The example in Figure 22-1 is in books1.html in the ch22 folder. Listing 22-1 shows how the HTML is structured. It consists of an HTML5 <section> element containing an <article> for each book. Only the first <article> is shown in detail.

**Listing 22-1.** HTML Structure for Book Descriptions

```
<section id="books">
    <article>
        <h3>HTML5 and CSS3 Web Design</h3>
        <p>A contemporary update of Craig Grannell's acclaimed. . .</p>
        <ul>
            <li>Learn the basics of HTML5 and CSS3 web design</li>
            <li>Implement effective layouts. . . </li>
        </ul>
        <figure><img src="images/html5_css3.png" width="277" height="350". . .></figure>
        <button>Buy Now</button>
    </article>
    <article>. . .</article>
    <article>. . .</article>
</section>
```

Notice that the image comes between the text and the button in the underlying HTML, yet it's displayed after the <h3> heading. The order of elements has been changed with CSS. That's something a table could never achieve.

In fact, to give my own book *PHP Solutions* more prominence, I promoted it to the first column in books2. html by adding this simple style rule:

```
article:last-child {
    order: -1;
}
```

If you check books1.html and books2.html, you'll see the HTML is identical in both files. But if you load books2.html into Chrome 21 or later, the order of columns has changed, as shown in Figure 22-2.

*Figure 22-2. Changing the order of flex items is trivially easy*

■ **Note**    This chapter describes what is expected to be the final syntax for flex layout. It does not discuss earlier, quite different versions of the syntax used by Firefox 14, Safari 6, older versions of Chrome, and the Developer Preview of IE 10. If you load books1.html and books2.html into a browser that doesn't understand flex layout, the `<article>` elements are stacked on top of each other, and the images are between the text and the *Buy Now* button.

## Understanding Flex Layout Terminology

Flex layout anticipates some changes to web layout that aren't currently supported by any browser. In particular, it's designed to work not only with left-to-right languages like English and other European languages, and right-to-left languages, such as Arabic. The Flexible Box Layout module also anticipates browser support for displaying Japanese and Chinese in the traditional top-to-bottom and right-to-left format. This affects the flow within a flex container, which can display items either in rows or columns.

To eliminate ambiguity when dealing with so many options, the W3C has created specific terminology to describe the main components of flex layout. Knowing what the terms refer to is important in understanding the values used for key properties in flex layout.

Figure 22-3 shows a diagrammatic representation of a flex container for a left-to-right language where the flex items are displayed in one or more rows.

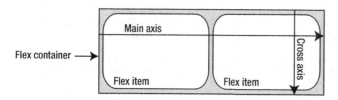

**Figure 22-3.** *A flex container has a main axis and a cross axis*

The <section> element in books1.html and books2.html is an example of this sort of flex container. It contains three flex items, the <article> elements that describe the books. In terms of flex layout terminology, they run across the flex container's *main axis*. In a right-to-left language, the main axis runs in the opposite direction. The container's *cross axis* runs perpendicular to the main axis.

In addition to being flex items, the <article> elements are flex containers in their own right, and they display their contents as a column. As Figure 22-4 shows, the main axis of a flex container that displays flex items in columns runs from the top to the bottom of the container, and the cross axis runs from left to right.

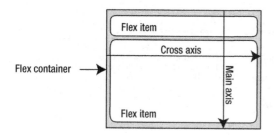

**Figure 22-4.** *When flex items are displayed in columns, the main and cross axes are transposed*

The following terms are used to refer to the different parts and dimensions of flex containers and flex items (Figure 22-5 shows them on a flex container where the main axis runs left to right):

*Main axis:* The primary axis along which flex items are laid out. When the items are laid out in rows, it runs from left-to-right in English and other European languages. For columns, it runs from top to bottom.

*Main-start:* The side of the flex container where the main axis begins.

*Main-end:* The side of the flex container where the main axis ends.

*Main size:* The size of a flex item or container measured along the main axis. In a row, it's the item's width. In a column, it's the item's height.

*Cross axis:* The axis perpendicular to the main axis is called the cross axis.

*Cross-start:* The side of the container where the cross axis begins. When the flex items are laid out in rows, it's the top. When they're laid out in columns in a left-to-right language, it's the left side.

*Cross-end:* The side where the cross axis ends.

*Cross size:* The size of a flex item or container measured along the cross axis. In a row, it's the item's height. In a column, it's the item's width.

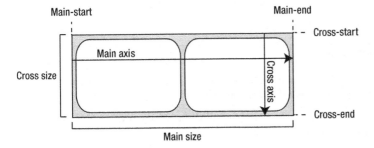

**Figure 22-5.** *The main parts and dimensions of a flex container*

■ **Note**   In traditional Chinese and Japanese layout, rows run vertically, and columns run from right to left.

## Creating a Flex Container

The Flexible Box Layout module adds two new values for the display property:

**flex** The element becomes a block-level flex container.

**inline-flex** The element becomes an inline flex container.

The difference between these two values lies in how the element interacts with surrounding elements. In the overwhelming majority of cases, flex is the value you'll need. Using inline-flex creates a flex container that is displayed inline in a similar way to setting display to inline-block (see "Understanding the Difference Between inline and inline-block" in Chapter 6).

■ **Note**   Because display is a standard property, browser-specific prefixes are added to the value rather than the property. For example, the source files use display: -webkit-flex to create a flex container in Chrome 21.

A flex container establishes a *flex formatting context* for all its contents. This has the following consequences:

- All child elements automatically become flex items.
- Floats do not intrude into the flex container.
- Adjacent vertical margins on flex items are not merged.
- You cannot use multi-column layout (see Chapter 18) inside a flex container.
- The float, clear, and vertical-align properties have no effect on flex items.

# Controlling the Flow in a Flex Container

In the standard CSS box model, the flow of a document displays elements in the order that they appear in the underlying HTML markup. Flex layout lets you control the direction of the flow inside a flex container using the properties listed in Table 22-1.

**Table 22-1.** *Properties that Control the Flow Inside a Flex Container*

| Property | Initial Value | Description |
|---|---|---|
| flex-direction | row | Sets the direction of the main axis. Flex items can be laid out in rows or columns in forward or reverse order. |
| flex-wrap | nowrap | Controls whether the container allows multiple rows or columns. Also affects the direction of the cross axis. |
| flex-flow | row nowrap | Shorthand property for flex-direction and flex-wrap. |

The properties in Table 22-1 apply to all flex items inside a flex container. As you'll learn later in this chapter, you can also reorder individual flex items using the order property.

The flex-direction property controls the direction of the flex container's main axis, laying out flex items in rows or columns. It accepts the following values:

**row** The main axis follows the same direction as the current language. In left-to-right languages like English, it starts at the left edge of the flex container and ends at the right edge. This is the default.

**row-reverse** Runs the main axis in the opposite direction to row.

**column** Runs the main axis in the same direction as blocks are laid out. In both left-to-right and right-to-left languages, this means from top to bottom. In traditional Chinese and Japanese layout, blocks are laid out from right to left.

**column-reverse** Runs the main axis in the opposite direction to column.

By default, flex containers display only a single row or column of flex items. To display multiple rows or columns, you need to use flex-wrap, which accepts the following values:

**nowrap** This is the default. The container creates only one row or column.

**wrap** The flex container is multi-line. In a left-to-right language like English, the cross axis runs in the direction indicated in Figures 22-3 through 22-5.

**wrap-reverse** The flex container is multi-line, but the cross-axis runs in the opposite direction from wrap.

The flex-flow property is a shorthand way of setting both flex-direction and flex-wrap in a single declaration. It accepts the same values as the individual properties. Because there is no ambiguity, the values can be in either order. If you omit the value for flex-direction, it defaults to row. And if you omit the value for flex-wrap, it defaults to nowrap.

Although these properties accept only a few values, the combination of flex-direction and flex-flow can be confusing because of the way they affect the main and cross axes. The following sections clarify the various options.

■ **Caution** Although flex layout gives you almost limitless control over the order in which items are displayed, the source order of the underlying HTML remains unchanged. For accessibility and search engine indexing, the HTML source order should follow a logical sequence. Flex layout is not intended to fix problems with poorly structured documents. Its primary role is to improve visual layout.

## Choosing Rows or Columns

A flex container can display its contents in rows or columns. To demonstrate various options, the examples in the following sections are based on the styles and HTML markup in Listing 22-2.

***Listing 22-2.*** Example Code for Flex Layout

```
<style>
#container {
    display: flex;
    border: 1px solid #000;
    width: 400px;
}
p {
    margin: 10px;
    font-family: "Lucida Sans Unicode", "Lucida Grande", sans-serif;
}
</style>

<div id="container">
    <p>Flex item 1</p>
    <p>Flex item 2</p>
    <p>Flex item 3</p>
    <p>Flex item 4</p>
</div>
```

## Single Row

The default values for flex-direction and flex-wrap are row and nowrap, respectively. So, if you omit them both, as in Listing 22-2 and row.html, the contents of the flex container are displayed as a single row in the same order as the underlying HTML source, as shown in Figure 22-6.

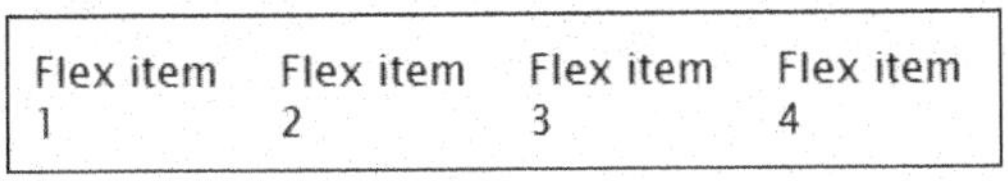

```
Flex item    Flex item    Flex item    Flex item
1            2            3            4
```

***Figure 22-6.*** *A default flex container displays a single row of items in the same order as the HTML source*

Because the <div> is a flex container, all its child paragraphs are automatically treated as flex items. You don't need to change their display property. The effect is very similar to floating the paragraphs left. However, the content of each paragraph has been wrapped because the flex container isn't wide enough to display all the paragraphs without doing so. If the paragraphs were floated, the final one would drop to the next line. But that's not possible in a flex container unless you explicitly define it to be multi-line.

In row_nowrap.html, the paragraphs have been given a minimum width of 100px. Because they also have a 10px margin all round, they're too wide to fit into the flex container. As Figure 22-7 shows, they spill out.

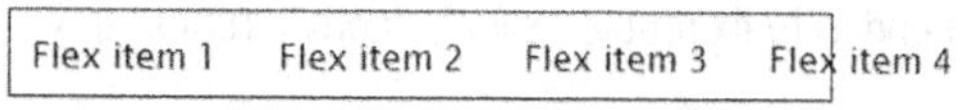

| Flex item 1 | Flex item 2 | Flex item 3 | Flex item 4 |

***Figure 22-7.*** *If the flex items are too wide for the container they spill out rather than wrap to another row*

Although you can set the overflow property (see "Handling Content That's Too Big" in Chapter 6) on the flex container, the normal way to deal with overflow is to make the container capable of handling multiple rows, as described later in this chapter.

## Single Column

To display the contents of a flex container in a single column, you need to set flex-direction to column as in column.html like this:

```
#container {
    display: flex;
    flex-direction: column;
    border: 1px solid #000;
    width: 400px;
}
```

Alternatively, you can set flex-flow to column like this:

```
#container {
    display: flex;
    flex-flow: column;
    border: 1px solid #000;
    width: 400px;
}
```

This creates a single column with the flex items displayed in the same order as the underlying source code, as shown in Figure 22-8.

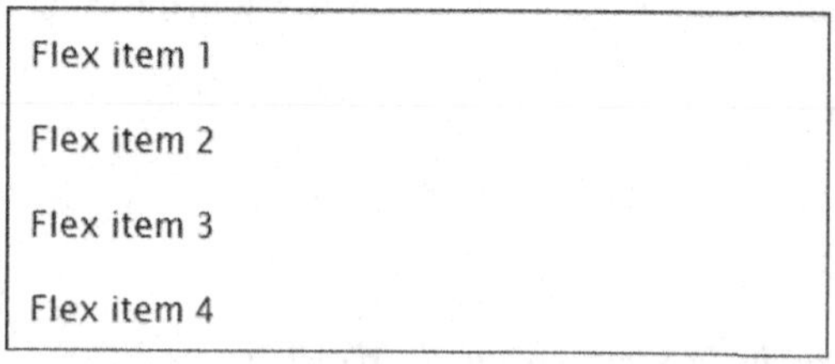

| Flex item 1 |
| Flex item 2 |
| Flex item 3 |
| Flex item 4 |

***Figure 22-8.*** *Setting flex-direction or flex-flow to column creates a single-column layout*

## Multiple Rows or Columns

To display multiple rows or columns in a flex container, set flex-wrap to wrap. For example, the style for the container <div> in row_wrap.html has been amended from Listing 22-2 like this:

```
#container {
    display: flex;
    flex-wrap: wrap;
    border: 1px solid #000;
    width: 400px;
}
```

As Figure 22-9 shows, the final item is now displayed on a separate row.

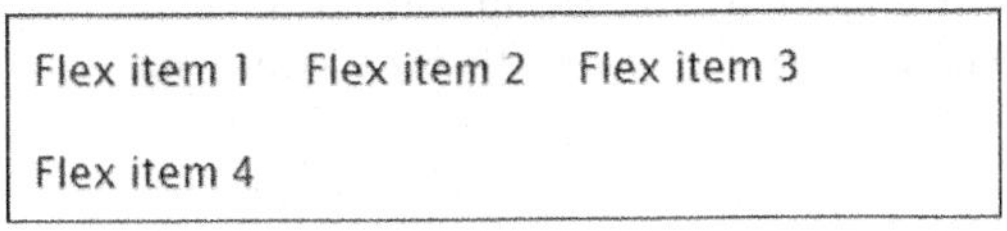

```
Flex item 1    Flex item 2    Flex item 3

Flex item 4
```

*Figure 22-9.* *The flex container now displays multiple rows*

The following shorthand flex-flow has exactly the same effect:

```
flex-flow: wrap;
```

To display multiple columns, set flex-direction to column and flex-flow to wrap. The styles for the container <div> in column_wrap.html have been given a height of 120px and changed like this:

```
#container {
    display: flex;
    flex-direction: column;
    flex-wrap: wrap;
    border: 1px solid #000;
    width: 400px;
    height: 120px;
}
```

As a result, the fourth item is moved to a second column, as shown in Figure 22-10.

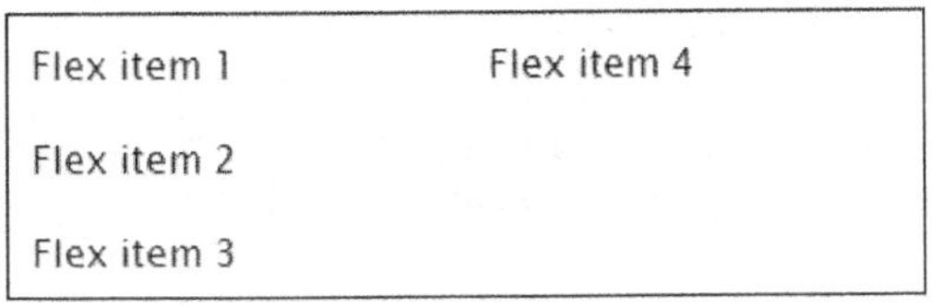

```
Flex item 1              Flex item 4

Flex item 2

Flex item 3
```

*Figure 22-10.* *The flex container has a fixed height, so the last item is moved to a new column*

Instead of using the individual properties, you can combine them in the shorthand `flex-flow` property like this:

```
flex-flow: column wrap;
```

---

■ **Note**   You cannot specify the number of rows or columns for a multi-line flex container. The choice is limited to single-line or multi-line.

---

In most cases, the options described in the preceding sections are likely to be all you need: single or multiple rows or columns with the flex items displayed in the order they appear in the underlying HTML. However, the `flex-direction` and `flex-wrap` properties (and the `flex-flow` shorthand) let you manipulate the direction of the main and cross axes, either independently or at the same time. The next three sections describe what happens in each combination.

## Reversing the Main Axis

The `flex-direction` property lets you reverse the direction of the main axis. The styles in row-reverse.html reverse the direction of a single-row flex container like this:

```
#container {
    display: flex;
    flex-direction: row-reverse;
    border: 1px solid #000;
    width: 400px;
}
```

The underlying HTML is still in the same order as Listing 22-2, but the flex items are displayed from right to left, as shown in Figure 22-11.

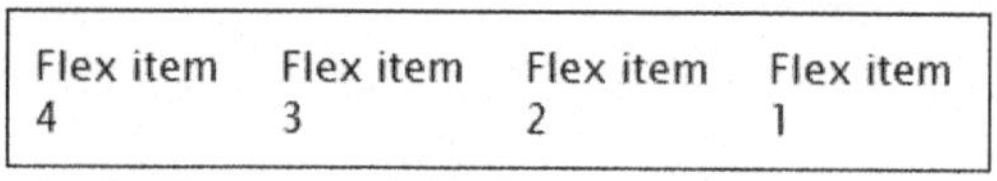

| Flex item | Flex item | Flex item | Flex item |
|---|---|---|---|
| 4 | 3 | 2 | 1 |

*Figure 22-11. The flex items are displayed in reverse order*

The same effect is achieved by setting the shorthand `flex-flow` to `row-reverse`.

You need to be careful when reversing the main axis of a single-row flex container. Figure 22-12 shows what happens when the paragraphs are given a minimum width of 100px (the code is in row-reverse_nowrap.html). The overflow disappears off the left of the browser viewport without spawning a scrollbar.

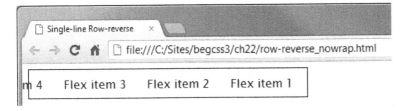

**Figure 22-12.** *The overflow runs offscreen when the main axis is reversed*

The overflow is moved onto a new row in row-reverse_wrap.html like this:

```
#container {
    display: flex;
    flex-direction: row-reverse;
    flex-wrap: wrap;
    border: 1px solid #000;
    width: 400px;
}
```

As Figure 22-13 shows, the final item is right-aligned. You'll learn later in this chapter how to change the alignment of items inside a flex container.

```
Flex item 3     Flex item 2     Flex item 1

                                Flex item 4
```

**Figure 22-13.** *When the main axis is reversed, rows are aligned to the new main-start edge*

The same effect is achieved by combining the individual properties like this (the values can be in either order):

```
flex-flow: wrap row-reverse;
```

To reverse the order of a single column, as shown in Figure 22-14, set flex-direction or flex-flow to column-reverse like this (the code is in column-reverse.html):

```
#container {
    display: flex;
    flex-direction: column-reverse;
    border: 1px solid #000;
    width: 400px;
}
```

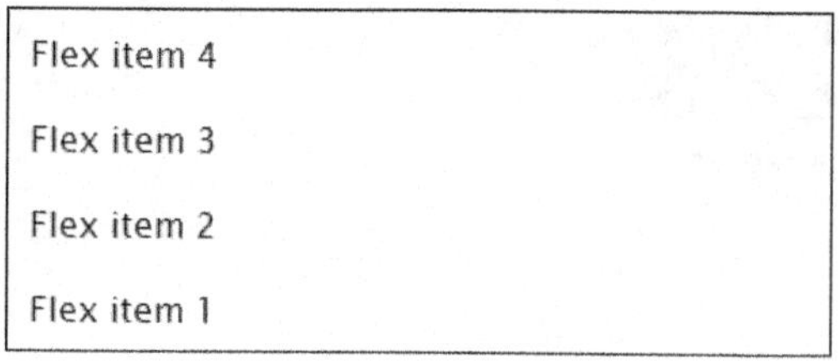

```
Flex item 4

Flex item 3

Flex item 2

Flex item 1
```

***Figure 22-14.*** *The column items are displayed in reverse order*

Figure 22-15 shows what happens in a multiple-column container when the main axis is reversed like this (the code is in column-reverse_wrap.html):

```
#container {
    display: flex;
    flex-direction: column-reverse;
    flex-wrap: wrap;
    border: 1px solid #000;
    width: 400px;
    height: 120px;
}
```

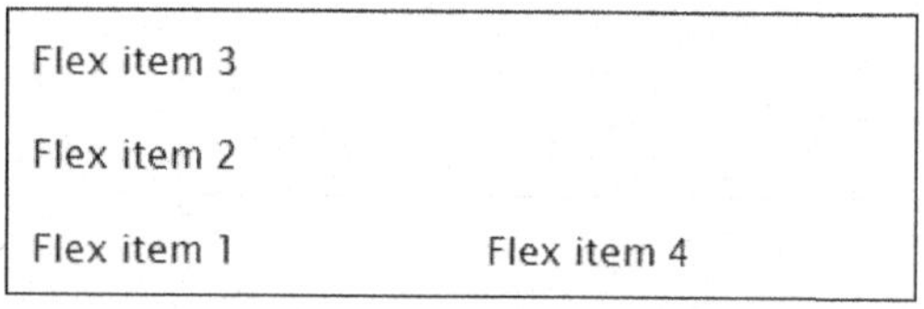

```
Flex item 3

Flex item 2

Flex item 1              Flex item 4
```

***Figure 22-15.*** *The new column begins at the bottom of the container when the main axis is reversed*

Notice that the new column begins at the bottom of the flex container. This is because reversing the main axis changes not only the display order, but also the main-start and main-end edges.

The same effect is achieved by the following shorthand:

```
flex-flow: column-reverse wrap;
```

■ **Tip**    Although it might not be immediately obvious, the browser doesn't reorder the flex items and then lay them out. It actually does reverse the axis along which they're displayed. That's why *Flex item 4* overflows to the left in Figure 22-12, and ends up in the next row or column in Figures 22-13 and 22-15.

## Reversing the Cross Axis

Setting the flex-wrap property to wrap-reverse not only allows the flex container to display multiple rows or columns, but it also reverses the cross axis. Let's see what effect that has when the main axis runs in the normal direction.

In the case of rows, reversing the cross axis means rows are stacked from bottom to top. The styles for the flex container in row_wrap-reverse.html look like this:

```
#container {
    display: flex;
    flex-flow: wrap-reverse;
    border: 1px solid #000;
    width: 400px;
}
```

This produces the result shown in Figure 22-16. The flex items are still laid out in the normal order along the main axis (left to right), but the cross axis has been changed, so the first row is at the bottom of the container.

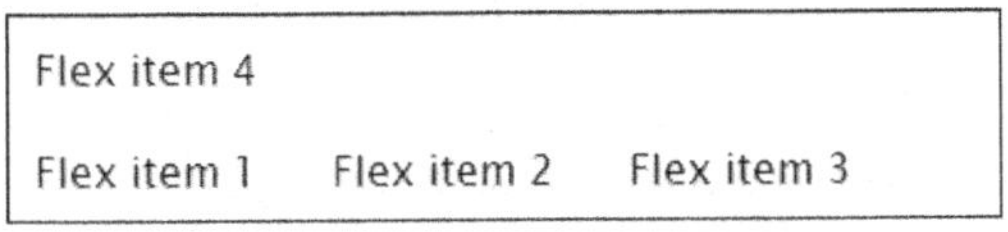

*Figure 22-16.*  *The rows run from left to right, but start at the bottom of the flex container*

In the case of columns, switching the cross axis in a left-to-right language like English results in the columns being laid out from right to left, as shown in Figure 22-17. The styles for the `container <div>` in column_wrap-reverse.html look like this:

```
#container {
    display: flex;
    flex-flow: wrap-reverse column;
    border: 1px solid #000;
    width: 400px;
    height: 120px;
}
```

| Flex item 4 | Flex item 1 |
|---|---|
|  | Flex item 2 |
|  | Flex item 3 |

*Figure 22-17.*  *The second column is displayed on the left*

## Reversing Both Axes

In row-reverse_wrap-reverse.html, both axes are reversed by setting flex-flow like this:

```
#container {
    display: flex;
    flex-flow: row-reverse wrap-reverse;
    border: 1px solid #000;
    width: 400px;
}
```

This produces the result shown in Figure 22-18. The first item is at the bottom-right of the container, the next two items are displayed in the same row going from right to left, and the final item is at the top-right.

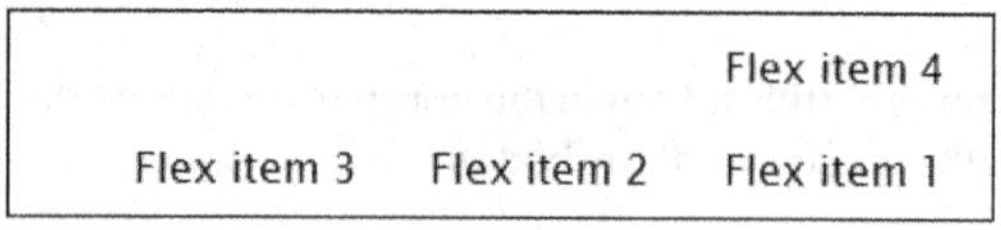

| | |
|---|---|
| | Flex item 4 |
| Flex item 3     Flex item 2 | Flex item 1 |

**Figure 22-18.** *Both axes have been reversed*

To show what happens when both axes are reversed in a multiple-column flex container, the styles in column-reverse_wrap-reverse.html look like this (see Figure 22-19):

```
#container {
    display: flex;
    flex-flow: column-reverse wrap-reverse;
    border: 1px solid #000;
    width: 400px;
    height: 120px;
}
```

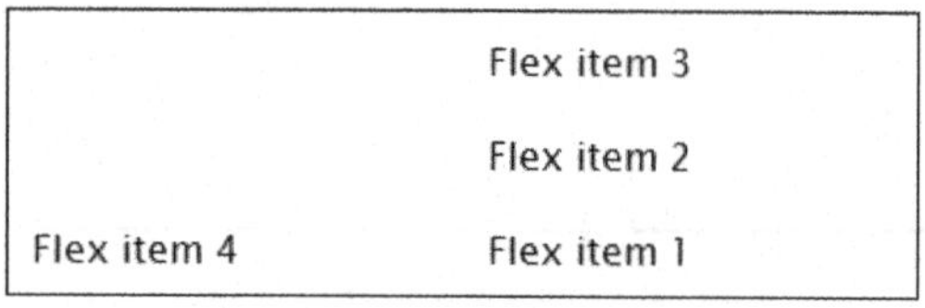

| | |
|---|---|
| | Flex item 3 |
| | Flex item 2 |
| Flex item 4 | Flex item 1 |

**Figure 22-19.** *The columns start at the bottom and continue to the left*

## Reordering Individual Flex Items

In addition to altering the flow within a flex container, flex layout lets you change the order in which individual flex items are displayed. You do this with the order property, which accepts as its value a positive or negative integer.

The default value of order is 0. All flex items with the same value are displayed in the same order as they appear in the underlying HTML markup. Although you can give each flex item a specific number to control its position, it's usually much simpler to give an item a negative number to move it to the first position, or a positive number to move it to the end. For example, the styles for books1.html (see Figure 22-1 at the beginning of this chapter) move the image of the book cover above the text by setting its order property to –1. The <h3> heading is kept in first position by setting its order to –2 like this:

```
article>figure {
    order: -1;
    margin-top: 0;
    margin-bottom: 0;
}
article>h3 {
    order: -2;
    margin-top: 0;
}
```

The order property is not set for the other items, so they all have the default value 0. As a result, they're displayed in their source order after the heading and image have been relocated.

---

■ **Caution** The final order in which items are displayed is determined by the direction of the flow inside the flex container, as the following example demonstrates.

---

It's important to realize that using order to move an item to the top of the display list doesn't override the effect of flex-direction, flex-wrap, or flex-flow. In order_row-reverse.html, the following style rule moves the second paragraph to the top of the display list:

```
p:nth-of-type(2) {
    order: -1;
}
```

However, the main axis is reversed by this rule:

```
#container {
    display: flex;
    flex-flow: row-reverse wrap;
    border: 1px solid #000;
    width: 400px;
}
```

As Figure 22-20 shows, *Flex item 2* is displayed at the top-right of the flex container because reversing the main axis changes the main-start to the right edge. In other words, it has become the first item within the container's reversed flow.

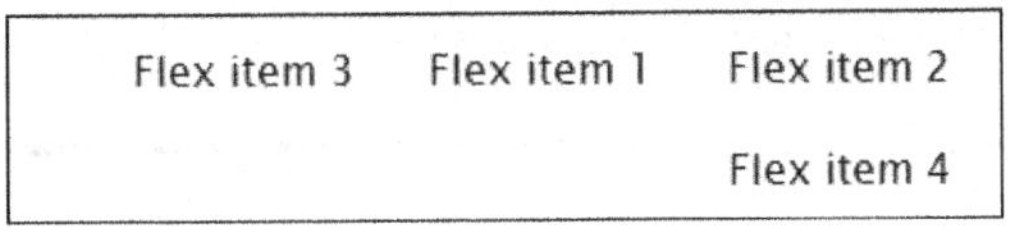

| Flex item 3 | Flex item 1 | Flex item 2 |
| | | Flex item 4 |

*Figure 22-20.* *The order of items is subject to the direction of the container's axes*

## Controlling the Dimensions of Flex Items

According to the Flexible Box Layout module, the "defining aspect of flex layout is the ability to make flex items *flex*, altering their width or height to fill the available space." This is achieved with the properties listed in Table 22-2. There are three independent properties and a shorthand one. However, the shorthand one is listed first because it's recommended to use it in preference to the individual ones.

**Table 22-2.** *Properties that Control the Flexibility of Flex Items*

| Property | Initial Value | Description |
|---|---|---|
| flex | 0 1 auto | Shorthand property that sets the individual flex-grow, flex-shrink, and flex-basis properties in a single declaration. The specification strongly recommends using the shorthand rather than the individual properties because it resets unspecified components correctly. |
| flex-grow | 0 | Sets the *flex grow ratio* expressed as a positive number. This determines how much the item will grow relative to other flex items when free space is distributed. |
| flex-shrink | 1 | Sets the *flex shrink ratio* expressed as a positive number. This determines how much the item will shrink relative to other flex items when there isn't sufficient space to fit them at their normal size. |
| flex-basis | auto | Sets the initial main size (see "Understanding Flex Layout Terminology" earlier in this chapter) of the flex item. Accepts as its value a length, percentage, or auto. Percentage values are relative to the flex container's inner main size. |

Understanding the flex property is probably the most difficult aspect of flexible layout. The order of values is significant. They must be a space-separated list in the following order: flex-grow, flex-shrink, flex-basis. You can omit one or more values from the flex shorthand, but the rules for doing so are rather unusual, as explained in the sidebar "Default Values in flex Shorthand."

## DEFAULT VALUES IN FLEX SHORTHAND

If you omit the values for flex-grow or flex-basis in the flex shorthand property, the substituted values are different from the initial values for the independent properties.

- If omitted from the flex shorthand, both the flex grow and flex shrink ratios default to 1.

- If omitted from the shorthand, the flex-basis component defaults to 0.

- To avoid ambiguity, if you set the flex-basis component to 0, it must be preceded by both the flex grow and flex shrink ratios. Alternatively, you must specify it with a unit, such as 0px.

- The flex shorthand property also accepts the keyword none, which is the equivalent of 0 0 auto.

■ **Tip**  The most important aspect of the flex property is that it overrides the flex item's main size—in other words, its width or height—in order to make it fit into the available space.

The flex-basis component of the flex property can be set to a length or percentage, indicating the flex item's optimum size. But setting it to zero or auto affects the way the flex grow and flex shrink ratios distribute space in a subtle, but important way.

Listing 22-3 contains the basic styles and HTML markup for the following examples that demonstrate the difference (the code is in no_distribution.html).

**Listing 22-3.** Basic Code for Space Distribution Examples

```
<style>
#container {
    display: flex;
    border: 1px solid #000;
    width: 500px;
}
p {
    margin: 2px;
    padding: 5px 0;
    text-align: center;
    background-color: #CCC;
    border: 1px solid #999;
    font-family: "Lucida Sans Unicode", "Lucida Grande", sans-serif;
}
</style>

<div id="container">
    <p>Item 1</p>
    <p>This is item 2</p>
    <p>Flex item 3</p>
</div>
```

The styles in Listing 22-3 display a single-row flex container with three paragraphs of differing lengths. The flex property is not set, so it defaults to 0 1 auto, which means no flex grow ratio, a flex shrink ratio of 1, and the main size set to auto. As a result, the width of each paragraph is controlled by its content, as shown in Figure 22-21.

**Figure 22-21.** *The flex items collapse to the width of their content*

## How Zero flex-basis Distributes Space

When the flex-basis component of the flex shorthand is set to zero, the flex grow and flex shrink ratios are applied to the full main size of the flex item.

The styles in flex-basis_zero.html adapt the paragraph styles in Listing 22-3 like this:

```
p {
    margin: 2px;
    padding: 5px 0;
    text-align: center;
    background-color: #CCC;
    border: 1px solid #999;
    font-family: "Lucida Sans Unicode", "Lucida Grande", sans-serif;
    flex: 1 1 0;
}
```

```
p:nth-of-type(2) {
    flex: 2 1 0;
}
```

The first style rule sets the flex grow and flex shrink ratios for all paragraphs to 1, and the flex-basis component to 0. The second rule resets the flex grow ratio for the second paragraph to 2.

As Figure 22-22 shows, the free space in the flex container is distributed to each paragraph by applying the flex grow ratio to the paragraph's full width. The second paragraph is twice as wide as the other two.

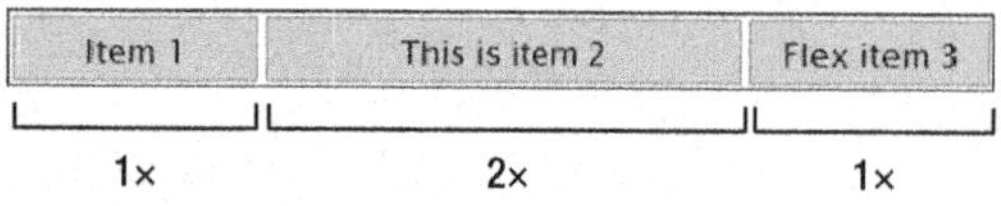

*Figure 22-22.* *The free space is distributed to each paragraph in direct proportion to its flex grow ratio*

## How auto flex-basis Distributes Space

In flex-basis_auto.html the final value in the flex properties has been set to auto like this:

```
p {
    margin: 2px;
    padding: 5px 0;
    text-align: center;
    background-color: #CCC;
    border: 1px solid #999;
    font-family: "Lucida Sans Unicode", "Lucida Grande", sans-serif;
    flex: 1 1 auto;
}
p:nth-of-type(2) {
    flex: 2 1 auto;
}
```

The browser sets the width of each paragraph based on its content, and then distributes any space that's left over to each one in proportion to the flex grow ratio, as shown in Figure 22-23.

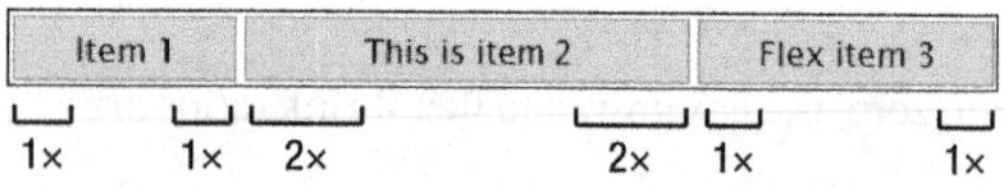

*Figure 22-23.* *Only the extra space is distributed when the flex-basis component is set to auto*

Even though the same flex grow ratio is applied to the first and third paragraphs, the third one is much wider because it contains more text.

---

■ **Note**    Flex items won't shrink below the size of the longest word or fixed-size element.

---

## Using Specific Dimensions with the flex Property

As noted earlier, the flex property overrides the main size of flex items. However, there's an important difference in the way it handles minimum dimensions. The following examples are based on the styles and HTML in Listing 22-4 (the code is in flex_width.html).

***Listing 22-4.*** Testing the Effect of the flex Property on width and min-width

```
<style>
#container {
    display: flex;
    flex-wrap: wrap;
    border: 1px solid #000;
    width: 400px;
}
p {
    font-family: "Lucida Sans Unicode", "Lucida Grande", sans-serif;
    background-color: #CCC;
    border: 1px solid #FFF;
    margin: 0;
    padding: 10px;
    width: 100px;
    flex: 1 0 0;
}
</style>

<div id="container">
    <p>Flex item 1</p>
    <p>Flex item 2</p>
    <p>Flex item 3</p>
    <p>Flex item 4</p>
</div>
```

This is an adaptation of Listing 22-2. The paragraphs have been given a background color and border to show how much of the flex container they occupy. The width of each paragraph is set to 100px. It also has 10px padding and a 1px border all round. This makes an overall width of 122px.

The value of the flex property is 1 0 0, which sets the flex shrink ratio to zero. Although you probably expect this to prevent the paragraphs from shrinking, all four paragraphs are squeezed into the 400px flex container, as shown in Figure 22-24.

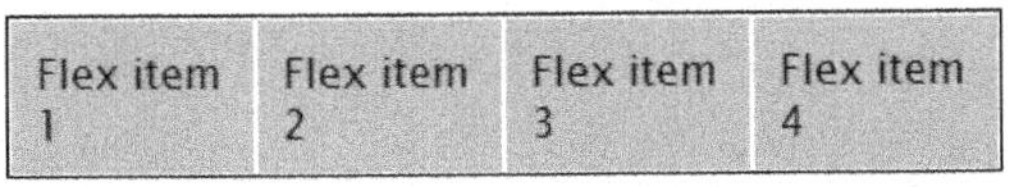

***Figure 22-24.*** *The flex property overrides the paragraphs' declared width*

The flex property ignores the fact that flex-wrap has been set to wrap, which would allow the final paragraph to move onto a second row. Because the flex-basis component has been set to zero, the flex items are resized in proportion to their flex grow ratio.

In flex_min-width.html, the style for the paragraphs is altered to specify a minimum width like this:

```
p {
    font-family: "Lucida Sans Unicode", "Lucida Grande", sans-serif;
    background-color: #CCC;
    border: 1px solid #FFF;
    margin: 0;
    padding: 10px;
    min-width: 100px;
    flex: 1 0 0;
}
```

The flex property doesn't override min-width or min-height, but setting the flex-basis component to zero causes the final paragraph to overflow the flex container, as shown in Figure 22-25.

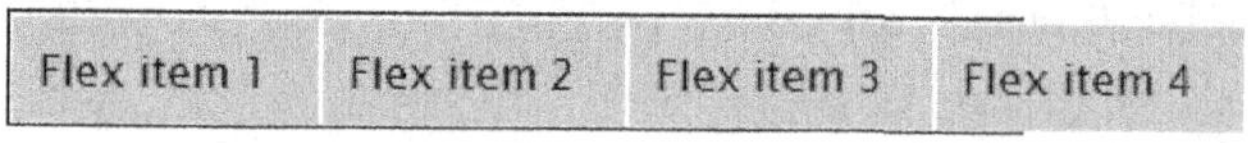

| Flex item 1 | Flex item 2 | Flex item 3 | Flex item 4 |

**Figure 22-25.** *The minimum width is honored, but the final item overflows*

To get the final item to move to another row, you need to set the flex-basis component to auto like this (the code is in flex_auto_width.html):

```
p {
    font-family: "Lucida Sans Unicode", "Lucida Grande", sans-serif;
    background-color: #CCC;
    border: 1px solid #FFF;
    margin: 0;
    padding: 10px;
    width: 100px;
    flex: 1 0 auto;
}
```

Alternatively, set the flex-basis component to the desired size like this (the code is in flex-basis_width.html):

```
p {
    font-family: "Lucida Sans Unicode", "Lucida Grande", sans-serif;
    background-color: #CCC;
    border: 1px solid #FFF;
    margin: 0;
    padding: 10px;
    flex: 1 0 100px;
}
```

Both produce the result shown in Figure 22-26. All four items have been resized using the value of width or the flex-basis component as the desired minimum. But they all fill the available space. As a result the final item is three times wider than the others.

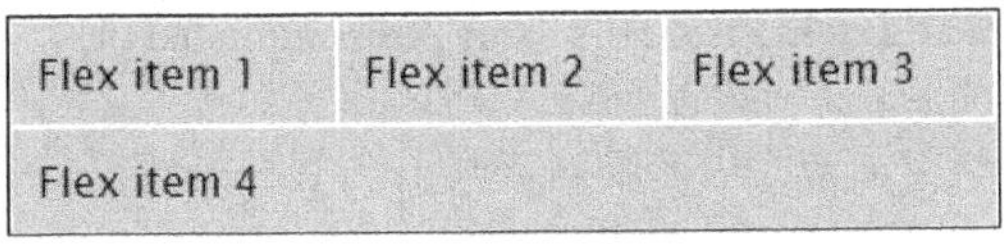

| Flex item 1 | Flex item 2 | Flex item 3 |
|---|---|---|
| Flex item 4 | | |

**Figure 22-26.** *The top row is based on the declared width, but the last item fills the bottom row*

This might be what you want. But if it isn't, it's important to remember that the flex property's role is to fill the available space. If you want elements to maintain their defined size, use the align properties described in the following section instead.

On the other hand, if you want to fill the available space with evenly sized items, adjust the flex-basis component accordingly. The paragraphs in flex-basis_even.html are styled like this:

```
p {
    font-family: "Lucida Sans Unicode", "Lucida Grande", sans-serif;
    background-color: #CCC;
    border: 1px solid #FFF;
    margin: 0;
    padding: 10px;
    flex: 1 0 178px;
}
```

This sets the flex-basis component to 178px, which is the size the paragraphs need to be to fit into the 400px space after taking the padding and borders into consideration. This produces the layout shown in Figure 22-27.

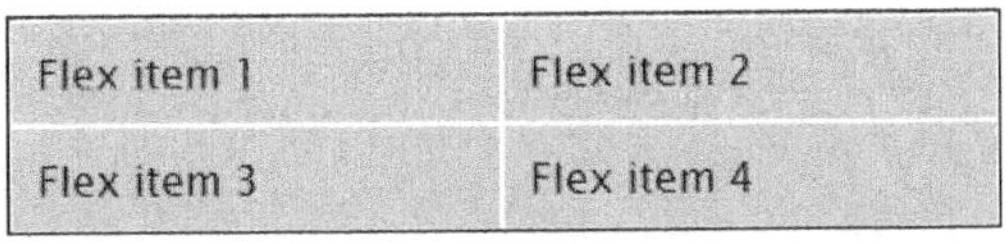

| Flex item 1 | Flex item 2 |
|---|---|
| Flex item 3 | Flex item 4 |

**Figure 22-27.** *The items are now all the same width*

## Aligning Flex Items

The Flexible Box Layout module defines four new properties to control the alignment of flex items. But before describing them, let's look at the way flex layout treats margins. Inside a flex container, margins don't collapse, so all margins on a flex item are preserved. That's not all. The value of auto takes on a new meaning when applied to a margin inside a flex container.

The style rule that controls the *Buy Now* button in books1.html and books2.html (see Figures 22-1 and 22-2 at the beginning of this chapter) looks like this:

```
article>button {
    margin-top: auto;
    align-self: center;
}
```

I'll explain align-self shortly. Setting margin-top to auto has the effect of pushing the button to the bottom of the flex container. Consequently, all the buttons are aligned at the bottom of their respective columns.

You can also set a margin to auto to align elements both left and right inside the same flex container. For example, split_nav.html contains the following <nav> element:

```
<nav>
    <ul>
        <li><a href="#">Home</a></li>
        <li><a href="#">Products</a></li>
        <li><a href="#">Services</a></li>
        <li><a href="#">About Us</a></li>
        <li id="login"><a href="#">Log In</a></li>
        <li>
            <form method="get" action="#">
                <label for="search">Search:</label>
                <input type="search" name="search">
                <input type="submit" name="find" value="Go">
            </form>
        </li>
    </ul>
</nav>
```

The styles convert the unordered list into a single-row flex container and set the left margin of the login list item like this:

```
nav>ul {
    display: flex;
    align-items: baseline;
    margin: 0;
    padding: 0;
}
#login {
    margin-left: auto;
}
```

This splits the list items into two groups, effectively aligning them on opposite sides of the navigation menu, as shown in Figure 22-28.

***Figure 22-28.*** *Setting the left margin of the Log In link to auto splits the menu into two groups*

## Using Flex Layout Alignment Properties

Table 22-3 describes the four properties designed to help control the alignment of flex items. Three of them apply to flex containers. The fourth applies to individual flex items.

**Table 22-3.** *Flex Alignment Properties*

| Property | Initial Value | Description |
|---|---|---|
| justify-content | flex-start | Aligns flex items along the main axis of the current line of the flex container. |
| align-content | stretch | Aligns the flex container's rows or columns within the flex container if there is any extra space on the cross axis. Applies only to multiple-row or multiple-column flex containers. |
| align-items | stretch | Sets the default alignment for flex items on the cross axis. |
| align-self | auto | Overrides align-items for individual flex items. |

The justify-content property accepts the following values:

**flex-start** Flex items are packed toward the start of the main axis. Each item is placed flush with the next. This is the default.

**flex-end** Flex items are packed toward the end of the main axis flush against each other.

**center** Flex items are packed flush against each other in the center of the row or column with equal free space at both ends. If the items overflow, they overflow by an equal amount at both ends.

**space-between** Flex items are spread evenly along the main axis with the first item flush against the main-start edge and the last one flush against the main-end. If items overflow or there's only one item, this value is equal to flex-start.

**space-around** Flex items are distributed evenly with half-size spaces at each end of the axis. If they overflow or there's only one item, this is equal to center.

Figure 22-29 shows an example of each value on a single-row flex container (the code is in justify-content.html).

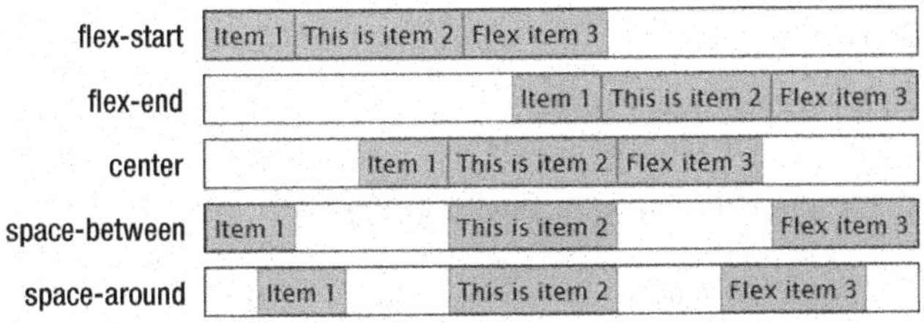

**Figure 22-29.** *Aligning flex items along the main axis with justify-content*

To distribute free space on the cross axis in a multiple-row or multiple-column flex container, use align-content, which accepts the same values as justify-content, but applies them to the cross axis rather than the main axis. It also accepts the following value:

**stretch** This is the default. Free space is split equally between all rows or columns increasing their cross size. If there is insufficient space, it has the same value as flex-start.

Figure 22-30 shows the effect of the different values for align-content on a multiple-row flex container with a fixed height (the code is in align-content.html).

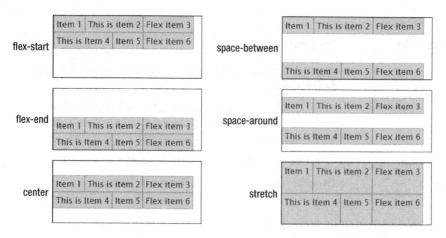

**Figure 22-30.** *Aligning rows along the cross axis in a multiple-row flex container*

The `align-items` property controls the alignment of flex items in the current row or column of a flex container, and is applied to the container.

The `align-self` property is applied to individual flex items, and overrides `align-items`. Both properties accept the following values:

**flex-start** The item's cross-start edge is flush with the container's cross-start.

**flex-end** The item's cross-end edge is flush with the container's cross-end.

**center** The item is centered on the cross axis. If it's too big, it overflows equally in both directions.

**baseline** The text baseline of each item is aligned with the baseline of the item with the largest font size.

**stretch** This is the default for `align-items`. The item stretches to fill the current row or column unless prevented by minimum and maximum width or height.

The `align-self` property also accepts the following value:

**auto** This is the default for `align-self`. It inherits the value of the parent's `align-items` property. If the item has no parent, it defaults to `stretch`.

Figure 22-31 shows the different values for `align-items` (the code is in align-items.html).

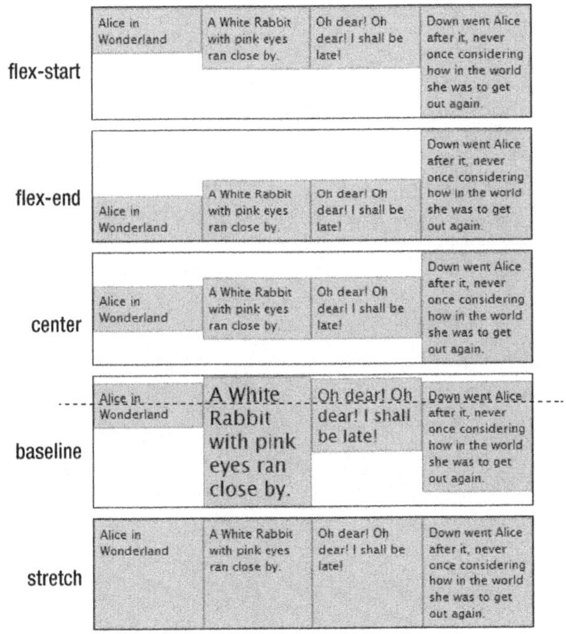

**Figure 22-31.** *Flex items can be aligned in a variety of ways in a flex container*

## EXERCISE: BOOK DESCRIPTIONS

The following exercise shows how to convert Listing 22-1 into a three-column display of books (see Figures 22-1 and 22-2) using flex layout.

Use as your starting point books_begin.html and styles/books_begin.css in the ch22 folder. At the time of this writing, the only browser that supports the final syntax of flex layout is Chrome 21 with the -webkit- browser-specific prefix. The instructions include both the prefixed and unprefixed properties. By the time you read this, other browsers are likely to have adopted the new syntax with or without prefixes. Check http://caniuse.com/#feat=flexbox for up-to-date details.

1. Load the page into a browser. It has been given a few basic styles, but all three book descriptions fill the width of the screen and are stacked on top of each other. Figure 22-32 shows the first book. Everything is left-aligned, and the book image is between the text and the *Buy Now* button.

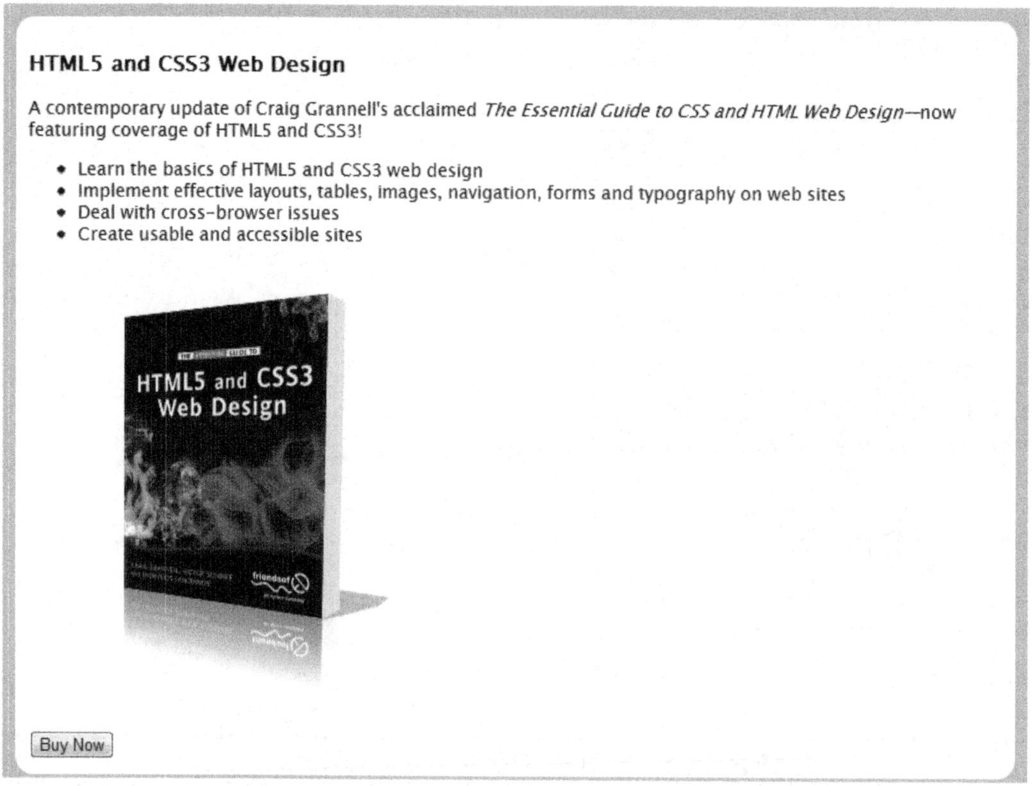

**HTML5 and CSS3 Web Design**

A contemporary update of Craig Grannell's acclaimed *The Essential Guide to CSS and HTML Web Design*—now featuring coverage of HTML5 and CSS3!

- Learn the basics of HTML5 and CSS3 web design
- Implement effective layouts, tables, images, navigation, forms and typography on web sites
- Deal with cross-browser issues
- Create usable and accessible sites

[ Buy Now ]

*Figure 22-32. Each book description fills the full width of the page*

2. Give the `<section>` element a fixed width and center it by setting its horizontal margins to `auto`. Also convert it into a flex container by setting its `display` property. The `<section>` has the ID `books`, so amend its style rule like this:

```
#books {
    background-color: #CCC;
    padding: 5px;
    width: 1000px;
    margin: 0 auto;
    display: -webkit-flex;
    display: flex;
}
```

3. Save the style sheet, and load the page into the latest version of Chrome or a browser that supports the final flex syntax. The flex container defaults to a single row because the styles for the `books` `<section>` don't set the `flex-direction` or `flex-flow` properties. As a result the three `<article>` elements have been laid out alongside each other in equal-height columns. But they're not of equal width, and the layout looks rather haphazard, as Figure 22-33 shows.

**Figure 22-33.** *Turning the parent element into a flex container has created three equal-height columns*

4. Because they're inside a flex container, the `<article>` elements have been converted automatically into flex items. To make them equal width, you could set the `flex-basis` component of the `flex` property to `33.3%`, but that commits the design to always having three columns. Instead, set the `flex` property to **1 1 0**. This gives each column the same width even if you add an extra `<article>` or remove one. Change the style rule for the `<article>` elements like this:

```
article {
    background-color: #FFF;
    margin: 5px;
    border-radius: 15px;
    padding: 10px;
    font-size: 14px;
    -webkit-flex: 1 1 0;
    flex: 1 1 0;
}
```

5. Setting the `flex` property alone greatly improves the layout, as Figure 22-34 shows. But the `<article>` elements need to be converted into flex containers as well. Their contents need to be displayed as columns, so add the following definitions to their style rule:

```
article {
    background-color: #FFF;
    margin: 5px;
    border-radius: 15px;
    padding: 10px;
    font-size: 14px;
    -webkit-flex: 1 1 0;
    display: -webkit-flex;
    -webkit-flex-flow: column;
    flex: 1 1 0;
    display: flex;
    flex-flow: column;
}
```

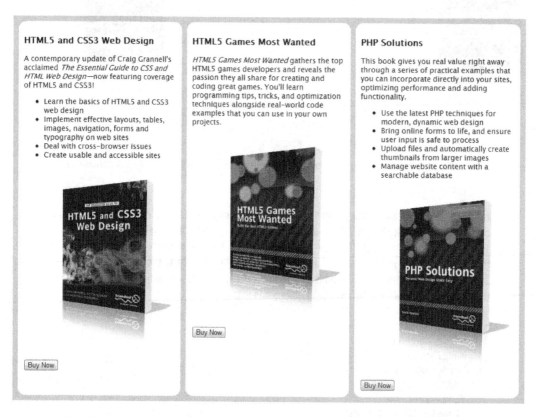

*Figure 22-34.* *The flex items are now all the same width*

6. Move the *Buy Now* button to the bottom of each column and center it by setting its top margin to auto and align-self to center like this:

```
article > button {
    margin-top: auto;
    -webkit-align-self: center;
    align-self: center;
}
```

7. Next, move the <figure> from below the text to just below the <h3> heading. Setting the order property of the <figure> to −1 moves it above the heading, so you also need to set the heading to a lower number. After adding the following styles, the page should look like Figure 22-35:

```
article > figure {
    -webkit-order: -1;
    order: -1;
    margin-top: 0;
    margin-bottom: 0;
}
article > h3 {
    -webkit-order: -2;
    order: -2;
    margin-top: 0;
}
```

**Figure 22-35.** *The buttons are aligned at the bottom, and the images have been moved up*

8. Reduce some of the vertical space by adding the following rule for the paragraphs:

```
article>p {
    margin: 0 0 0.5em 0;
}
```

9. Save the style sheet, and test the page. It now looks like Figure 22-1 at the beginning of this chapter.

10. Promote the last column to first (see Figure 22-36) by adding the following style:

```
article:last-child {
    -webkit-order: -1;
    order: -1;
}
```

**PHP Solutions**

This book gives you real value right away through a series of practical examples that you can incorporate directly into your sites, optimizing performance and adding functionality.

- Use the latest PHP techniques for modern, dynamic web design
- Bring online forms to life, and ensure user input is safe to process
- Upload files and automatically create thumbnails from larger images
- Manage website content with a searchable database

Buy Now

**HTML5 and CSS3 Web Design**

A contemporary update of Craig Grannell's acclaimed *The Essential Guide to CSS and HTML Web Design*—now featuring coverage of HTML5 and CSS3!

- Learn the basics of HTML5 and CSS3 web design
- Implement effective layouts, tables, images, navigation, forms and typography on web sites
- Deal with cross-browser issues
- Create usable and accessible sites

Buy Now

**HTML5 Games Most Wanted**

*HTML5 Games Most Wanted* gathers the top HTML5 games developers and reveals the passion they all share for creating and coding great games. You'll learn programming tips, tricks, and optimization techniques alongside real-world code examples that you can use in your own projects.

Buy Now

***Figure 22-36.*** *The last column has been promoted to the first*

Compare your styles with book2.css if necessary.

Obviously, this book display represents only a page fragment. But it shouldn't be too difficult to envisage how it could be adapted as the center section of a page by making the middle column proportionately wider than the others. Assuming the middle column contains the most important content, it would come before the others in the underlying HTML and be repositioned using the order property. For an example, see flex_layout.html in the ch22 folder.

# Other Features to Look Forward To

In the remaining pages, I briefly describe new CSS features that are being actively developed. Some have already started to appear in browsers. Others are still ideas that may or may not come to fruition. All the features described in the following sections are subject to change.

## Checking Whether a Browser Supports a Feature

Not knowing whether visitors to your site have a browser capable of displaying a particular feature is one of the most frustrating aspects of web design. The CSS3 Conditional Rules module (http://dev.w3.org/csswg/css3-conditional/) proposes a simple way of checking with an @supports rule, which works in a similar way to media queries (see Chapter 17).

The proposed syntax for @supports resembles media queries in the following respects:

- Conditions must be wrapped in parentheses.

- Multiple conditions can be specified using the keyword and.

- A negative set of conditions is created by placing the keyword not at the beginning.

However, alternative conditions are separated by the keyword or rather than commas.
For example, you can test whether a browser supports flex layout like this:

```
@supports (display: flex) or (display: -webkit-flex) {
    /* Flex layout rules go here */
}
```

A browser capable of handling the final flex layout syntax that also understands @supports rules applies the styles inside the curly braces. Other browsers ignore the rules. So, you could use the cascade to provide basic rules to older browsers, and then override them by placing the @supports rule last.

When multiple conditions create ambiguity, you indicate precedence by wrapping an extra pair of parentheses around conditions that need to be considered together. For example, the following is ambiguous:

```
@supports (transform: scale(2)) and (border-radius: 15px) or (linear-gradient(#FFF, #000))
```

Does it mean that scale() and border-radius need to be supported, and if not, linear-gradient() is the alternative? Or does it mean that scale() and either border-radius or linear-gradient() must be supported? If it's the first case, the rule needs to be rewritten like this:

```
@supports ((transform: scale(2)) and (border-radius: 15px)) or (linear-gradient(#FFF, #000))
```

In the second case, you need this:

```
@supports (transform: scale(2)) and ((border-radius: 15px) or (linear-gradient(#FFF, #000))
```

One of the most ingenious aspects of @supports is that it eliminates problems with partial support for CSS features. The @supports rule tests not only the property, but also the value supplied. If the value fails, so does the rule. For example, all browsers support the display property, but they don't all support flex as one of its values.

---

■ **Tip**  While waiting for @supports to be implemented by browsers, you can use a lightweight JavaScript library called Modernizr (http://modernizr.com/) to test browser support for CSS3 features. If a feature isn't supported, it injects a class, such as no-boxshadow, into the web page's <html> tag. This allows you to create different style rules for browsers that don't support particular features. You can learn how to use Modernizr from my tutorial at www. adobe.com/devnet/dreamweaver/articles/using-modernizr.html.

---

# Hyphenation

The draft CSS3 Text module (http://dev.w3.org/csswg/css3-text/) proposes a new hyphens property, which accepts the following values:

**none** This is the default. Words are not hyphenated.

**manual** Words are hyphenated only when they contain characters—such as the HTML soft hyphen entity &shy;—that explicitly suggest hyphenation opportunities.

**auto** Words may be hyphenated either as determined by hyphenation characters or the browser's language-appropriate hyphenation resource.

For the browser to know which hyphenation resource to use, you need to add the lang attribute with the appropriate language code in the opening tag of the element, or in the opening <html> tag for the whole page. For example, to indicate that the text is in English, add lang = "en".

Firefox, Safari, and IE 10 have started supporting hyphenation on an experimental basis with browser-specific prefixes.

## 3D Transforms

All mainstream browsers except Opera have begun supporting three-dimensional transforms with browser-specific prefixes. These are similar to the 2D transforms described in Chapter 20, but they add a third axis to create a 3D illusion.

3D transforms rely on new properties that control perspective and whether the reverse side of the element is shown when facing the user. There are dedicated 3D transform functions for rotating, scaling, and translating elements, and for setting the perspective.

I haven't covered 3D transforms in this book because they're still fairly experimental. To learn more, study the specification at http://dev.w3.org/csswg/css3-transforms/#transform-3d-rendering.

## CSS Variables

Often you find yourself using the same value repeatedly in different parts of your style sheets, especially when defining colors. Not only are color values difficult to remember, but it's a major pain to have to update them all if the color scheme changes. So, web designers have long been demanding the ability to use variables that need to be defined only once for their values to be available throughout a style sheet.

The CSS Variables module (http://dev.w3.org/csswg/css-variables/) proposes doing just that. However, just as this book was going to press, the module's editors decided to change an important part of the original proposals.

The proposed method of defining a variable property remains the same. You create a name prefixed by var- and assign it a value. For example, let's say you want to define the primary color for use throughout the site, you could create the following style rule using the :root pseudo-class:

```
:root {
    var-primary: #008B8B; /* dark cyan */
}
```

To apply the primary color to headings, it was originally proposed using $ followed by the variable name—in this case, $primary. However, that idea has been dropped—at least for the time being. Instead, you access the value using the var() function like this:

```
h1, h2, h3 {
    color: var(primary);
}
```

This applies the color defined as var-primary to the top three levels of headings. If you change the value of var-primary, the new color is automatically applied to the headings, as well as to any other elements that use the same variable.

Optionally, you can add a second argument to var() to define the value of the variable if it hasn't already been defined.

Once finally implemented, this should make a major difference to working with large style sheets.

# CSS4 Selectors

Even though many CSS3 modules are still a long way from implementation, work has already begun on the CSS4 Selectors module (http://dev.w3.org/csswg/selectors4/). Among the new selectors being planned, two stand out as being particularly useful. One is the :matches() pseudo-class. The other lets you select a parent element.

The :matches() pseudo-class takes as its argument a list of selectors and matches any of them. This is extremely useful in situations where you need to repeat the same ancestor or parent multiple times in a group selector. For example, flex_layout.html uses the following group selector to target <section>, <nav>, and <aside> elements that are direct children of a <div> with the ID main:

```
#main > section, #main > nav, #main > aside
```

This involves repeating #main > three times. With the :matches() pseudo-class, this group selector can be rewritten like this:

```
#main > :matches(section, nav, aside)
```

In this rather trivial example, it doesn't save much typing, but group selectors can become extremely verbose. Let's say you want special link styles for the <nav> and <aside> elements, the group selector currently looks like this:

```
#main > nav a:link, #main > nav a:visited,
#main > aside a:link, #main > aside a:visited
```

With :matches(), it can be reduced to this:

```
#main > :matches(nav, aside) a:matches(:link, :visited)
```

---

■ **Tip**  At the time of this writing, WebKit-based browsers and Firefox support the same functionality as :matches() using the nonstandard :-webkit-any() and :-moz-any() pseudo-classes.

---

The other change to selectors that looks particularly significant is what I like to think of as the "parent" selector. It's not officially called that, but it describes what it does. Descendant and child selectors target styles at elements nested inside another element, but there's currently no way of styling a parent element. Let's say, for example, that you link to a heading inside a page using a URL fragment, you can style the heading with the :target pseudo-class with the following selector:

```
h3:target
```

But what if you could style the whole <div> or <article> that you've just linked to rather than just the heading?

The CSS4 Selectors module proposes letting you determine the *subject of a selector*, in effect turning a child selector into a parent selector. The first draft of the specification proposed prefixing the subject with a dollar sign ($). This has since changed to an exclamation mark (!), and it might change yet again. However, this is how it's proposed to identify the parent <div> of a heading that's the target of a link:

```
!div > h3:target
```

This would apply the styles to the <div> rather than to the <h3> heading.

## Advanced Layout and Effects

Many new specifications are actively being worked on. Some of the most interesting include:

- CSS Grid Layout (http://dev.w3.org/csswg/css3-grid-layout/)

- CSS Exclusions and Shapes (http://dev.w3.org/csswg/css3-exclusions/)

- CSS Regions (http://dev.w3.org/csswg/css3-regions/)

- Compositing and Blending (http://www.w3.org/TR/compositing/)

- Filter Effects (www.w3.org/TR/filter-effects/)

- CSS Masking (www.w3.org/TR/css-masking/)

■ **Note** The initial drafts for Filter Effects and CSS Masking hadn't been officially published when this book went to press. The URLs for the specifications are where they are expected to be located, but might change.

Many of the ideas have been put forward by Adobe, and are based on the company's extensive experience with print design. Some of them—such as CSS exclusions, shapes, and regions—emulate print layout by flowing text around irregular shapes or linking dynamically between text boxes. These features are particularly suited to electronic books and magazines. Compositing and blending brings Photoshop-like effects to the browser, and filters create cinematic effects.

Although Adobe has been the prime mover behind these developments, it's working closely with Microsoft, Opera, and other manufacturers. You can find more information, including examples, at http://html.adobe.com/webstandards/.

# Summary

That concludes our in-depth exploration of CSS3 as it currently stands in the second half of 2012. Although it will probably have moved on even before the ink is dry on the pages of the printed book, I've deliberately tried to describe the new aspects of CSS as they're intended to work rather than focus on browser shortcomings. Browsers will continue to improve, catching up with the specification. If you master even only half of the properties described in this book, you'll have a solid foundation for years to come. The great strength of CSS lies in the way it's designed to be both backward- and forward-compatible. Old browsers silently ignore new properties and rules they don't understand, and new features are designed to build on top of existing ones.

This chapter has attempted to peek into the future of CSS. I concentrated heavily on flex layout, even though the formal syntax is currently supported by only one browser. Flex layout promises to revolutionize the way pages are laid out. It's probably more suited to sections of a page than laying out complete pages. Flex layout is very powerful, but grasping the implications of reverse axes and understanding how the flex property works can be a challenge.

Looking ahead to some of the new features proposed for CSS, it's becoming an increasingly technical discipline. In the course of the book, I've recommended online tools that help generate the necessary code. No doubt, dedicated software or new online tools will emerge in response to developments in CSS. But even if you don't write the code yourself, understanding how it works will remain an essential part of being a successful web designer.

I hope you've found this book useful as you go forward and make the Web a beautiful and useful place.

# Index

## ■ U

## ■ V

## ■ W, X, Y

## ■ Z

CPSIA information can be obtained at www.ICGtesting.com
Printed in the USA
LVOW03s2150211214

419883LV00015B/573/P